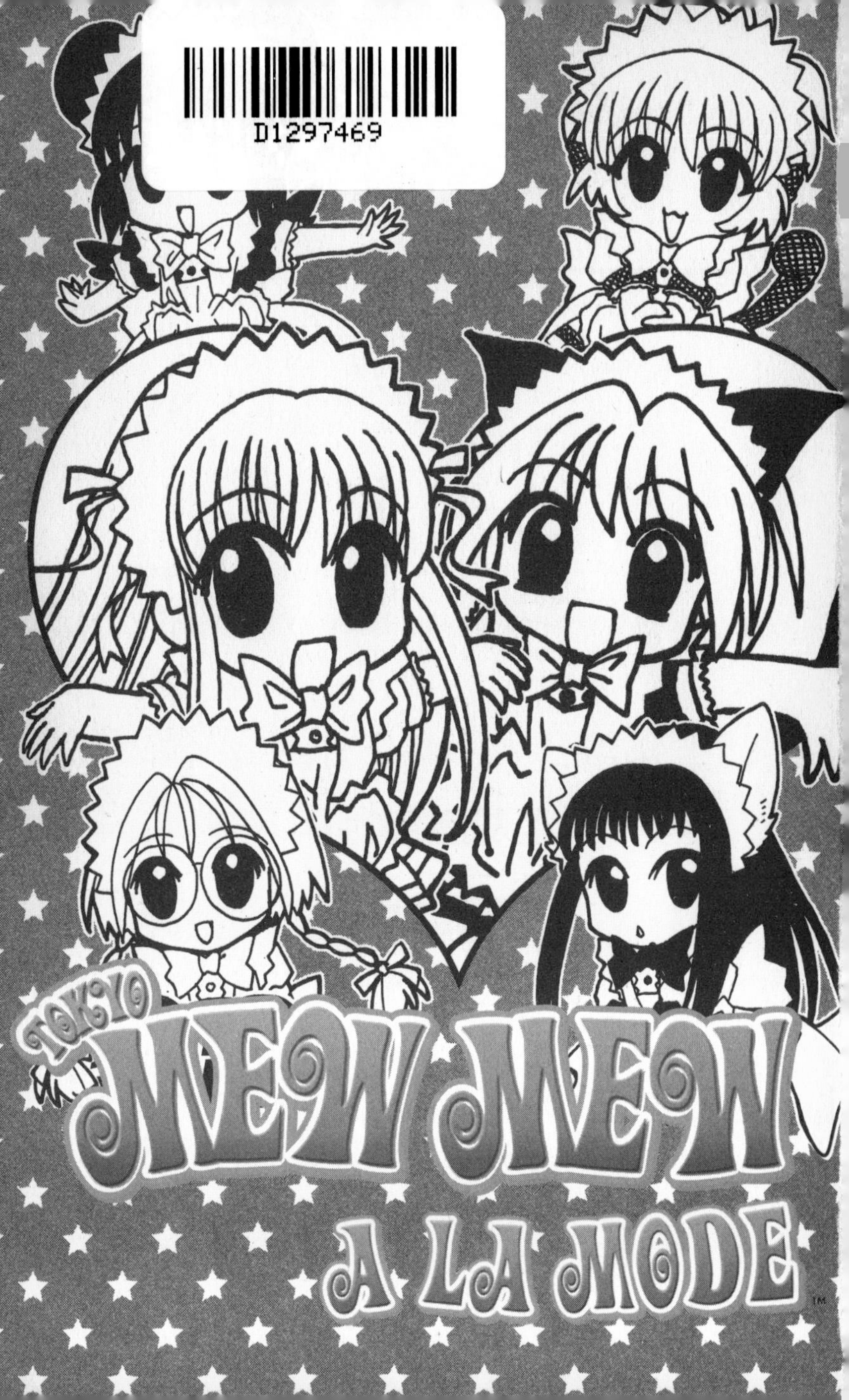
TOKYO
MEW MEW
A LA MODE
™

Tokyo Mew Mew a la Mode Vol. 2
Art by Mia Ikumi
Original Concept by Kodansha

Translation - Yoohae Yang
English Adaptation - Stuart Hazleton
Associate Editor - Peter Ahlstrom
Retouch and Lettering - Irene Woori Choi
Production Artist - Rafael Najarian
Cover Design - Christian Lownds

Editor - Carol Fox
Digital Imaging Manager - Chris Buford
Production Managers - Jennifer Miller and Mutsumi Miyazaki
Managing Editor - Jill Freshney
VP of Production - Ron Klamert
Publisher and E.I.C. - Mike Kiley
President and C.O.O. - John Parker
C.E.O. - Stuart Levy

A  Manga

TOKYOPOP Inc.
5900 Wilshire Blvd. Suite 2000
Los Angeles, CA 90036

E-mail: info@TOKYOPOP.com
Come visit us online at www.TOKYOPOP.com

ISBN: 1-59532-790-8

First TOKYOPOP printing: September 2005
10 9 8 7 6 5 4 3 2 1
Printed in Canada

TOKYO MEW MEW A LA MODE

ART BY MIA IKUMI
ORIGINAL CONCEPT BY KODANSHA

VOLUME 2

HAMBURG // LONDON // LOS ANGELES // TOKYO

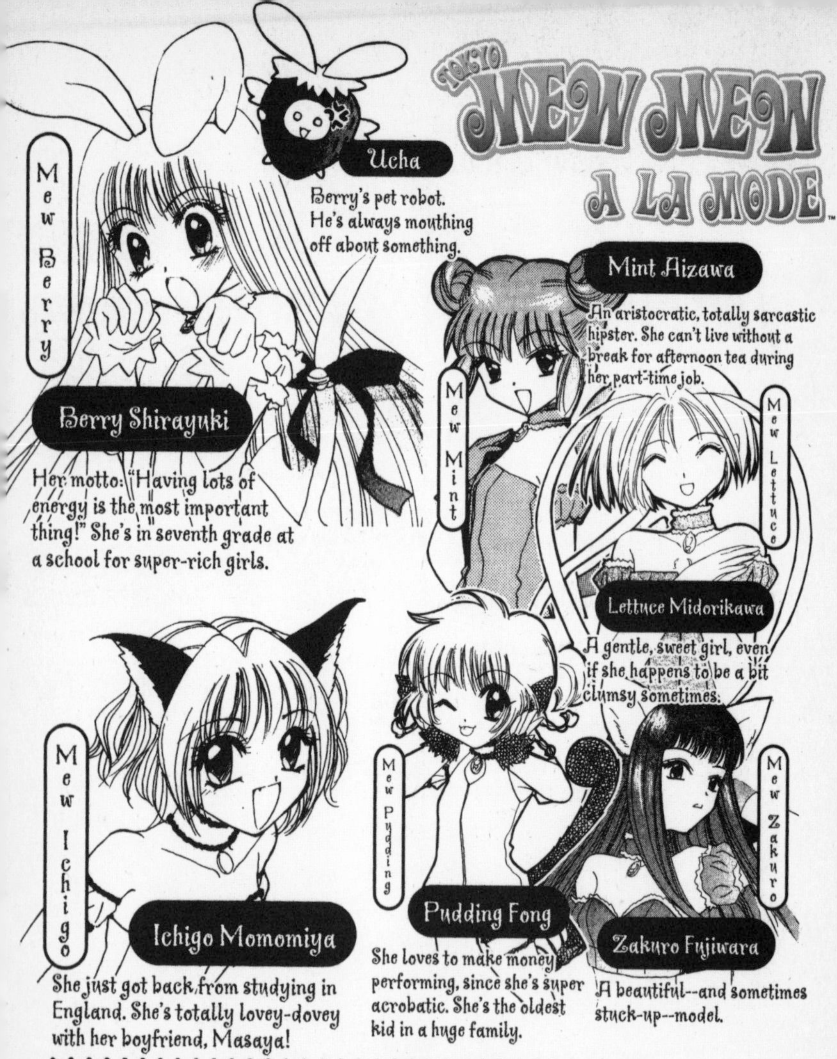
TOKYO MEW MEW A LA MODE™
Ucha
Berry's pet robot. He's always mouthing off about something.
Mew Berry
Berry Shirayuki
Her motto: "Having lots of energy is the most important thing!" She's in seventh grade at a school for super-rich girls.
Mint Aizawa
An aristocratic, totally sarcastic hipster. She can't live without a break for afternoon tea during her part-time job.
Mew Mint
Mew Lettuce
Lettuce Midorikawa
A gentle, sweet girl, even if she happens to be a bit clumsy sometimes.
Mew Ichigo
Ichigo Momomiya
She just got back from studying in England. She's totally lovey-dovey with her boyfriend, Masaya!
Mew Pudding
Pudding Fong
She loves to make money performing, since she's super acrobatic. She's the oldest kid in a huge family.
Mew Zakuro
Zakuro Fujiwara
A beautiful--and sometimes stuck-up--model.

☆ Berry Shirayuki, a seventh grader, was starting to get nervous around her childhood friend, Tasuku--a crush, maybe? But soon she had bigger problems--when she stopped by a mysterious cafe after school, she was transformed into a Mew Mew!

☆ Berry joined forces with Ichigo and the other Tokyo Mew Mew members to protect the people of Earth from the Saint Rose Crusaders--who, unfortunately for the rest of us, are scheming to take over the world. Meanwhile, Berry is starting to feel even more strange around Tasuku--who's developed the annoying (endearing?) habit of rescuing her!

CONTENTS

Ryou Shirogane

One half of the brains behind Tokyo Mew Mew. Cafe Mew Mew is the headquarters where he can usually be found.

Keiichirou Akasaka

Ryou's partner and manager of Cafe Mew Mew.

Tasuku Meguro

Berry's neighbor and childhood friend. His official hobby is hugging Berry as often as he possibly can!

The Saint Rose Crusaders

Each member has a unique and amazing ability. They're scheming to take over the world.

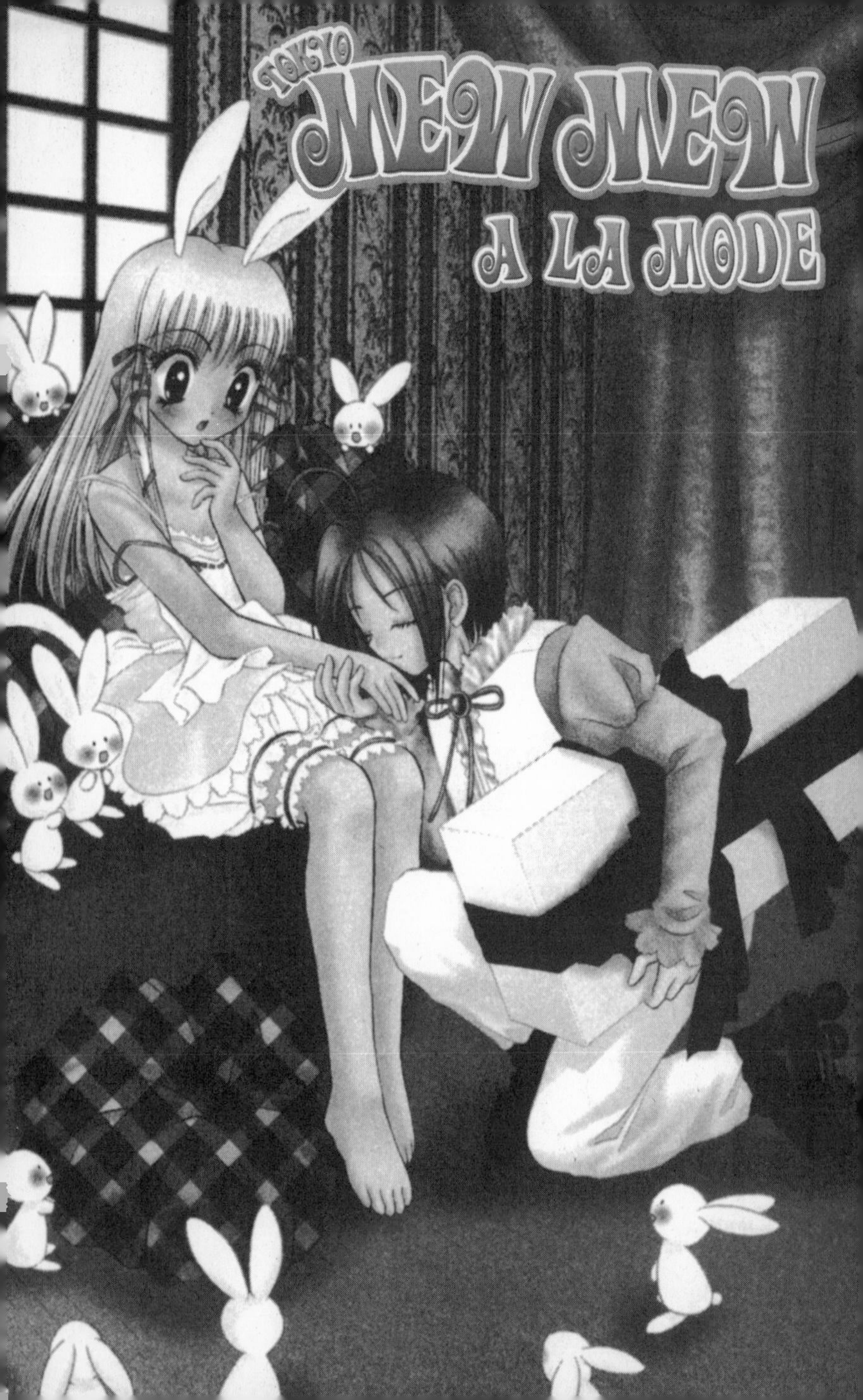
TOKYO
MEW MEW
A LA MODE

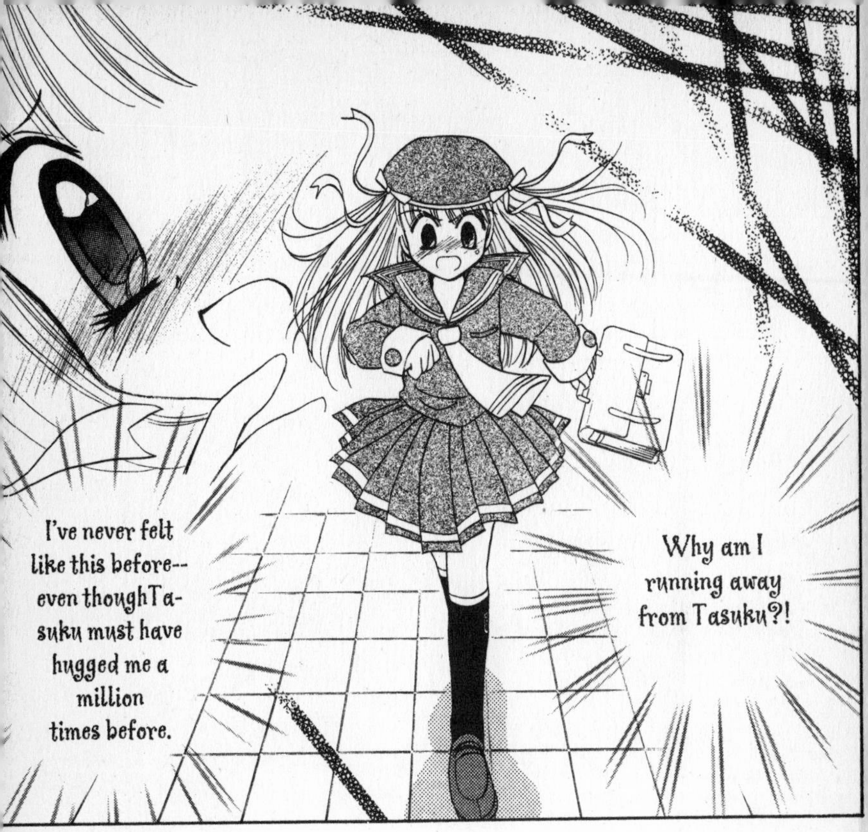
Why am I running away from Tasuku?!
I've never felt like this before-- even thoughTa-suku must have hugged me a million times before.

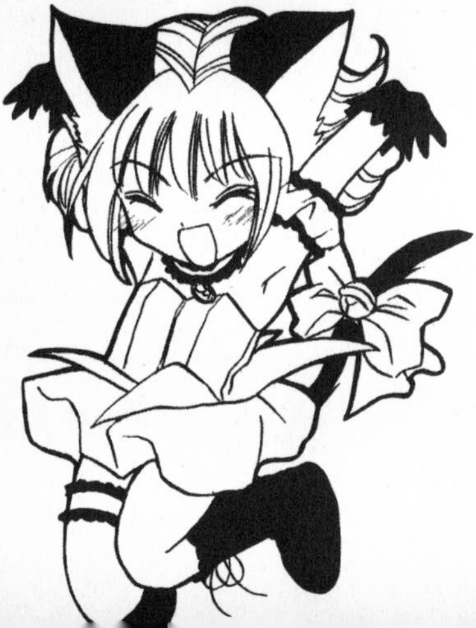

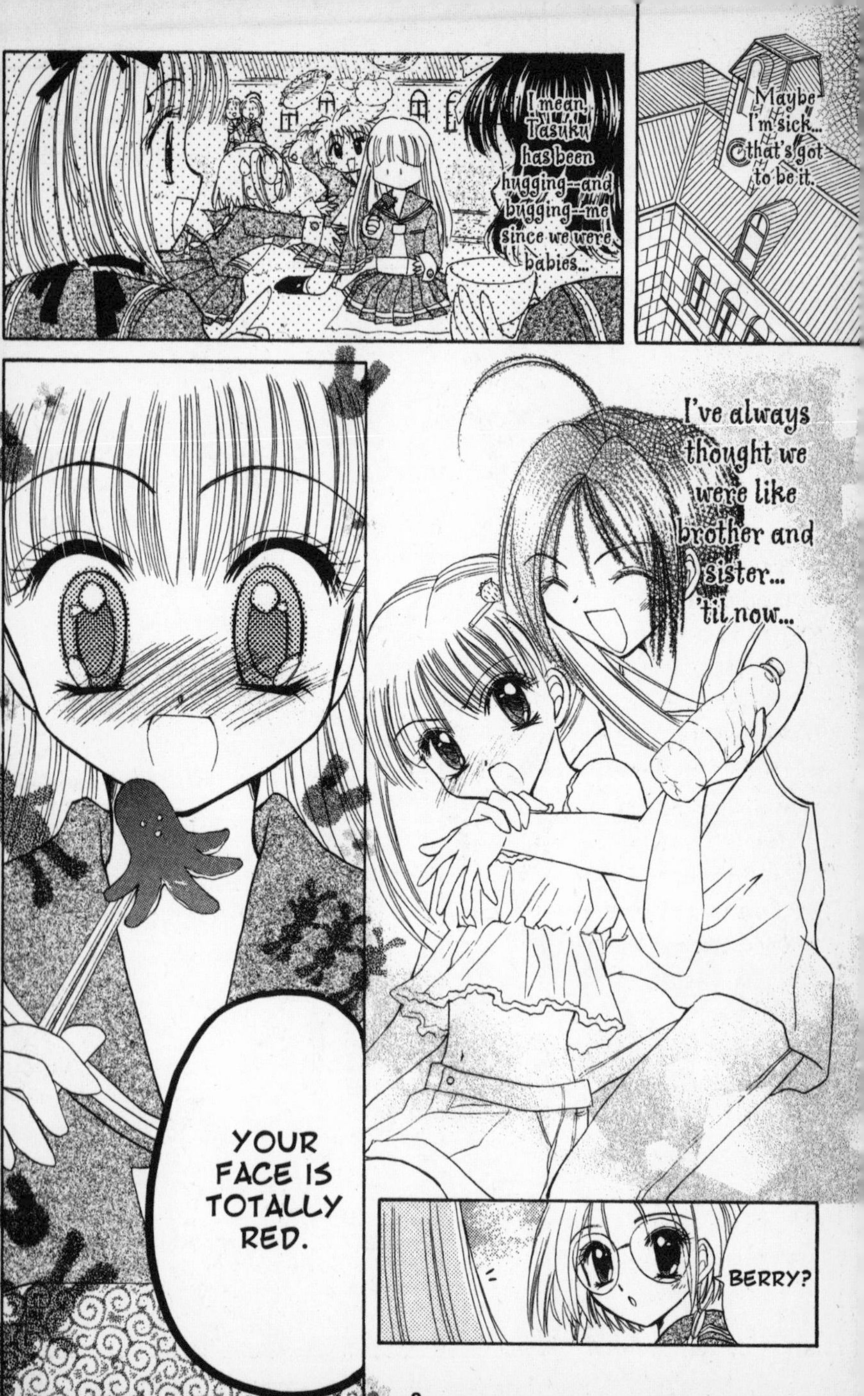
Maybe I'm sick... that's got to be it.
I mean, Tasuku has been hugging--and bugging--me since we were babies...
I've always thought we were like brother and sister... 'til now...
YOUR FACE IS TOTALLY RED.
BERRY?

Hi there!
Mia Ikumi here!

Long time no see! How is everyone out there? This is Ikumi bringing you volume two of *Tokyo Mew Mew a la Mode*! ♡

I've often heard comments like, "sometimes it seemed like that manga took a long time to make, and sometimes the time seemed to pass so quickly!" Well, for me, it just plain felt like forever. (Laugh) I almost felt like I'd be working on the Tokyo Mew Mew manga until I was a little old woman! But everything must come to an end eventually, and I must admit I'm a little sad to be finished.

So please...enjoy the last volume of *Tokyo Mew Mew*! ♡

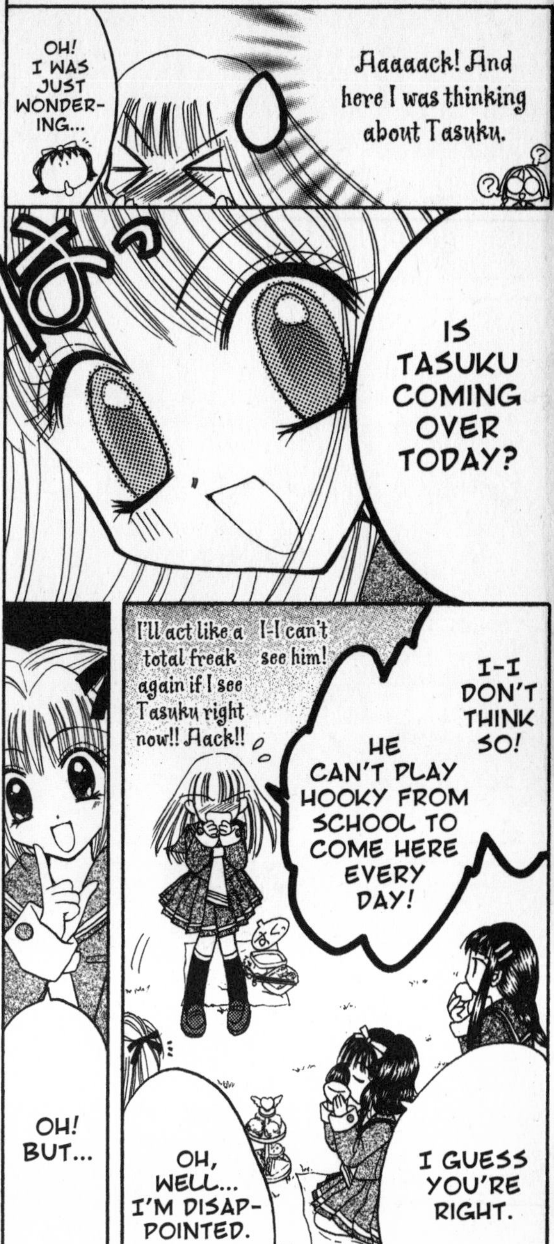

Aaaaack! And here I was thinking about Tasuku.
OH! I WAS JUST WONDERING...
IS TASUKU COMING OVER TODAY?
はっ
I-I DON'T THINK SO!
HE CAN'T PLAY HOOKY FROM SCHOOL TO COME HERE EVERY DAY!
I-I can't see him!
I'll act like a total freak again if I see Tasuku right now!! Aack!!
I GUESS YOU'RE RIGHT.
OH, WELL... I'M DISAPPOINTED.
OH! BUT...

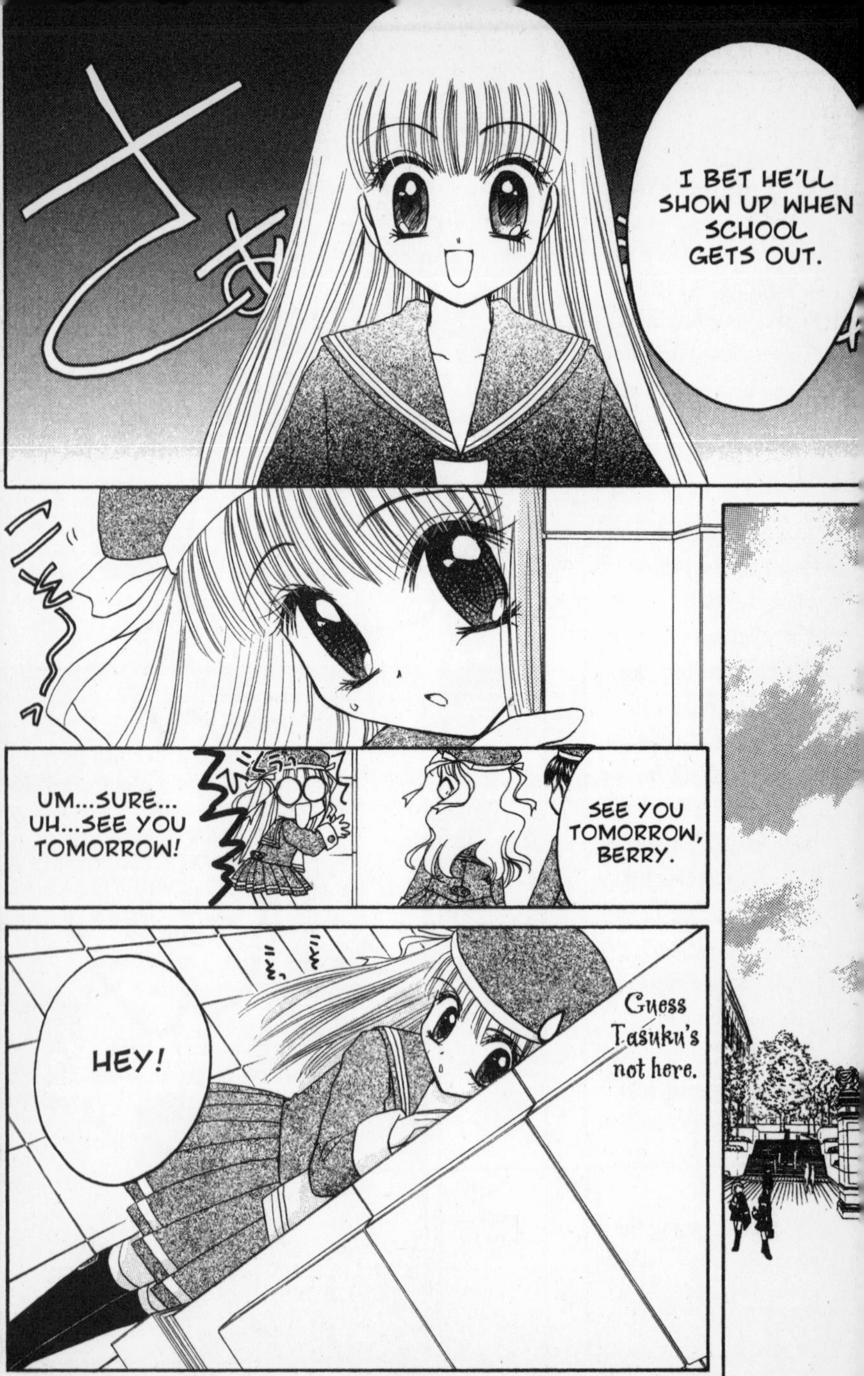
I BET HE'LL SHOW UP WHEN SCHOOL GETS OUT.
SEE YOU TOMORROW, BERRY.
UM...SURE... UH...SEE YOU TOMORROW!
Guess Tasuku's not here.
HEY!

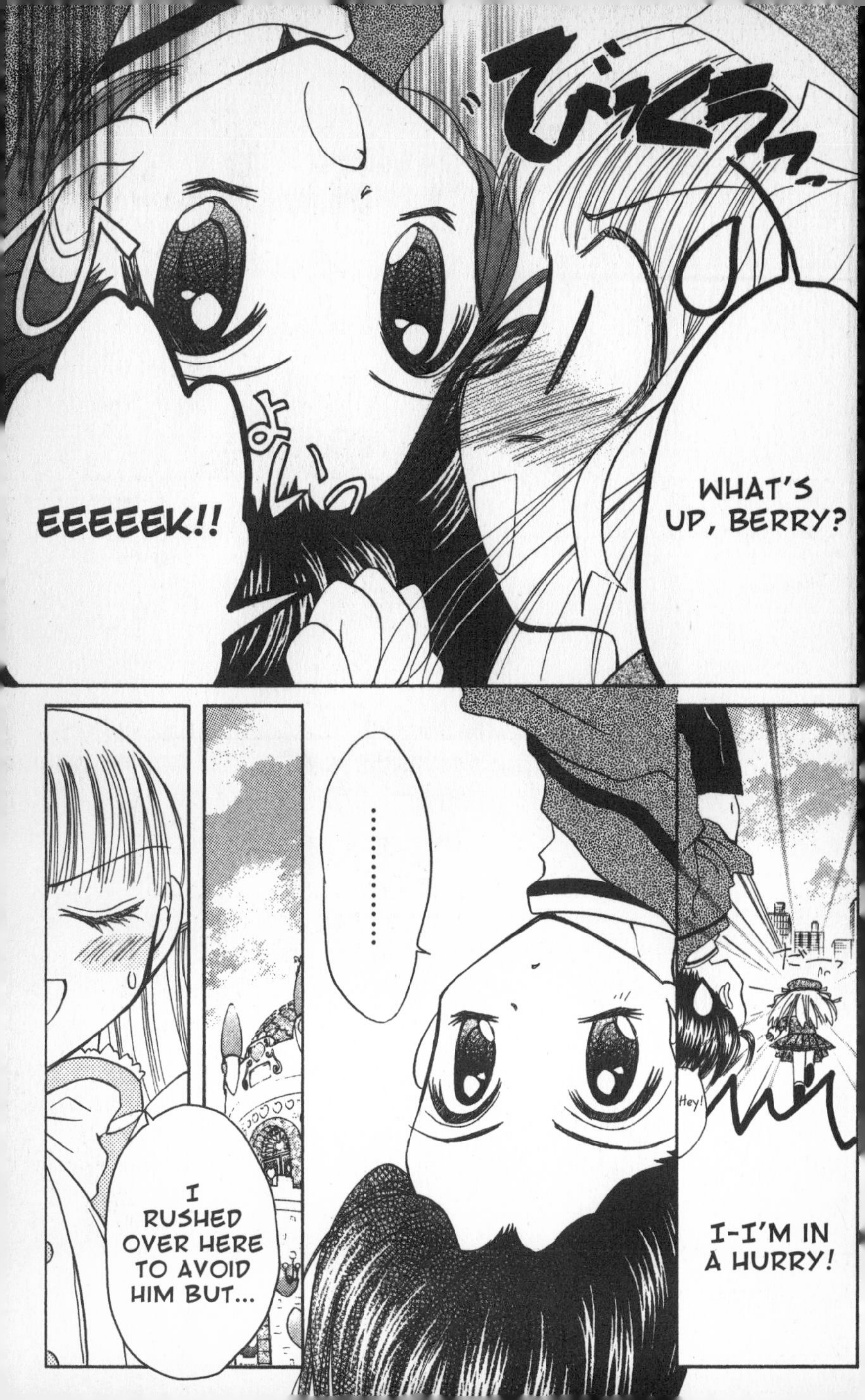
WHAT'S UP, BERRY?
EEEEEK!!
I-I'M IN A HURRY!
Hey!
......
I RUSHED OVER HERE TO AVOID HIM BUT...

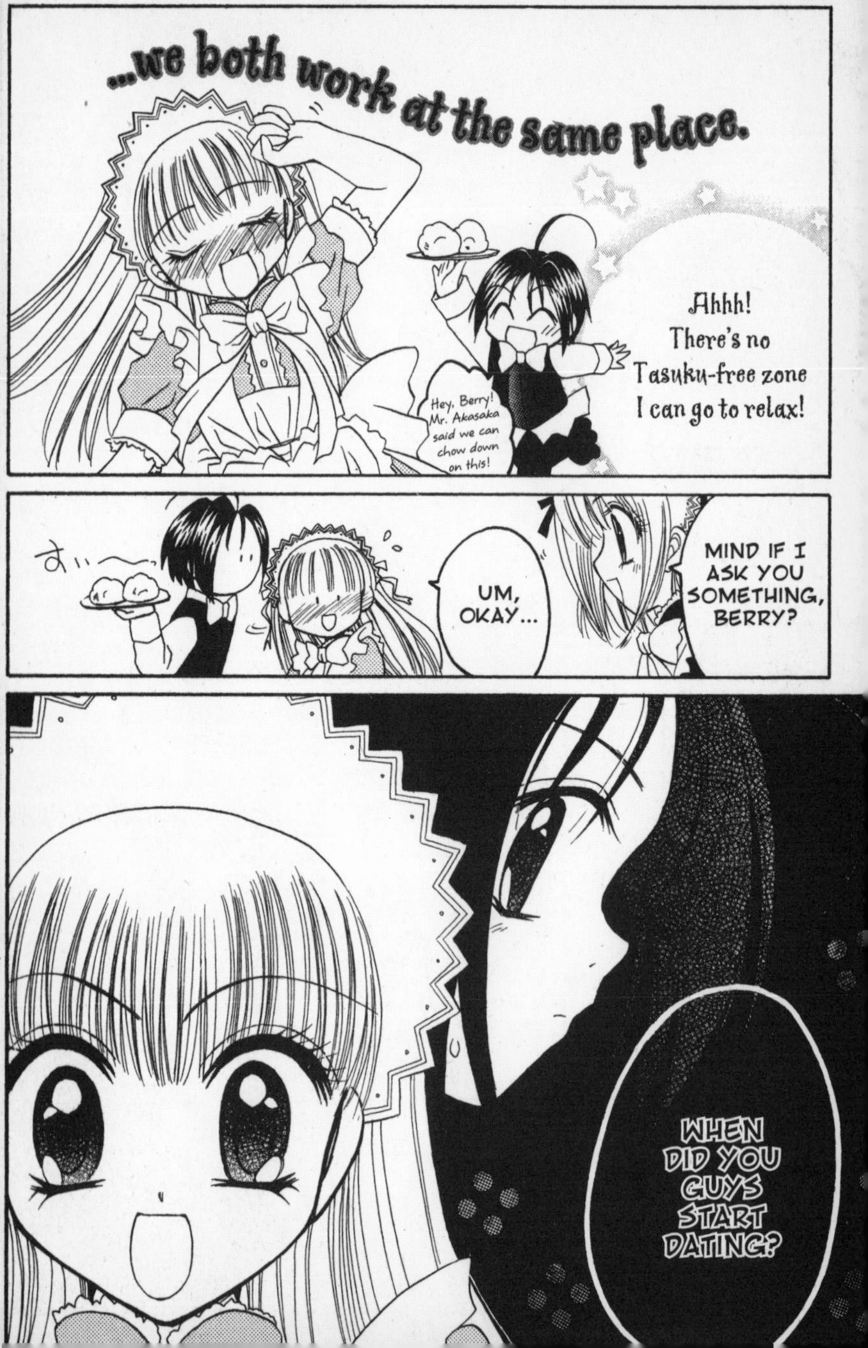
...we both work at the same place.
Ahhh! There's no Tasuku-free zone I can go to relax!
Hey, Berry! Mr. Akasaka said we can chow down on this!
MIND IF I ASK YOU SOMETHING, BERRY?
UM, OKAY...
WHEN DID YOU GUYS START DATING?

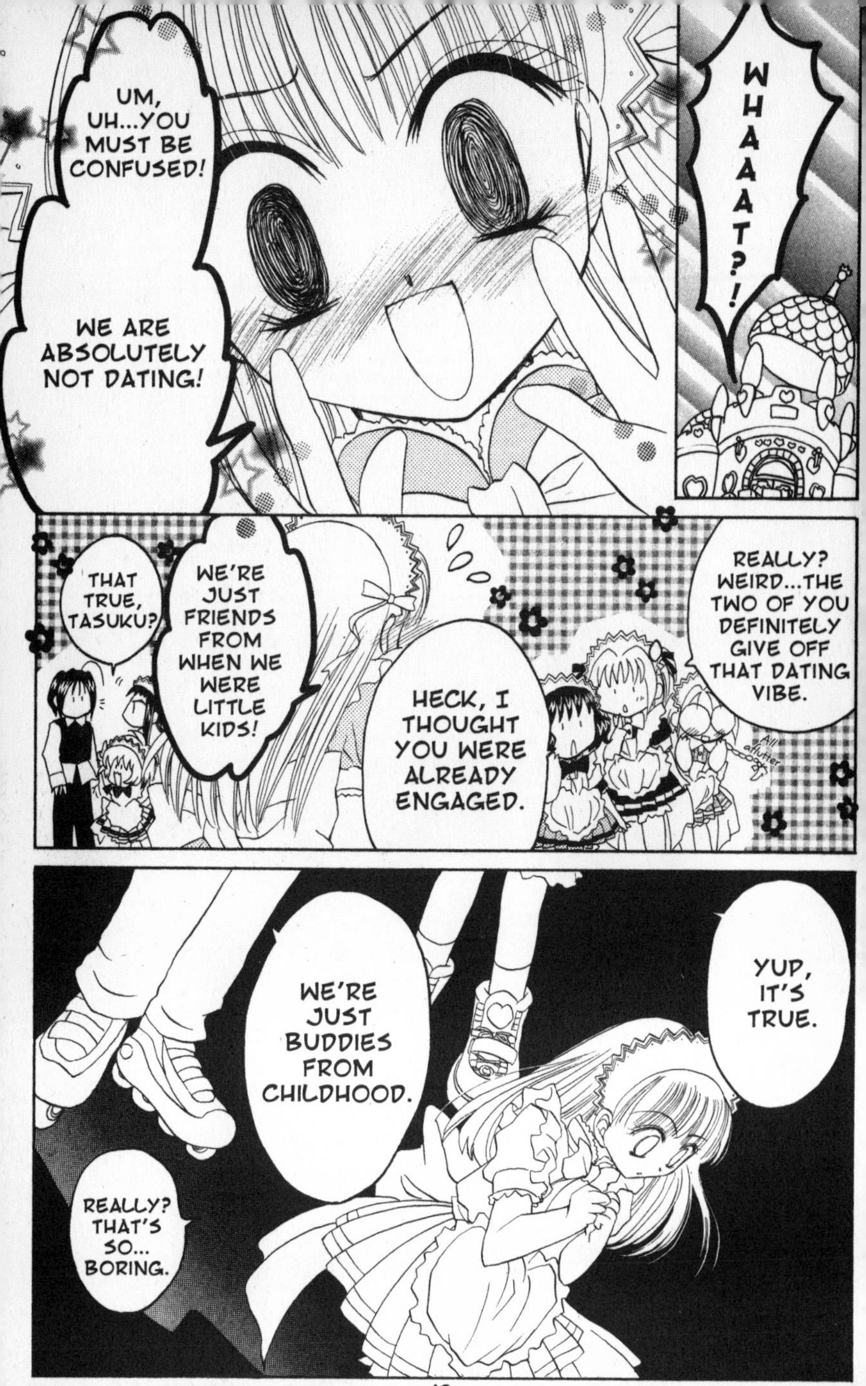
WHAAAT?!
UM, UH...YOU MUST BE CONFUSED!
WE ARE ABSOLUTELY NOT DATING!
REALLY? WEIRD...THE TWO OF YOU DEFINITELY GIVE OFF THAT DATING VIBE.
All aflutter
HECK, I THOUGHT YOU WERE ALREADY ENGAGED.
WE'RE JUST FRIENDS FROM WHEN WE WERE LITTLE KIDS!
THAT TRUE, TASUKU?
YUP, IT'S TRUE.
WE'RE JUST BUDDIES FROM CHILDHOOD.
REALLY? THAT'S SO... BORING.

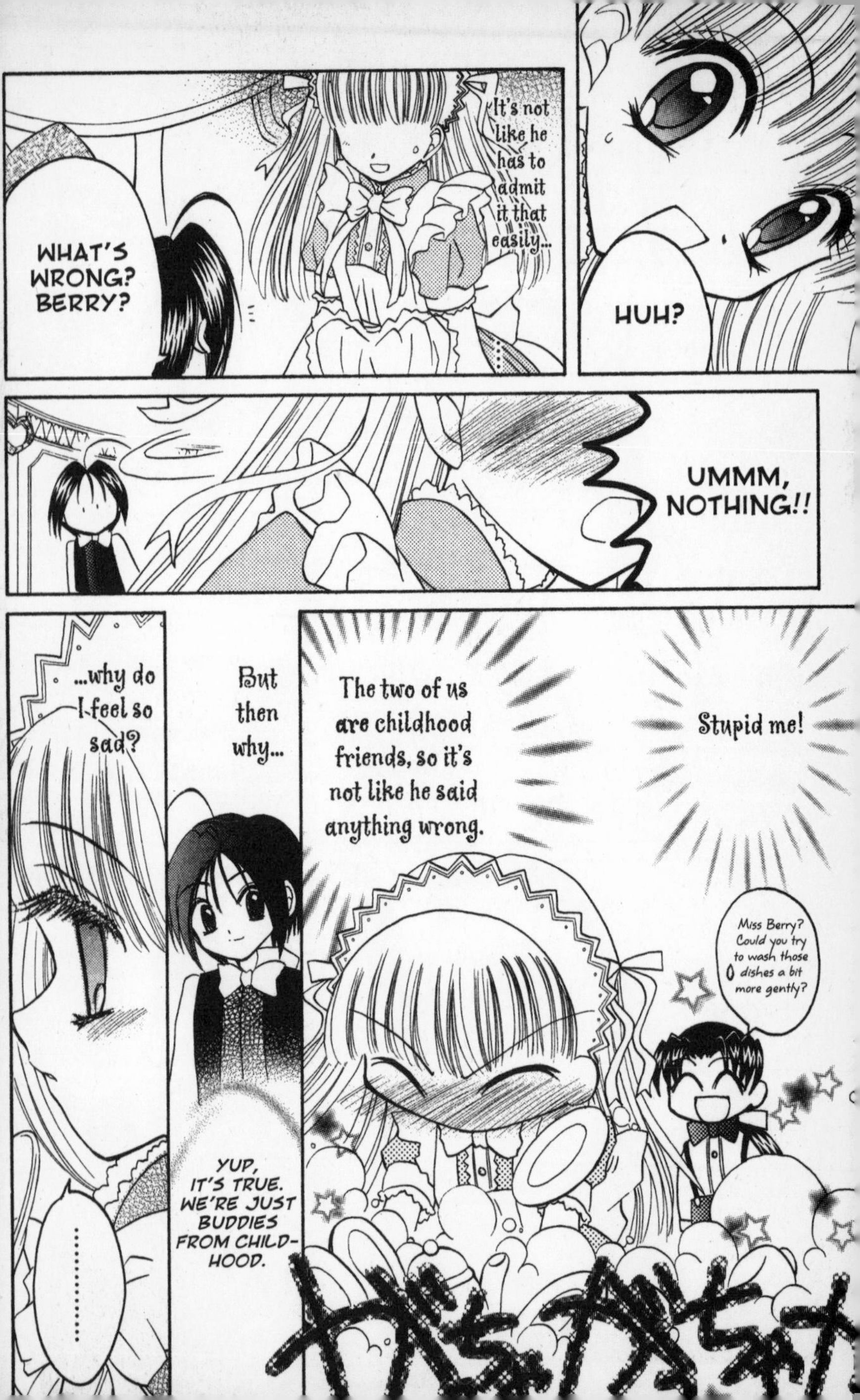

It's not like he has to admit it that easily...
WHAT'S WRONG? BERRY?
HUH?
UMMM, NOTHING!!
Stupid me!
The two of us are childhood friends, so it's not like he said anything wrong.
Miss Berry? Could you try to wash those dishes a bit more gently?
But then why...
YUP, IT'S TRUE. WE'RE JUST BUDDIES FROM CHILD-HOOD.
...why do I feel so sad?
....

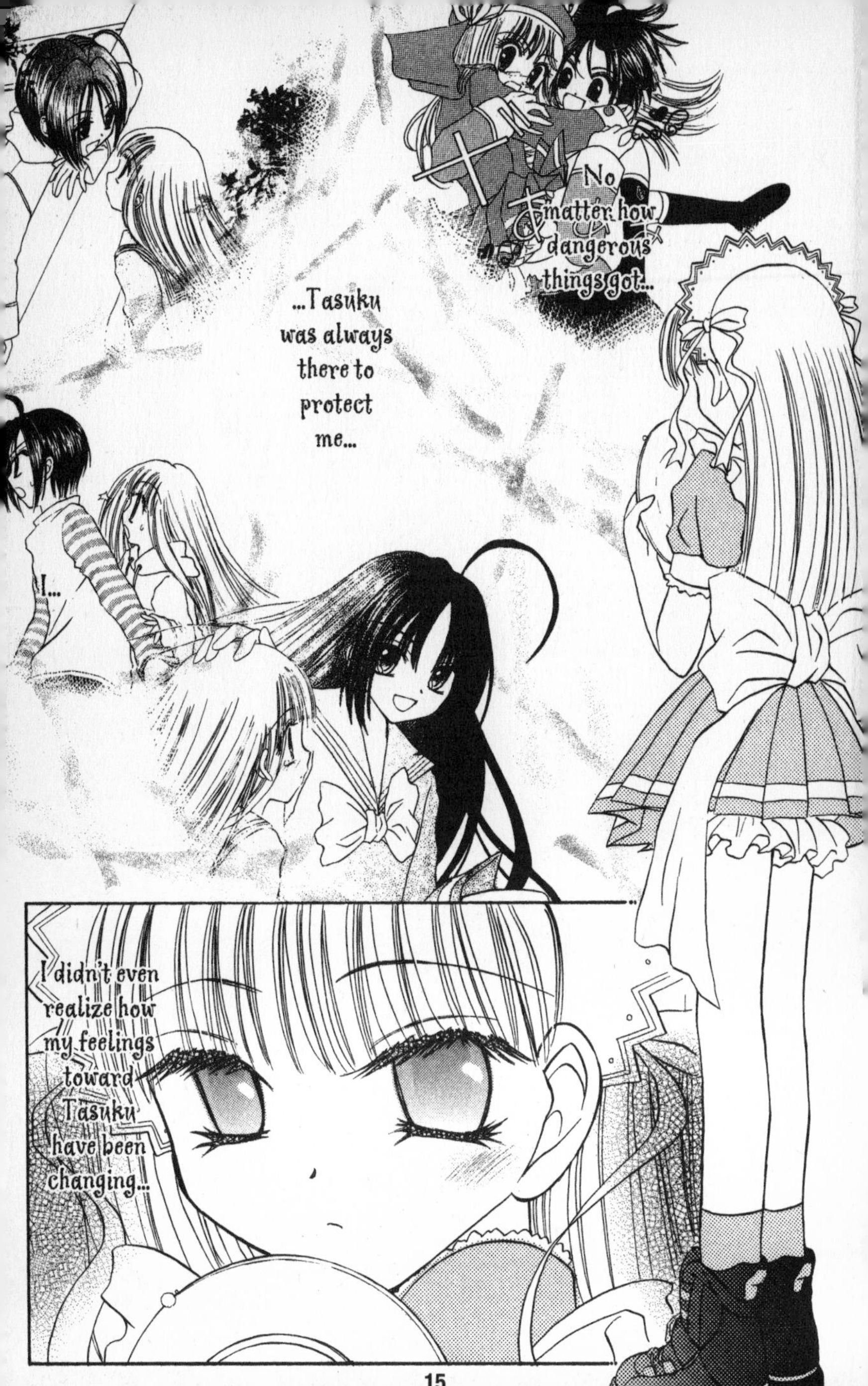
No matter how dangerous things got...
...Tasuku was always there to protect me...
I...
I didn't even realize how my feelings toward Tasuku have been changing...

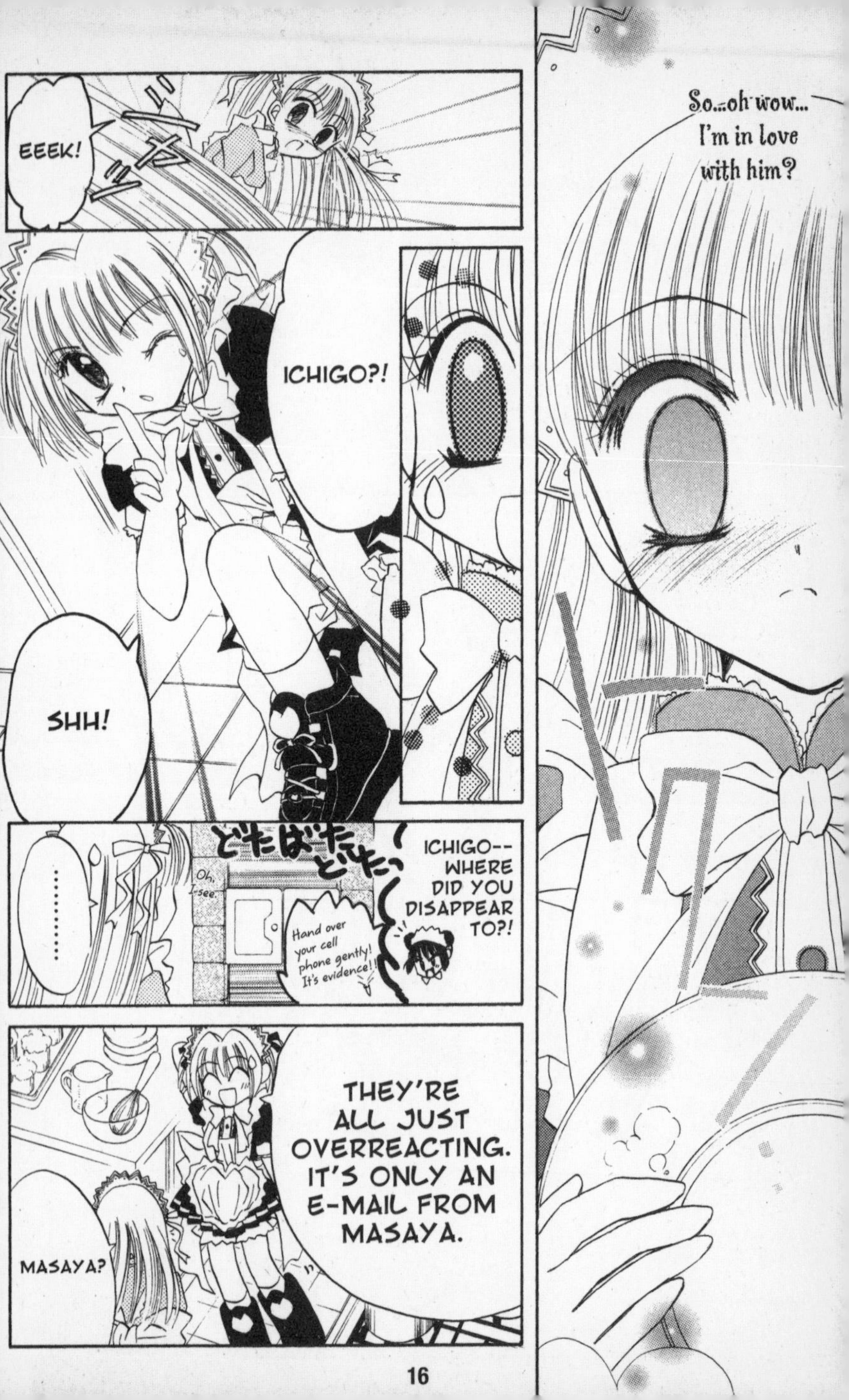
So...oh wow... I'm in love with him?
EEEK!
ICHIGO?!
SHH!
ICHIGO-- WHERE DID YOU DISAPPEAR TO?!
どたばたどたっ
Hand over your cell phone gently! It's evidence!!
Oh, I-see.
....
THEY'RE ALL JUST OVERREACTING. IT'S ONLY AN E-MAIL FROM MASAYA.
MASAYA?

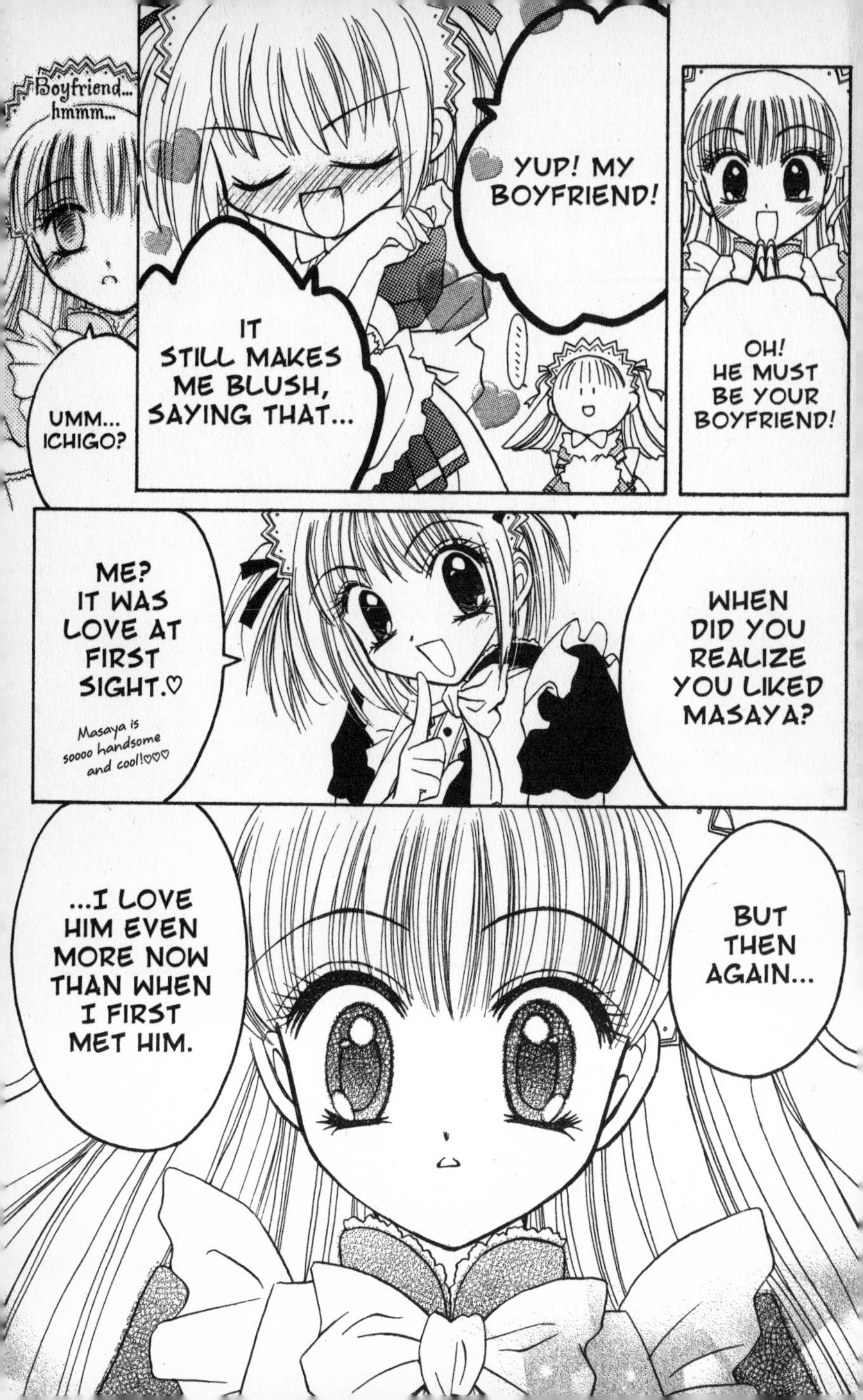
OH! HE MUST BE YOUR BOYFRIEND!
YUP! MY BOYFRIEND!
IT STILL MAKES ME BLUSH, SAYING THAT...
Boyfriend... hmmm...
UMM... ICHIGO?
WHEN DID YOU REALIZE YOU LIKED MASAYA?
ME? IT WAS LOVE AT FIRST SIGHT.♡
Masaya is soooo handsome and cool!♡♡♡
BUT THEN AGAIN...
...I LOVE HIM EVEN MORE NOW THAN WHEN I FIRST MET HIM.

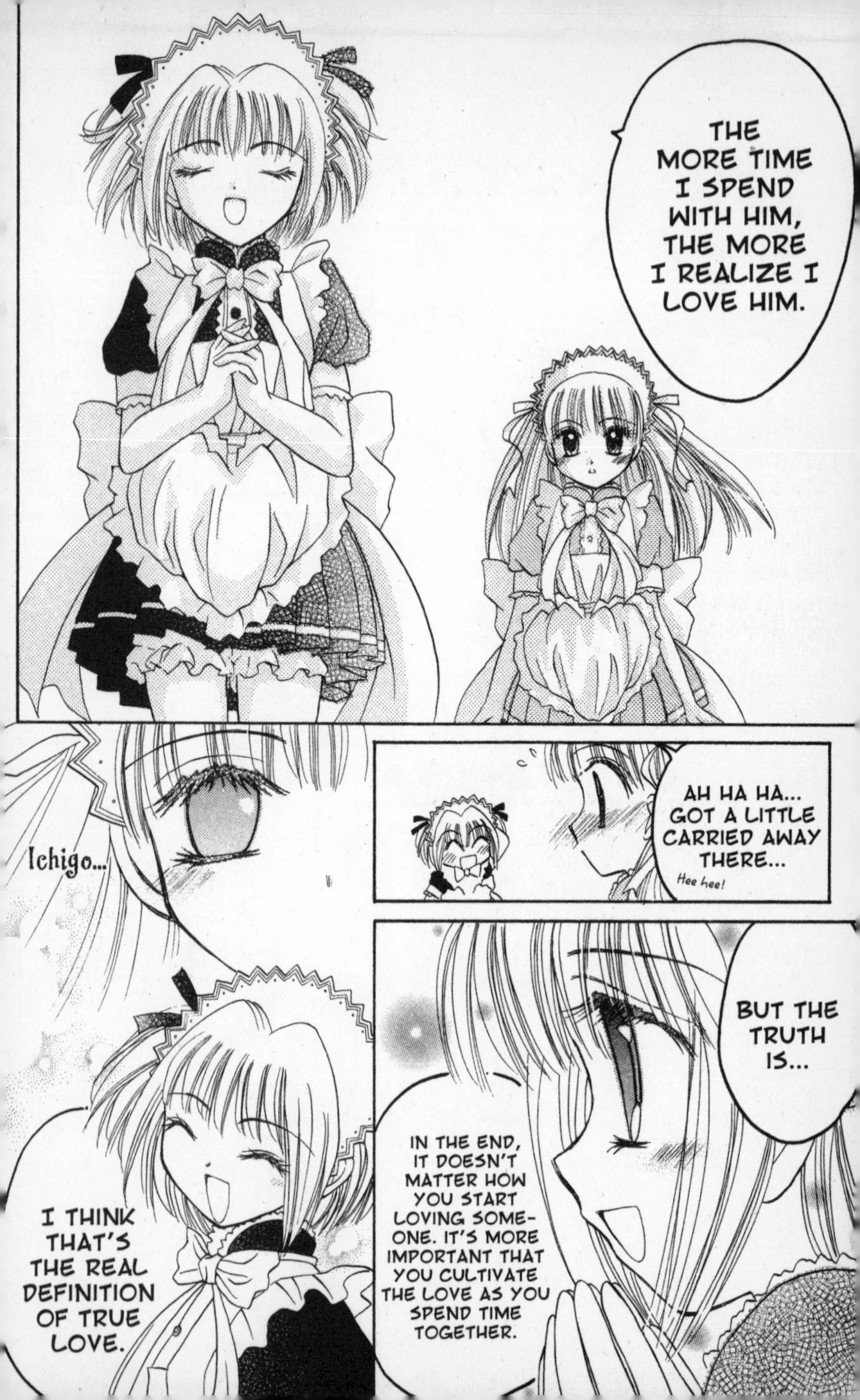
THE MORE TIME I SPEND WITH HIM, THE MORE I REALIZE I LOVE HIM.
AH HA HA... GOT A LITTLE CARRIED AWAY THERE...
Hee hee!
Ichigo...
BUT THE TRUTH IS...
IN THE END, IT DOESN'T MATTER HOW YOU START LOVING SOME-ONE. IT'S MORE IMPORTANT THAT YOU CULTIVATE THE LOVE AS YOU SPEND TIME TOGETHER.
I THINK THAT'S THE REAL DEFINITION OF TRUE LOVE.

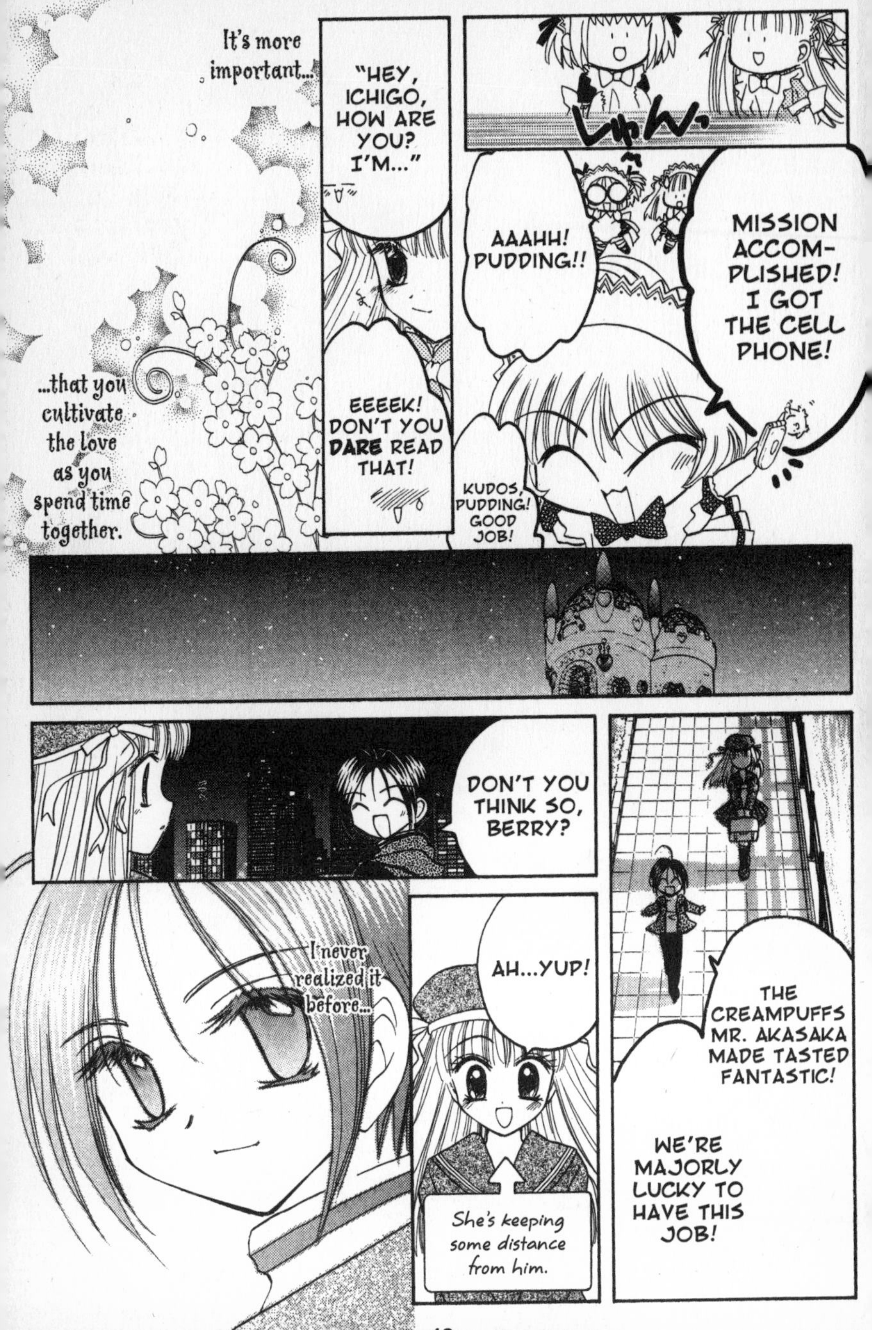
しゅん
MISSION ACCOMPLISHED! I GOT THE CELL PHONE!
AAAHH! PUDDING!!
KUDOS, PUDDING! GOOD JOB!
"HEY, ICHIGO, HOW ARE YOU? I'M..."
EEEEK! DON'T YOU DARE READ THAT!
It's more important...
...that you cultivate the love as you spend time together.
THE CREAMPUFFS MR. AKASAKA MADE TASTED FANTASTIC!
WE'RE MAJORLY LUCKY TO HAVE THIS JOB!
DON'T YOU THINK SO, BERRY?
AH...YUP!
She's keeping some distance from him.
I never realized it before...

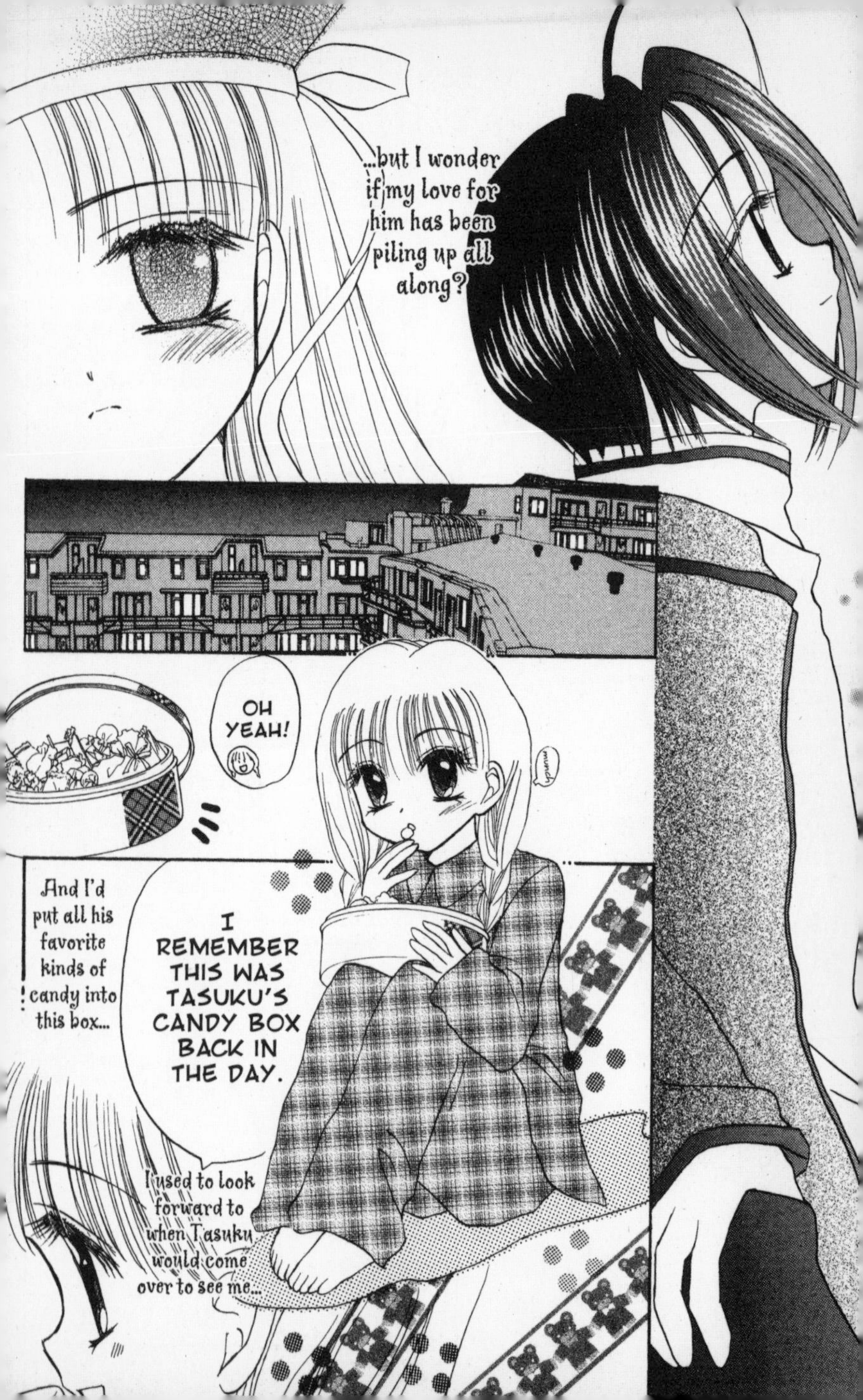
...but I wonder if my love for him has been piling up all along?
OH YEAH!
munch
I REMEMBER THIS WAS TASUKU'S CANDY BOX BACK IN THE DAY.
And I'd put all his favorite kinds of candy into this box...
I used to look forward to when Tasuku would come over to see me...

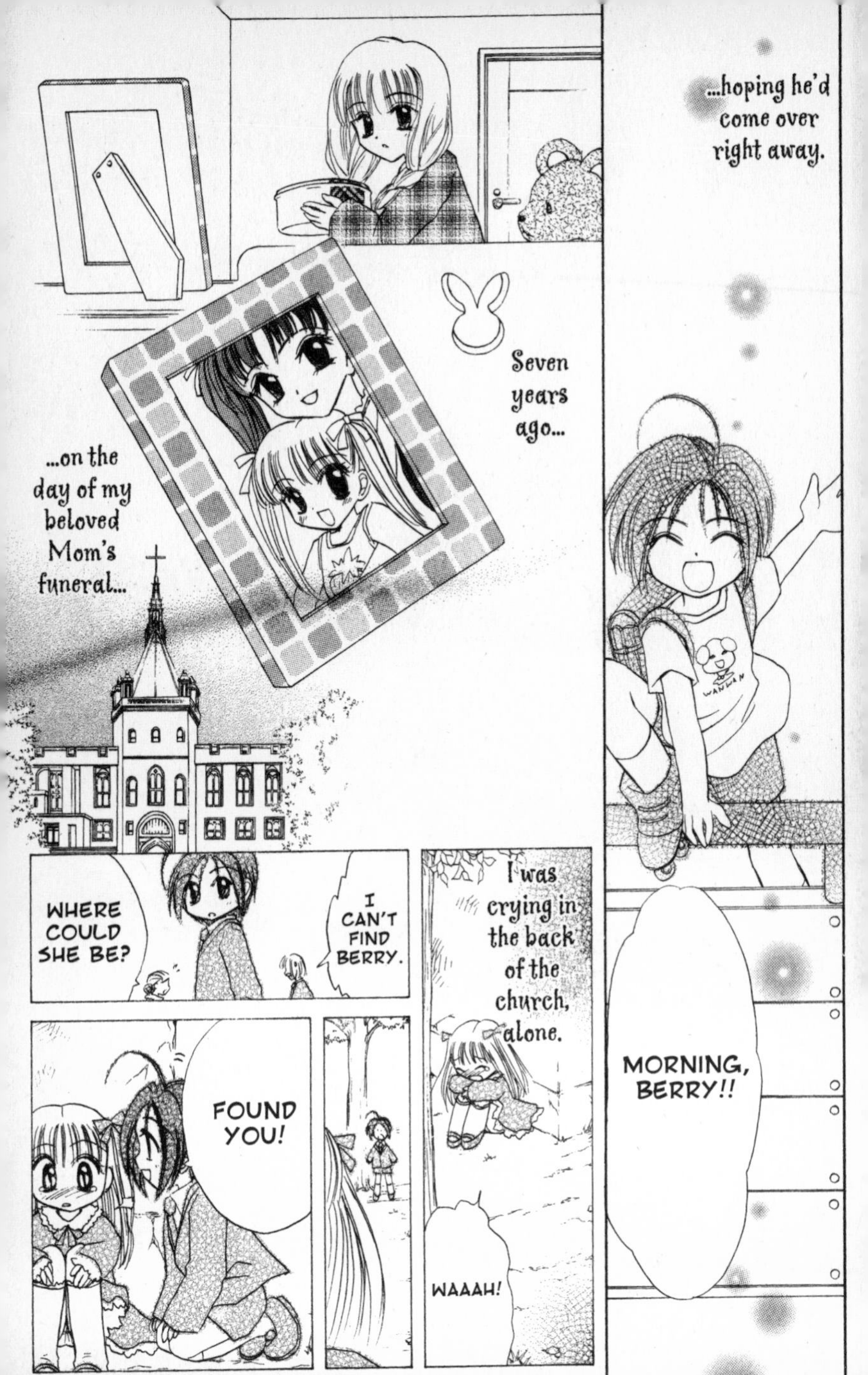
...hoping he'd come over right away.
MORNING, BERRY!!
Seven years ago...
...on the day of my beloved Mom's funeral...
I was crying in the back of the church, alone.
I CAN'T FIND BERRY.
WHERE COULD SHE BE?
WAAAH!
FOUND YOU!

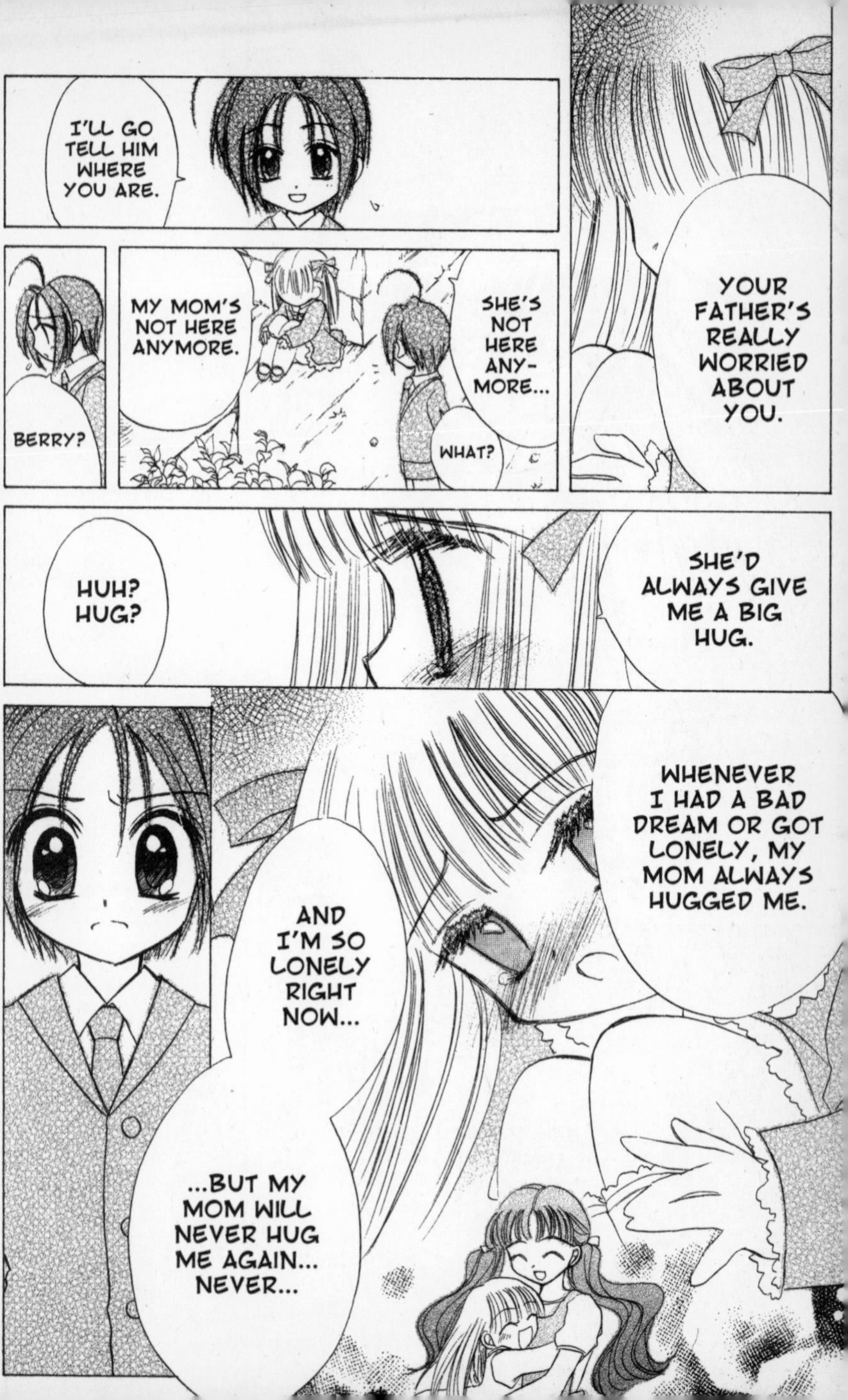
YOUR FATHER'S REALLY WORRIED ABOUT YOU.
I'LL GO TELL HIM WHERE YOU ARE.
SHE'S NOT HERE ANY-MORE...
WHAT?
MY MOM'S NOT HERE ANYMORE.
BERRY?
SHE'D ALWAYS GIVE ME A BIG HUG.
HUH? HUG?
WHENEVER I HAD A BAD DREAM OR GOT LONELY, MY MOM ALWAYS HUGGED ME.
AND I'M SO LONELY RIGHT NOW...
...BUT MY MOM WILL NEVER HUG ME AGAIN... NEVER...

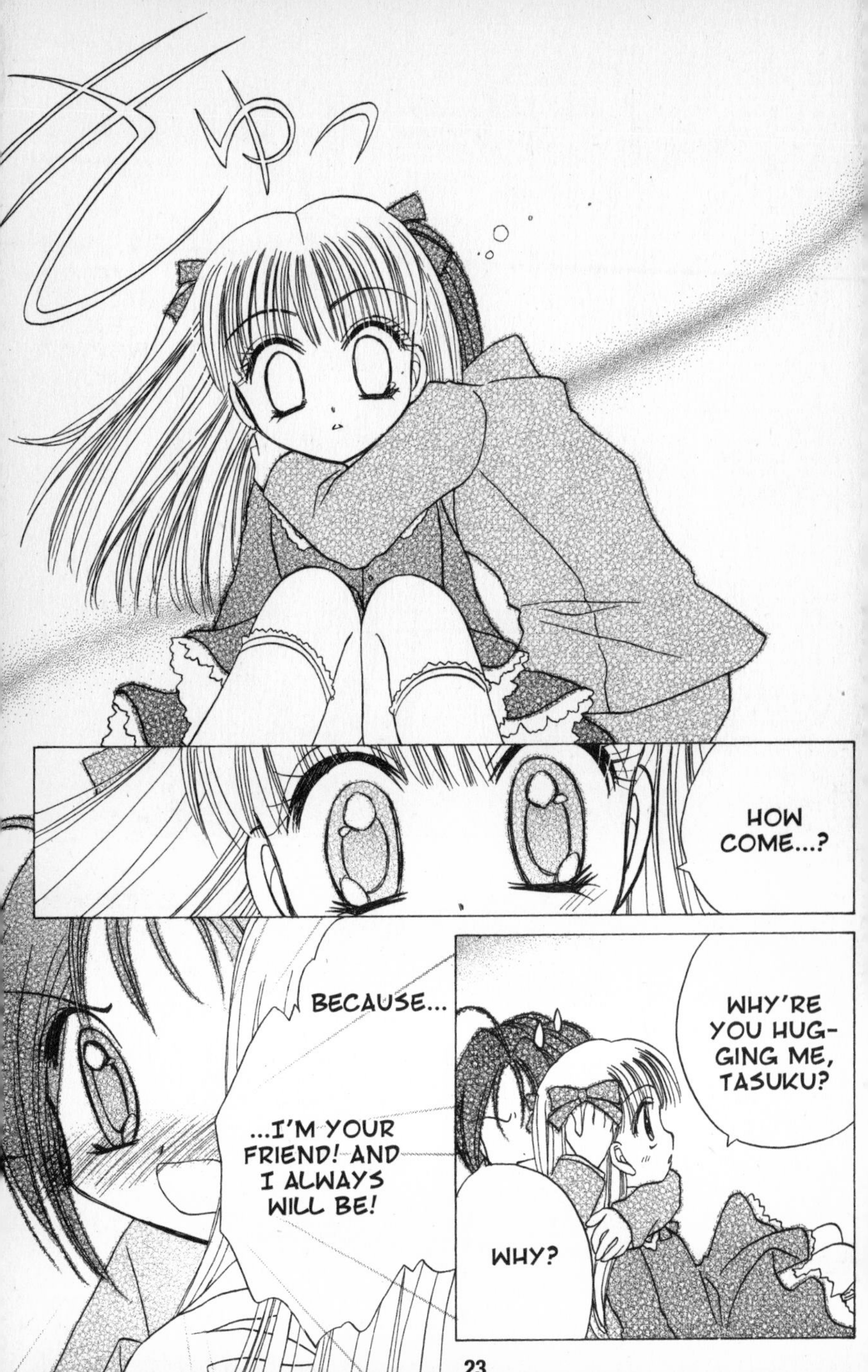
HOW COME...?
WHY'RE YOU HUG-GING ME, TASUKU?
WHY?
BECAUSE...
...I'M YOUR FRIEND! AND I ALWAYS WILL BE!

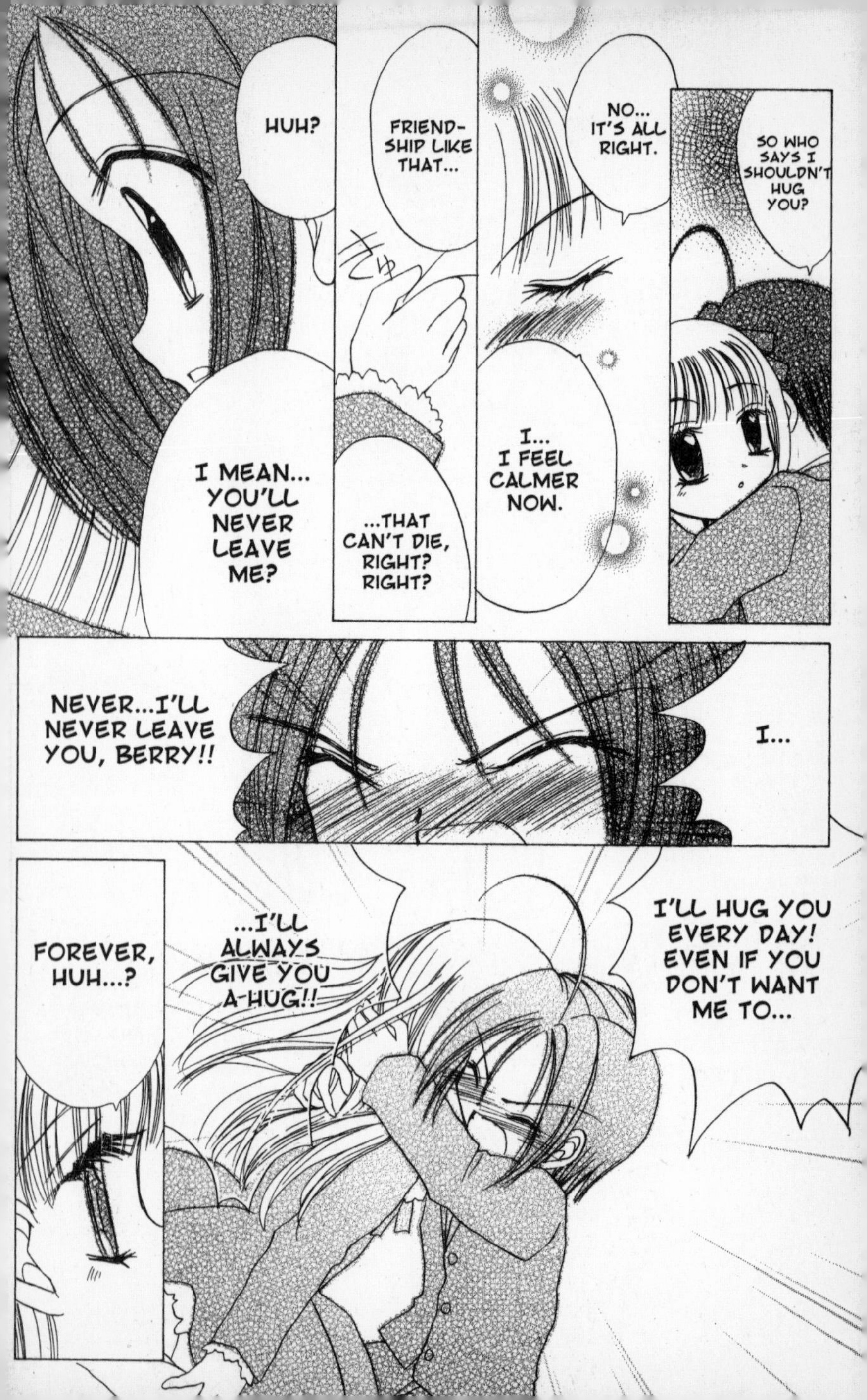
SO WHO SAYS I SHOULDN'T HUG YOU?
NO... IT'S ALL RIGHT.
I... I FEEL CALMER NOW.
FRIEND-SHIP LIKE THAT...
きゅ
...THAT CAN'T DIE, RIGHT? RIGHT?
HUH?
I MEAN... YOU'LL NEVER LEAVE ME?
I...
NEVER...I'LL NEVER LEAVE YOU, BERRY!!
I'LL HUG YOU EVERY DAY! EVEN IF YOU DON'T WANT ME TO...
...I'LL ALWAYS GIVE YOU A-HUG!!
FOREVER, HUH...?

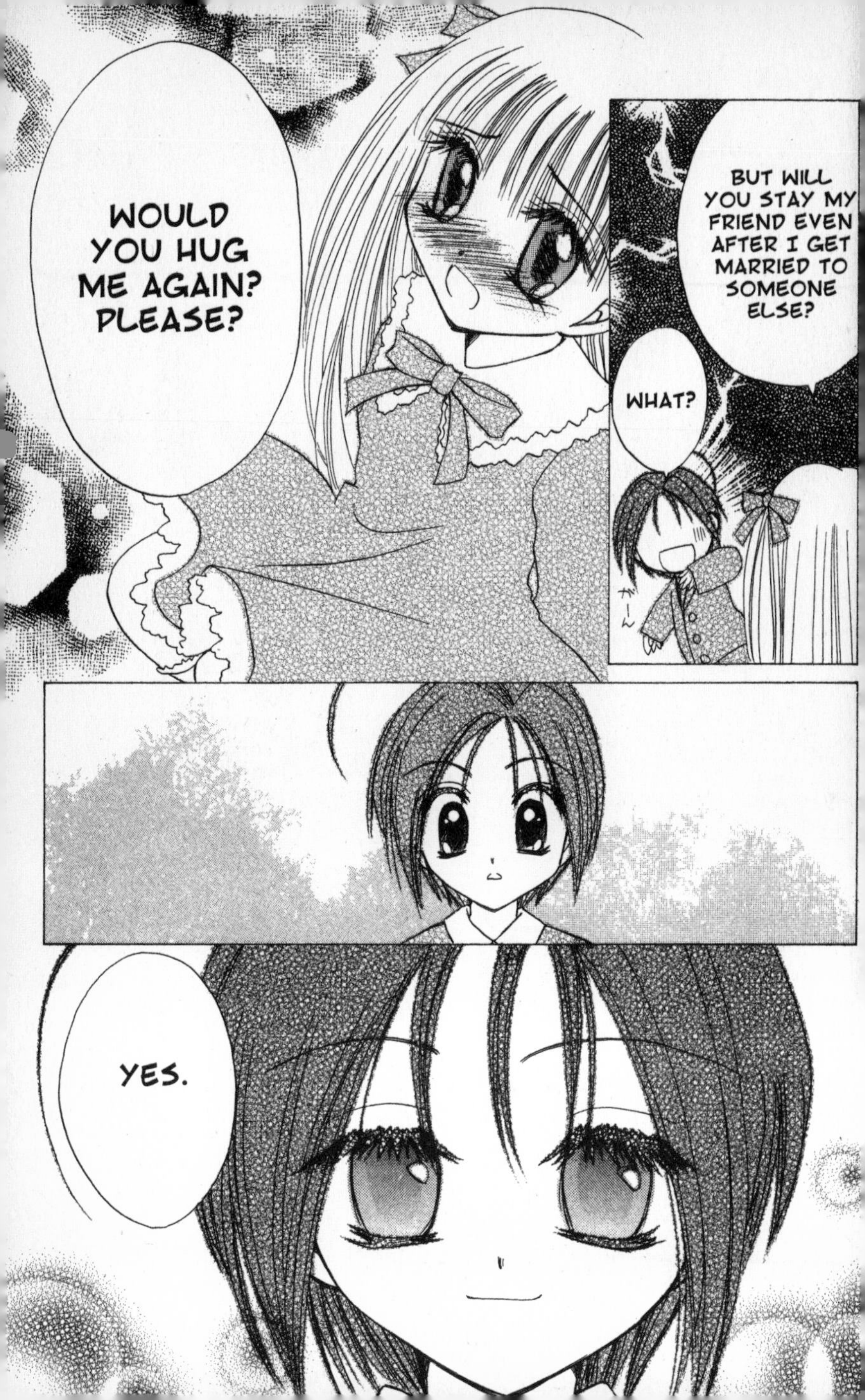
BUT WILL YOU STAY MY FRIEND EVEN AFTER I GET MARRIED TO SOMEONE ELSE?
WHAT?
WOULD YOU HUG ME AGAIN? PLEASE?
YES.

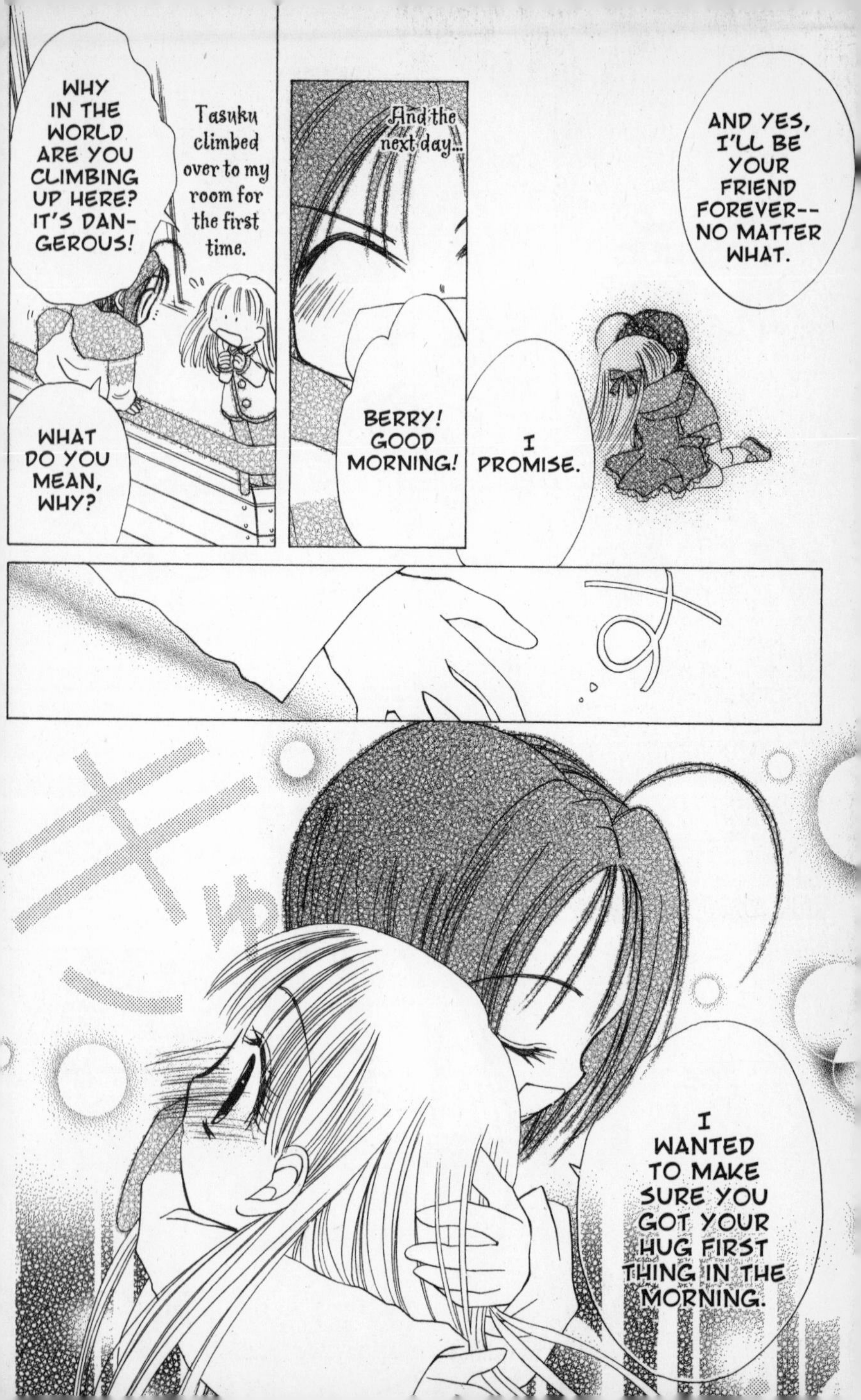
AND YES, I'LL BE YOUR FRIEND FOREVER--NO MATTER WHAT.
I PROMISE.
And the next day...
BERRY! GOOD MORNING!
Tasuku climbed over to my room for the first time.
WHY IN THE WORLD ARE YOU CLIMBING UP HERE? IT'S DANGEROUS!
WHAT DO YOU MEAN, WHY?
I WANTED TO MAKE SURE YOU GOT YOUR HUG FIRST THING IN THE MORNING.

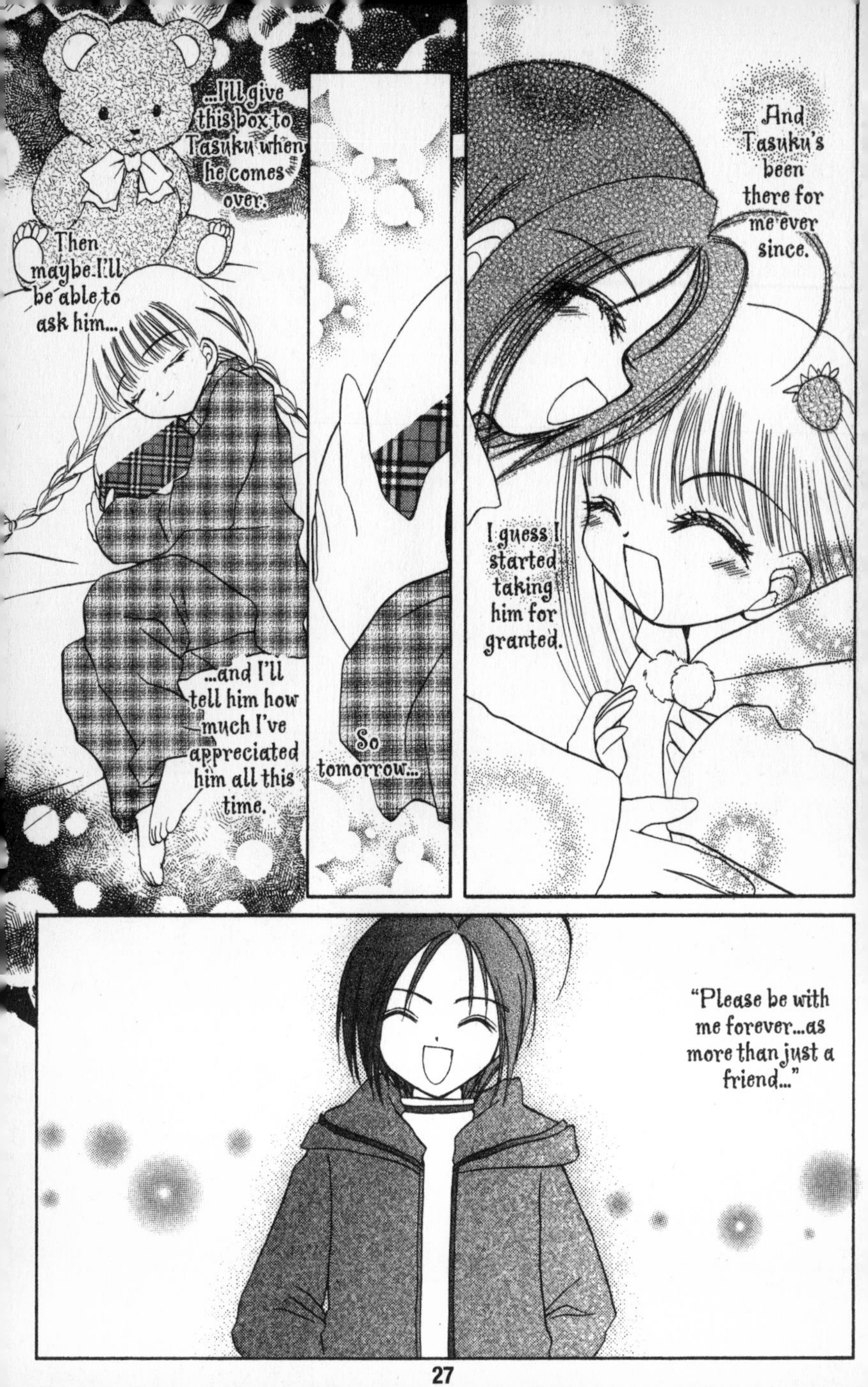

And Tasuku's been there for me ever since.
I guess I started taking him for granted.
...I'll give this box to Tasuku when he comes over.
Then maybe I'll be able to ask him...
So tomorrow...
...and I'll tell him how much I've appreciated him all this time.
"Please be with me forever...as more than just a friend..."

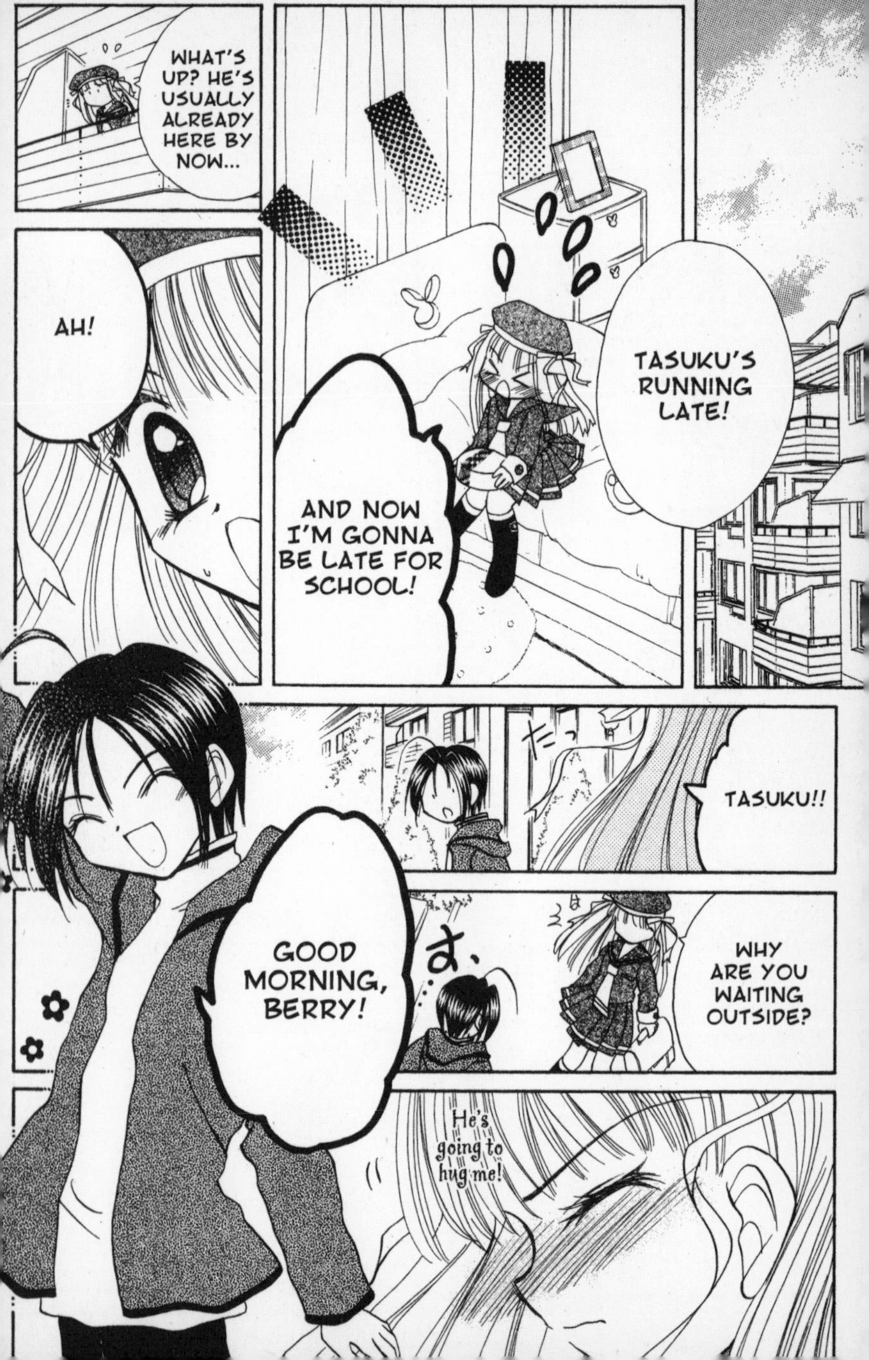

WHAT'S UP? HE'S USUALLY ALREADY HERE BY NOW...
TASUKU'S RUNNING LATE!
AND NOW I'M GONNA BE LATE FOR SCHOOL!
AH!
たっ
TASUKU!!
WHY ARE YOU WAITING OUTSIDE?
す、
GOOD MORNING, BERRY!
He's going to hug me!

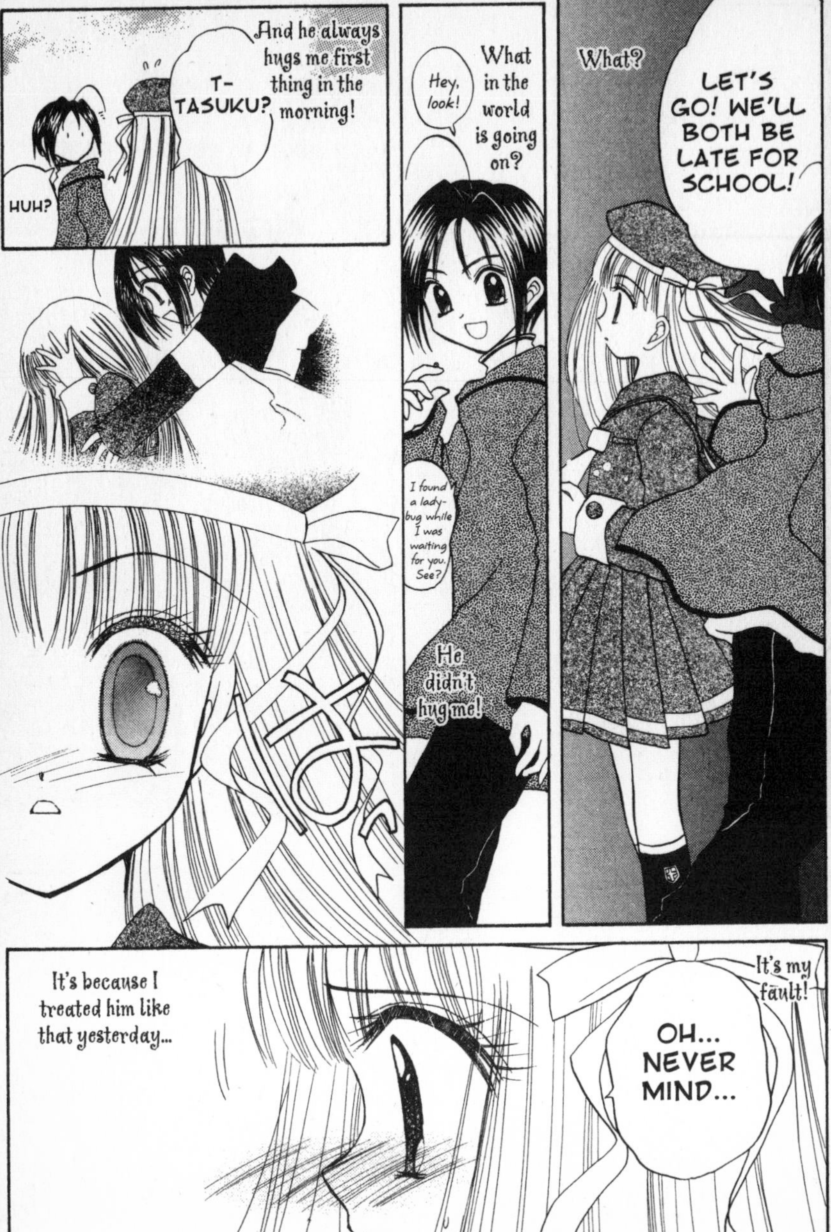

What?
LET'S GO! WE'LL BOTH BE LATE FOR SCHOOL!
Hey, look!
What in the world is going on?
I found a lady-bug while I was waiting for you. See?
He didn't hug me!
And he always hugs me first thing in the morning!
T-TASUKU?
HUH?
It's my fault!
OH... NEVER MIND...
It's because I treated him like that yesterday...

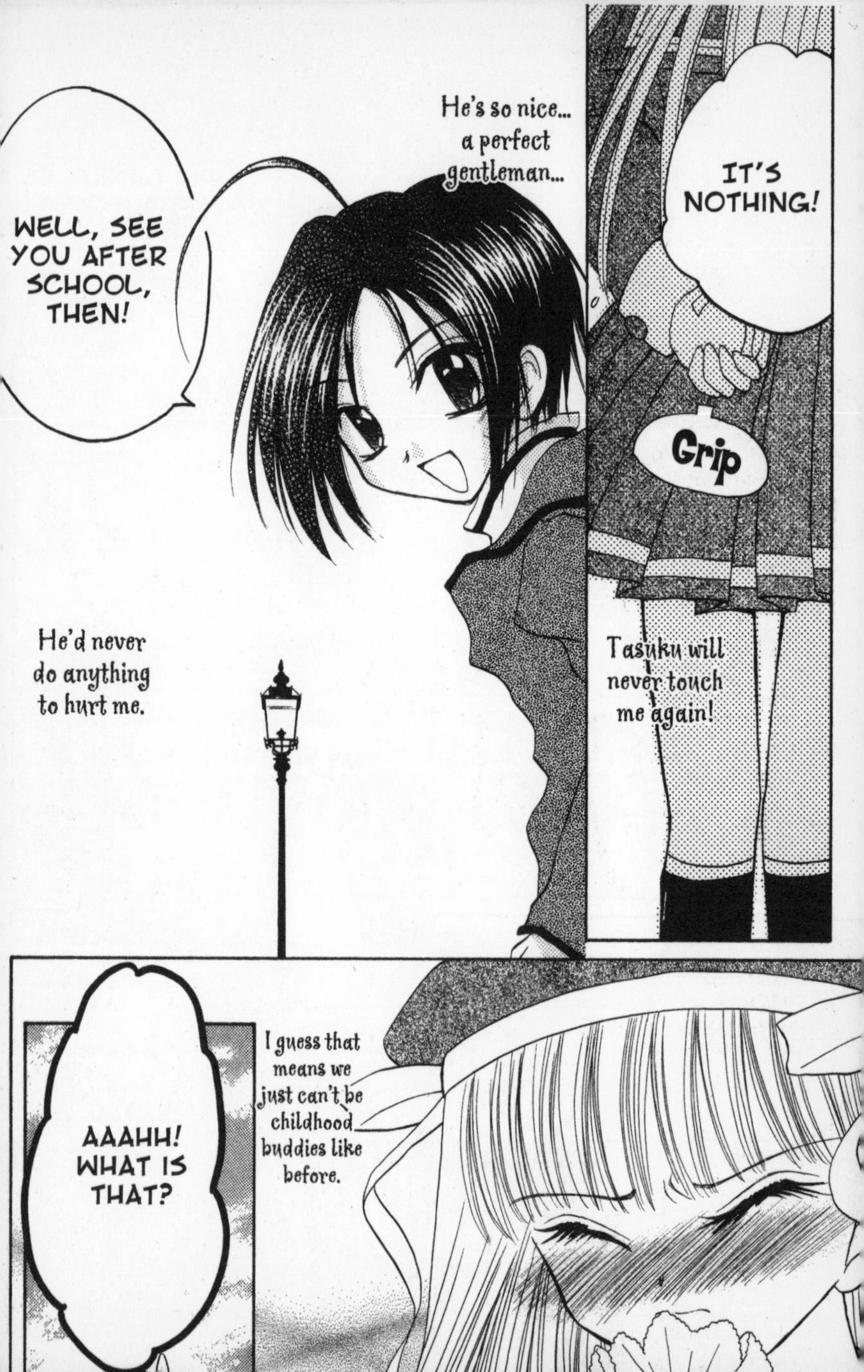
IT'S NOTHING!
Grip
Tasuku will never touch me again!
He's so nice... a perfect gentleman...
WELL, SEE YOU AFTER SCHOOL, THEN!
He'd never do anything to hurt me.
I guess that means we just can't be childhood buddies like before.
AAAHH! WHAT IS THAT?

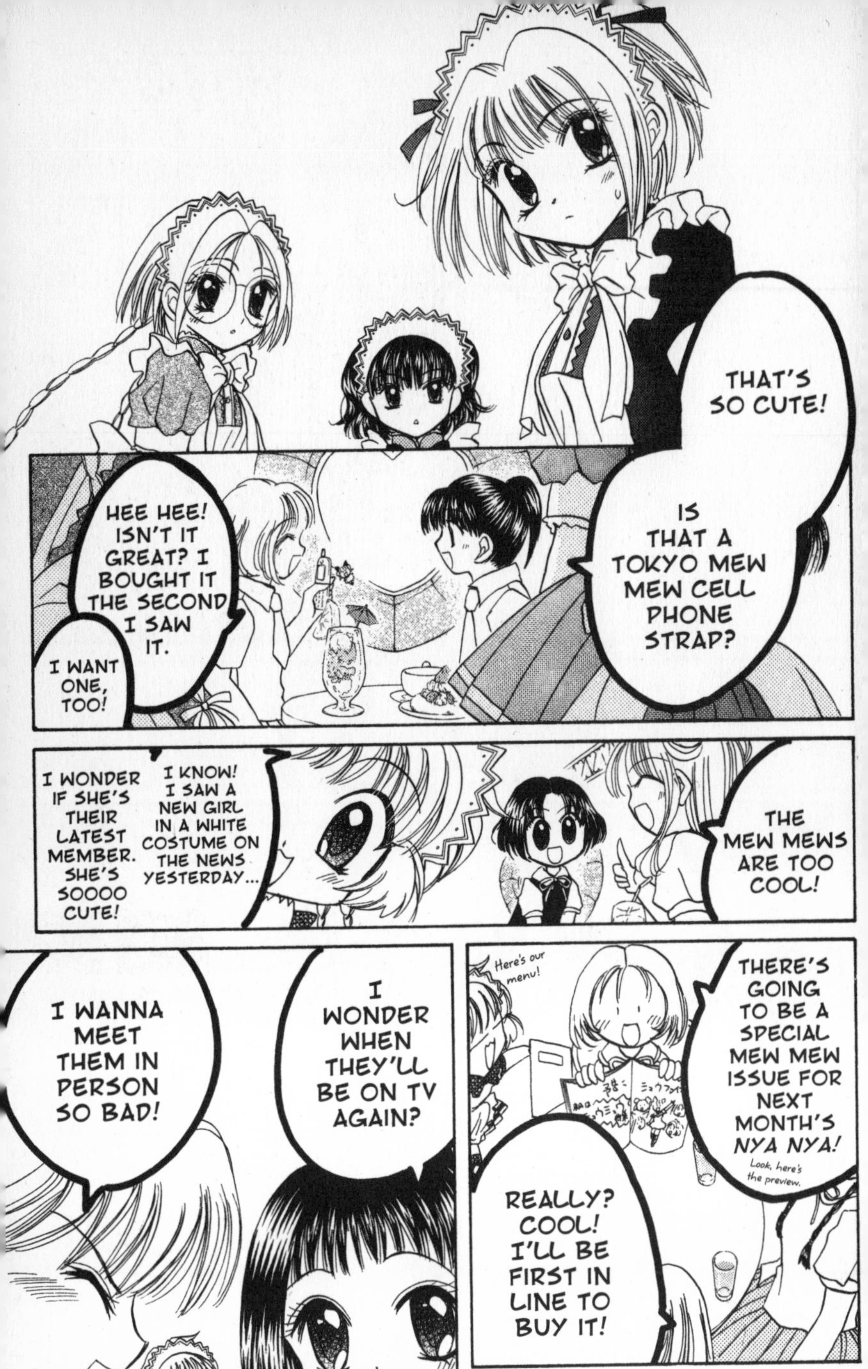

THAT'S SO CUTE!
IS THAT A TOKYO MEW MEW CELL PHONE STRAP?
HEE HEE! ISN'T IT GREAT? I BOUGHT IT THE SECOND I SAW IT.
I WANT ONE, TOO!
THE MEW MEWS ARE TOO COOL!
I KNOW! I SAW A NEW GIRL IN A WHITE COSTUME ON THE NEWS YESTERDAY...
I WONDER IF SHE'S THEIR LATEST MEMBER. SHE'S SOOOO CUTE!
THERE'S GOING TO BE A SPECIAL MEW MEW ISSUE FOR NEXT MONTH'S *NYA NYA*!
Look, here's the preview.
Here's our menu!
REALLY? COOL! I'LL BE FIRST IN LINE TO BUY IT!
I WONDER WHEN THEY'LL BE ON TV AGAIN?
I WANNA MEET THEM IN PERSON SO BAD!

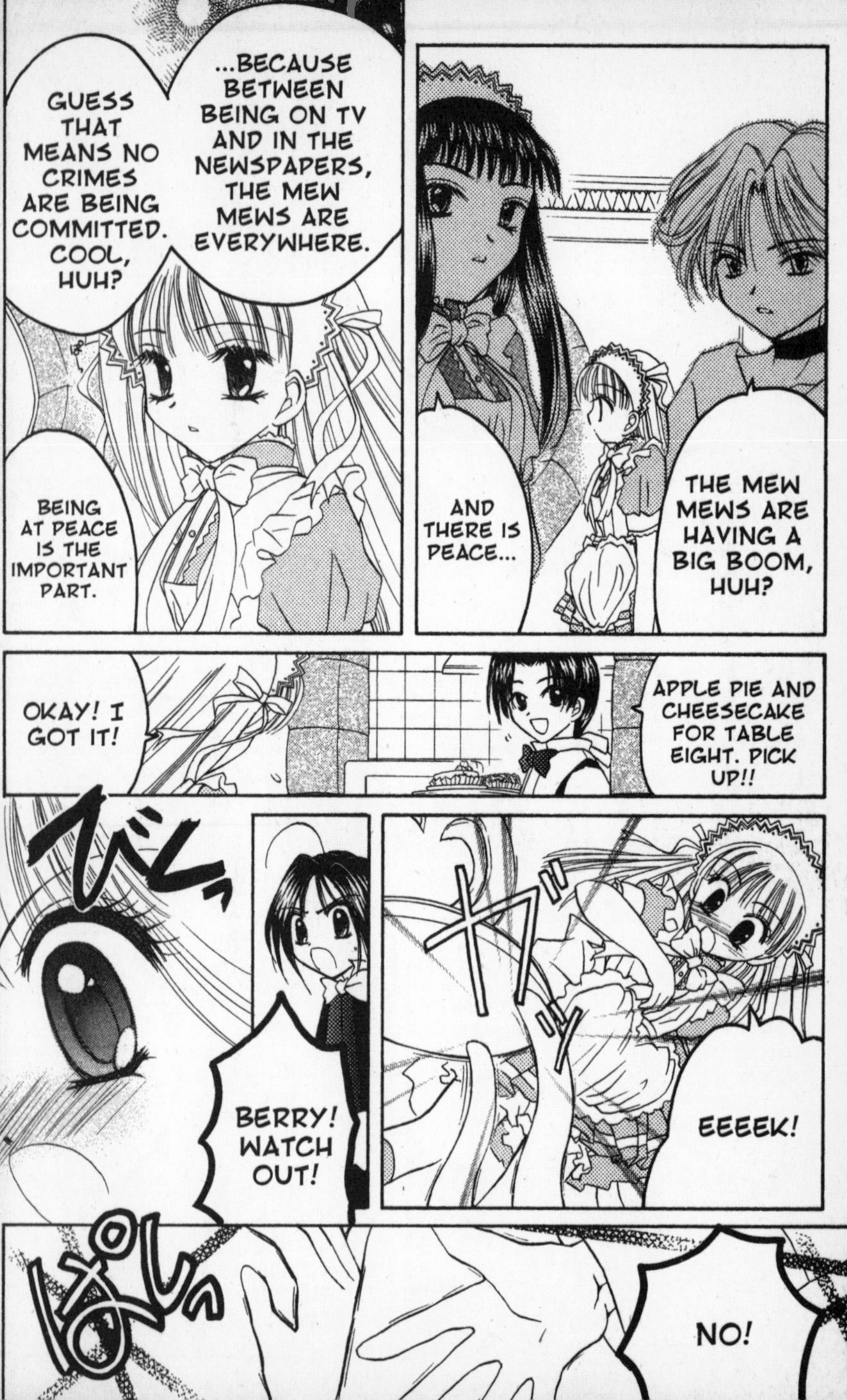

THE MEW MEWS ARE HAVING A BIG BOOM, HUH?
AND THERE IS PEACE...
...BECAUSE BETWEEN BEING ON TV AND IN THE NEWSPAPERS, THE MEW MEWS ARE EVERYWHERE.
GUESS THAT MEANS NO CRIMES ARE BEING COMMITTED. COOL, HUH?
BEING AT PEACE IS THE IMPORTANT PART.
APPLE PIE AND CHEESECAKE FOR TABLE EIGHT. PICK UP!!
OKAY! I GOT IT!
EEEEK!
BERRY! WATCH OUT!
NO!

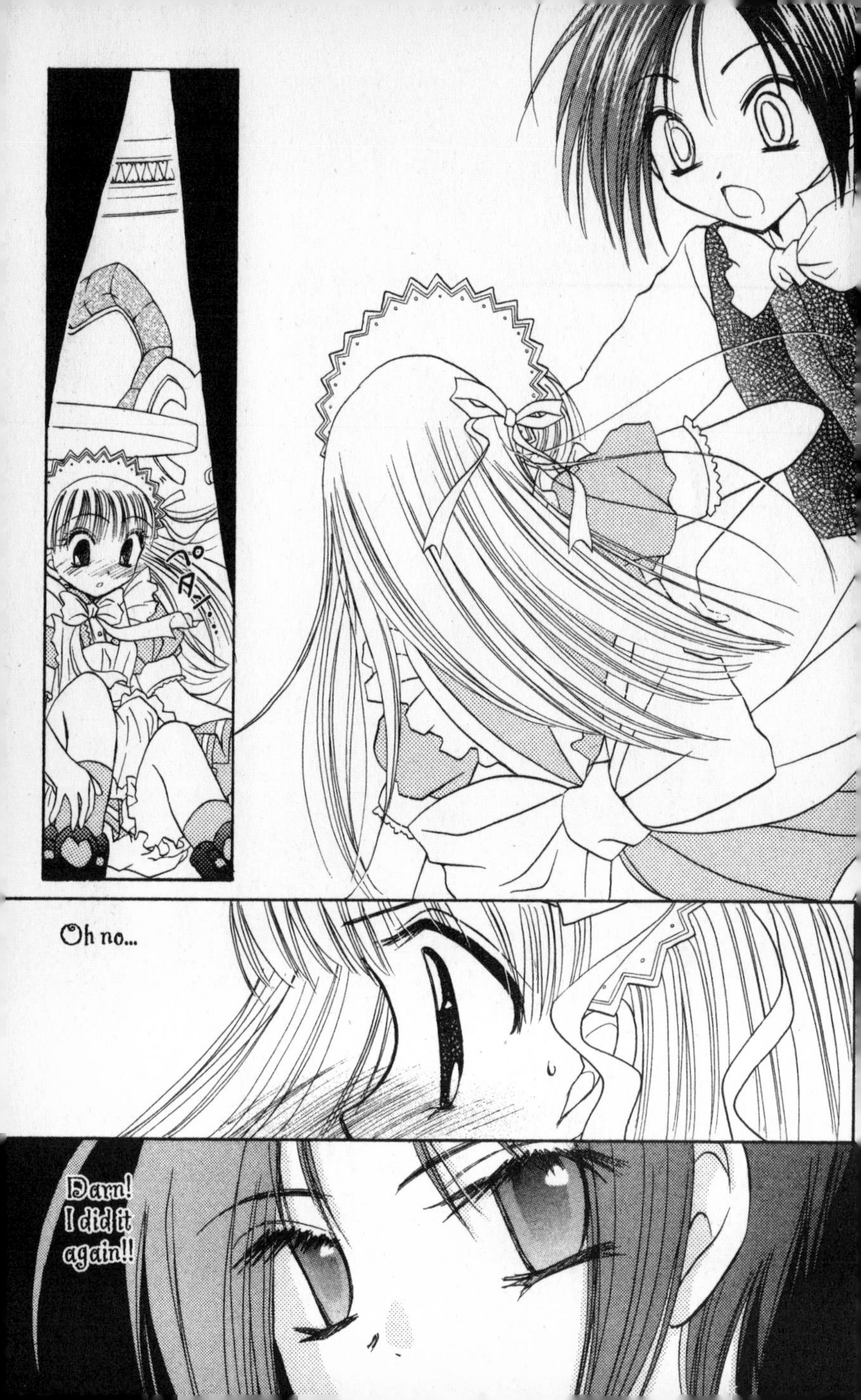
Oh no...
Darn! I did it again!!

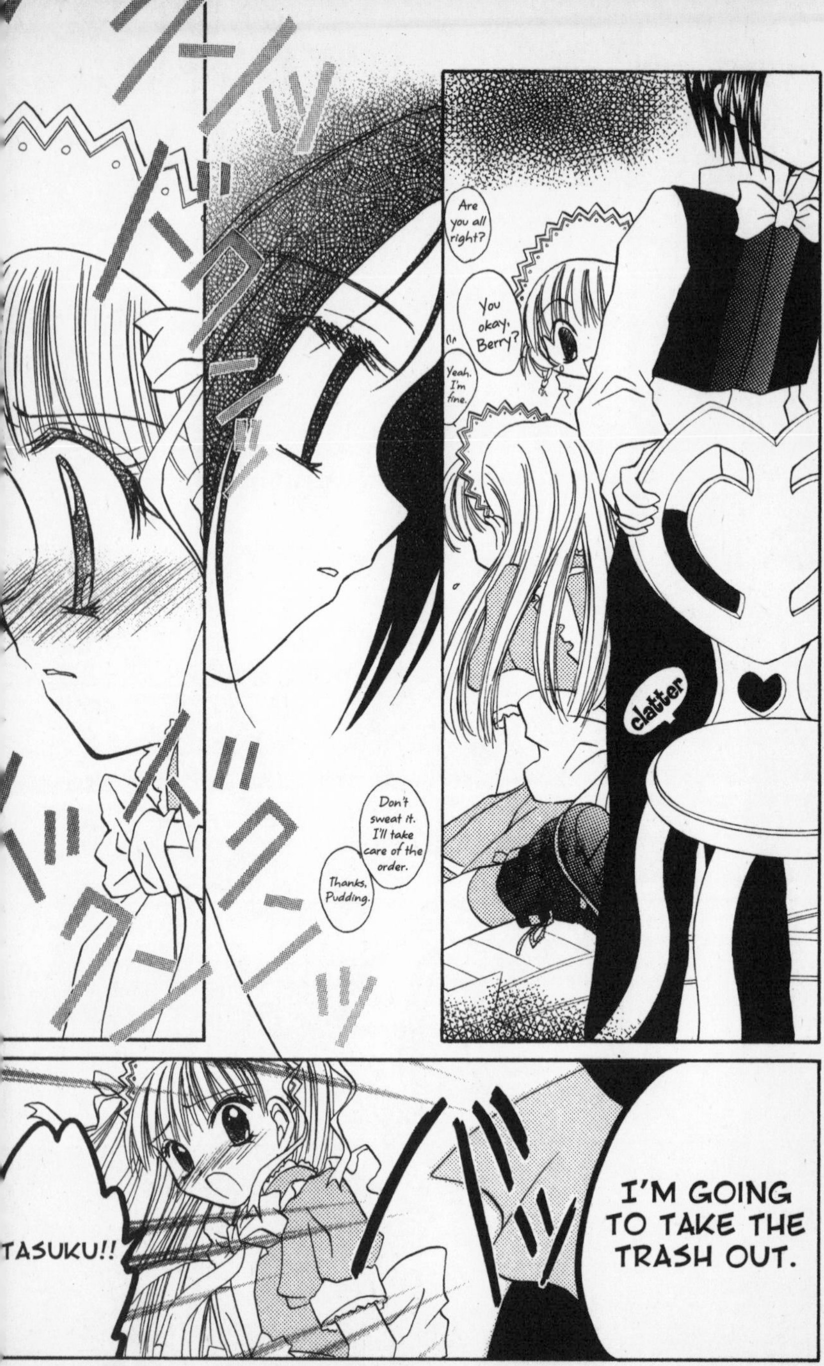
Are you all right?
You okay, Berry?
Yeah. I'm fine.
clatter
Don't sweat it. I'll take care of the order.
Thanks, Pudding.
I'M GOING TO TAKE THE TRASH OUT.
TASUKU!!

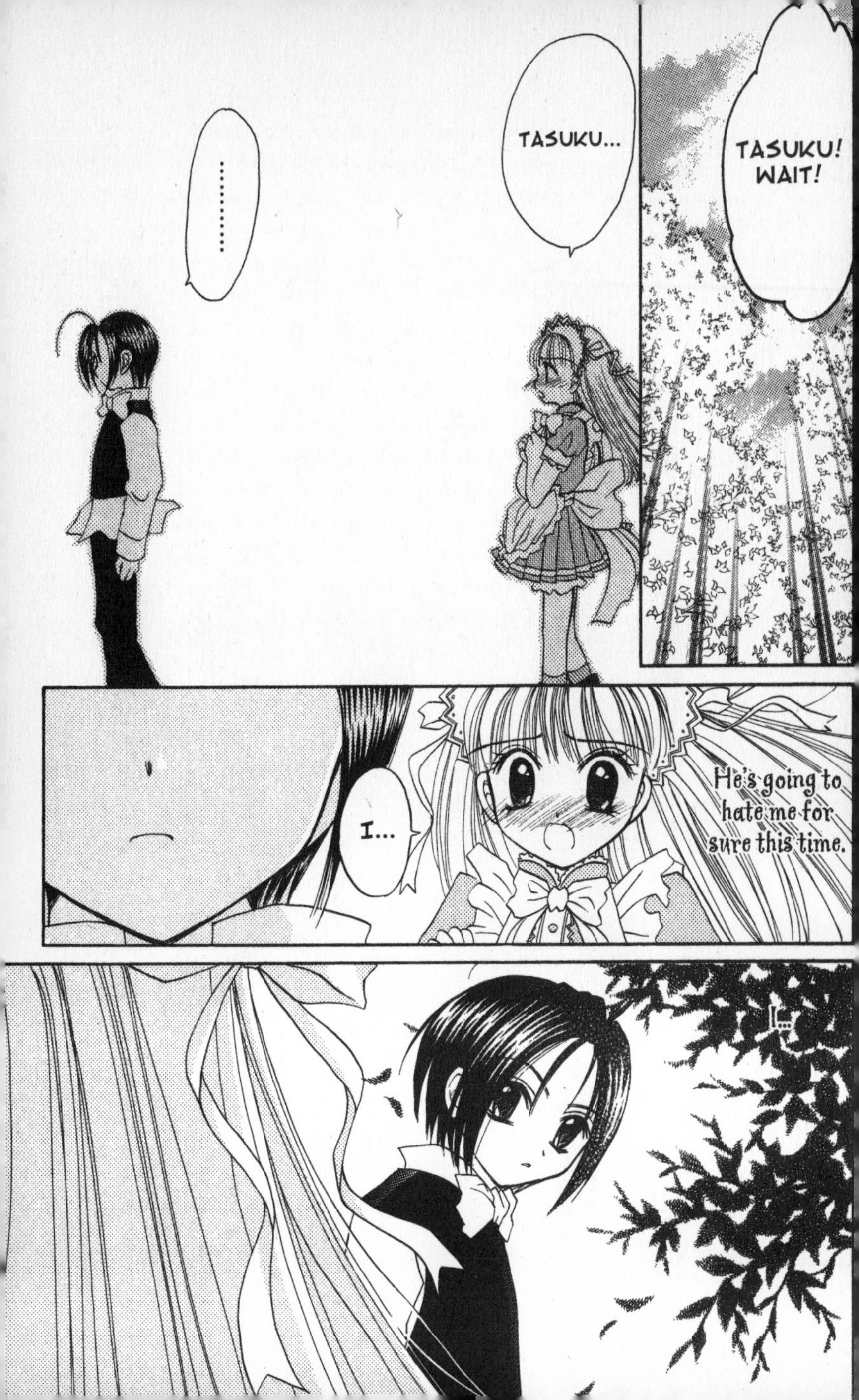
TASUKU! WAIT!
TASUKU...
......
He's going to hate me for sure this time.
I...
I...

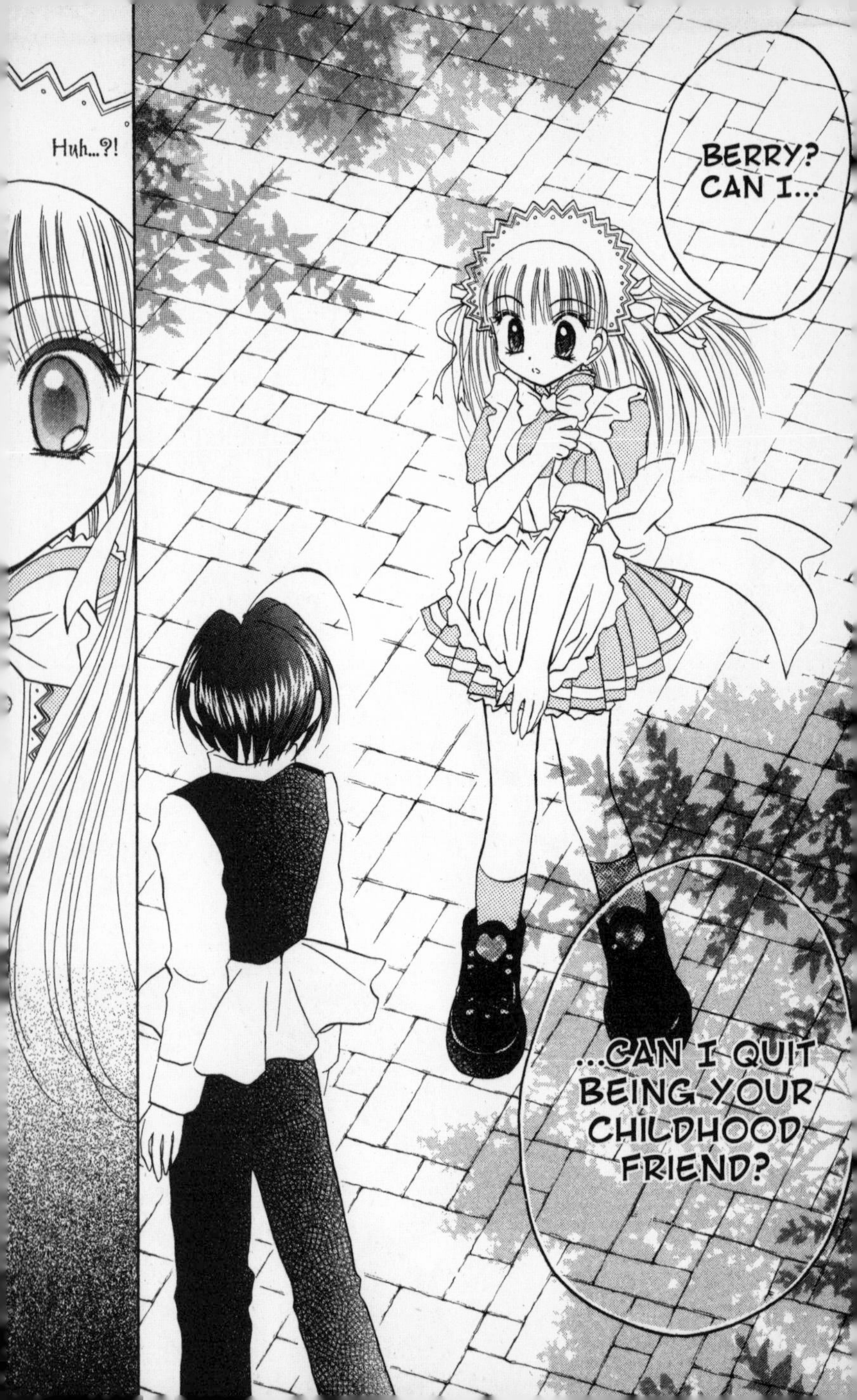
Berry? Can I...
...Can I quit being your childhood friend?
Huh...?!

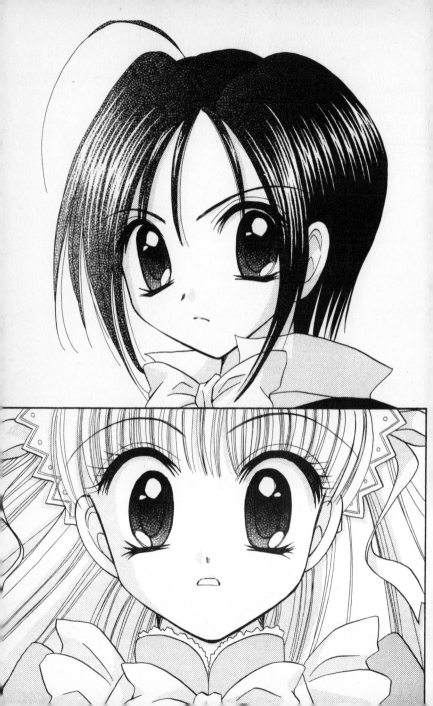

Special manga extra!

Berry's rush report ☆*1

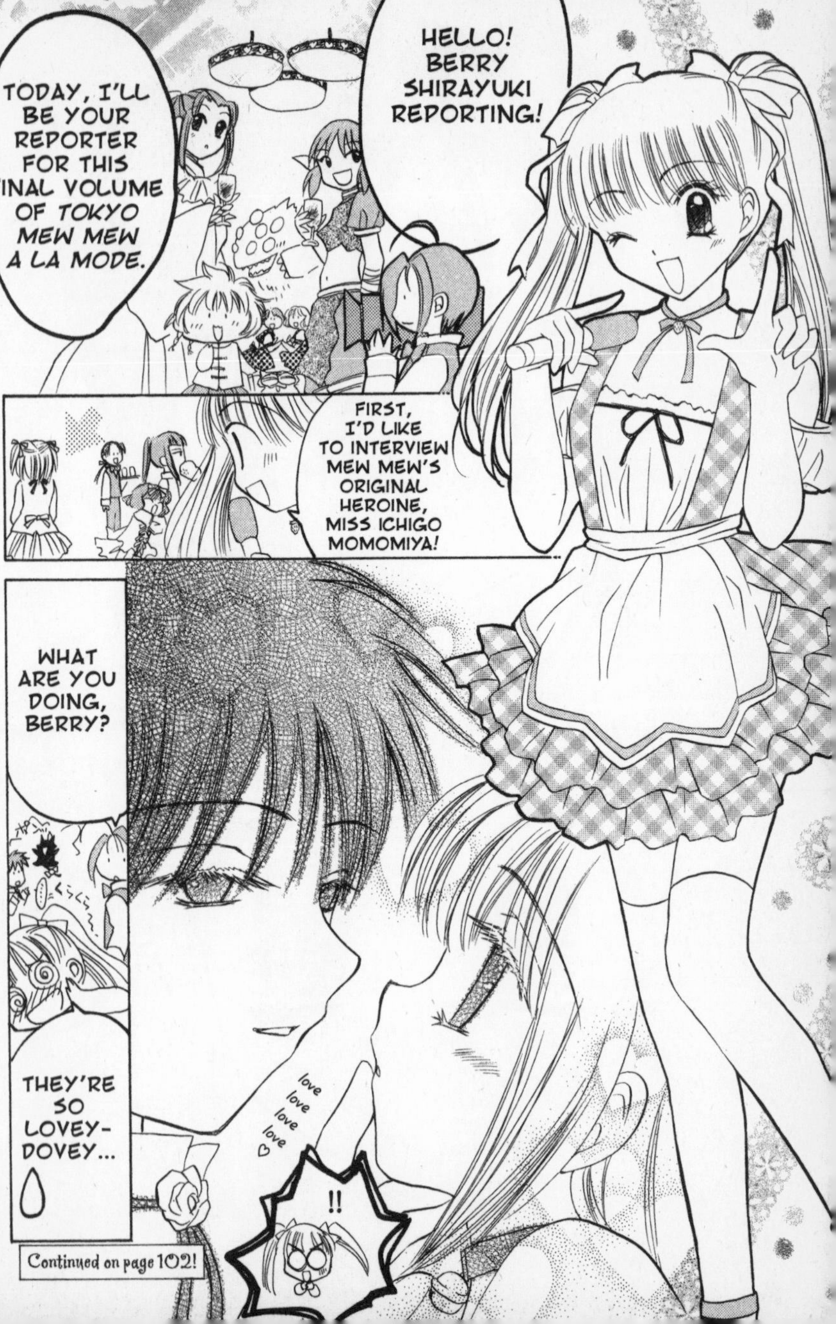
HELLO! BERRY SHIRAYUKI REPORTING!
TODAY, I'LL BE YOUR REPORTER FOR THIS FINAL VOLUME OF *TOKYO MEW MEW A LA MODE.*
FIRST, I'D LIKE TO INTERVIEW MEW MEW'S ORIGINAL HEROINE, MISS ICHIGO MOMOMIYA!
WHAT ARE YOU DOING, BERRY?
love love love love ♡
THEY'RE SO LOVEY-DOVEY...
!!

Continued on page 102!

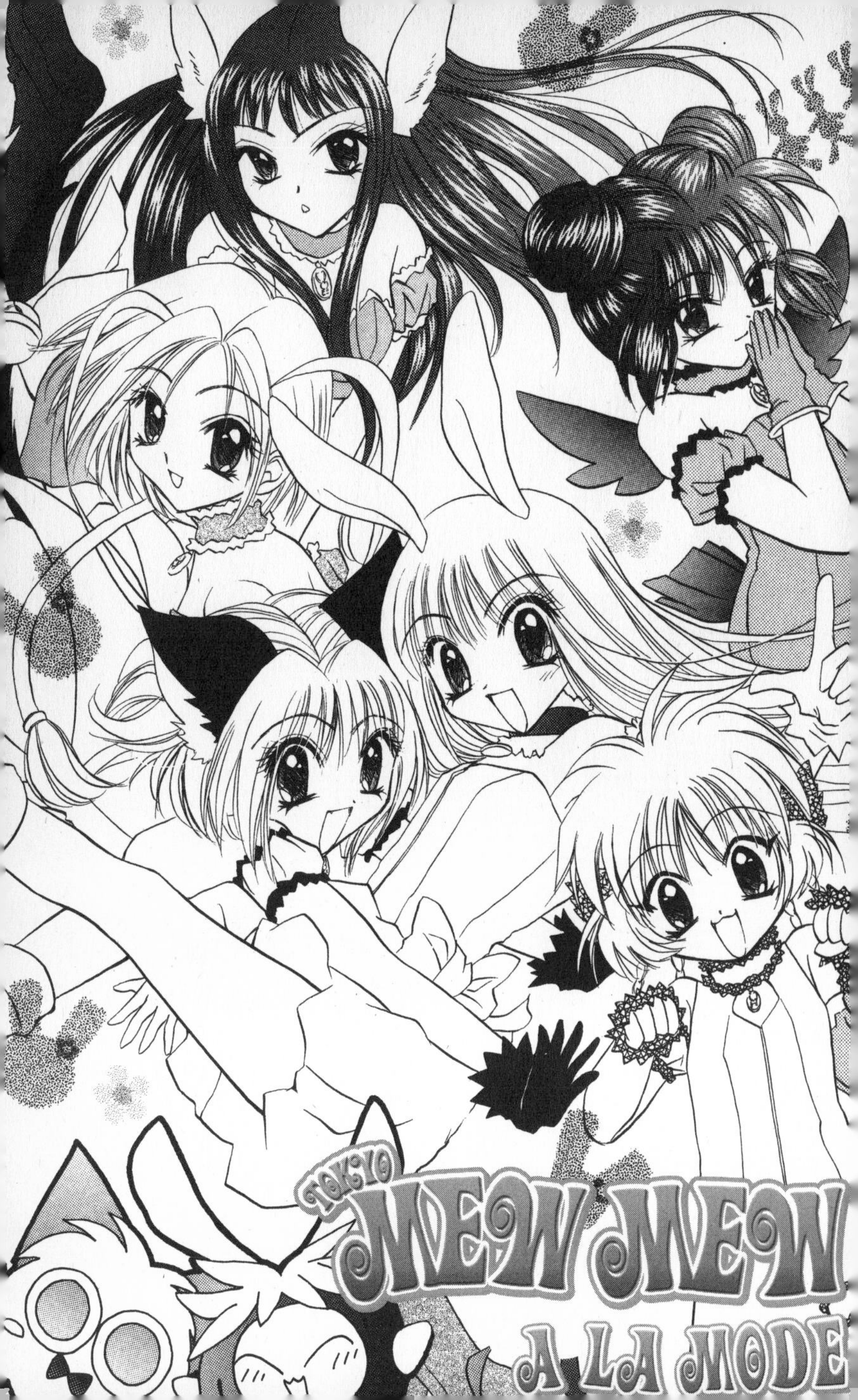
TOKYO
MEW MEW
A LA MODE

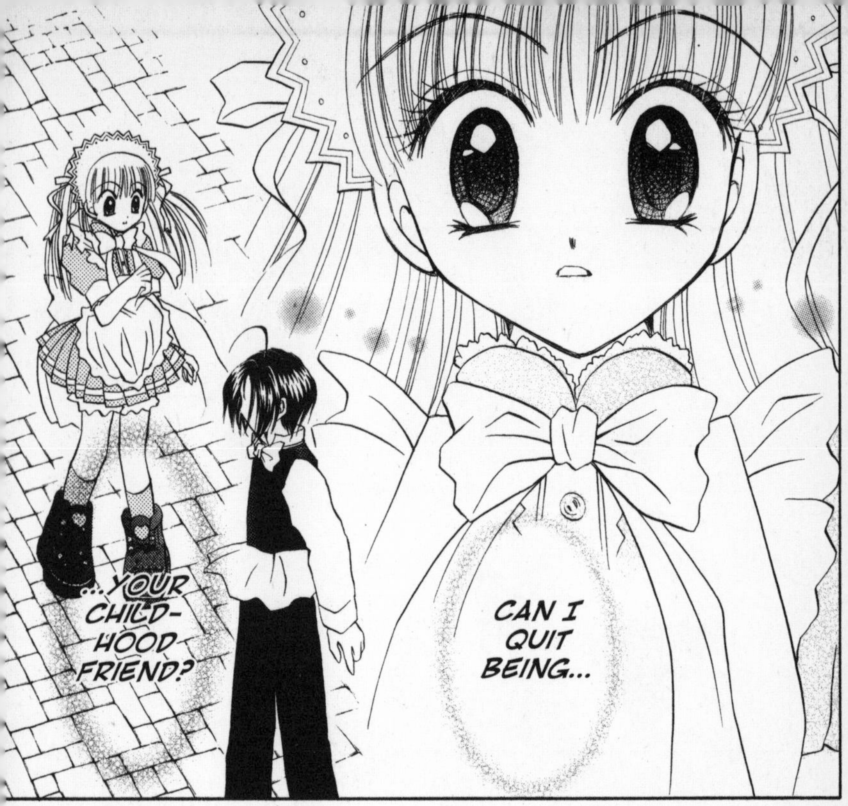
CAN I QUIT BEING...
...YOUR CHILD-HOOD FRIEND?

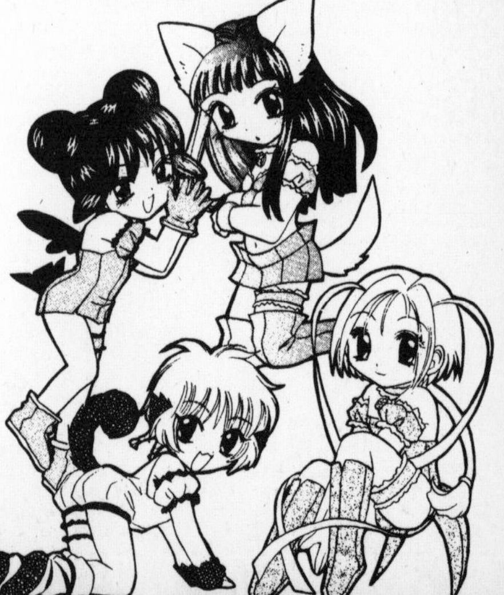

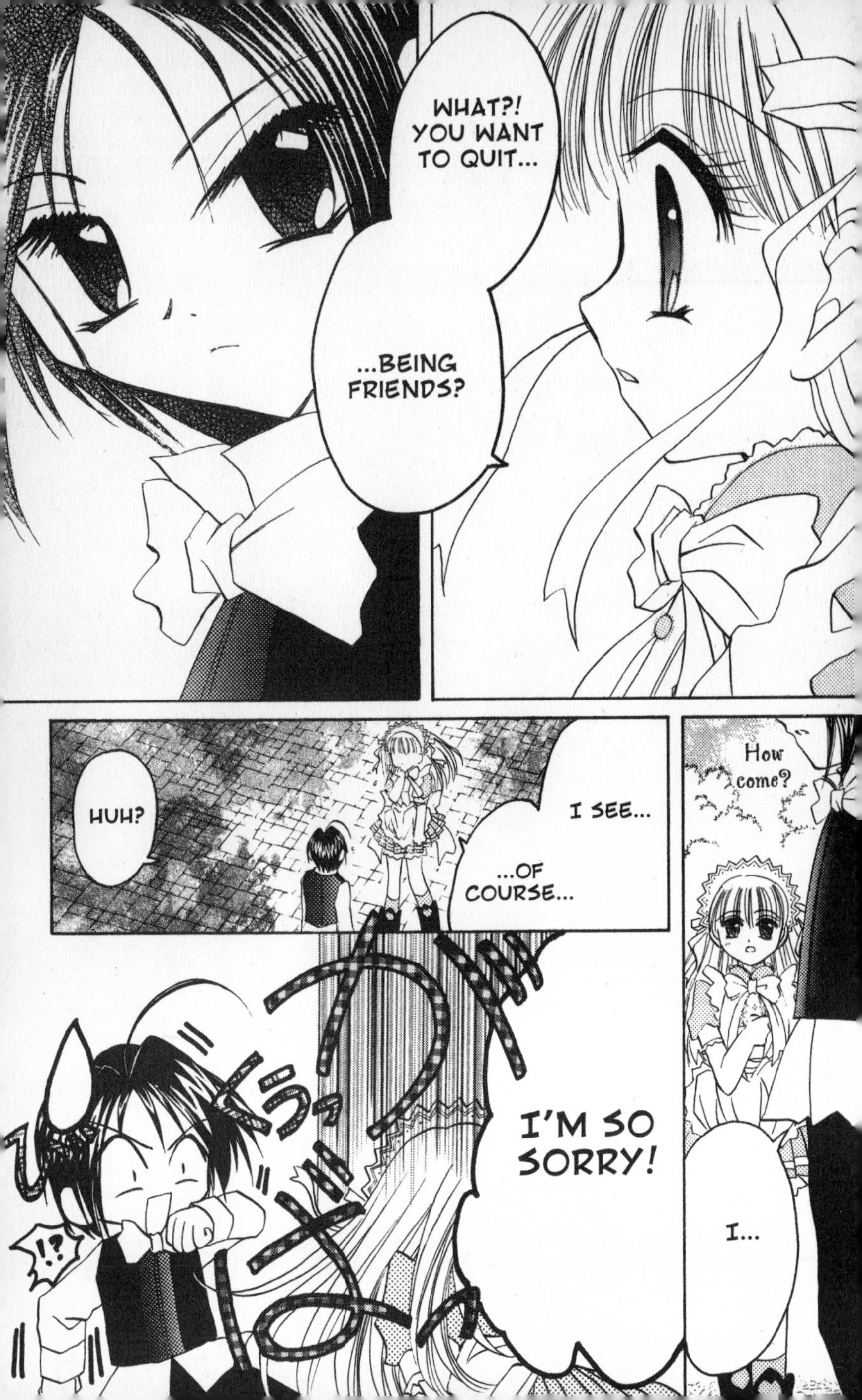
WHAT?! YOU WANT TO QUIT...
...BEING FRIENDS?
How come?
I...
I SEE...
...OF COURSE...
HUH?
I'M SO SORRY!
!?

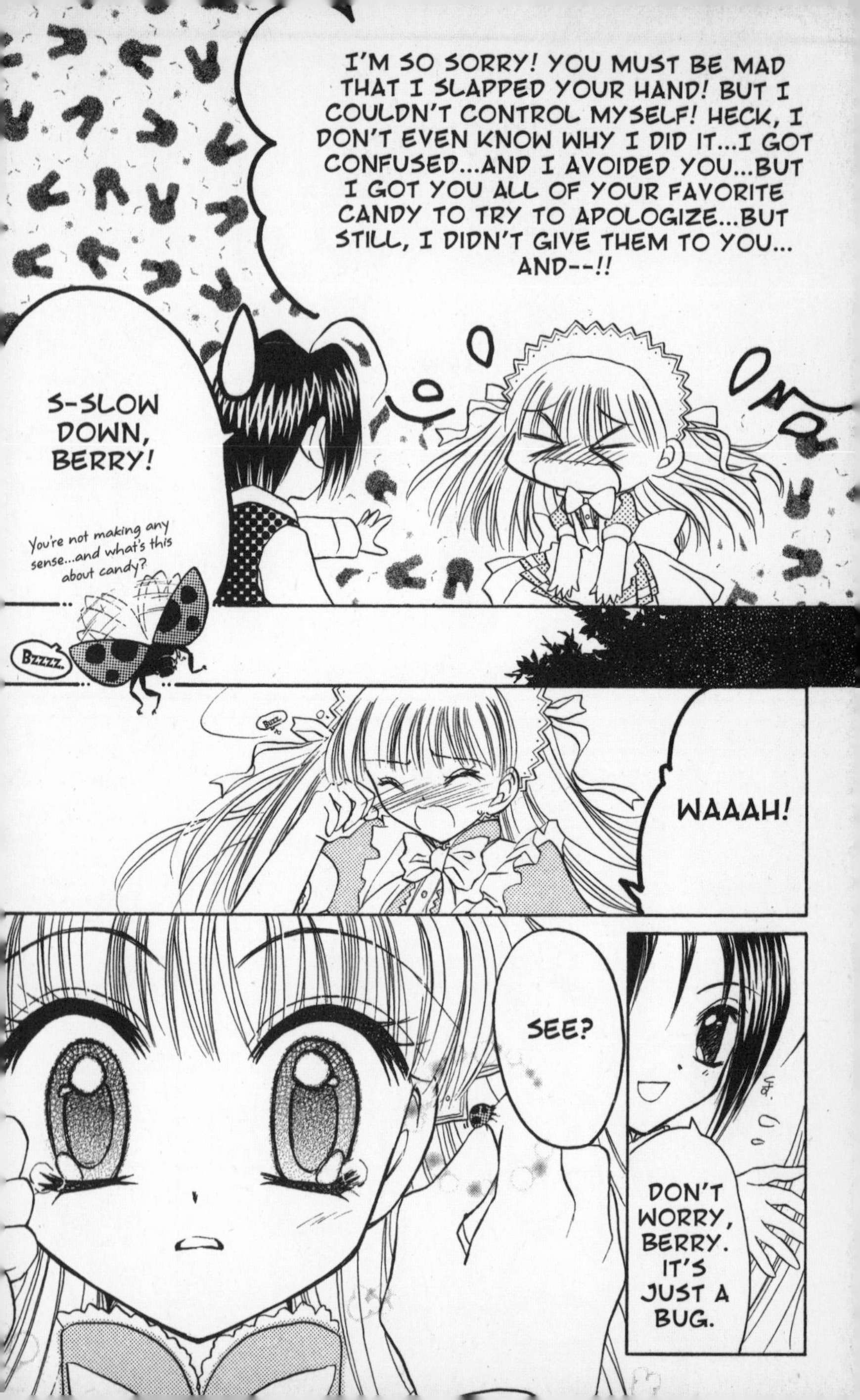
I'M SO SORRY! YOU MUST BE MAD THAT I SLAPPED YOUR HAND! BUT I COULDN'T CONTROL MYSELF! HECK, I DON'T EVEN KNOW WHY I DID IT...I GOT CONFUSED...AND I AVOIDED YOU...BUT I GOT YOU ALL OF YOUR FAVORITE CANDY TO TRY TO APOLOGIZE...BUT STILL, I DIDN'T GIVE THEM TO YOU... AND--!!
S-SLOW DOWN, BERRY!
You're not making any sense...and what's this about candy?
Bzzzz.
WAAAH!
DON'T WORRY, BERRY. IT'S JUST A BUG.
SEE?

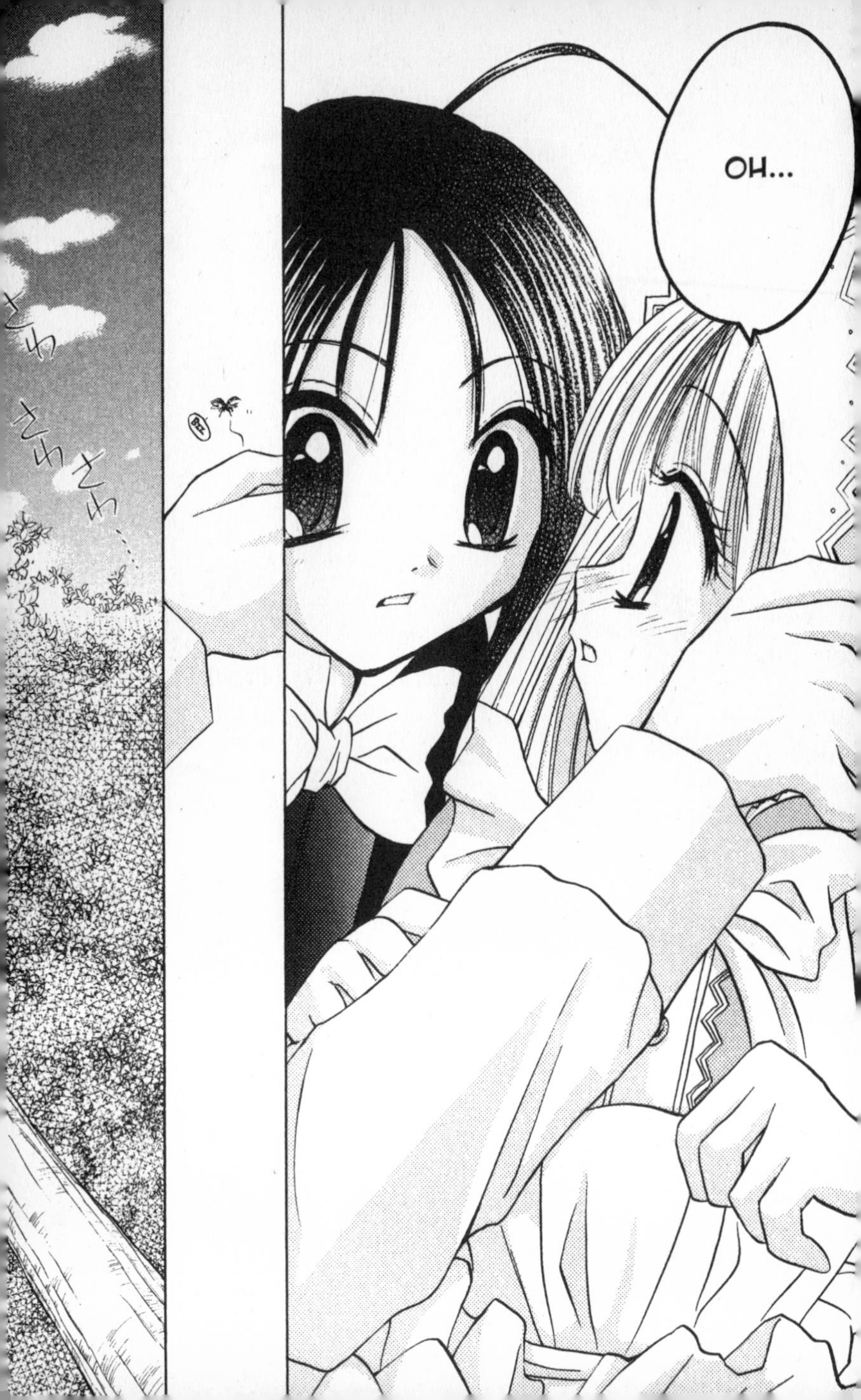
OH...
BZZ
さわ
さわさわ...

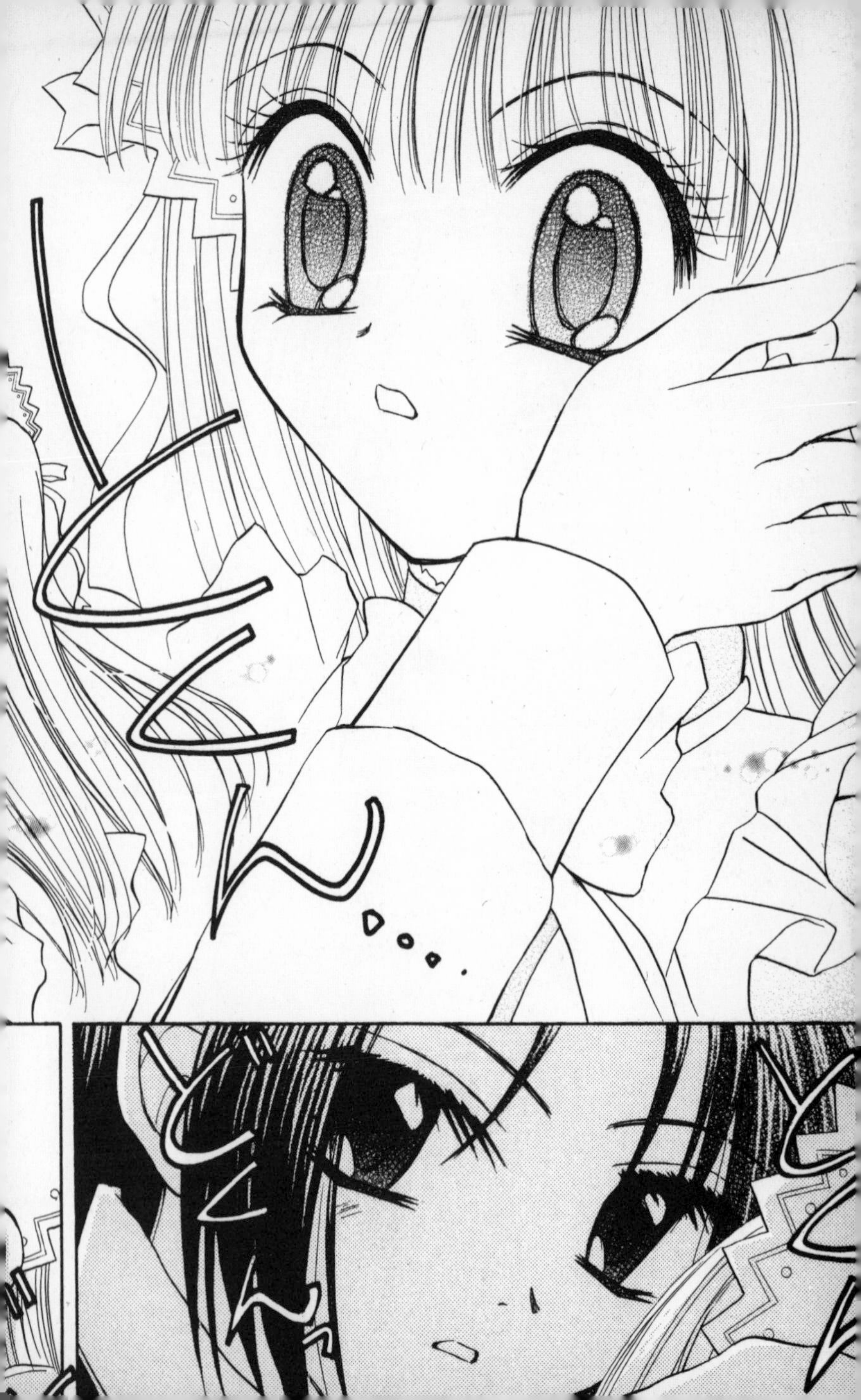

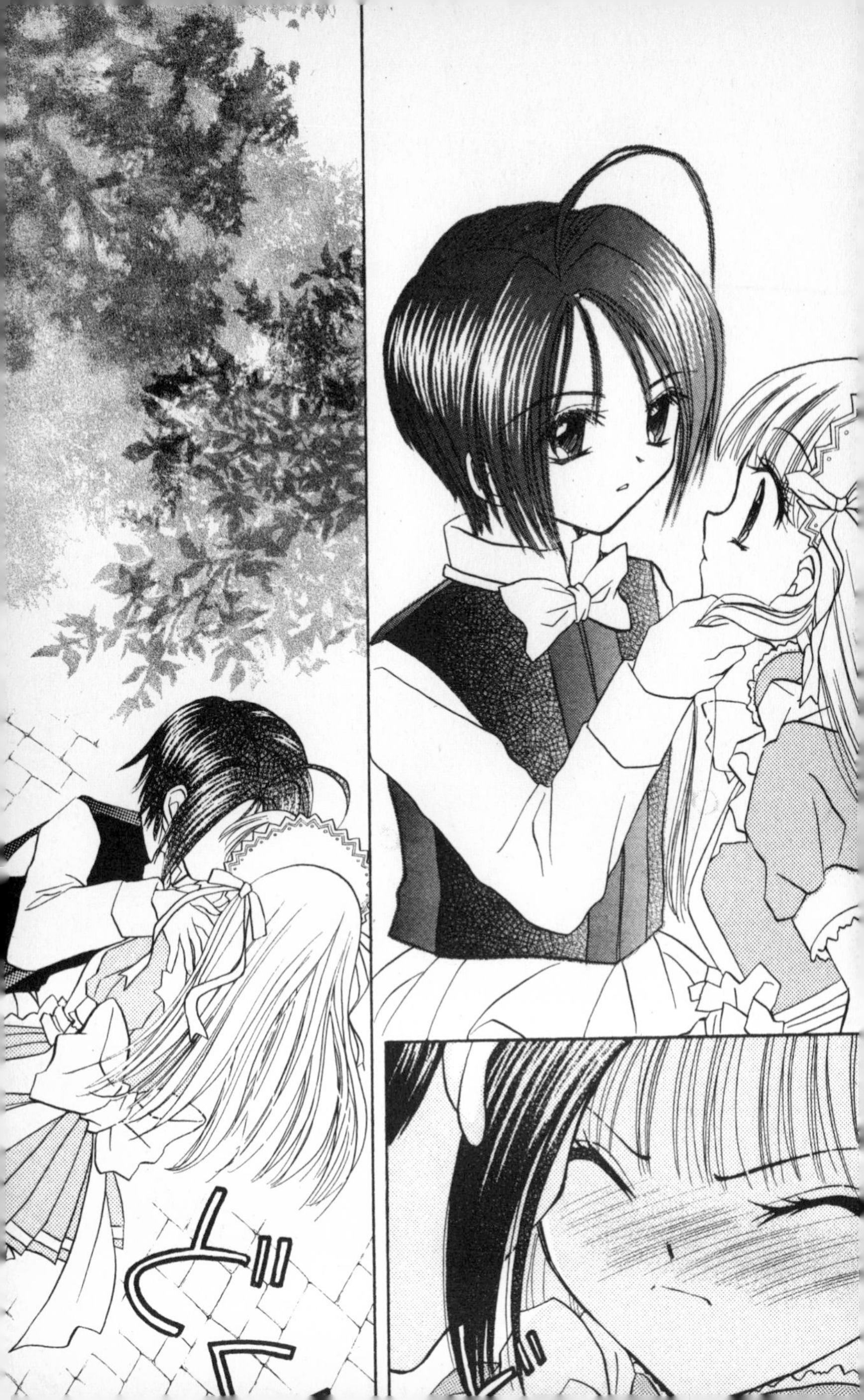

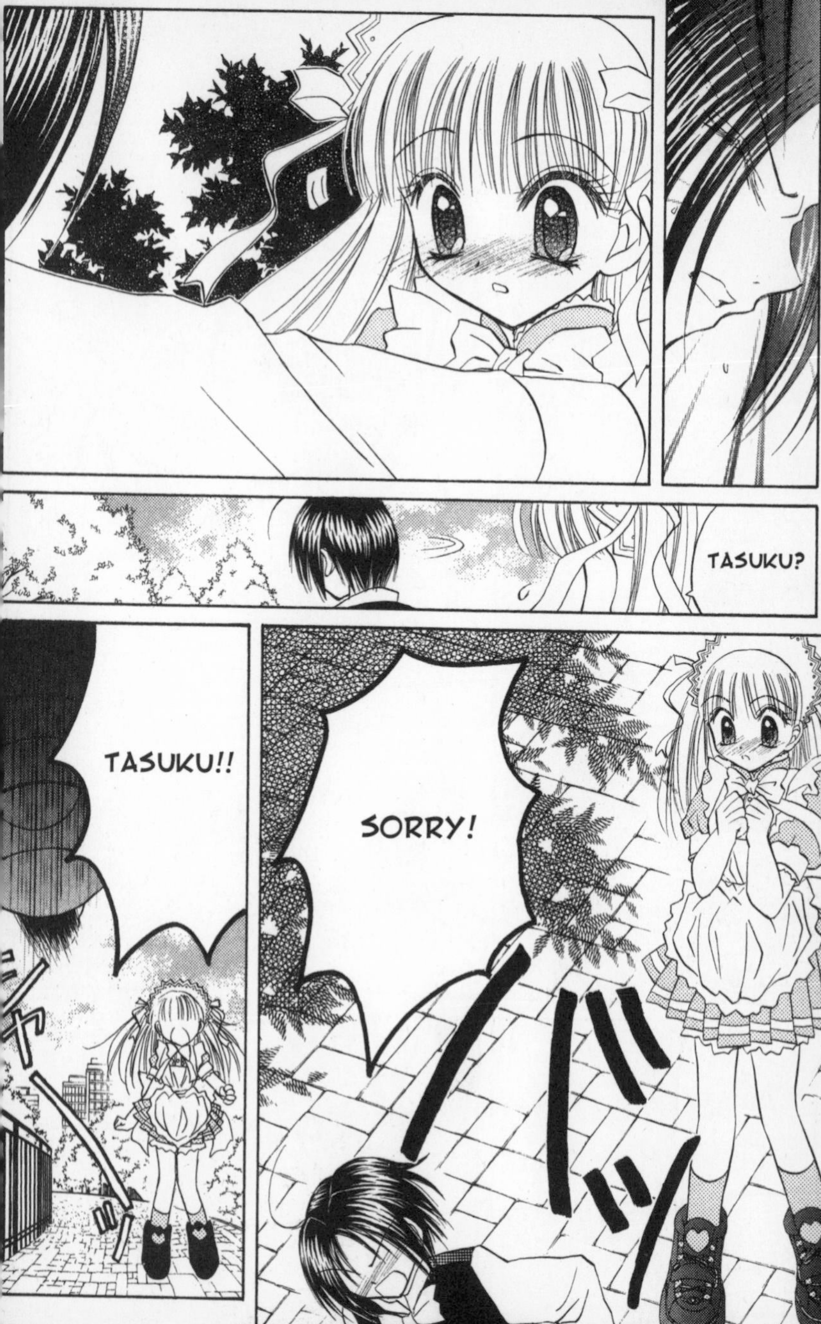
TASUKU?
SORRY!
バッ
TASUKU!!

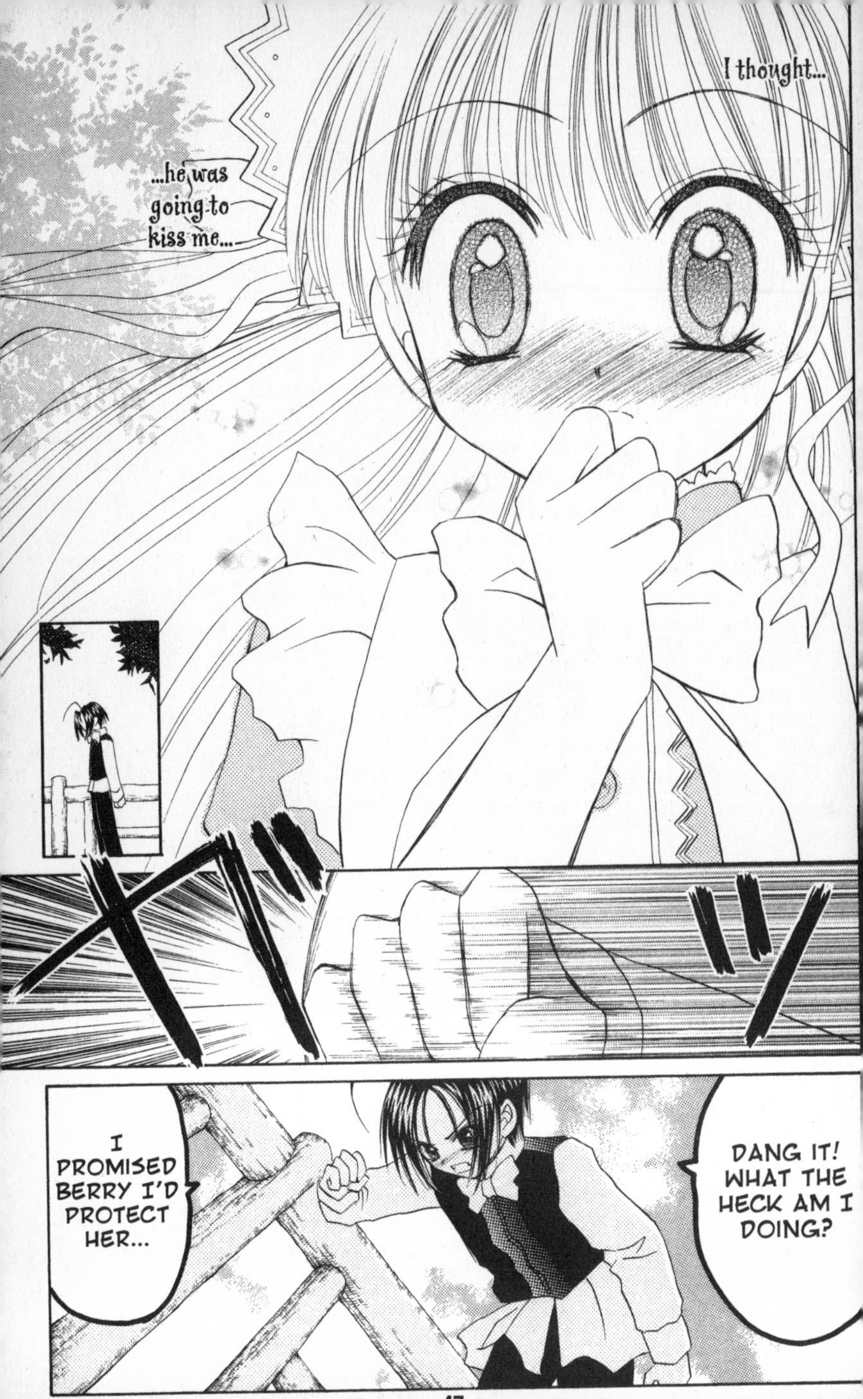
I thought...
...he was going to kiss me...
DANG IT! WHAT THE HECK AM I DOING?
I PROMISED BERRY I'D PROTECT HER...

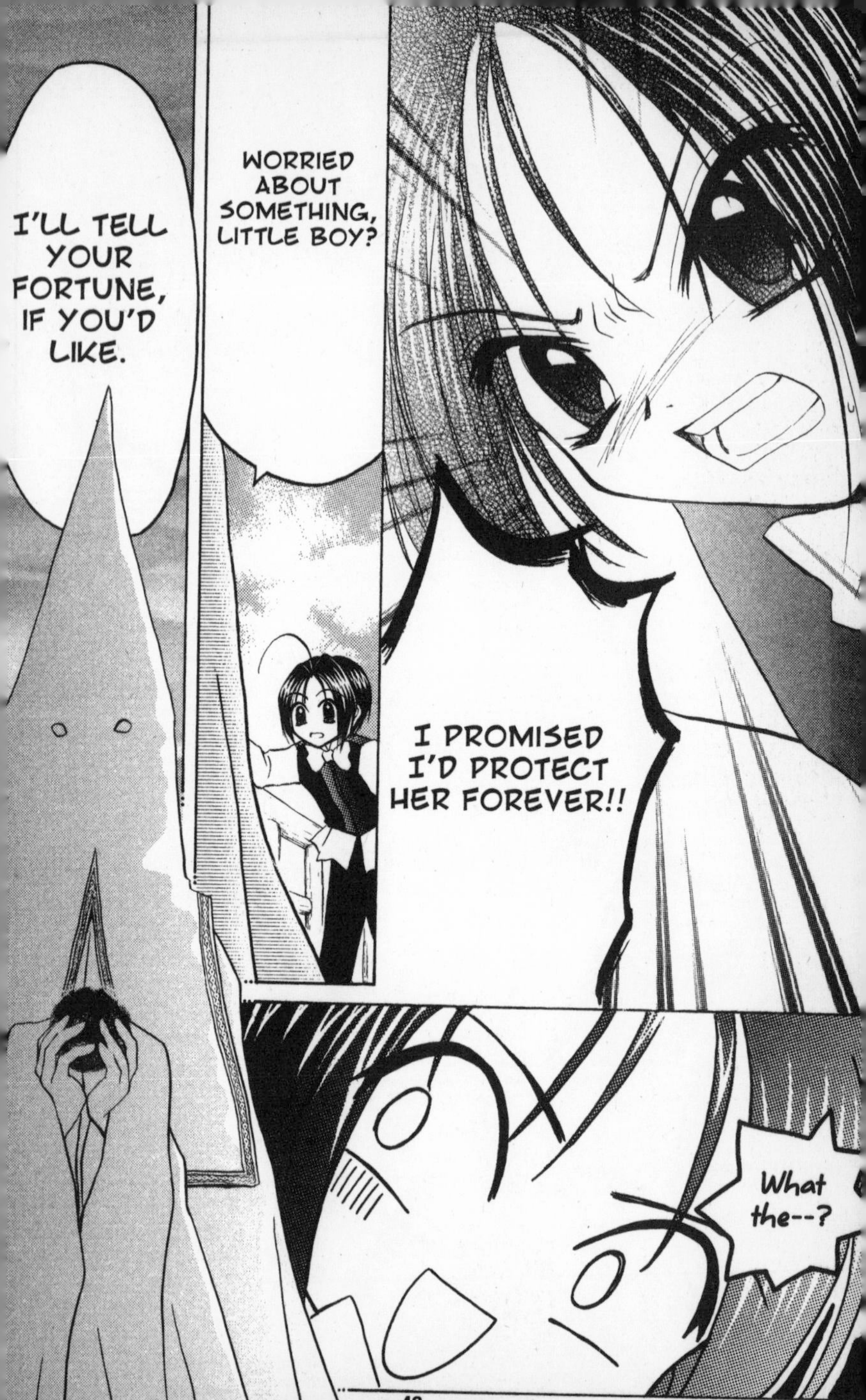
I PROMISED I'D PROTECT HER FOREVER!!
WORRIED ABOUT SOMETHING, LITTLE BOY?
What the--?
I'LL TELL YOUR FORTUNE, IF YOU'D LIKE.

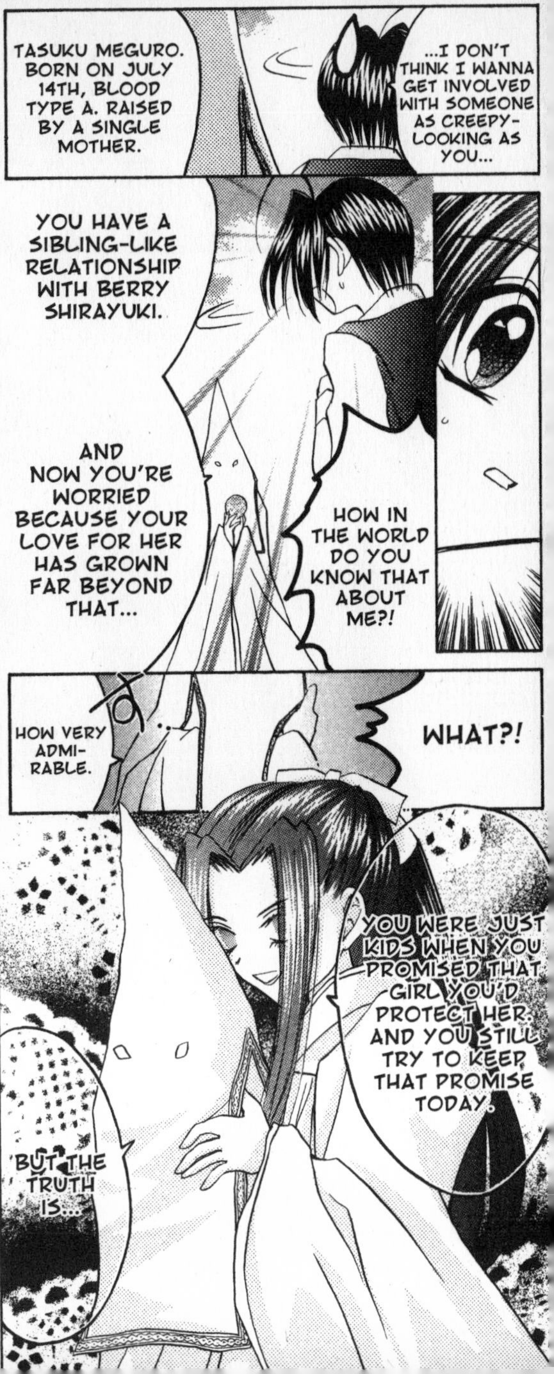
...I DON'T THINK I WANNA GET INVOLVED WITH SOMEONE AS CREEPY-LOOKING AS YOU...
TASUKU MEGURO. BORN ON JULY 14TH, BLOOD TYPE A. RAISED BY A SINGLE MOTHER.
YOU HAVE A SIBLING-LIKE RELATIONSHIP WITH BERRY SHIRAYUKI.
AND NOW YOU'RE WORRIED BECAUSE YOUR LOVE FOR HER HAS GROWN FAR BEYOND THAT...
HOW IN THE WORLD DO YOU KNOW THAT ABOUT ME?!
WHAT?!
HOW VERY ADMI-RABLE.
YOU WERE JUST KIDS WHEN YOU PROMISED THAT GIRL YOU'D PROTECT HER. AND YOU STILL TRY TO KEEP THAT PROMISE TODAY.
BUT THE TRUTH IS...

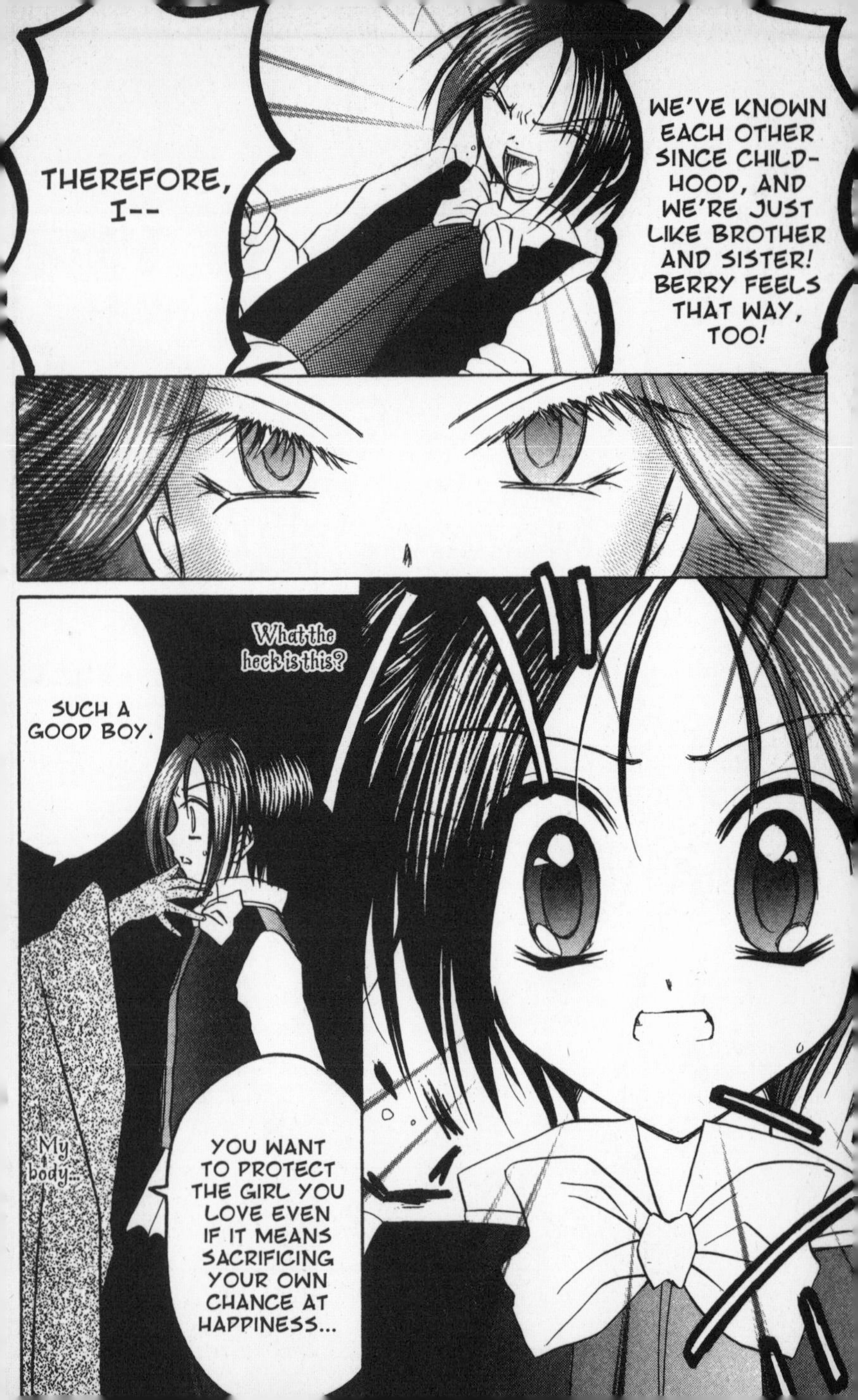
WE'VE KNOWN EACH OTHER SINCE CHILDHOOD, AND WE'RE JUST LIKE BROTHER AND SISTER! BERRY FEELS THAT WAY, TOO!
THEREFORE, I--
What the heck is this?
SUCH A GOOD BOY.
YOU WANT TO PROTECT THE GIRL YOU LOVE EVEN IF IT MEANS SACRIFICING YOUR OWN CHANCE AT HAPPINESS...
My body...

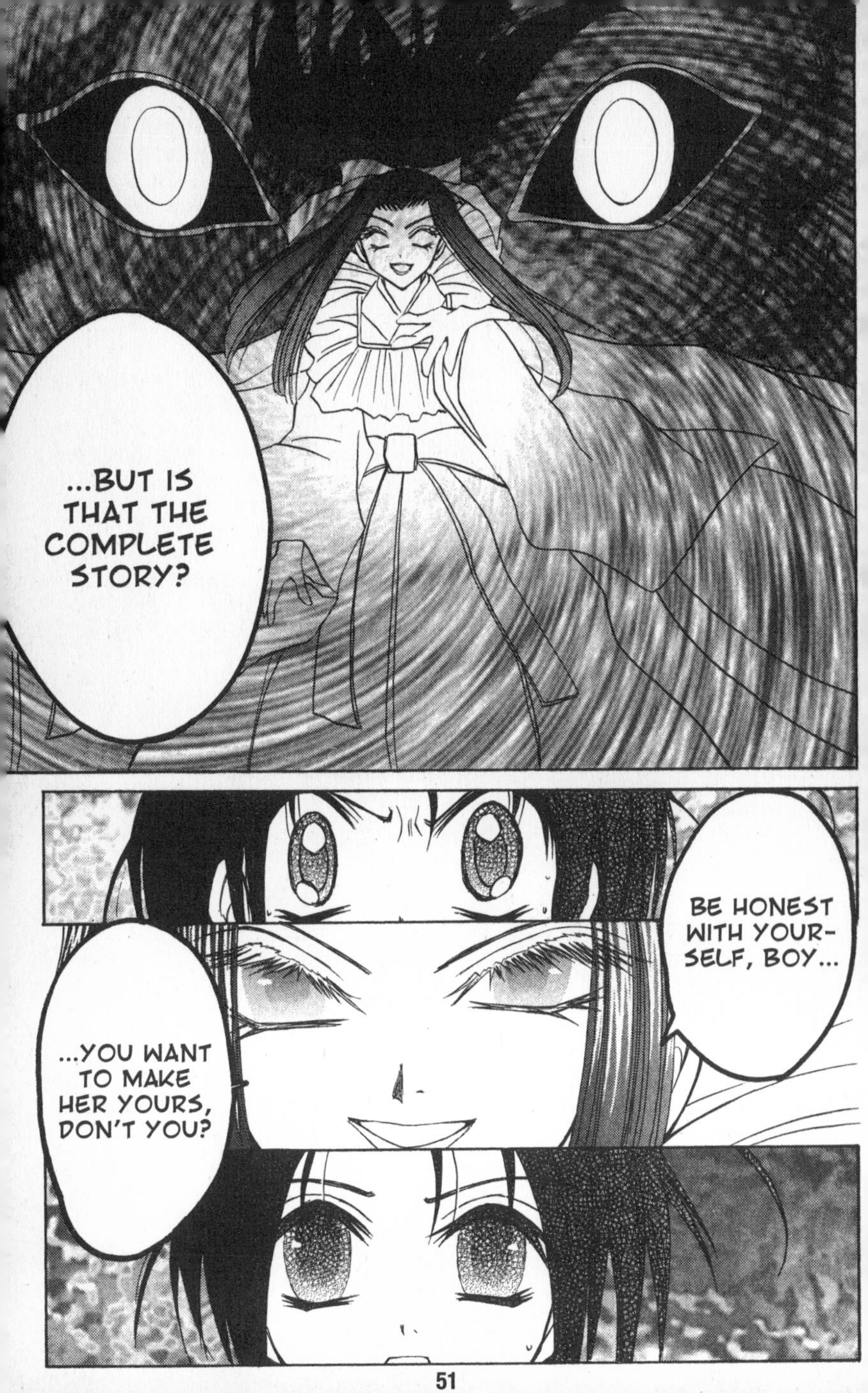
...BUT IS THAT THE COMPLETE STORY?
BE HONEST WITH YOUR-SELF, BOY...
...YOU WANT TO MAKE HER YOURS, DON'T YOU?

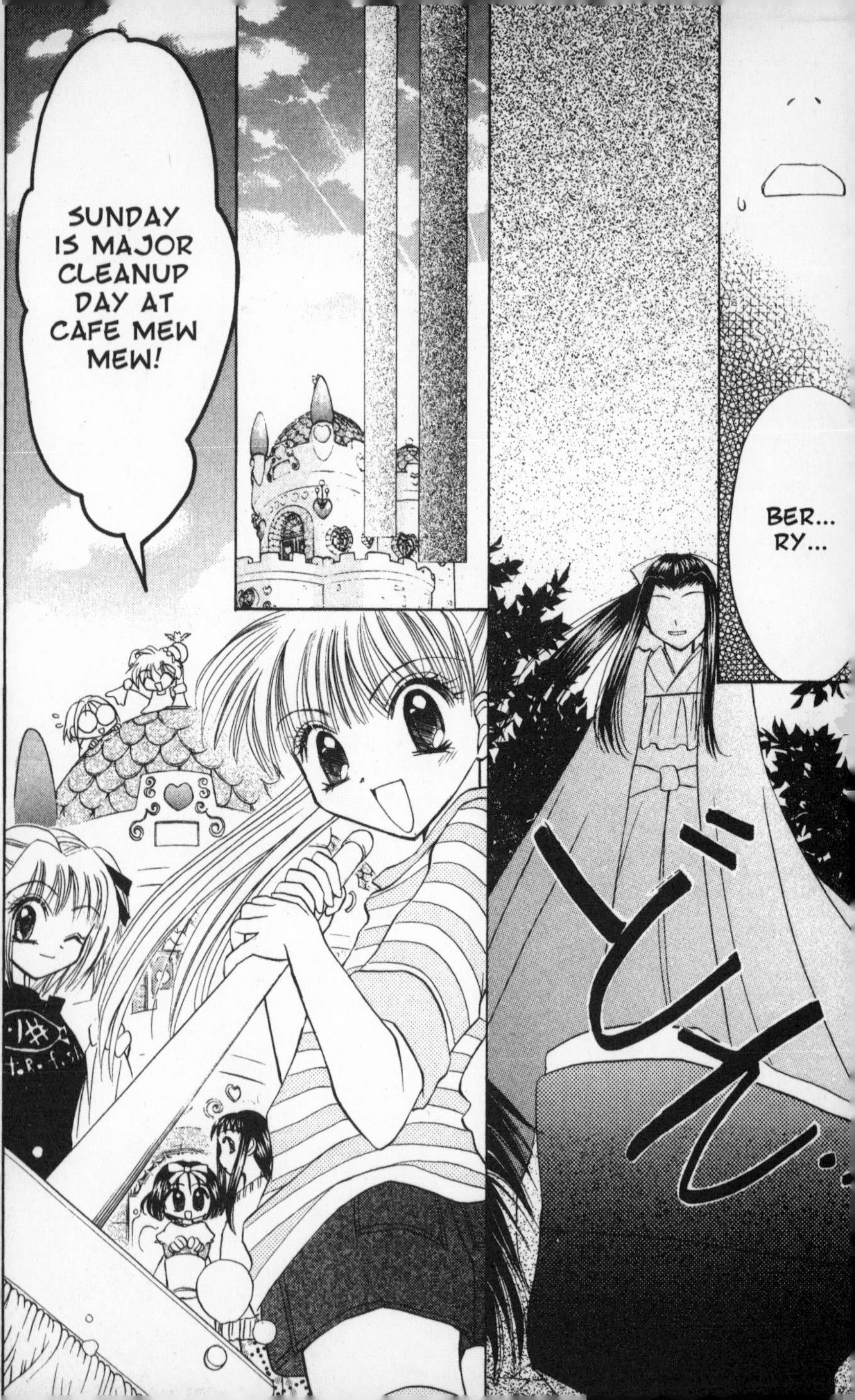
BER... RY...
SUNDAY IS MAJOR CLEANUP DAY AT CAFE MEW MEW!

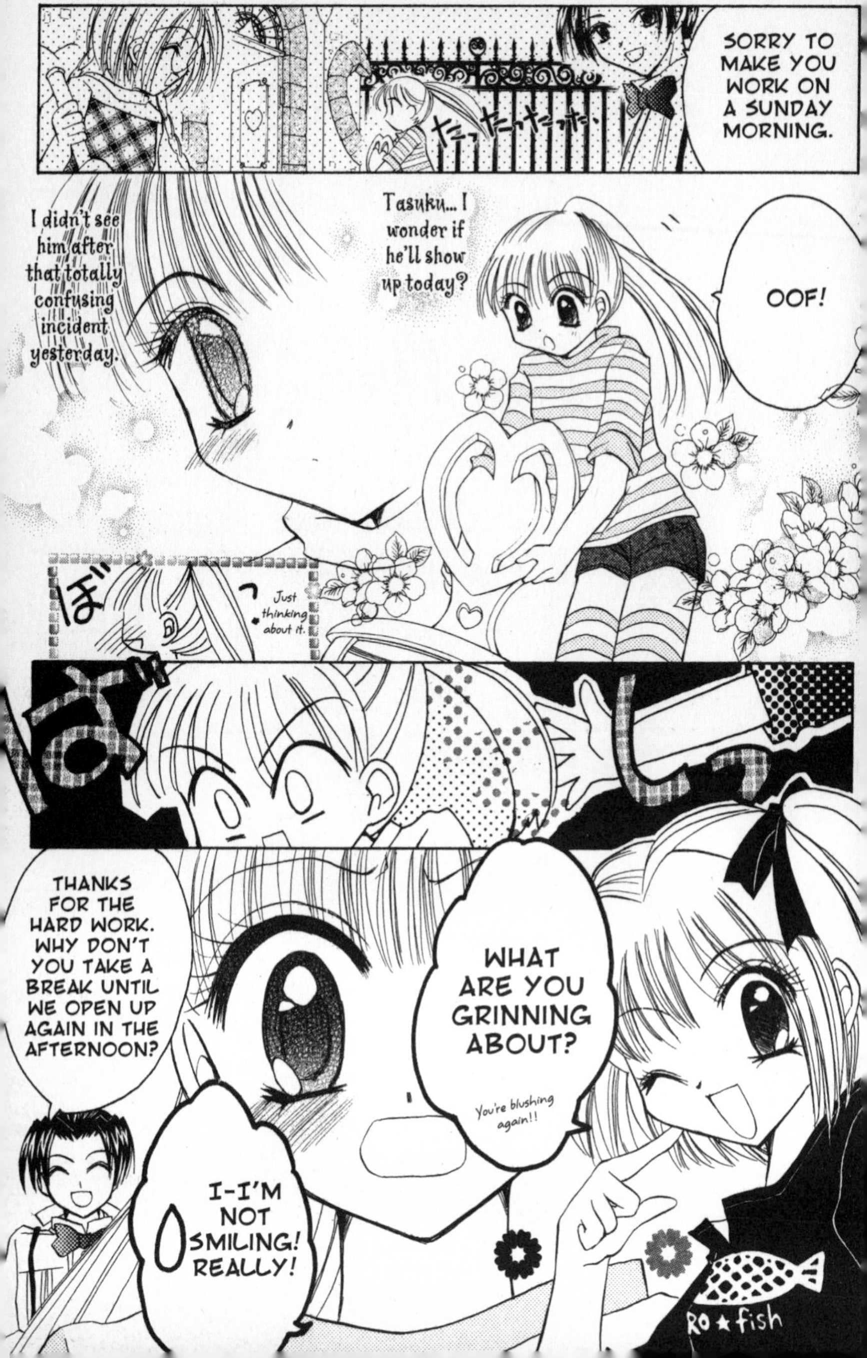
SORRY TO MAKE YOU WORK ON A SUNDAY MORNING.
OOF!
Tasuku... I wonder if he'll show up today?
I didn't see him after that totally confusing incident yesterday.
Just thinking about it.
WHAT ARE YOU GRINNING ABOUT?
You're blushing again!!
THANKS FOR THE HARD WORK. WHY DON'T YOU TAKE A BREAK UNTIL WE OPEN UP AGAIN IN THE AFTERNOON?
I-I'M NOT SMILING! REALLY!
RO ★ fish

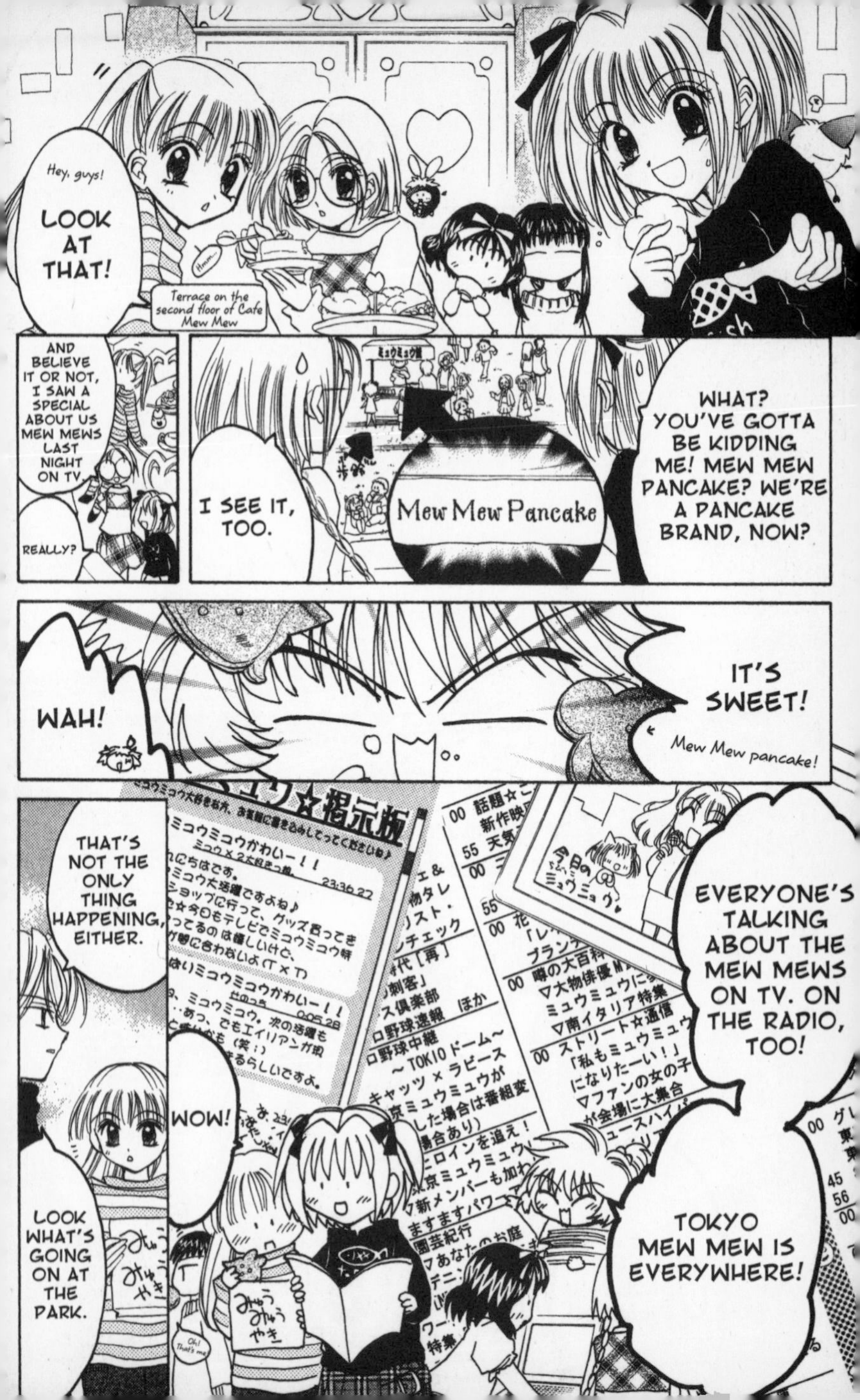
Terrace on the second floor of Cafe Mew Mew
Hmm...
Hey, guys!
LOOK AT THAT!
WHAT? YOU'VE GOTTA BE KIDDING ME! MEW MEW PANCAKE? WE'RE A PANCAKE BRAND, NOW?
Mew Mew Pancake
I SEE IT, TOO.
AND BELIEVE IT OR NOT, I SAW A SPECIAL ABOUT US MEW MEWS LAST NIGHT ON TV.
REALLY?
IT'S SWEET!
Mew Mew pancake!
WAH!
EVERYONE'S TALKING ABOUT THE MEW MEWS ON TV. ON THE RADIO, TOO!
TOKYO MEW MEW IS EVERYWHERE!
THAT'S NOT THE ONLY THING HAPPENING, EITHER.
WOW!
LOOK WHAT'S GOING ON AT THE PARK.
Oh! That's me!

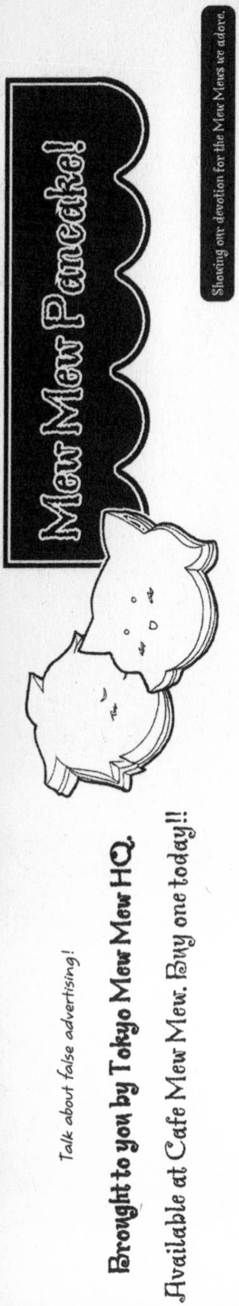

Mew Mew Pancake!
Showing our devotion for the Mew Mews we adore.
Talk about false advertising!
Brought to you by Tokyo Mew Mew HQ.
Available at Cafe Mew Mew. Buy one today!!

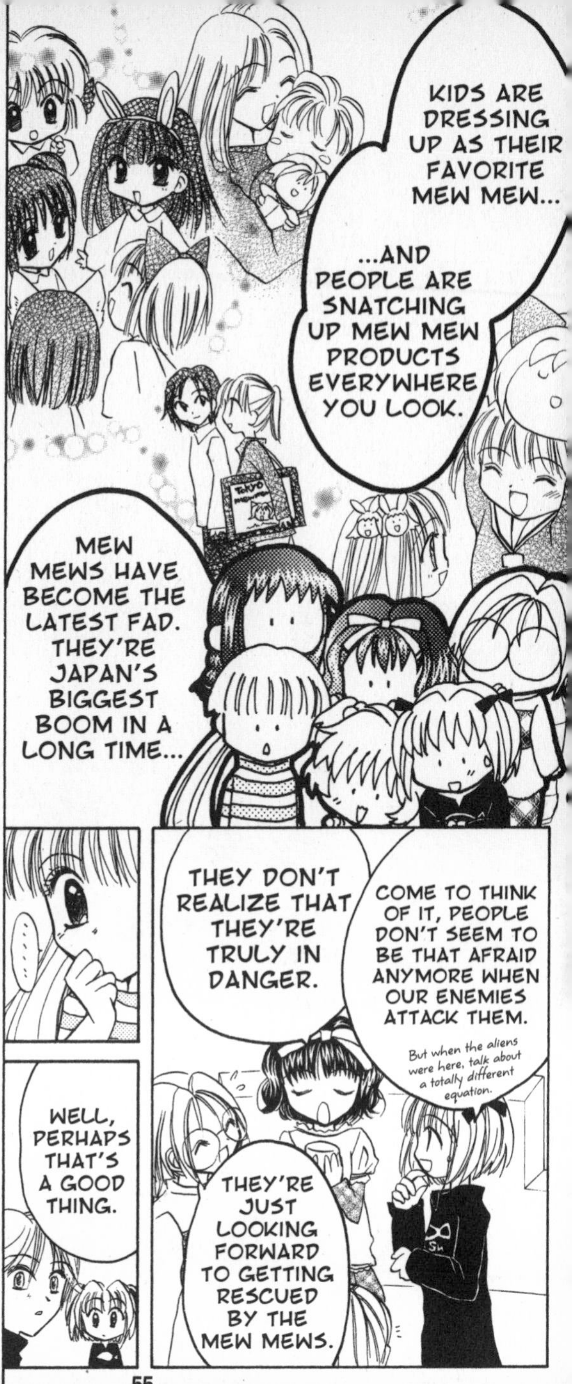

KIDS ARE DRESSING UP AS THEIR FAVORITE MEW MEW...
...AND PEOPLE ARE SNATCHING UP MEW MEW PRODUCTS EVERYWHERE YOU LOOK.
MEW MEWS HAVE BECOME THE LATEST FAD. THEY'RE JAPAN'S BIGGEST BOOM IN A LONG TIME...
COME TO THINK OF IT, PEOPLE DON'T SEEM TO BE THAT AFRAID ANYMORE WHEN OUR ENEMIES ATTACK THEM.
But when the aliens were here, talk about a totally different equation.
THEY DON'T REALIZE THAT THEY'RE TRULY IN DANGER.
......
THEY'RE JUST LOOKING FORWARD TO GETTING RESCUED BY THE MEW MEWS.
WELL, PERHAPS THAT'S A GOOD THING.

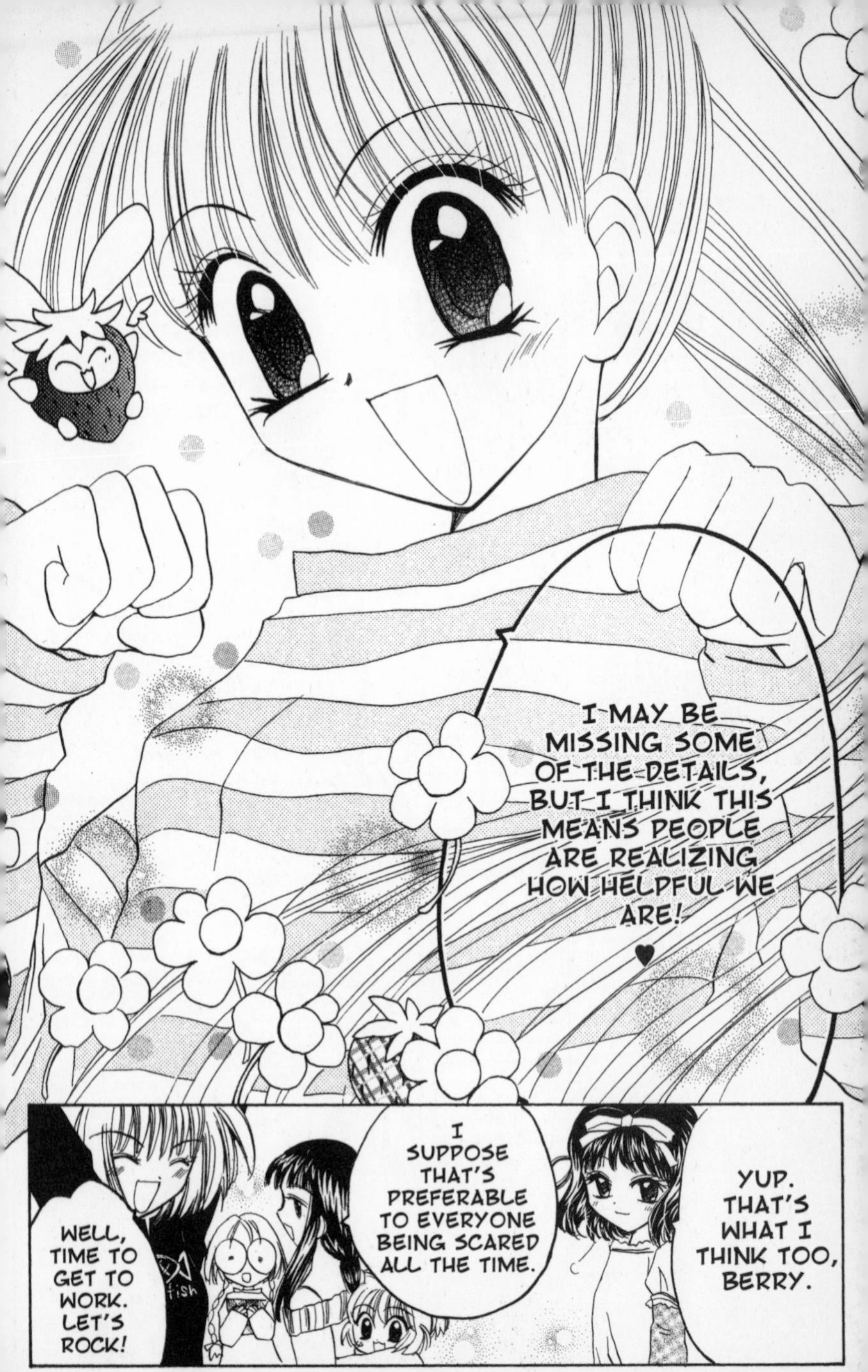
I MAY BE MISSING SOME OF THE DETAILS, BUT I THINK THIS MEANS PEOPLE ARE REALIZING HOW HELPFUL WE ARE! ♥
YUP. THAT'S WHAT I THINK TOO, BERRY.
I SUPPOSE THAT'S PREFERABLE TO EVERYONE BEING SCARED ALL THE TIME.
WELL, TIME TO GET TO WORK. LET'S ROCK!

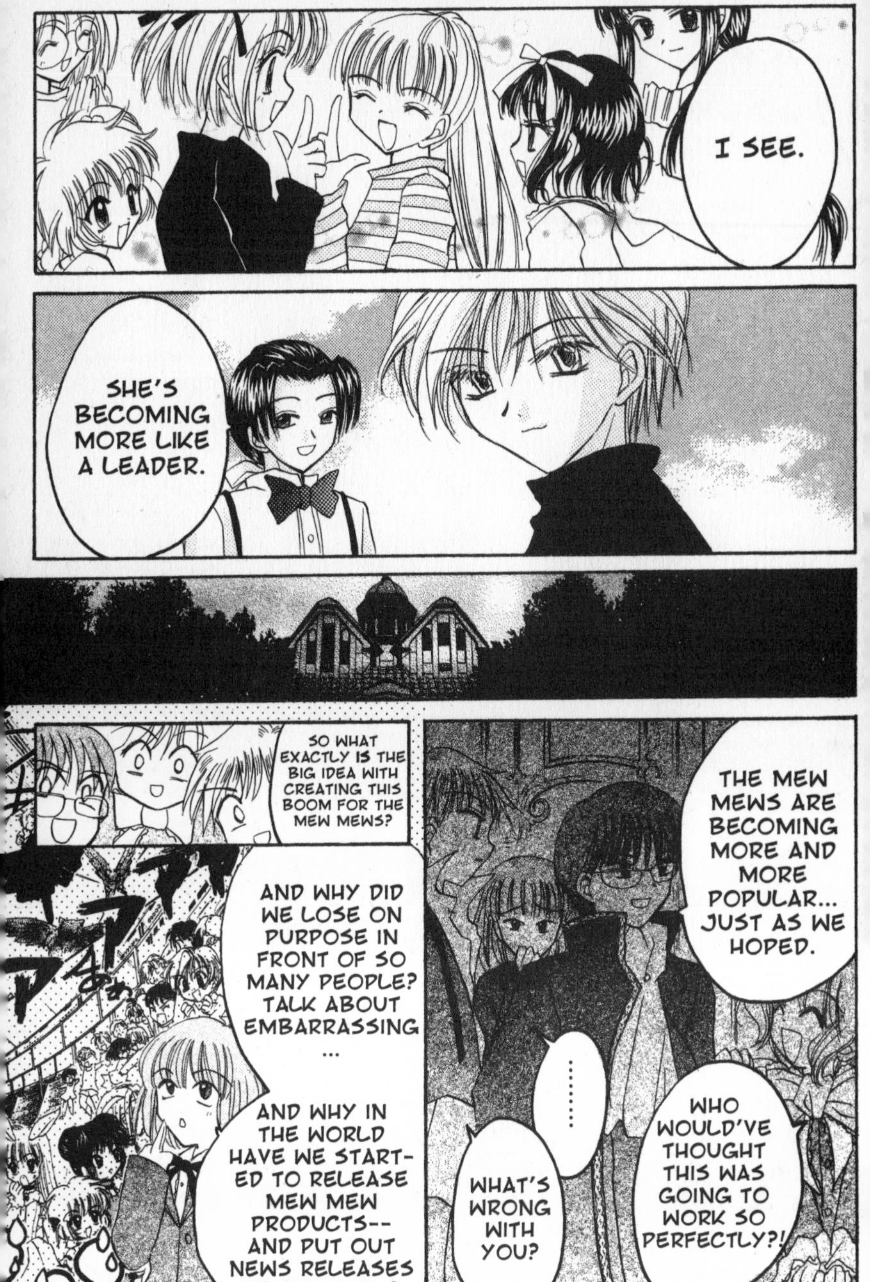
I SEE.
SHE'S BECOMING MORE LIKE A LEADER.
THE MEW MEWS ARE BECOMING MORE AND MORE POPULAR... JUST AS WE HOPED.
WHO WOULD'VE THOUGHT THIS WAS GOING TO WORK SO PERFECTLY?!
......
WHAT'S WRONG WITH YOU?
SO WHAT EXACTLY IS THE BIG IDEA WITH CREATING THIS BOOM FOR THE MEW MEWS?
AND WHY DID WE LOSE ON PURPOSE IN FRONT OF SO MANY PEOPLE? TALK ABOUT EMBARRASSING...
AND WHY IN THE WORLD HAVE WE START-ED TO RELEASE MEW MEW PRODUCTS-- AND PUT OUT NEWS RELEASES ABOUT THEM?

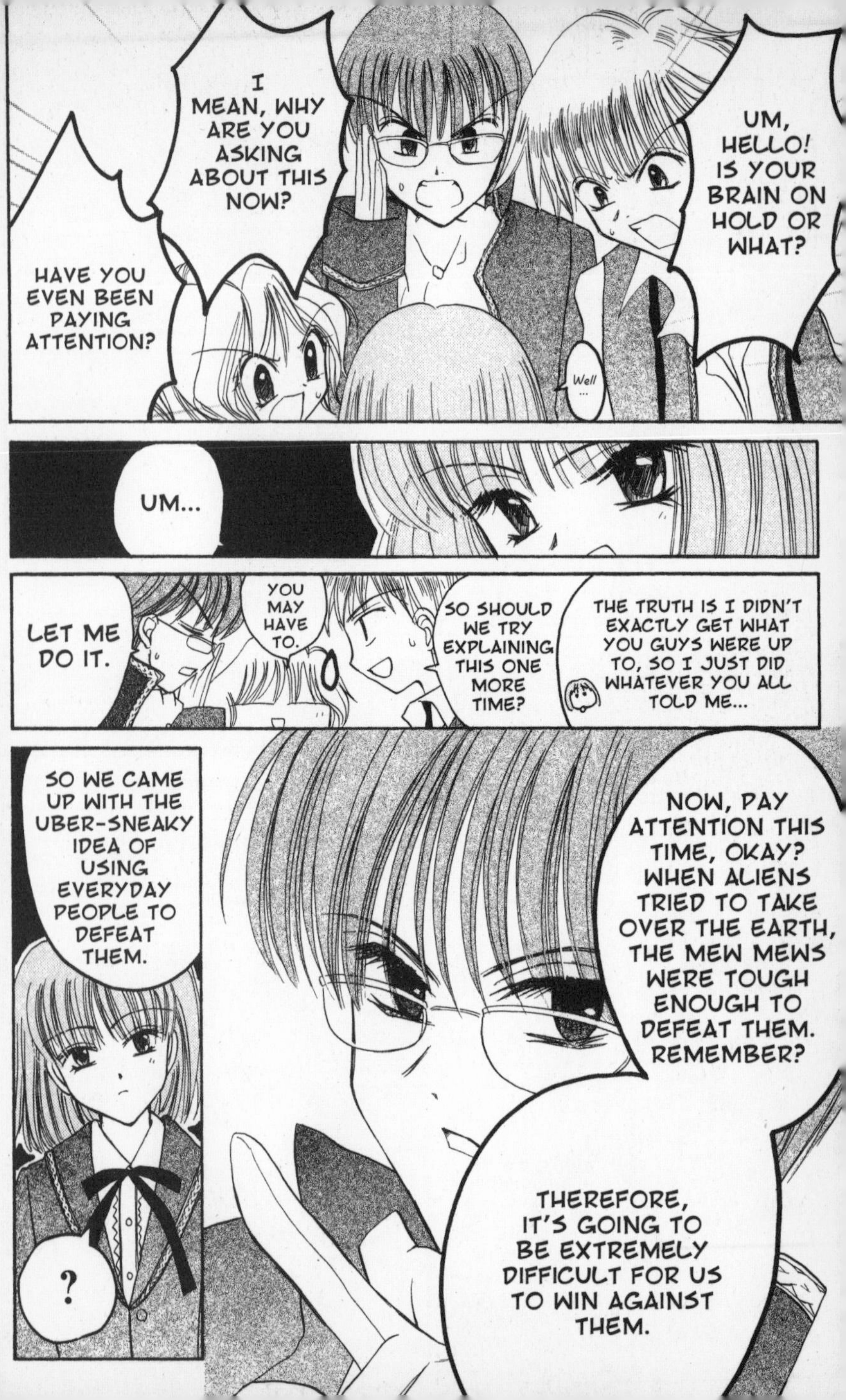
UM, HELLO! IS YOUR BRAIN ON HOLD OR WHAT?
I MEAN, WHY ARE YOU ASKING ABOUT THIS NOW?
HAVE YOU EVEN BEEN PAYING ATTENTION?
Well...
UM...
THE TRUTH IS I DIDN'T EXACTLY GET WHAT YOU GUYS WERE UP TO, SO I JUST DID WHATEVER YOU ALL TOLD ME...
SO SHOULD WE TRY EXPLAINING THIS ONE MORE TIME?
YOU MAY HAVE TO.
LET ME DO IT.
NOW, PAY ATTENTION THIS TIME, OKAY? WHEN ALIENS TRIED TO TAKE OVER THE EARTH, THE MEW MEWS WERE TOUGH ENOUGH TO DEFEAT THEM. REMEMBER?
THEREFORE, IT'S GOING TO BE EXTREMELY DIFFICULT FOR US TO WIN AGAINST THEM.
SO WE CAME UP WITH THE UBER-SNEAKY IDEA OF USING EVERYDAY PEOPLE TO DEFEAT THEM.
?

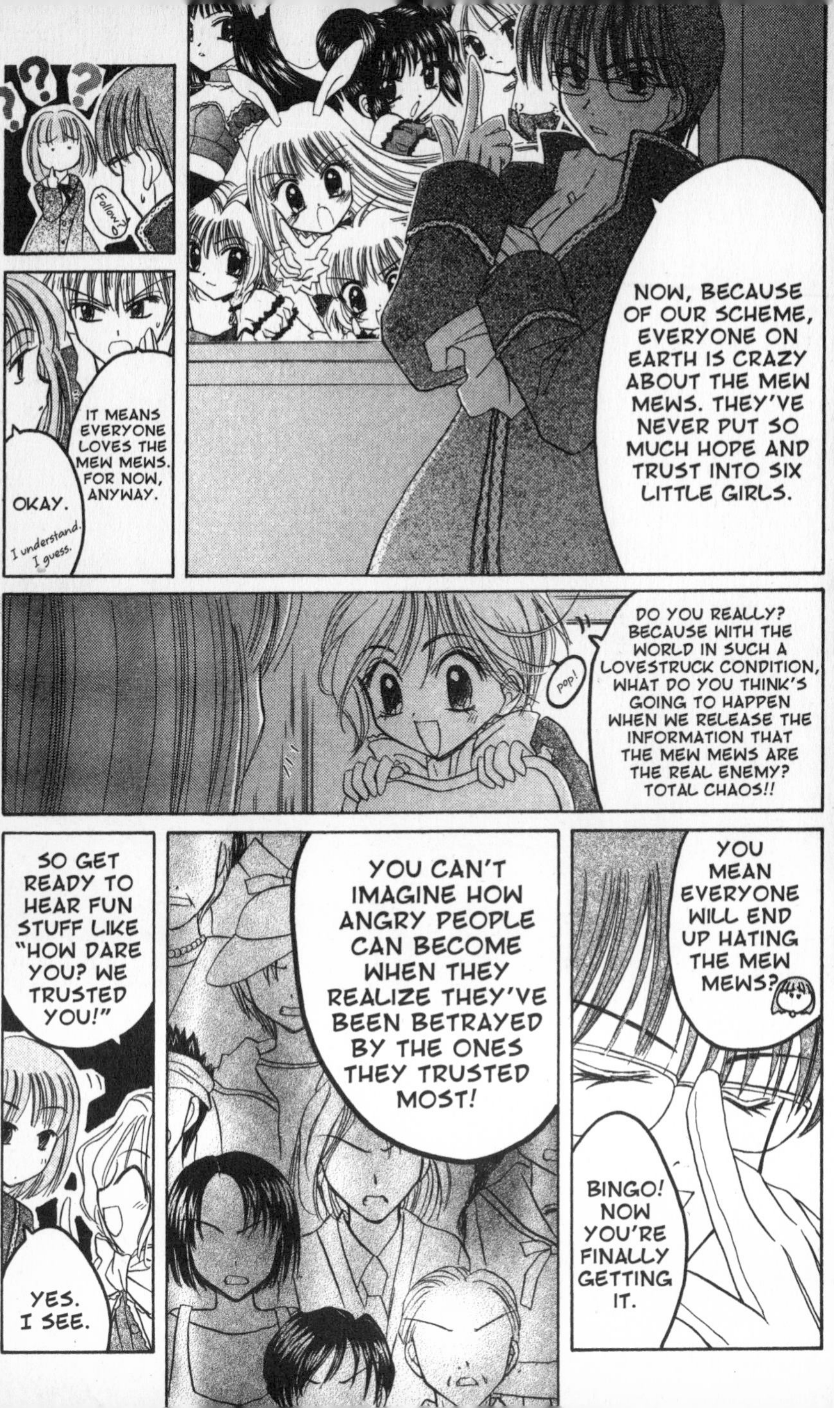
NOW, BECAUSE OF OUR SCHEME, EVERYONE ON EARTH IS CRAZY ABOUT THE MEW MEWS. THEY'VE NEVER PUT SO MUCH HOPE AND TRUST INTO SIX LITTLE GIRLS.
Follow?
IT MEANS EVERYONE LOVES THE MEW MEWS. FOR NOW, ANYWAY.
OKAY.
I understand. I guess.
DO YOU REALLY? BECAUSE WITH THE WORLD IN SUCH A LOVESTRUCK CONDITION, WHAT DO YOU THINK'S GOING TO HAPPEN WHEN WE RELEASE THE INFORMATION THAT THE MEW MEWS ARE THE REAL ENEMY? TOTAL CHAOS!!
pop!
YOU MEAN EVERYONE WILL END UP HATING THE MEW MEWS?
BINGO! NOW YOU'RE FINALLY GETTING IT.
YOU CAN'T IMAGINE HOW ANGRY PEOPLE CAN BECOME WHEN THEY REALIZE THEY'VE BEEN BETRAYED BY THE ONES THEY TRUSTED MOST!
SO GET READY TO HEAR FUN STUFF LIKE "HOW DARE YOU? WE TRUSTED YOU!"
YES. I SEE.

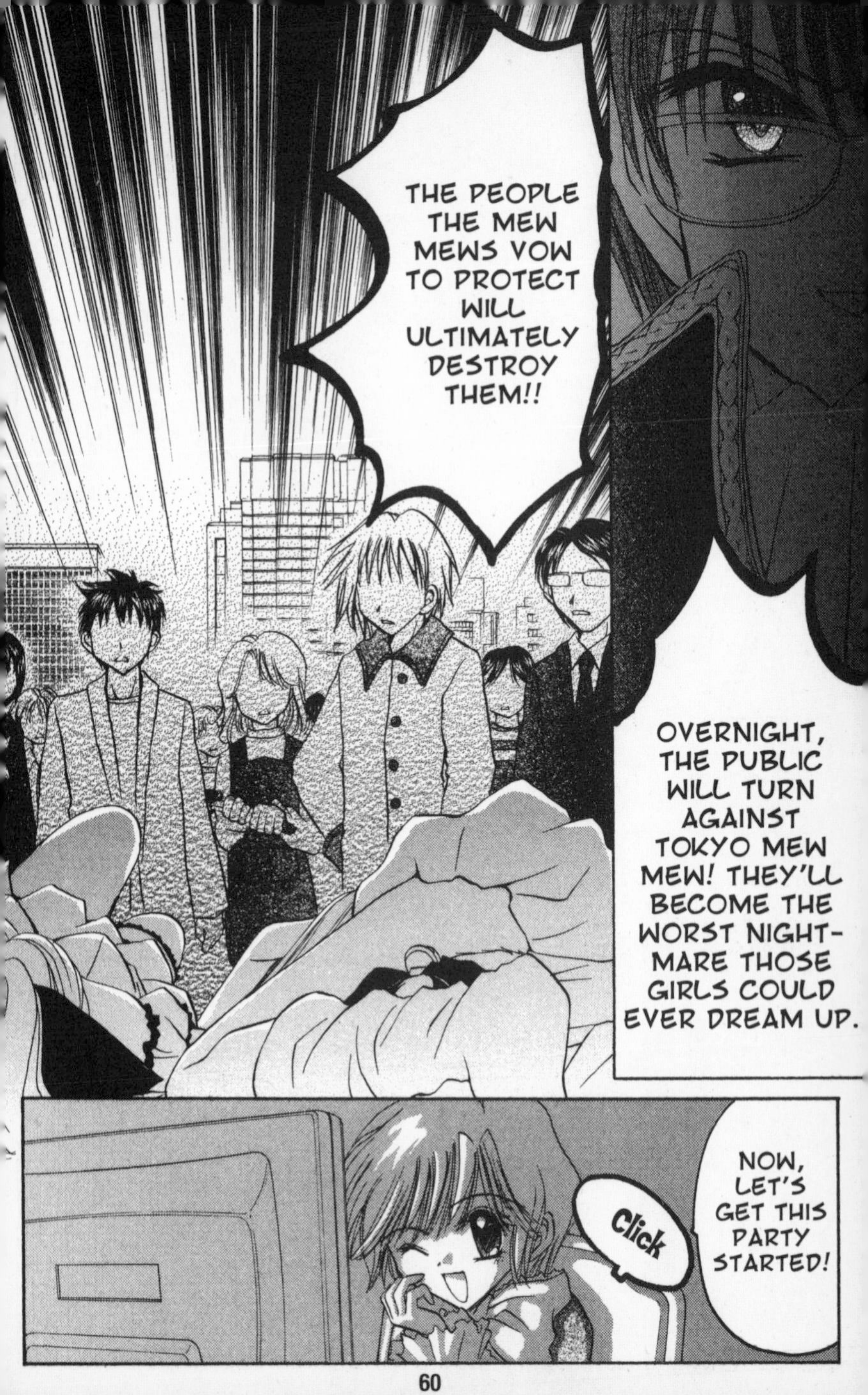
THE PEOPLE THE MEW MEWS VOW TO PROTECT WILL ULTIMATELY DESTROY THEM!!
OVERNIGHT, THE PUBLIC WILL TURN AGAINST TOKYO MEW MEW! THEY'LL BECOME THE WORST NIGHT-MARE THOSE GIRLS COULD EVER DREAM UP.
NOW, LET'S GET THIS PARTY STARTED!
Click

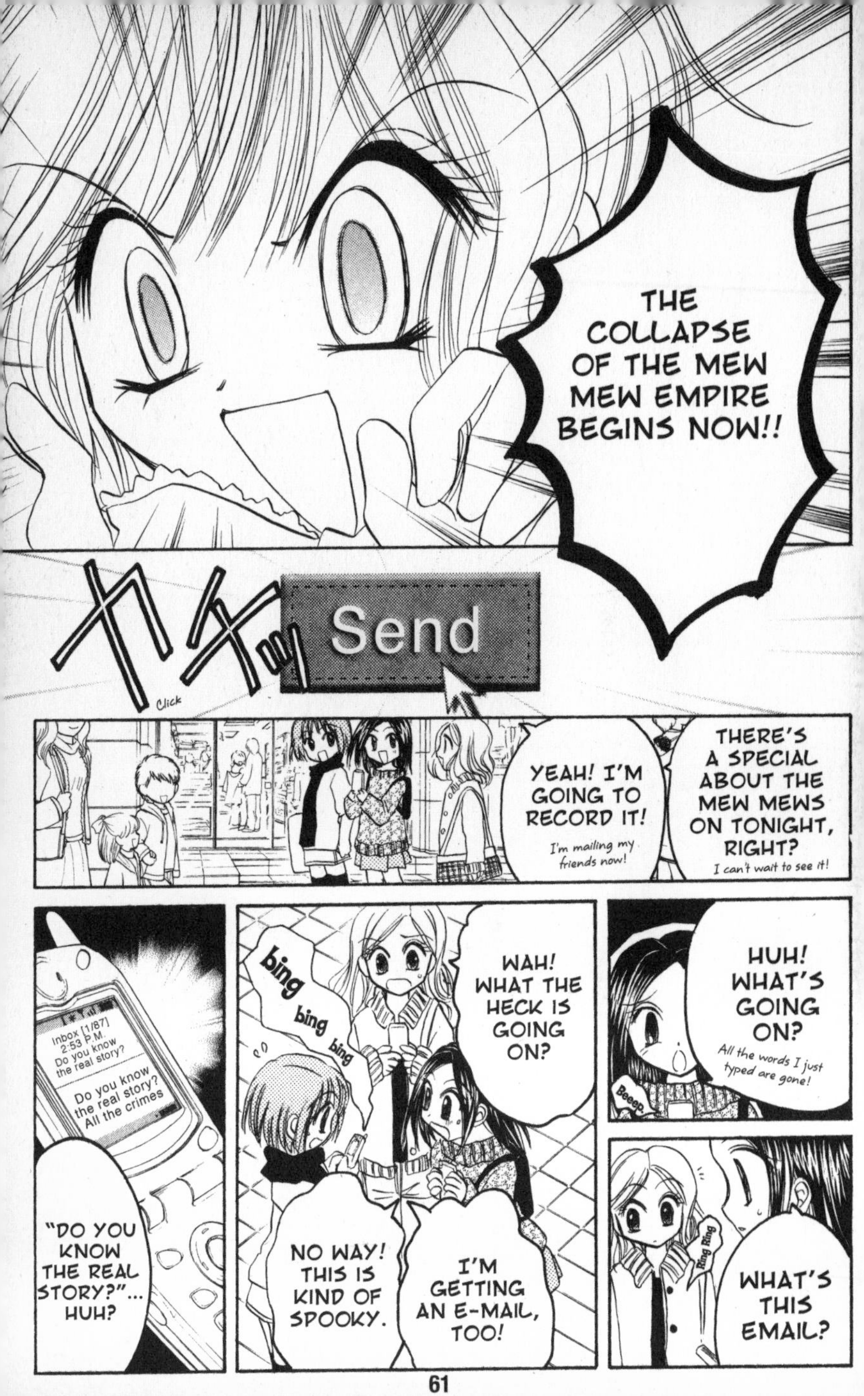
THE COLLAPSE OF THE MEW MEW EMPIRE BEGINS NOW!!
Click
Send
THERE'S A SPECIAL ABOUT THE MEW MEWS ON TONIGHT, RIGHT?
I can't wait to see it!
YEAH! I'M GOING TO RECORD IT!
I'm mailing my friends now!
HUH! WHAT'S GOING ON?
All the words I just typed are gone!
Beeep
WAH! WHAT THE HECK IS GOING ON?
bing bing bing
Inbox [1/87]
2:53 P.M.
Do you know the real story?
Do you know the real story? All the crimes
WHAT'S THIS EMAIL?
Ring Ring
I'M GETTING AN E-MAIL, TOO!
NO WAY! THIS IS KIND OF SPOOKY.
"DO YOU KNOW THE REAL STORY?"... HUH?

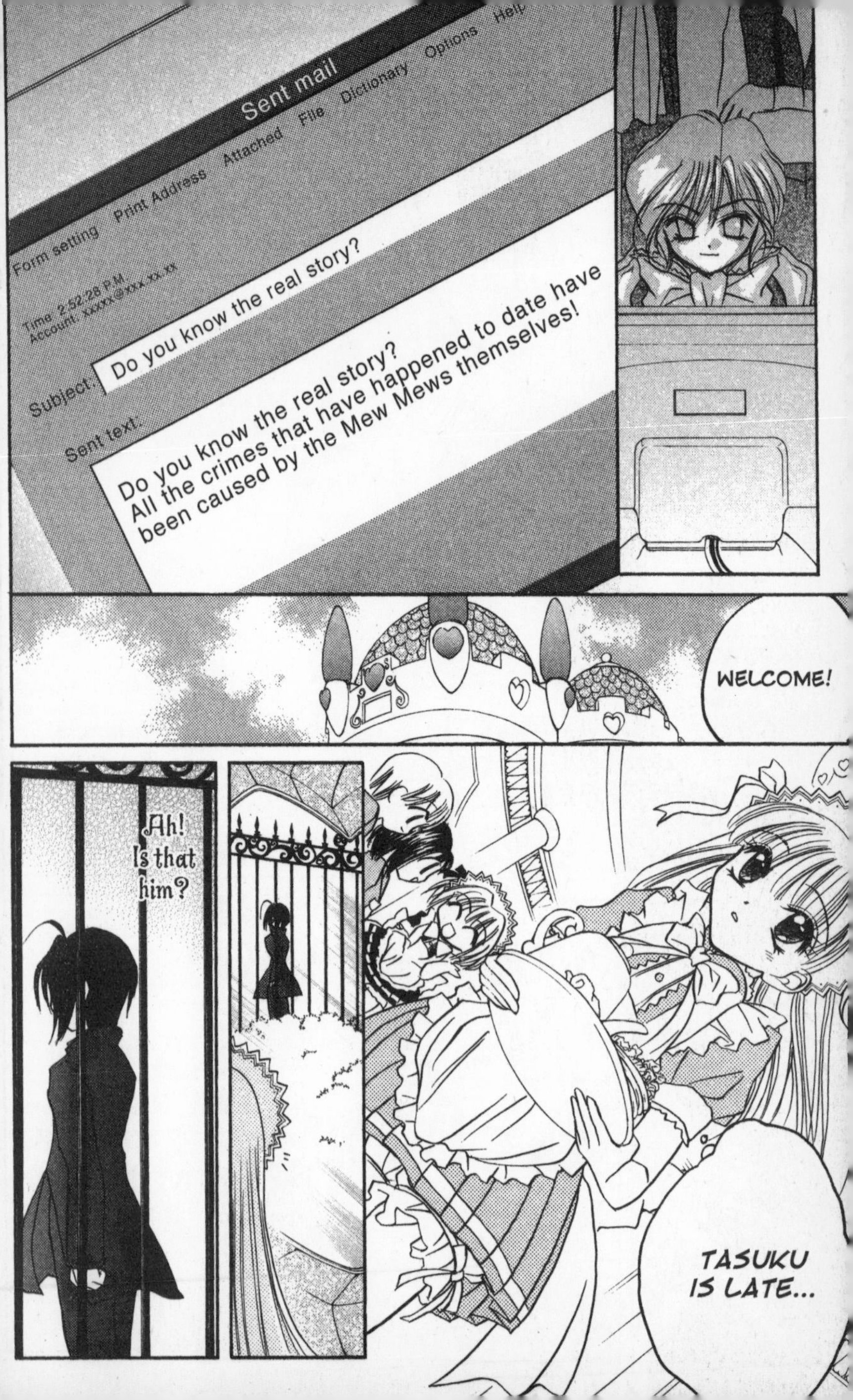

Sent mail
Form setting Print Address Attached File Dictionary Options Help
Time 2:52:28 P.M
Account: xxxxx@xxx.xx.xx
Subject: Do you know the real story?
Sent text:
Do you know the real story?
All the crimes that have happened to date have been caused by the Mew Mews themselves!
WELCOME!
TASUKU IS LATE...
Ah! Is that him?

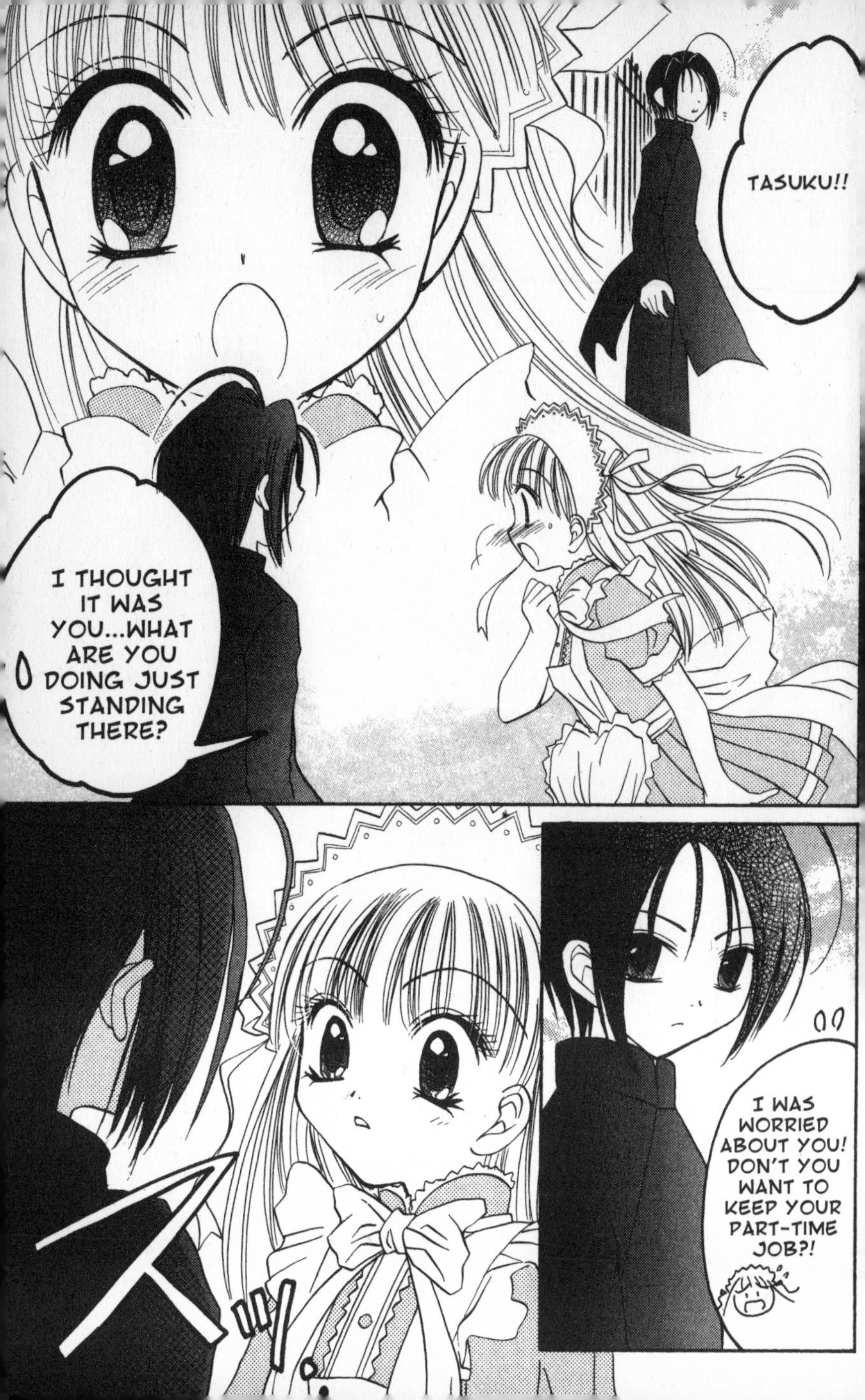
TASUKU!!
I THOUGHT IT WAS YOU...WHAT ARE YOU DOING JUST STANDING THERE?
I WAS WORRIED ABOUT YOU! DON'T YOU WANT TO KEEP YOUR PART-TIME JOB?!

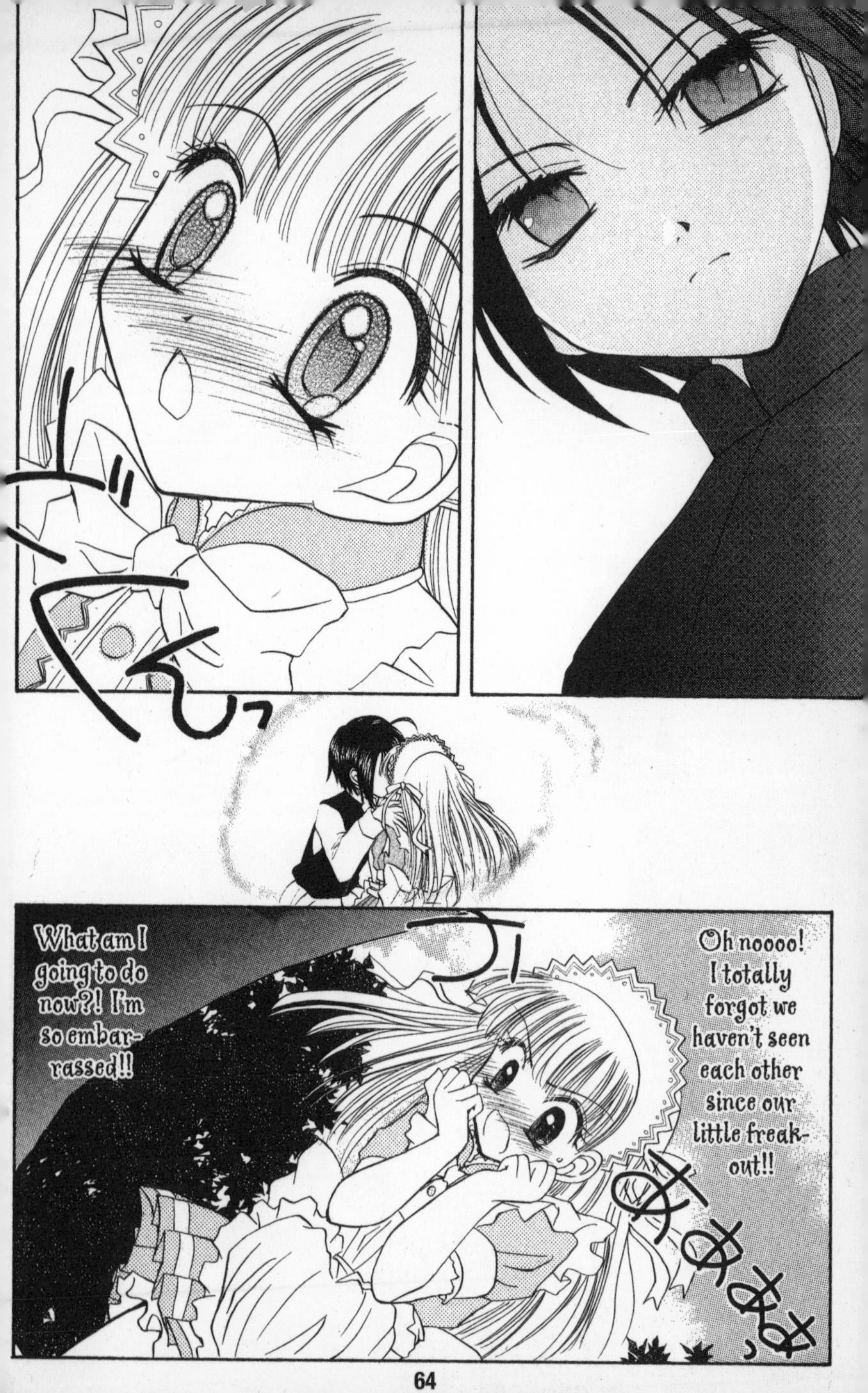

Oh noooo! I totally forgot we haven't seen each other since our little freak-out!!
What am I going to do now?! I'm so embar-rassed!!

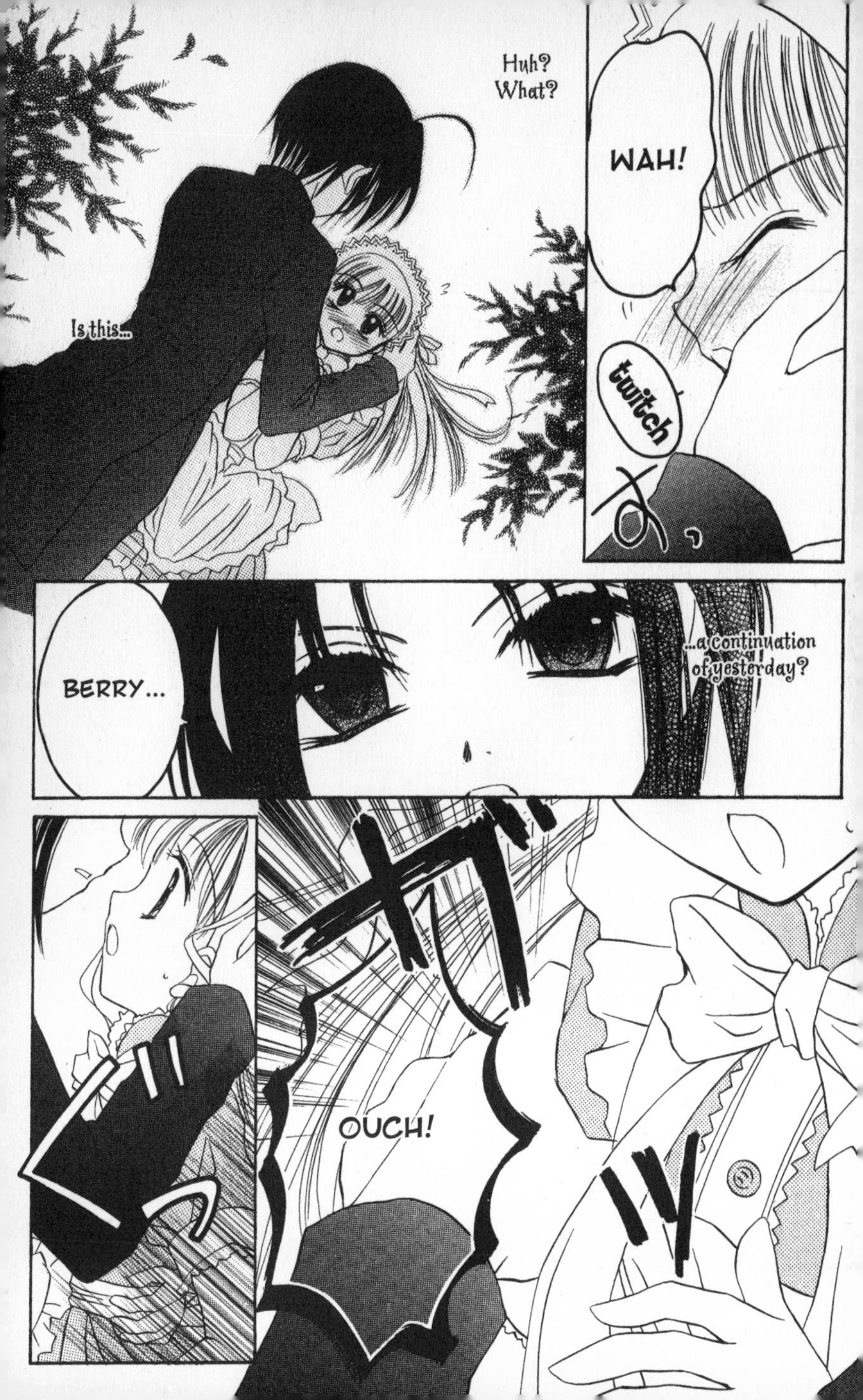
WAH!
twitch
Huh? What?
Is this...
...a continuation of yesterday?
BERRY...
OUCH!

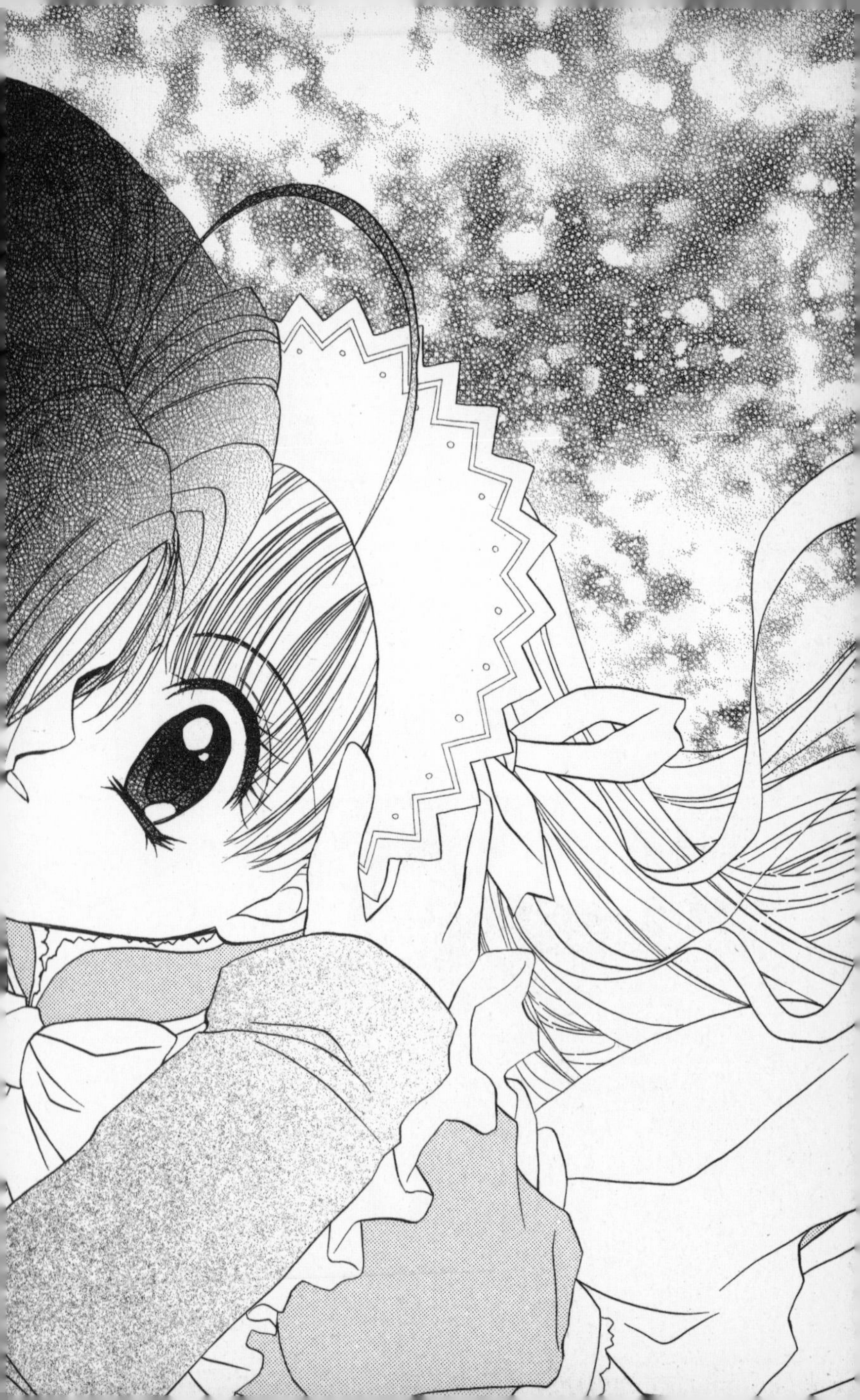

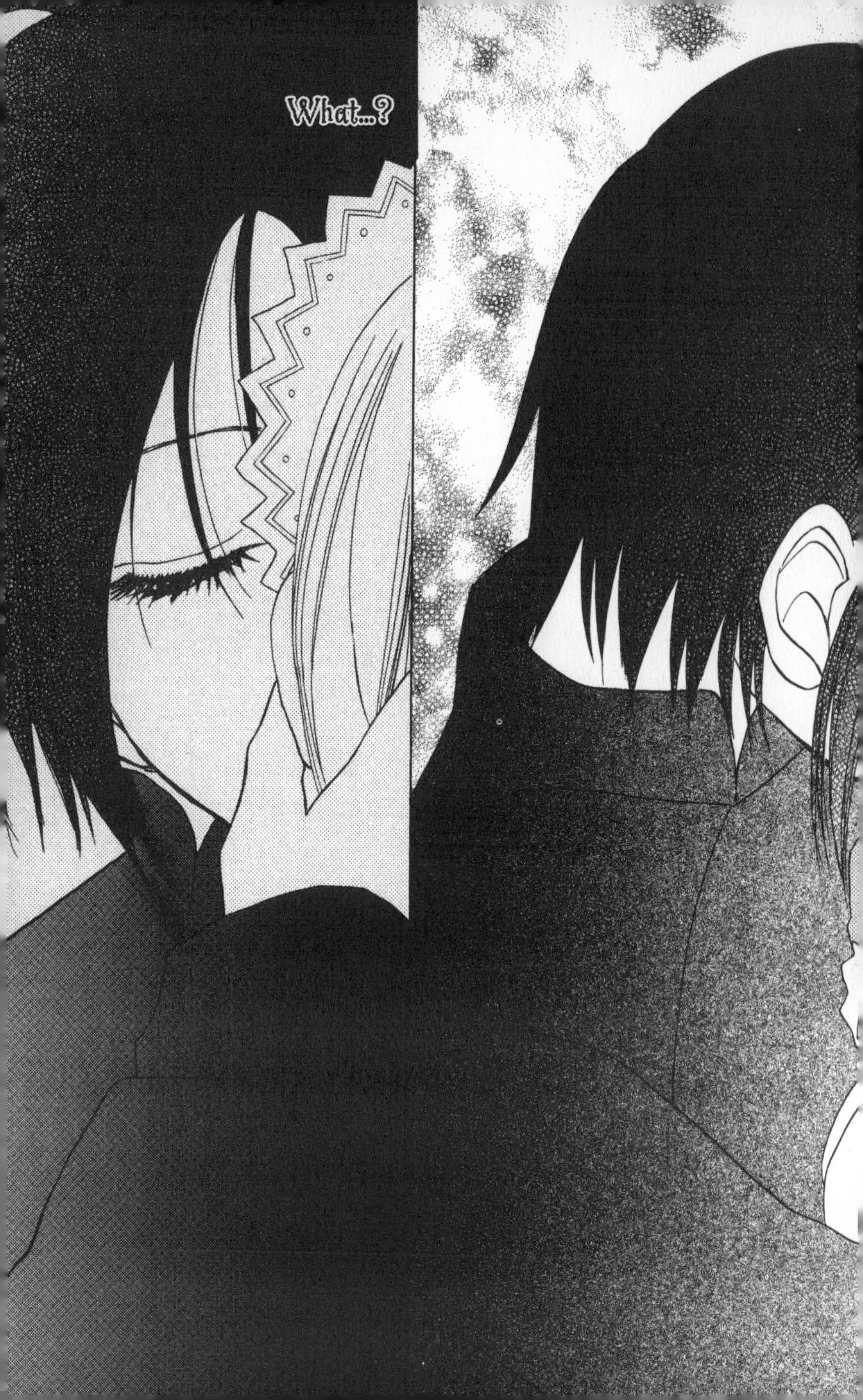
What...?

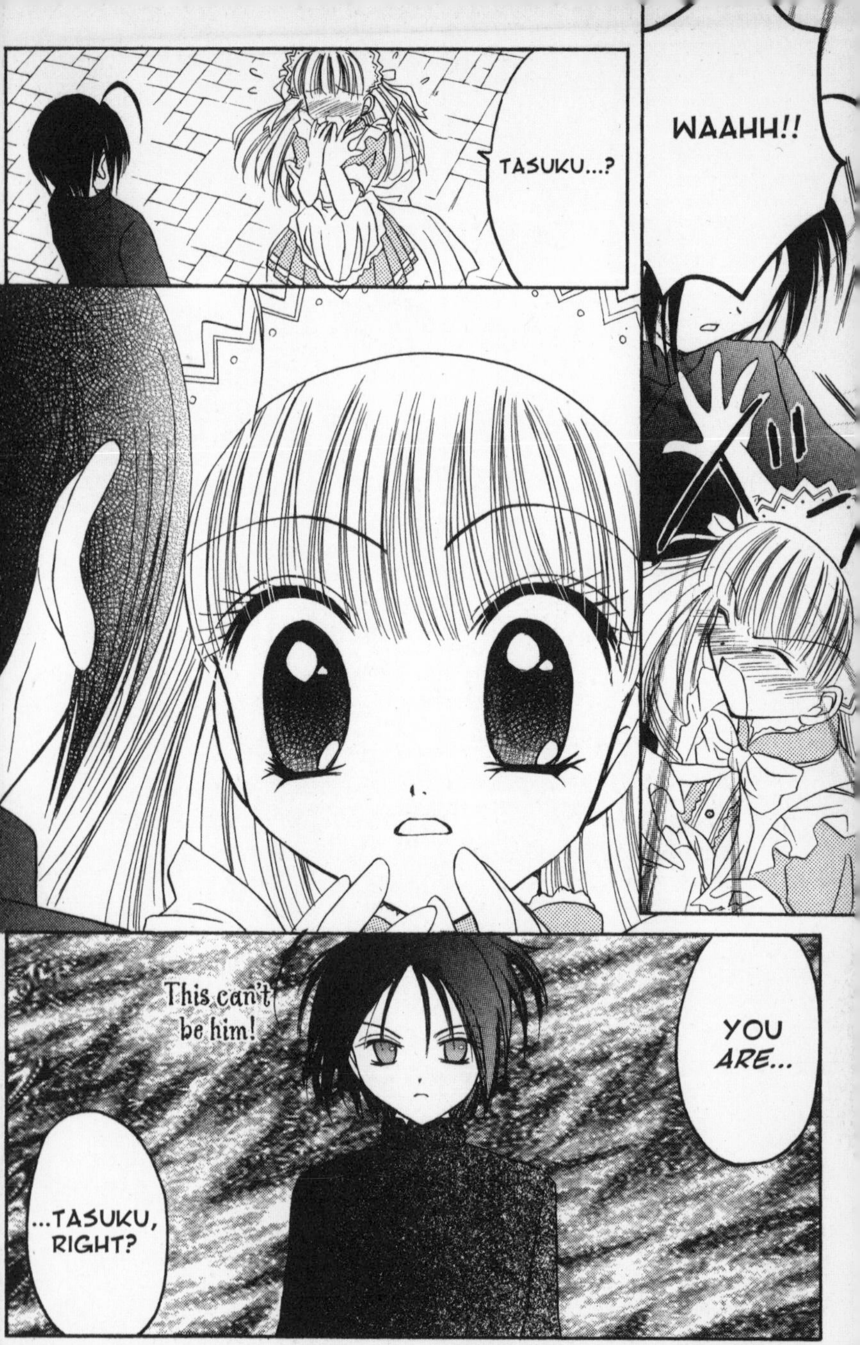
WAAHH!!
TASUKU...?
YOU ARE...
This can't be him!
...TASUKU, RIGHT?

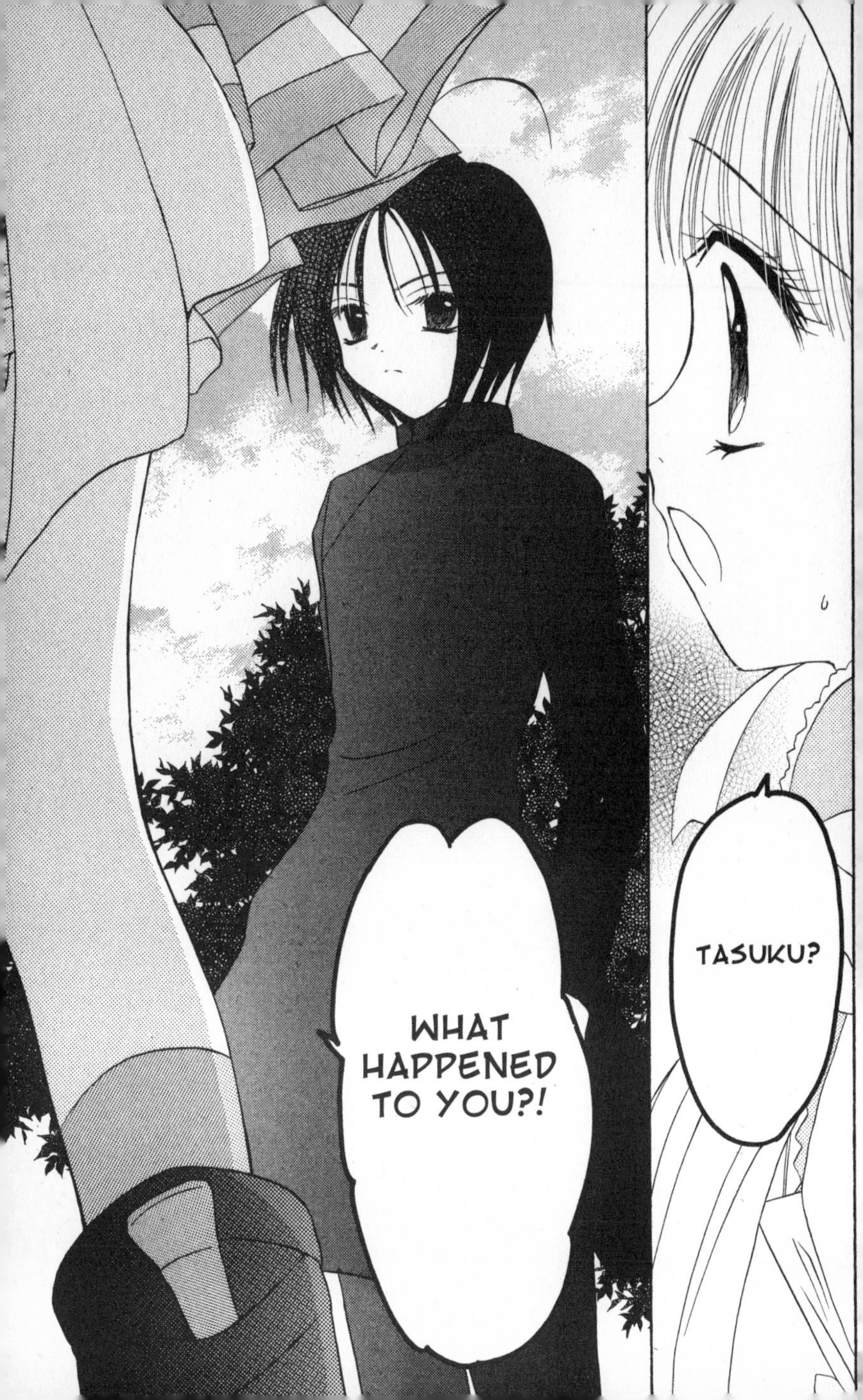
TASUKU?
WHAT HAPPENED TO YOU?!

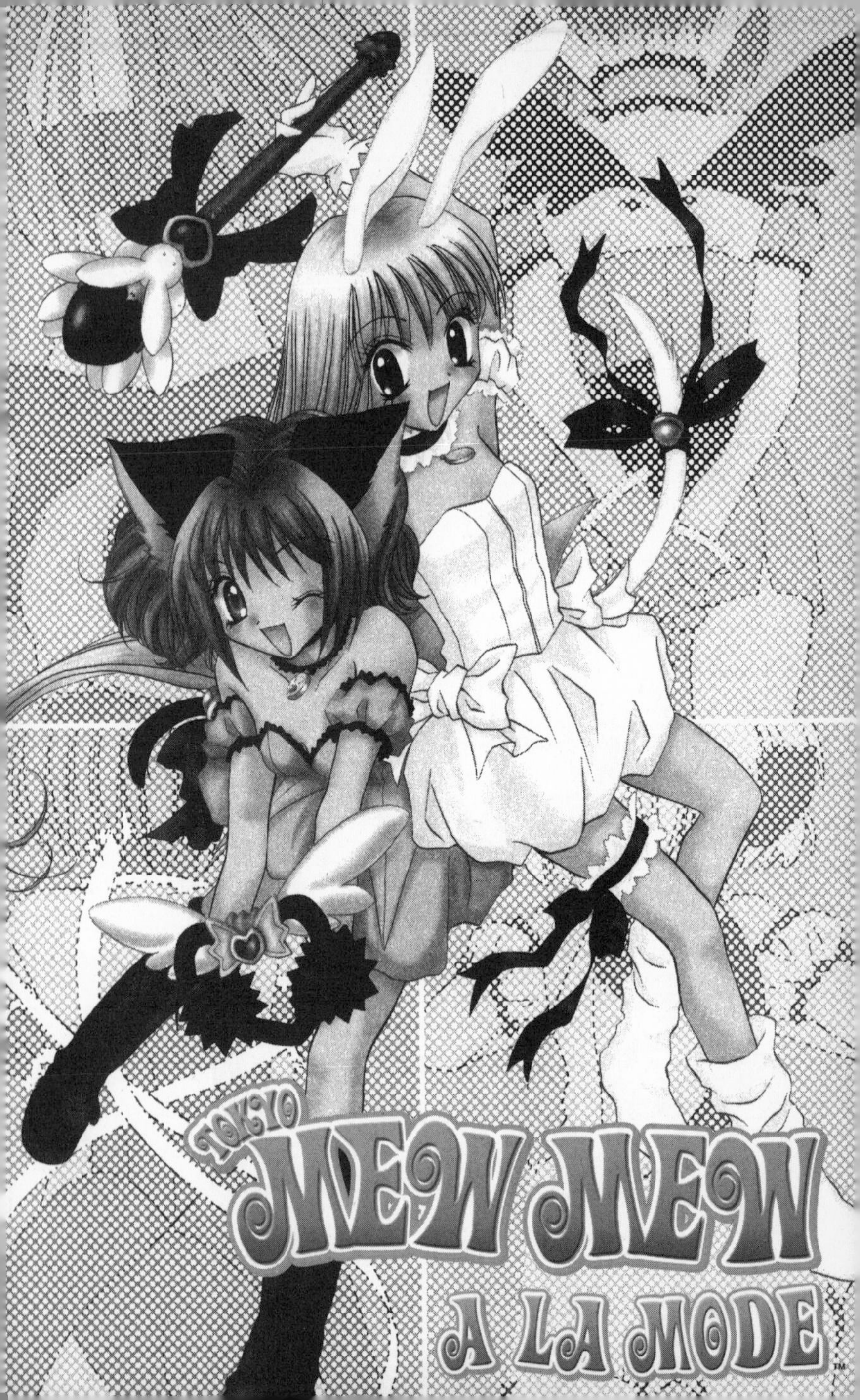
TOKYO MEW MEW A LA MODE™

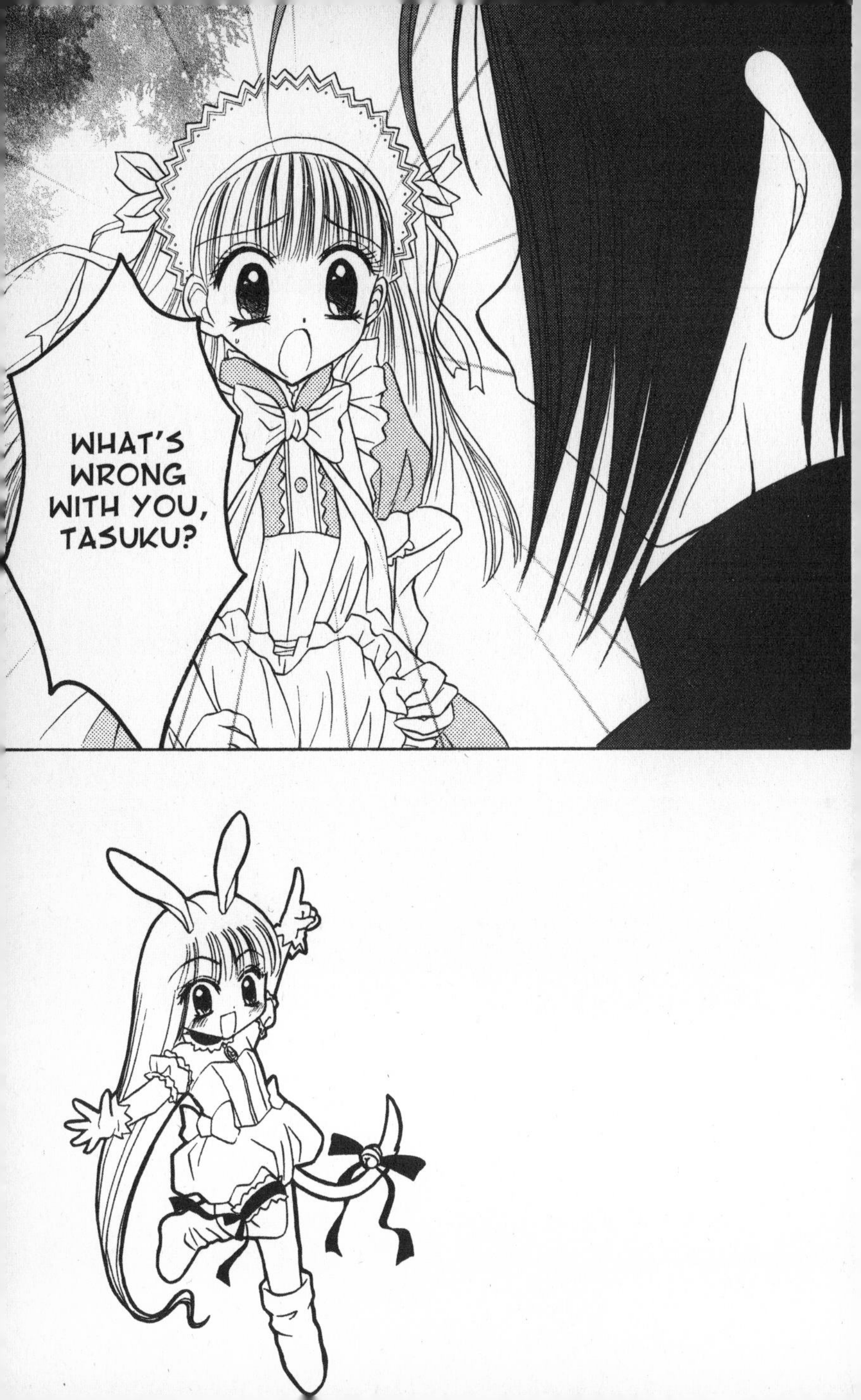
WHAT'S WRONG WITH YOU, TASUKU?

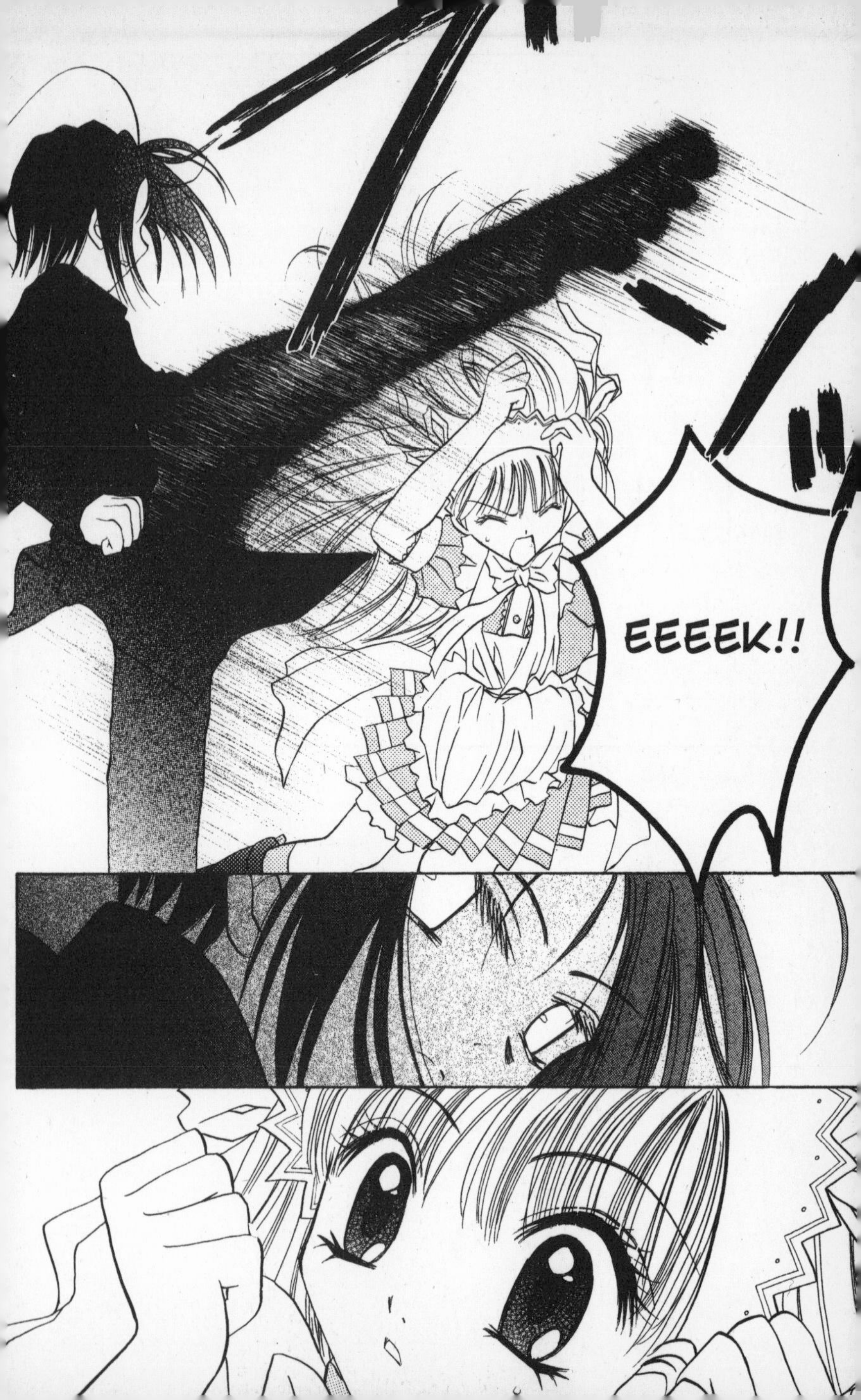
EEEEK!!

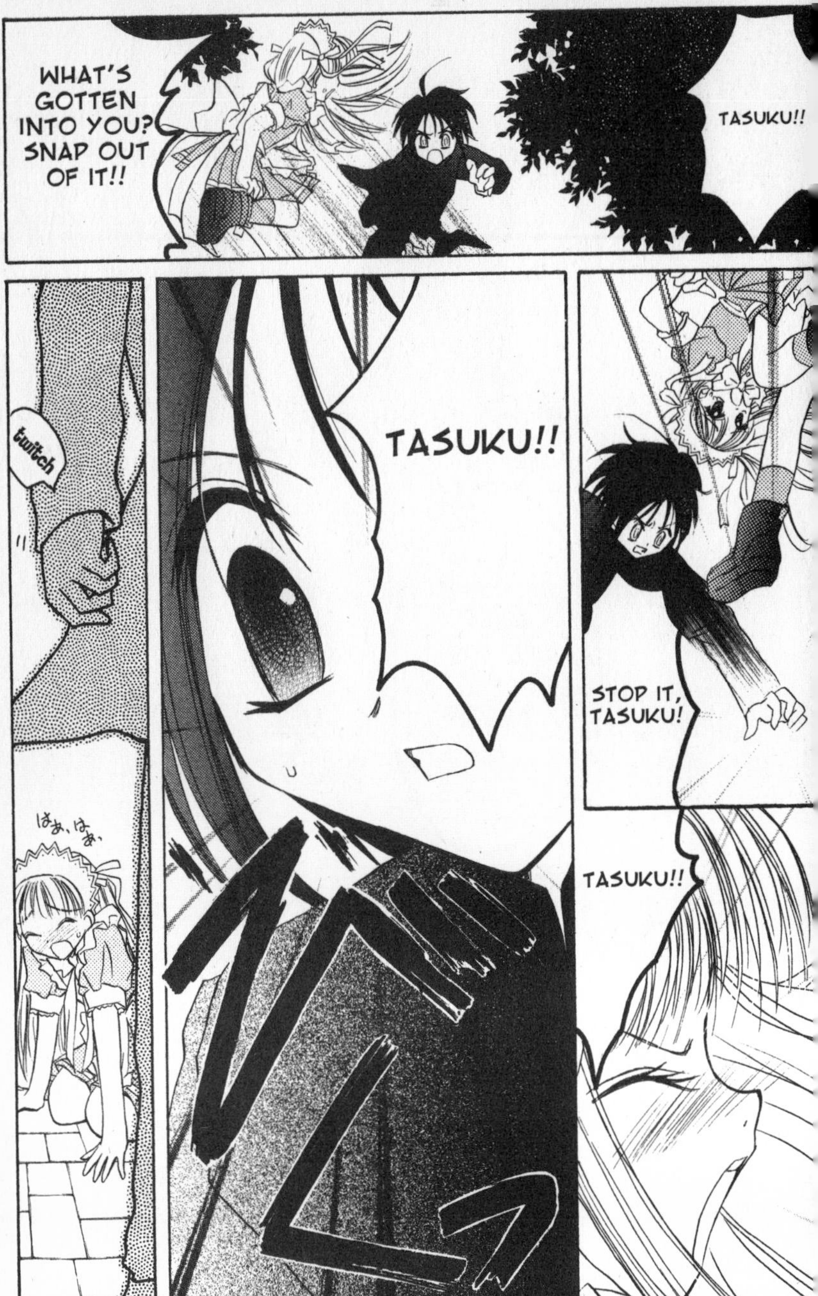
TASUKU!!
WHAT'S GOTTEN INTO YOU? SNAP OUT OF IT!!
STOP IT, TASUKU!
TASUKU!!
TASUKU!!
twitch
はぁ、はぁ、

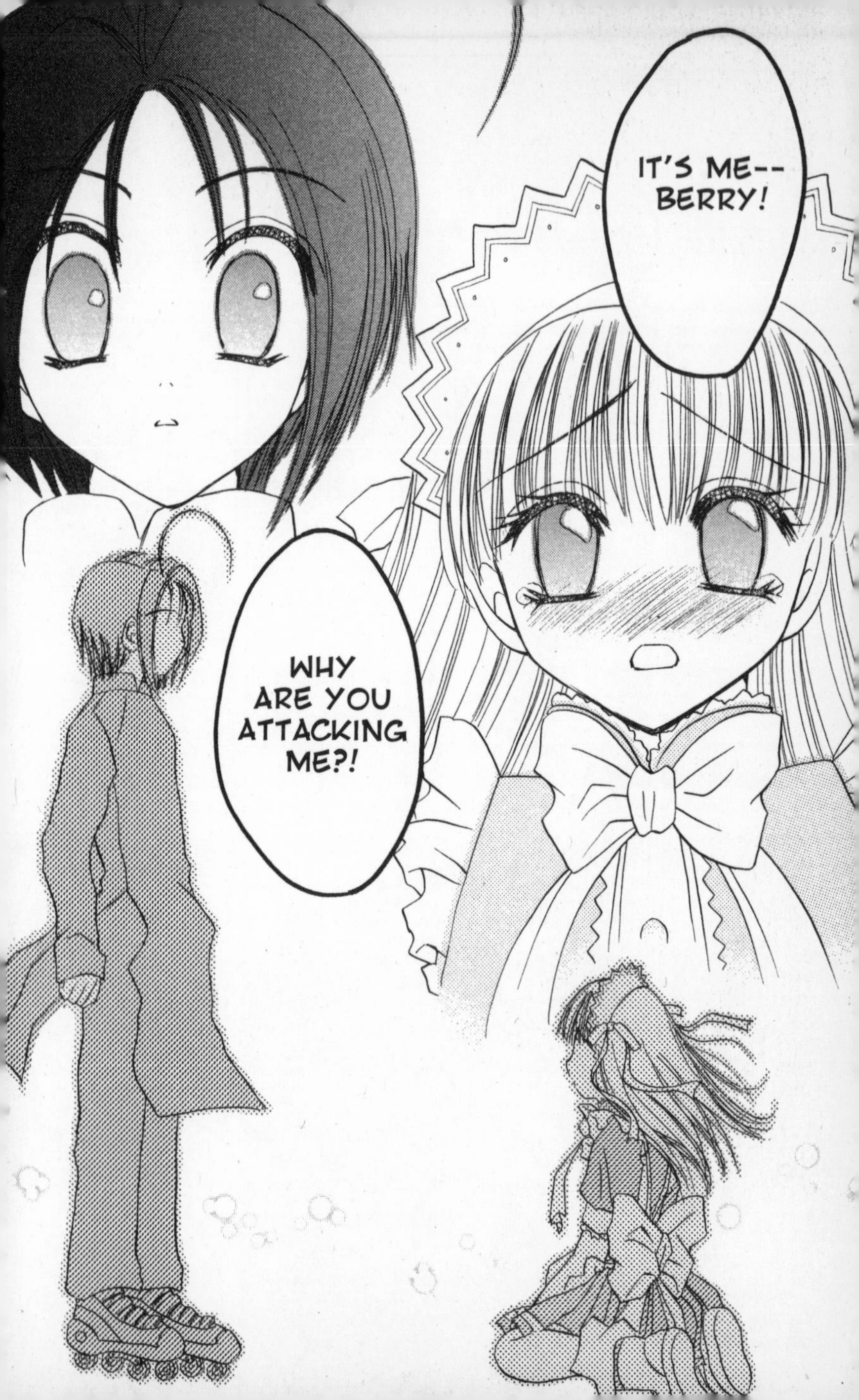
IT'S ME--BERRY!
WHY ARE YOU ATTACKING ME?!

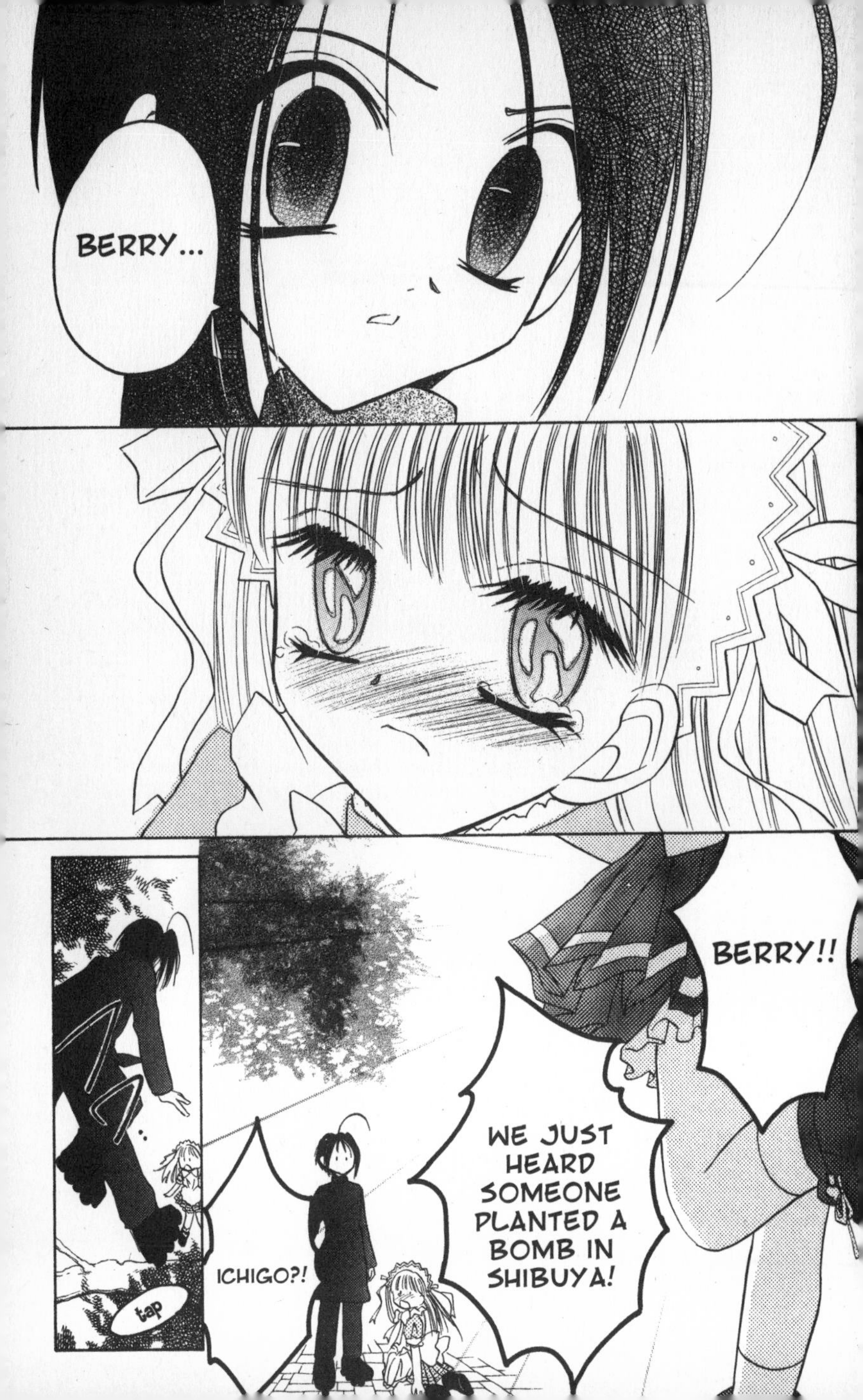

BERRY...
BERRY!!
WE JUST HEARD SOMEONE PLANTED A BOMB IN SHIBUYA!
ICHIGO?!
..
tap

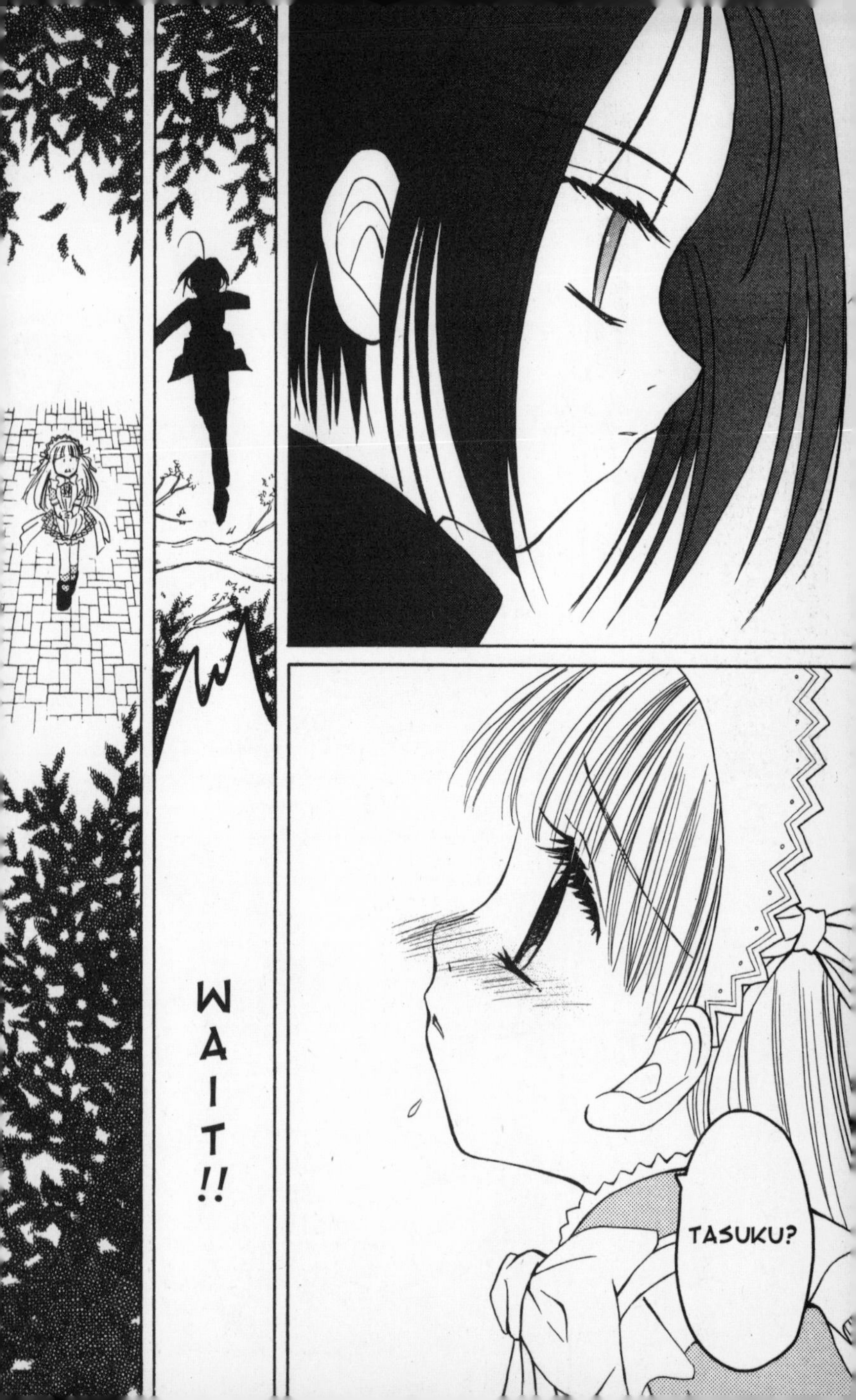

WAIT!!
TASUKU?

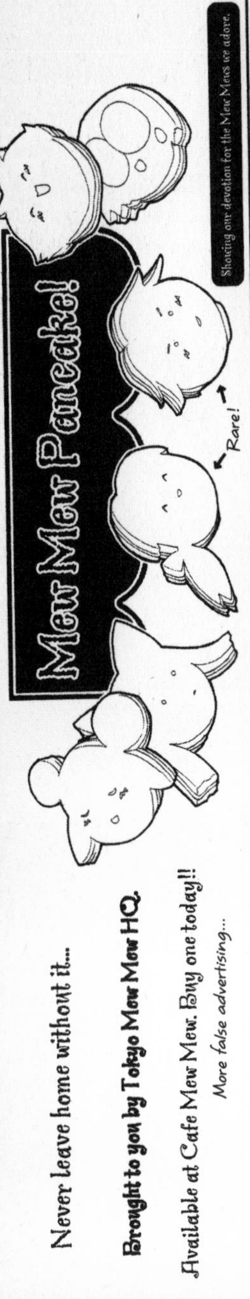
Mew Mew Pancake!
Showing our devotion for the Mew Mews we adore.
Rare!
Never leave home without it...
Brought to you by Tokyo Mew Mew HQ.
Available at Cafe Mew Mew. Buy one today!!
More false advertising...

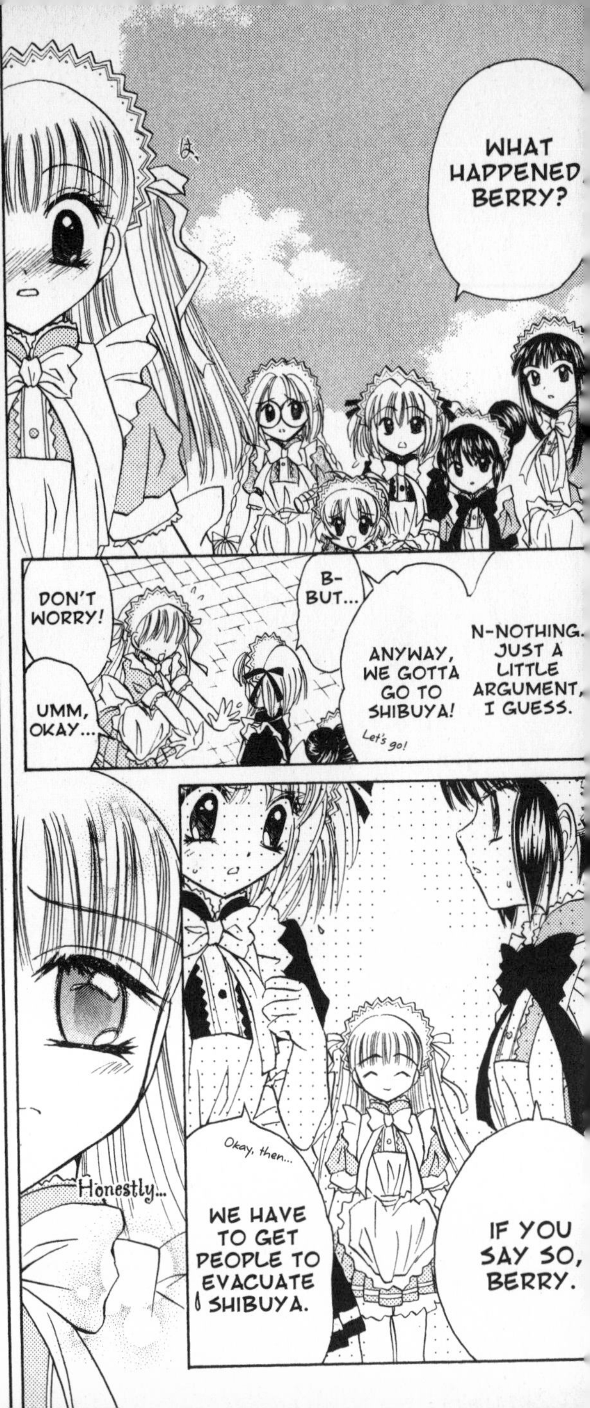
WHAT HAPPENED BERRY?
N-NOTHING. JUST A LITTLE ARGUMENT, I GUESS.
B-BUT...
ANYWAY, WE GOTTA GO TO SHIBUYA!
Let's go!
DON'T WORRY!
UMM, OKAY...
IF YOU SAY SO, BERRY.
Okay, then...
WE HAVE TO GET PEOPLE TO EVACUATE SHIBUYA.
Honestly...

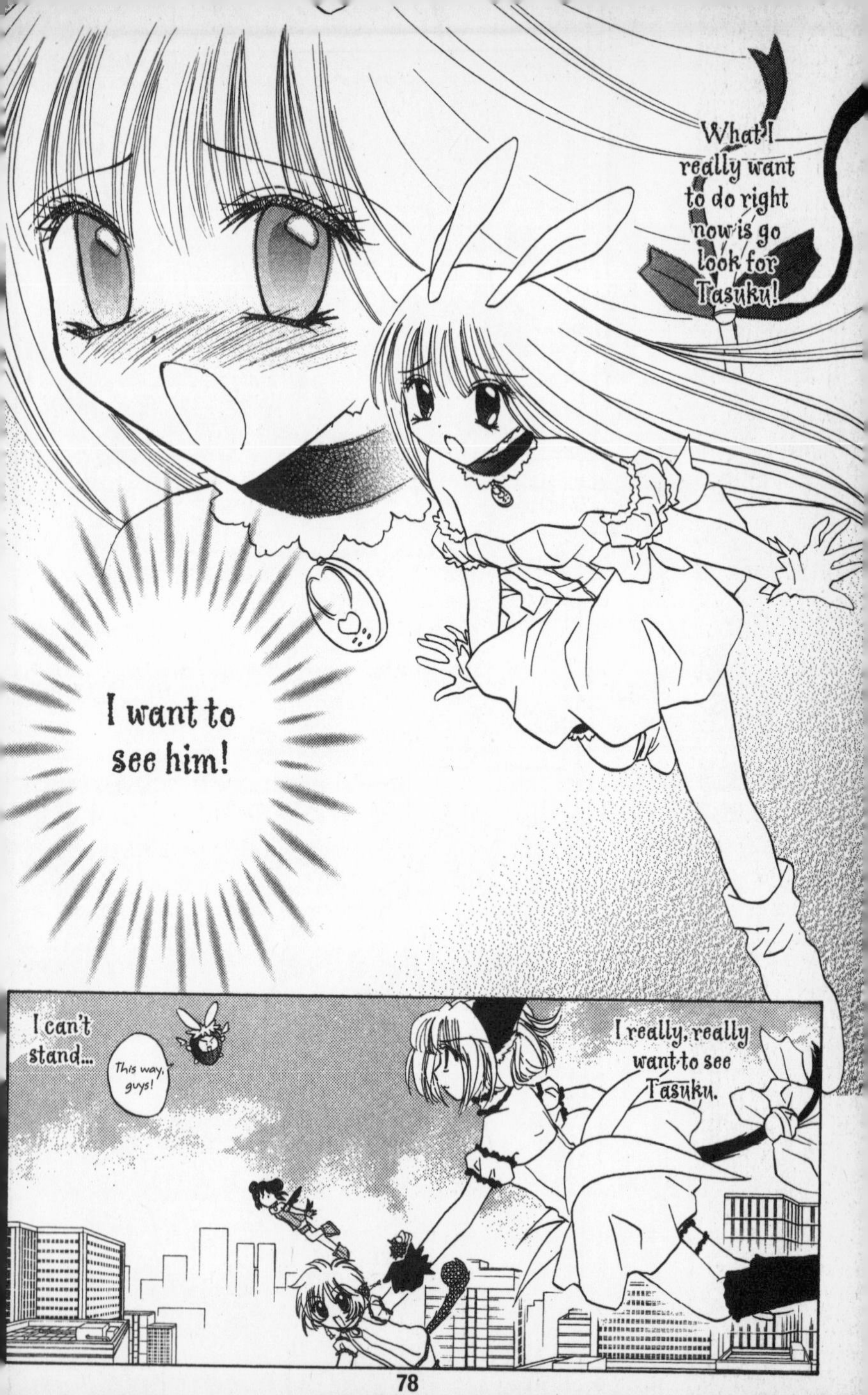

What I really want to do right now is go look for Tasuku!
I want to see him!
I really, really want to see Tasuku.
This way, guys!
I can't stand...

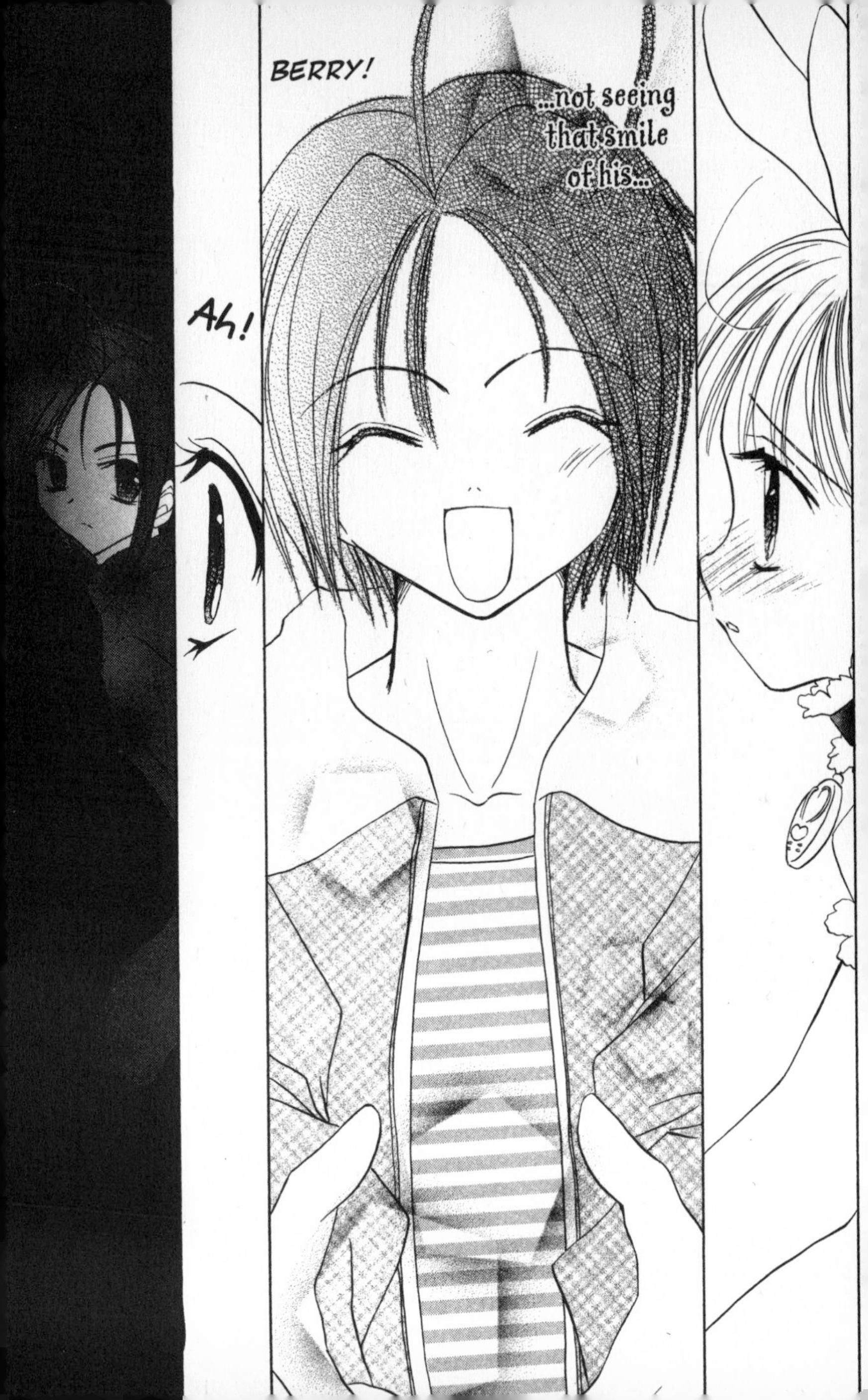
...not seeing that smile of his...
BERRY!
Ah!

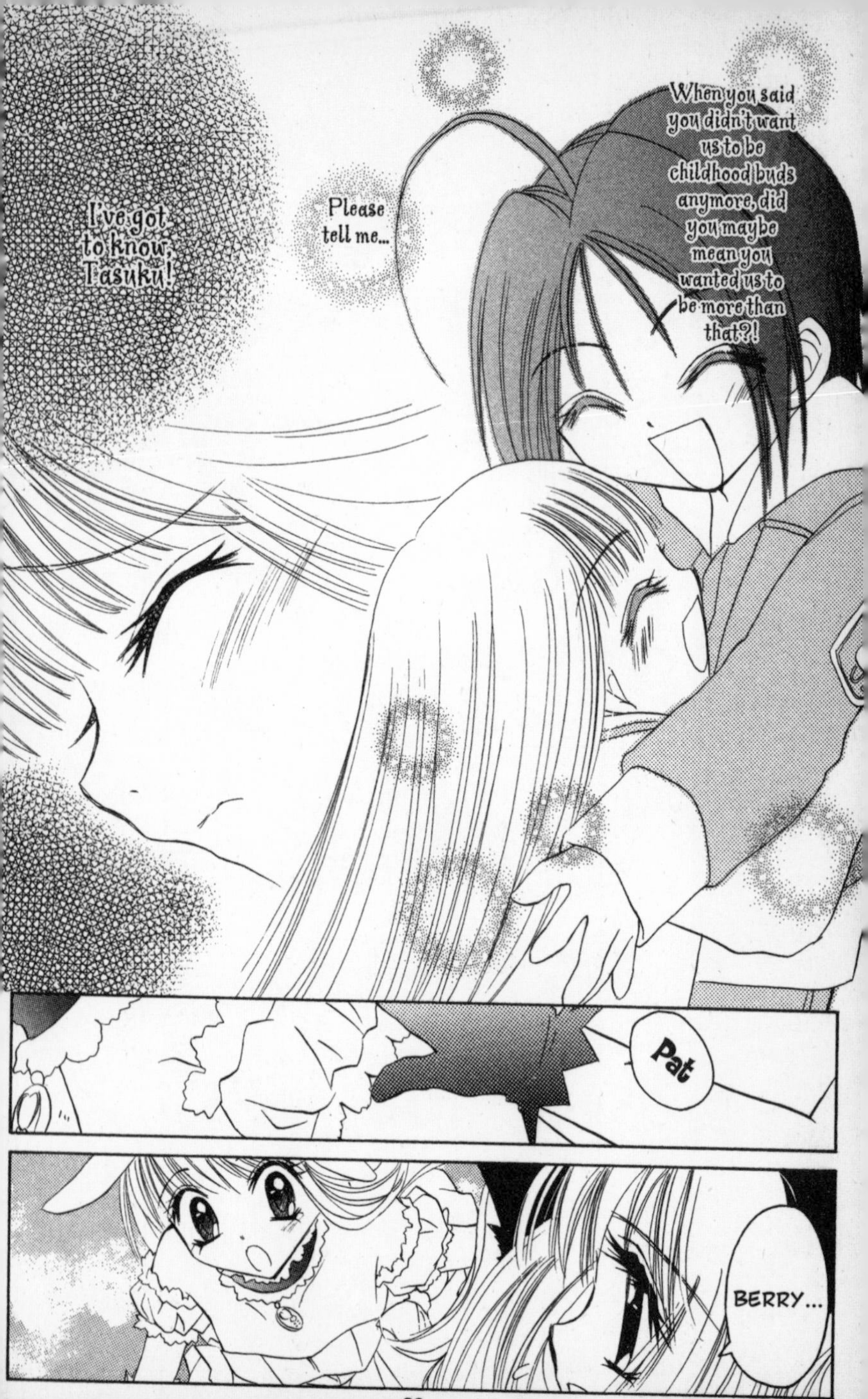
When you said you didn't want us to be childhood buds anymore, did you maybe mean you wanted us to be more than that?!
Please tell me...
I've got to know, Tasuku!
Pat
BERRY...

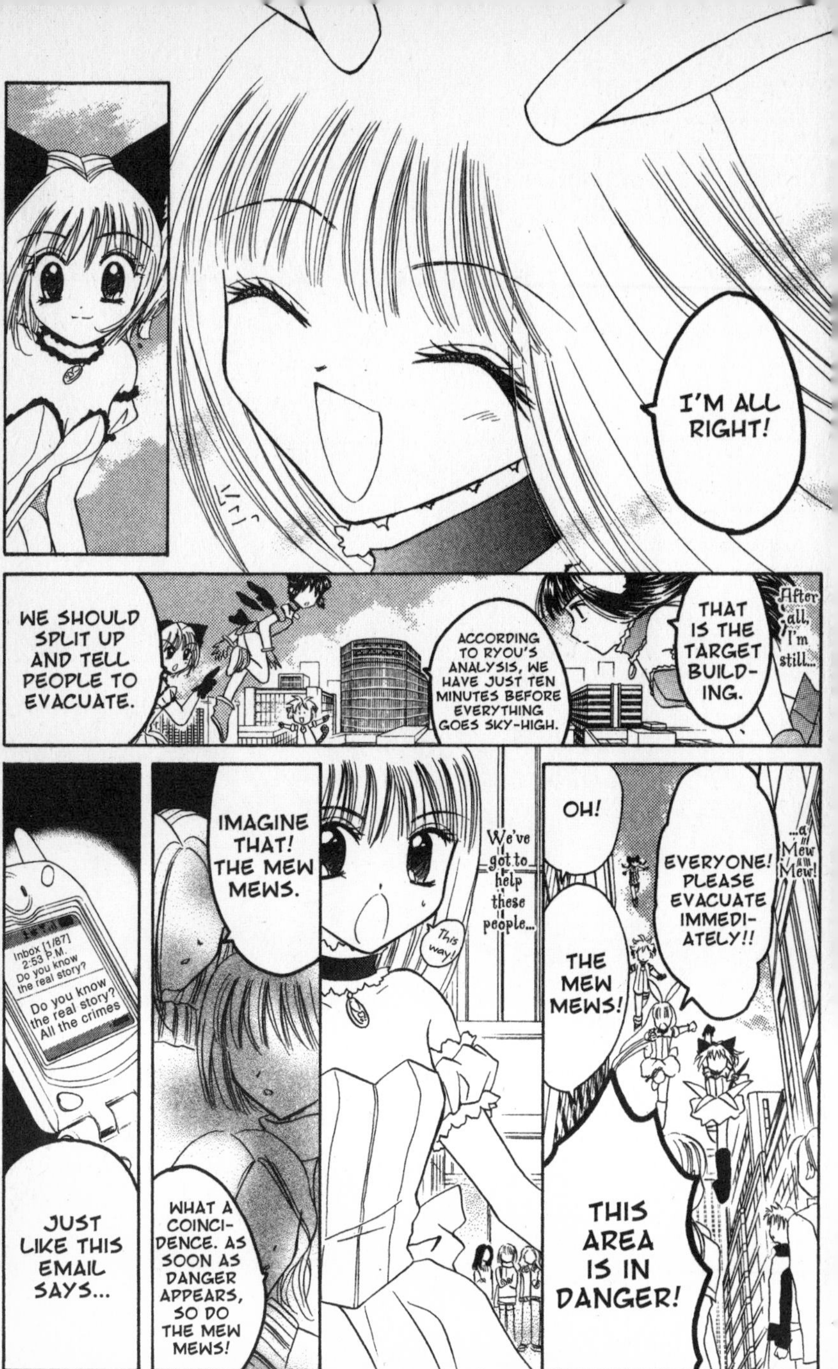
I'M ALL RIGHT!
After all, I'm still...
THAT IS THE TARGET BUILDING.
ACCORDING TO RYOU'S ANALYSIS, WE HAVE JUST TEN MINUTES BEFORE EVERYTHING GOES SKY-HIGH.
WE SHOULD SPLIT UP AND TELL PEOPLE TO EVACUATE.
...a Mew Mew!
EVERYONE! PLEASE EVACUATE IMMEDIATELY!!
OH!
THE MEW MEWS!
THIS AREA IS IN DANGER!
We've got to help these people...
IMAGINE THAT! THE MEW MEWS.
This way!
WHAT A COINCIDENCE. AS SOON AS DANGER APPEARS, SO DO THE MEW MEWS!
Inbox [1/87]
2:53 P.M.
Do you know the real story?
Do you know the real story? All the crimes
JUST LIKE THIS EMAIL SAYS...

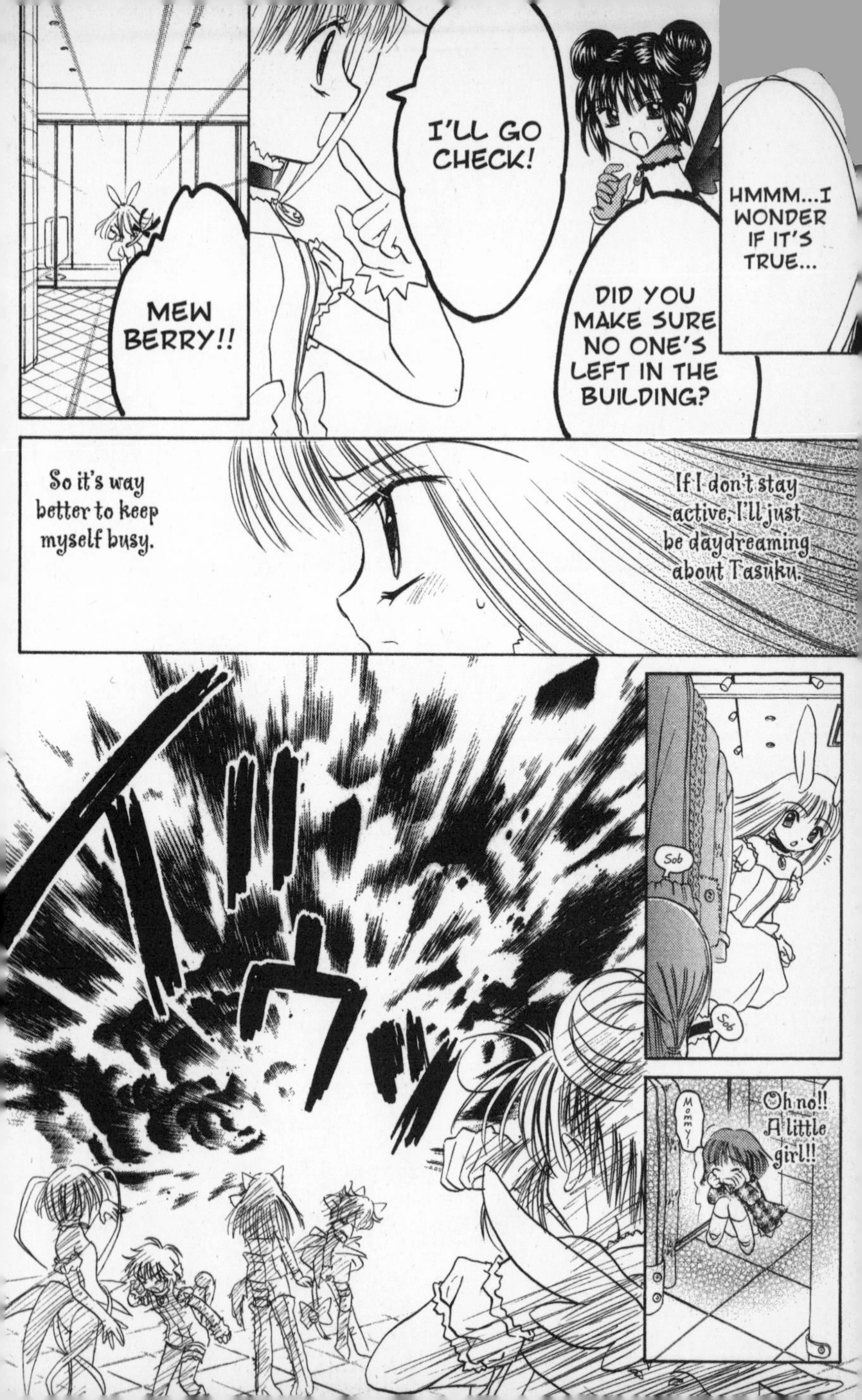

HMMM...I WONDER IF IT'S TRUE...
DID YOU MAKE SURE NO ONE'S LEFT IN THE BUILDING?
I'LL GO CHECK!
MEW BERRY!!
If I don't stay active, I'll just be daydreaming about Tasuku.
So it's way better to keep myself busy.
Sob
Sob
Oh no!! A little girl!!
Mommy!

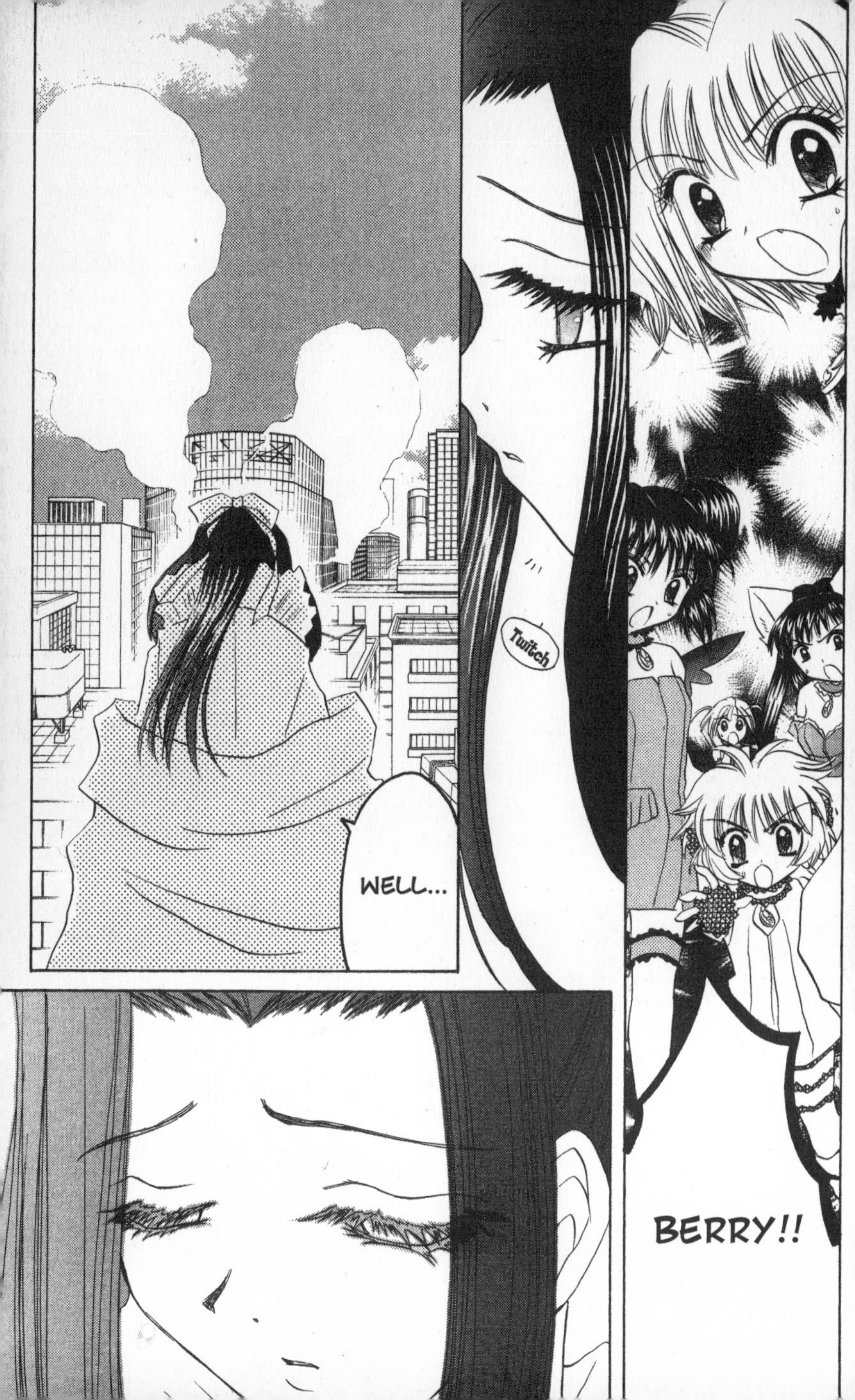
BERRY!!
Twitch
WELL...

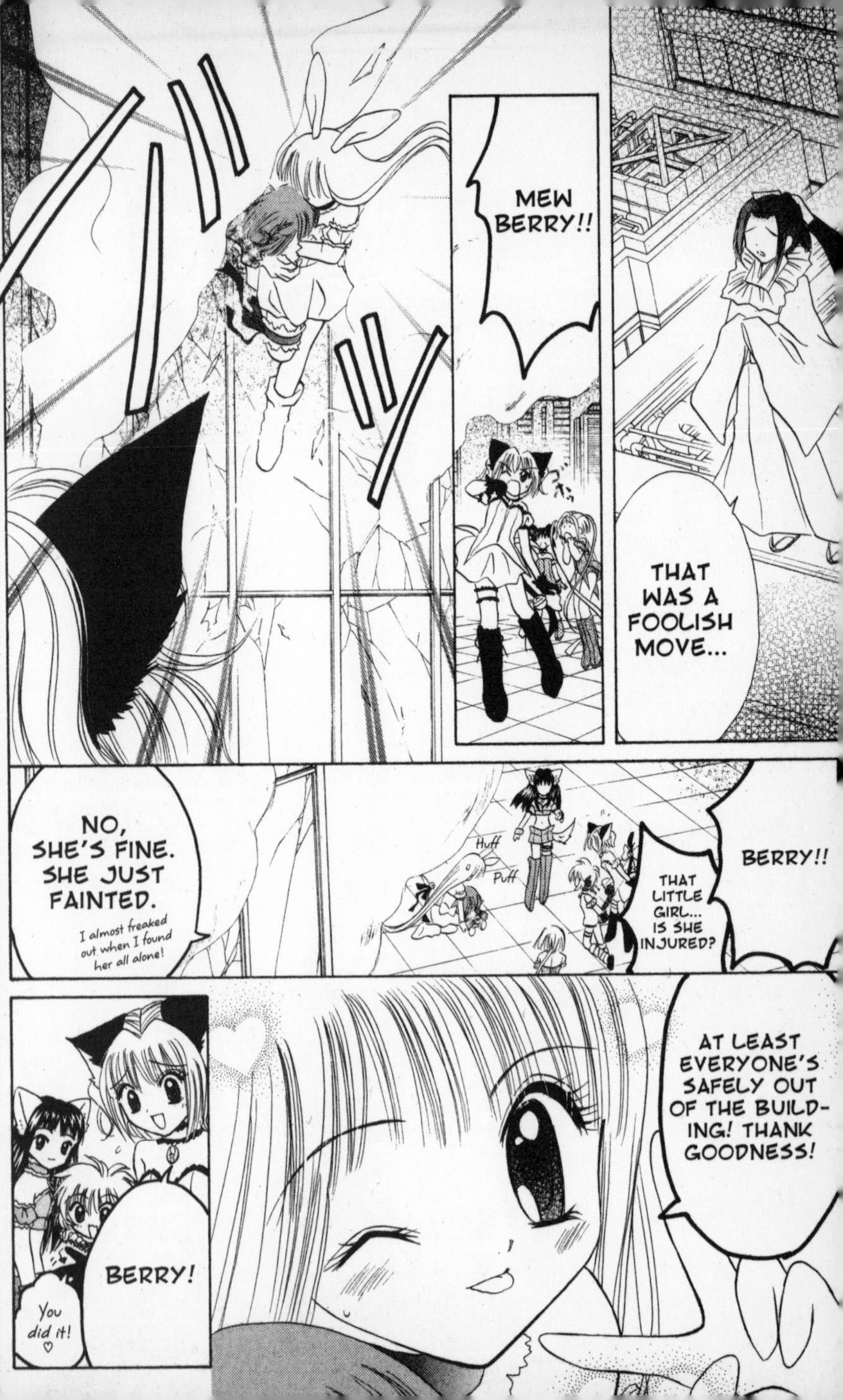
THAT WAS A FOOLISH MOVE...
MEW BERRY!!
BERRY!!
THAT LITTLE GIRL... IS SHE INJURED?
Huff
Puff
NO, SHE'S FINE. SHE JUST FAINTED.
I almost freaked out when I found her all alone!
AT LEAST EVERYONE'S SAFELY OUT OF THE BUILD-ING! THANK GOODNESS!
BERRY!
You did it! ♡

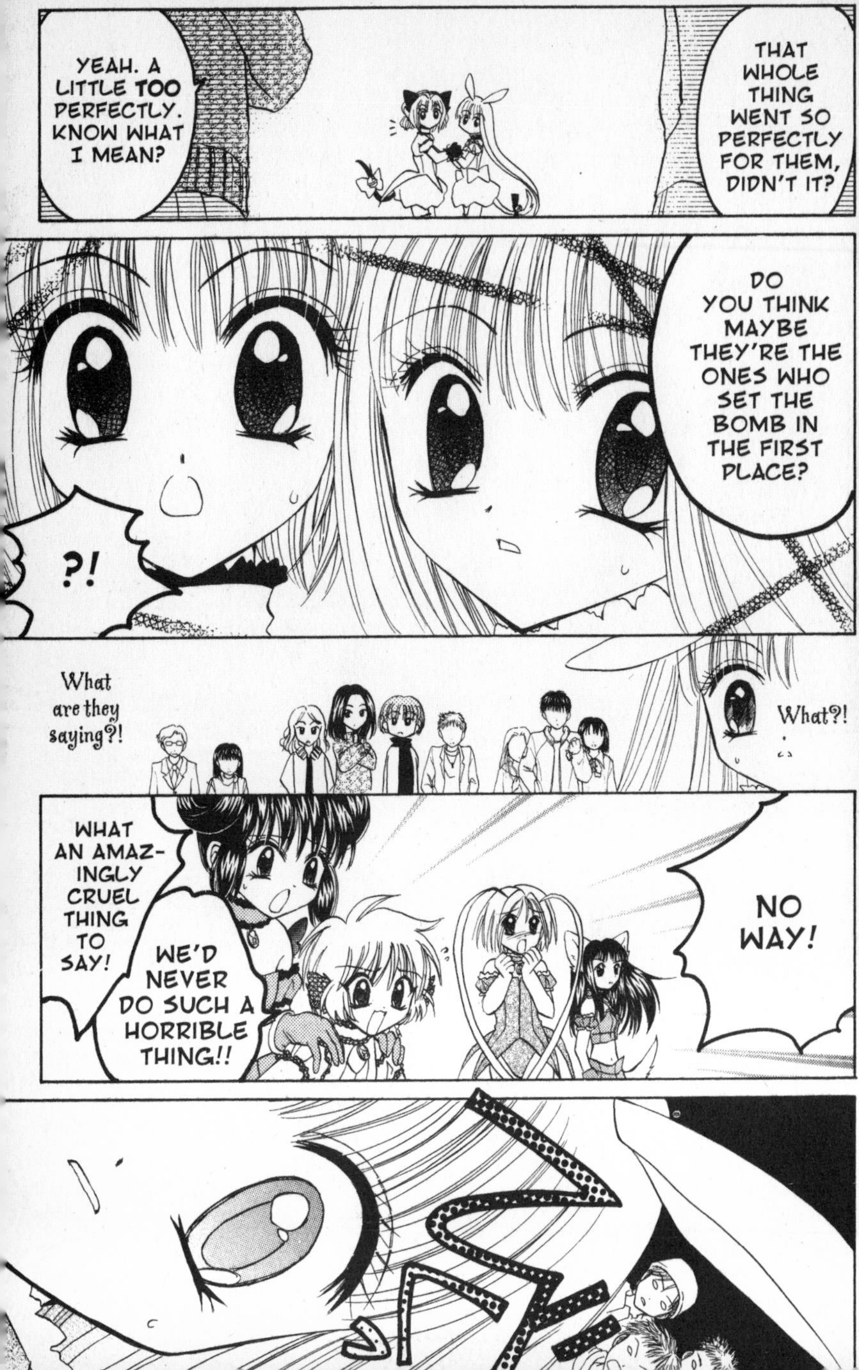
THAT WHOLE THING WENT SO PERFECTLY FOR THEM, DIDN'T IT?
YEAH. A LITTLE TOO PERFECTLY. KNOW WHAT I MEAN?
DO YOU THINK MAYBE THEY'RE THE ONES WHO SET THE BOMB IN THE FIRST PLACE?
?!
What?!
What are they saying?!
NO WAY!
WHAT AN AMAZINGLY CRUEL THING TO SAY!
WE'D NEVER DO SUCH A HORRIBLE THING!!

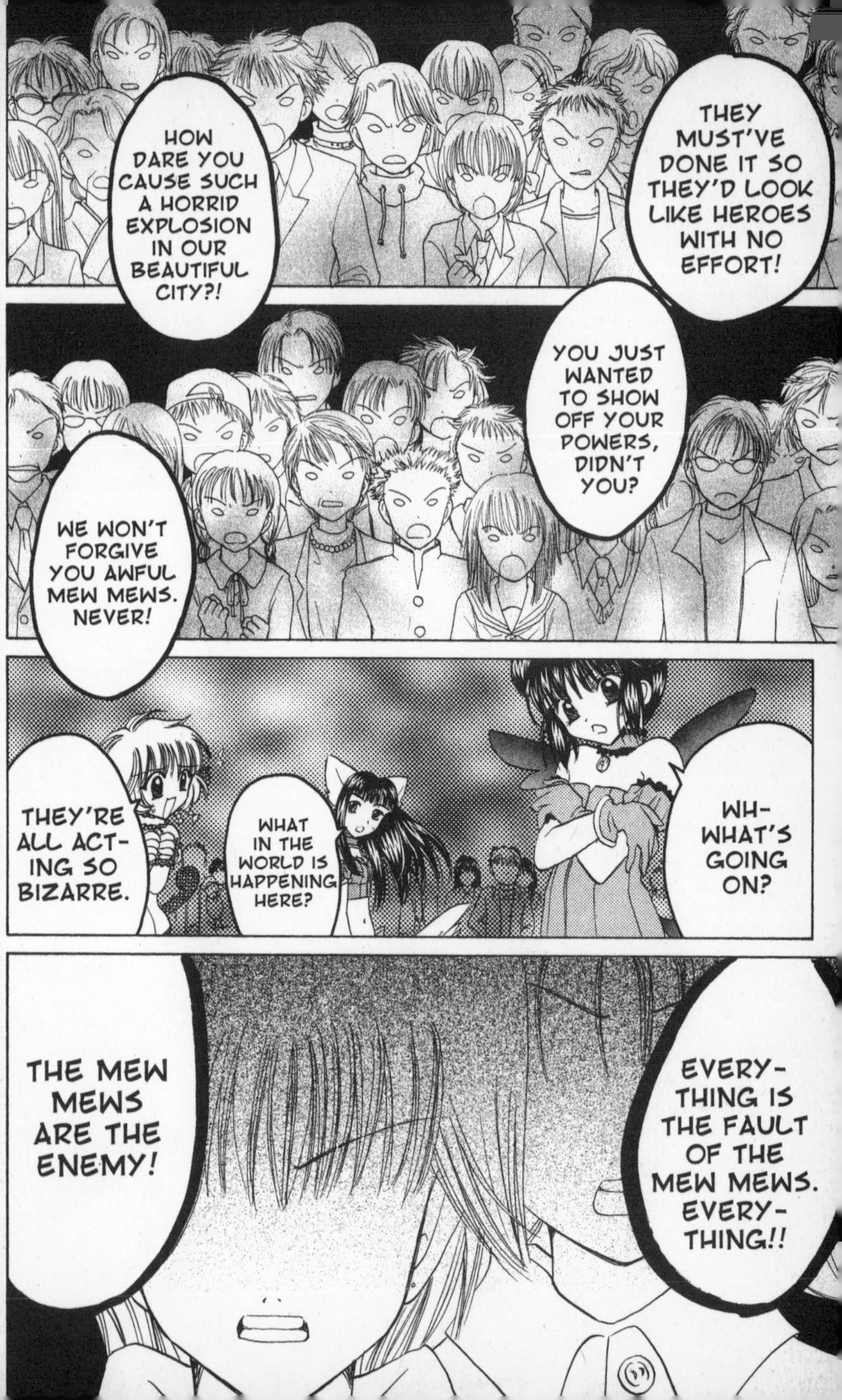

THEY MUST'VE DONE IT SO THEY'D LOOK LIKE HEROES WITH NO EFFORT!
HOW DARE YOU CAUSE SUCH A HORRID EXPLOSION IN OUR BEAUTIFUL CITY?!
YOU JUST WANTED TO SHOW OFF YOUR POWERS, DIDN'T YOU?
WE WON'T FORGIVE YOU AWFUL MEW MEWS. NEVER!
WH- WHAT'S GOING ON?
WHAT IN THE WORLD IS HAPPENING HERE?
THEY'RE ALL ACT-ING SO BIZARRE.
EVERY-THING IS THE FAULT OF THE MEW MEWS. EVERY-THING!!
THE MEW MEWS ARE THE ENEMY!

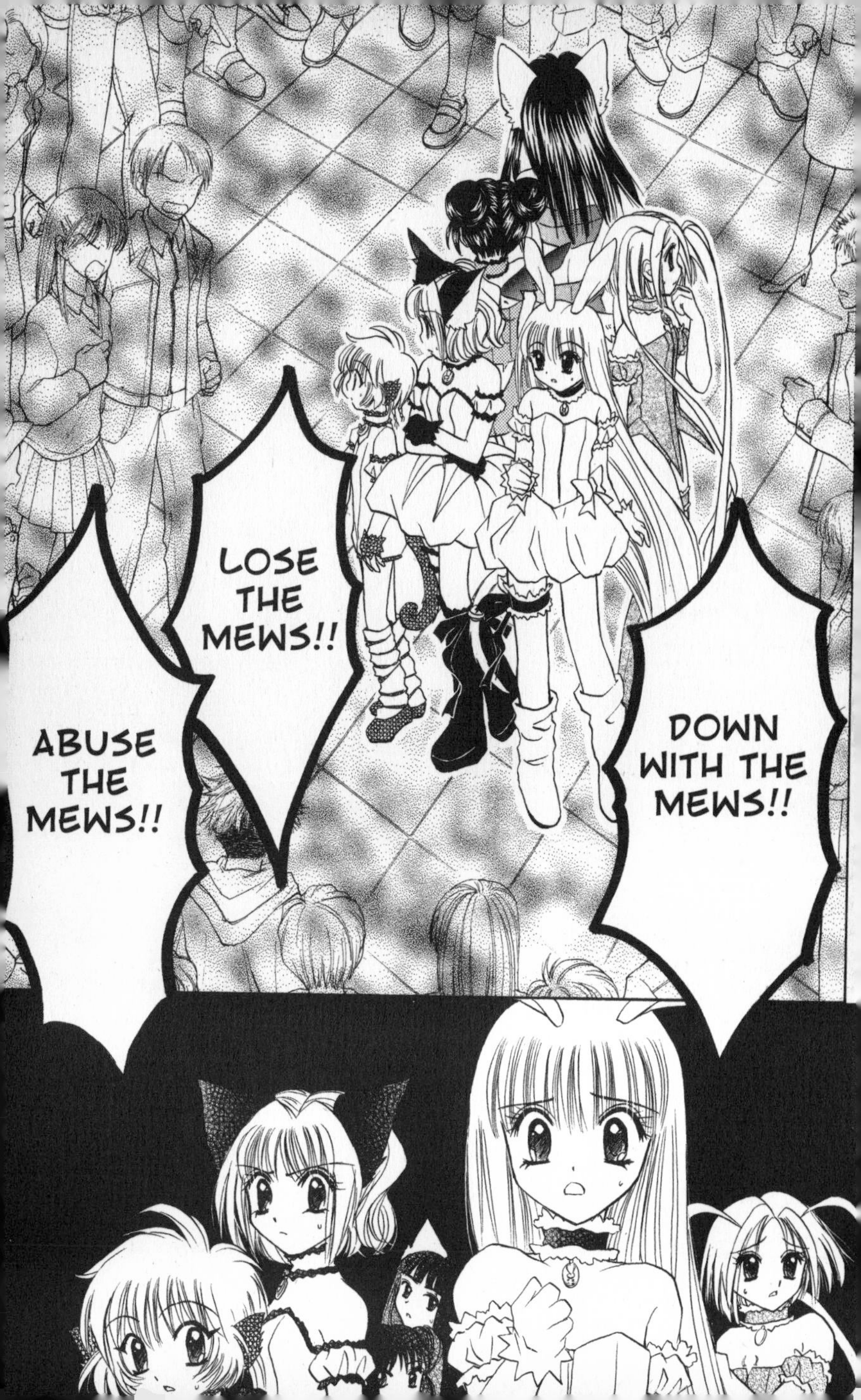
DOWN WITH THE MEWS!!
LOSE THE MEWS!!
ABUSE THE MEWS!!

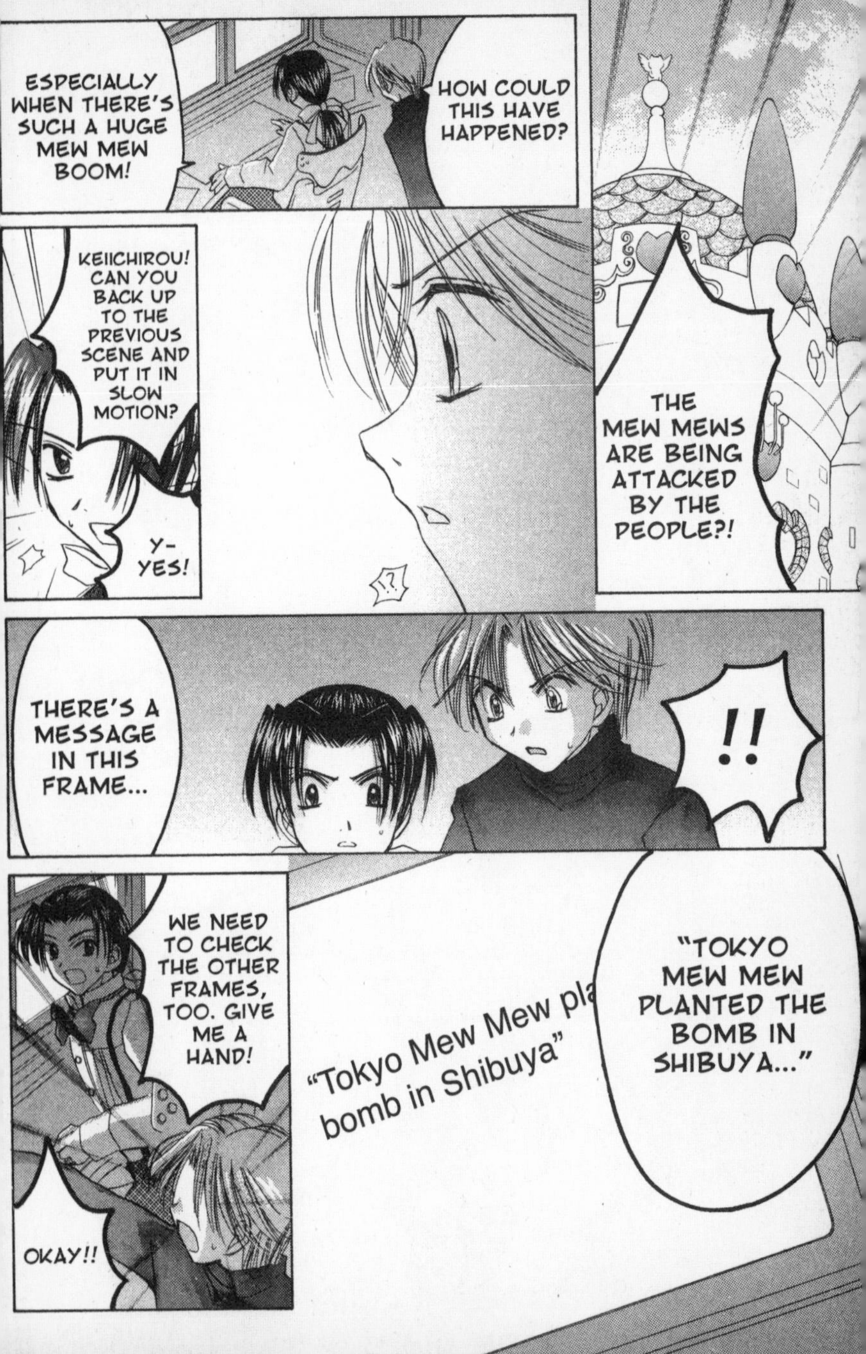
THE MEW MEWS ARE BEING ATTACKED BY THE PEOPLE?!
HOW COULD THIS HAVE HAPPENED?
ESPECIALLY WHEN THERE'S SUCH A HUGE MEW MEW BOOM!
!?
KEIICHIROU! CAN YOU BACK UP TO THE PREVIOUS SCENE AND PUT IT IN SLOW MOTION?
Y-YES!
!!
THERE'S A MESSAGE IN THIS FRAME...
"TOKYO MEW MEW PLANTED THE BOMB IN SHIBUYA..."
"Tokyo Mew Mew pla
bomb in Shibuya"
WE NEED TO CHECK THE OTHER FRAMES, TOO. GIVE ME A HAND!
OKAY!!

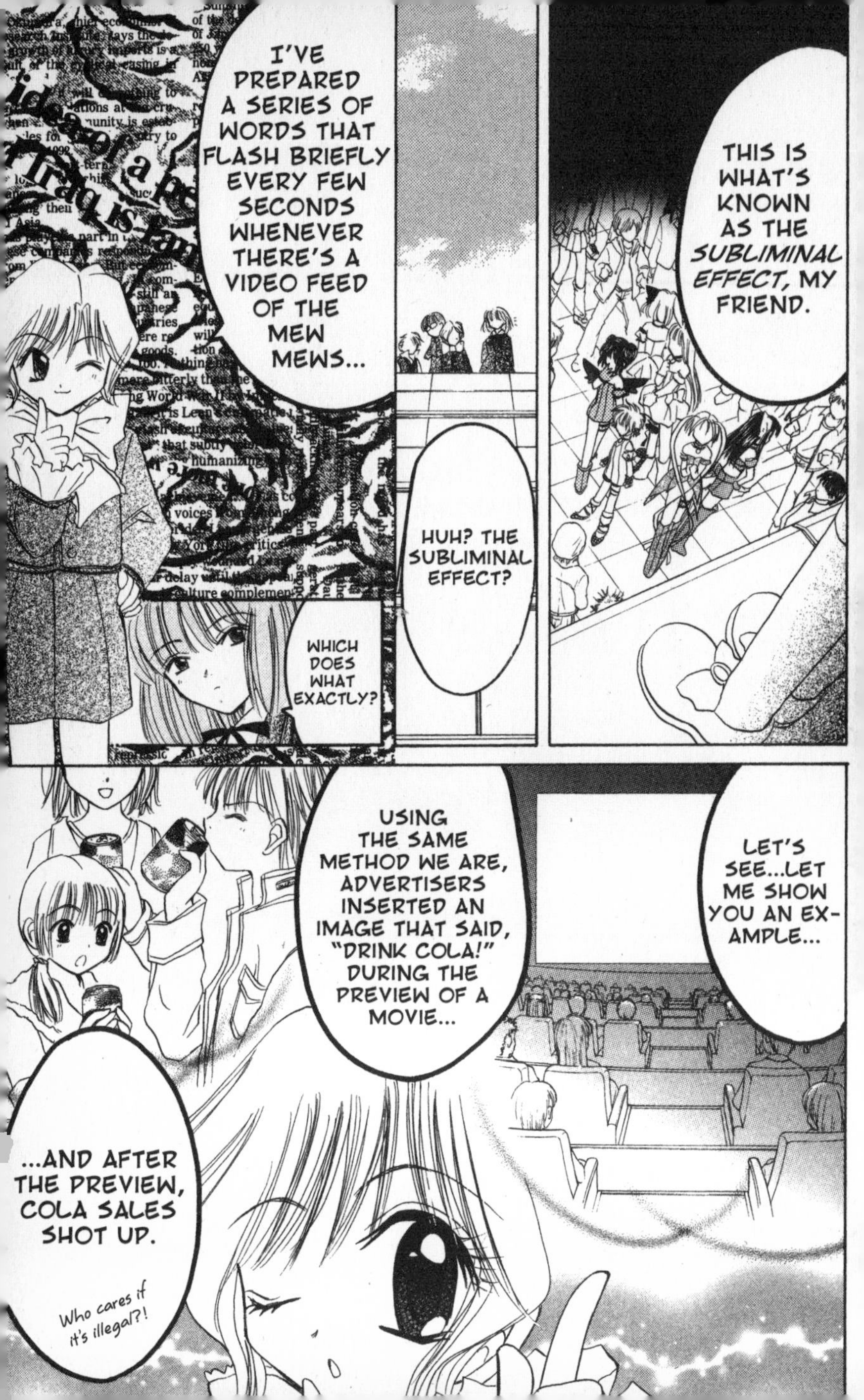
I'VE PREPARED A SERIES OF WORDS THAT FLASH BRIEFLY EVERY FEW SECONDS WHENEVER THERE'S A VIDEO FEED OF THE MEW MEWS...
THIS IS WHAT'S KNOWN AS THE *SUBLIMINAL EFFECT*, MY FRIEND.
HUH? THE SUBLIMINAL EFFECT?
WHICH DOES WHAT EXACTLY?
LET'S SEE...LET ME SHOW YOU AN EX-AMPLE...
USING THE SAME METHOD WE ARE, ADVERTISERS INSERTED AN IMAGE THAT SAID, "DRINK COLA!" DURING THE PREVIEW OF A MOVIE...
...AND AFTER THE PREVIEW, COLA SALES SHOT UP.
Who cares if it's illegal?!

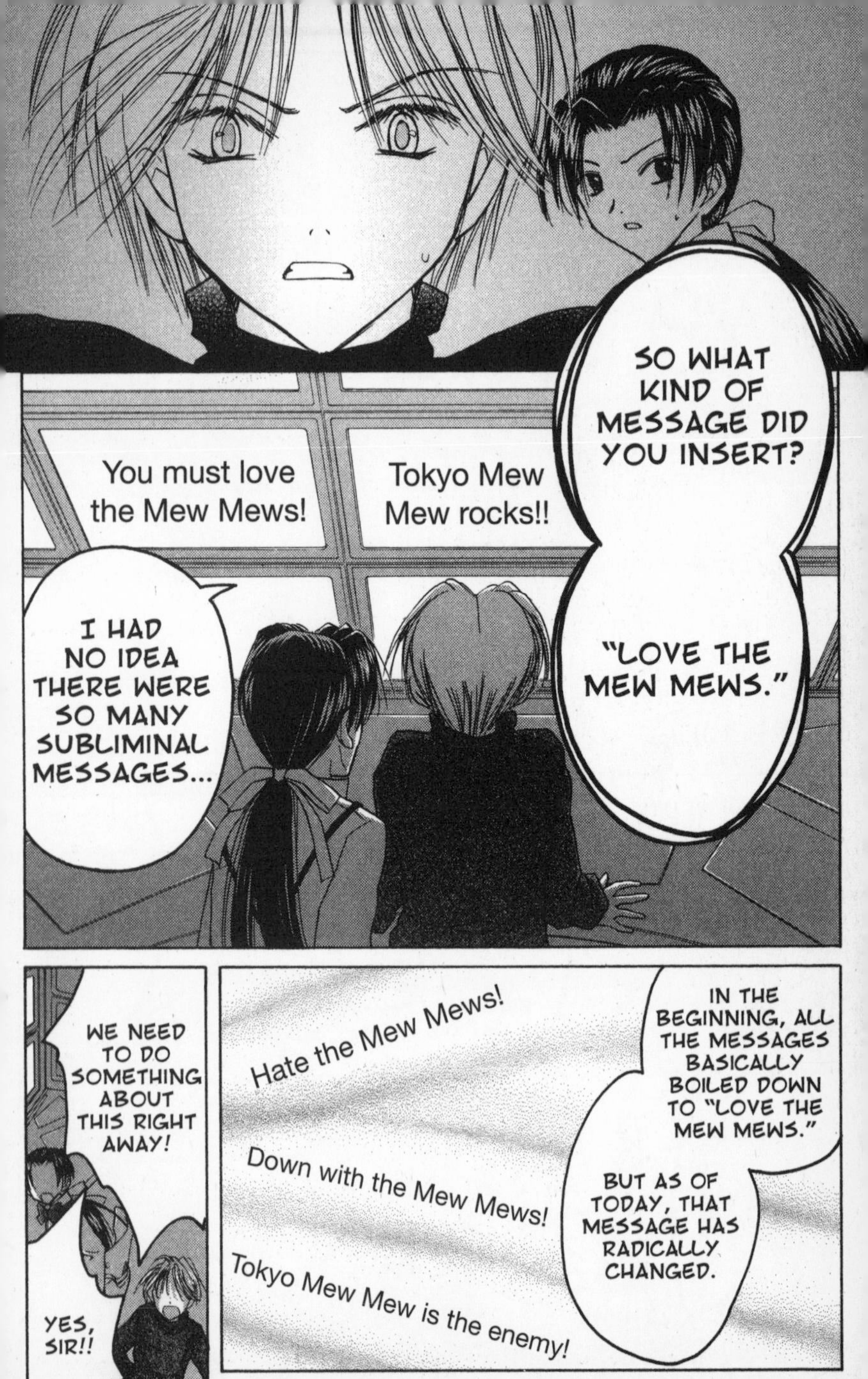
SO WHAT KIND OF MESSAGE DID YOU INSERT?
"LOVE THE MEW MEWS."
Tokyo Mew Mew rocks!!
You must love the Mew Mews!
I HAD NO IDEA THERE WERE SO MANY SUBLIMINAL MESSAGES...
IN THE BEGINNING, ALL THE MESSAGES BASICALLY BOILED DOWN TO "LOVE THE MEW MEWS."
BUT AS OF TODAY, THAT MESSAGE HAS RADICALLY CHANGED.
Hate the Mew Mews!
Down with the Mew Mews!
Tokyo Mew Mew is the enemy!
WE NEED TO DO SOMETHING ABOUT THIS RIGHT AWAY!
YES, SIR!!

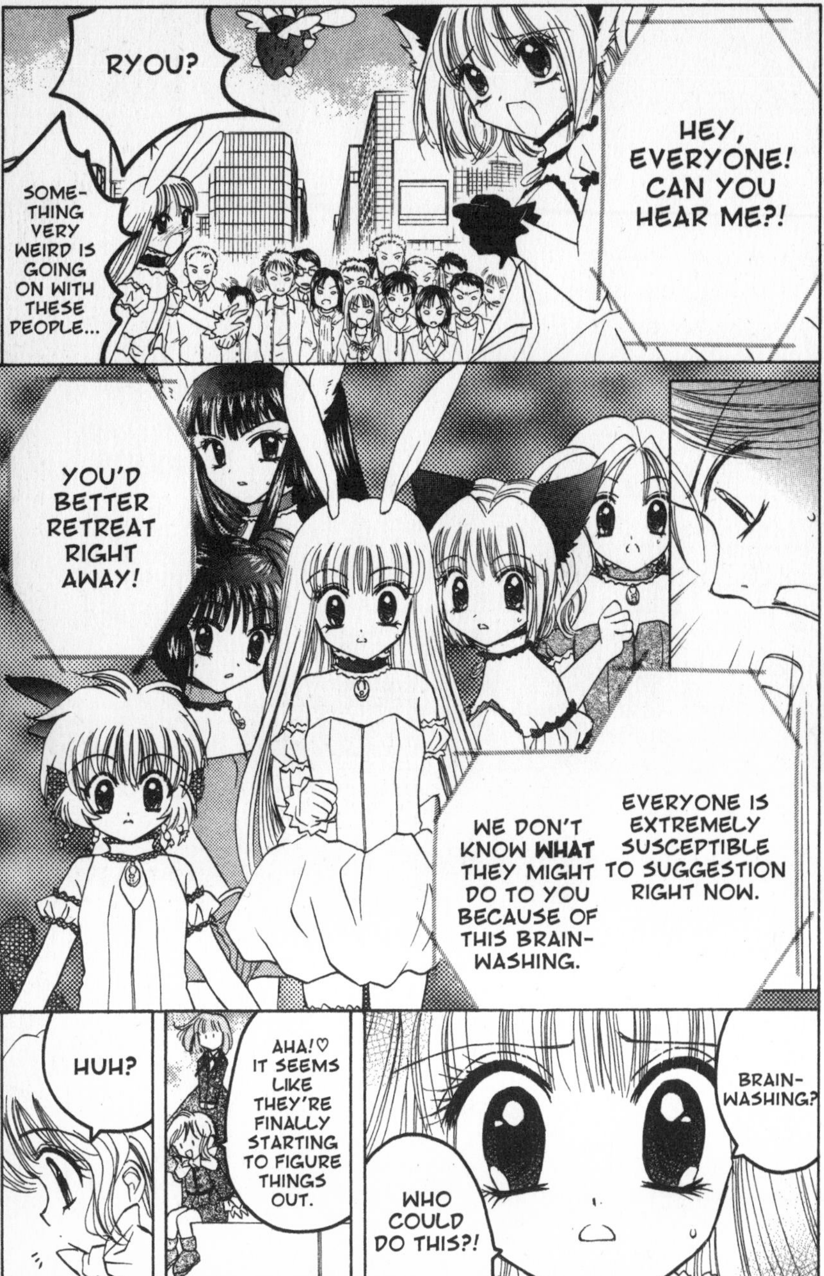
HEY, EVERYONE! CAN YOU HEAR ME?!
RYOU?
SOMETHING VERY WEIRD IS GOING ON WITH THESE PEOPLE...
EVERYONE IS EXTREMELY SUSCEPTIBLE TO SUGGESTION RIGHT NOW.
WE DON'T KNOW **WHAT** THEY MIGHT DO TO YOU BECAUSE OF THIS BRAIN-WASHING.
YOU'D BETTER RETREAT RIGHT AWAY!
BRAIN-WASHING?
WHO COULD DO THIS?!
AHA!♡ IT SEEMS LIKE THEY'RE FINALLY STARTING TO FIGURE THINGS OUT.
HUH?

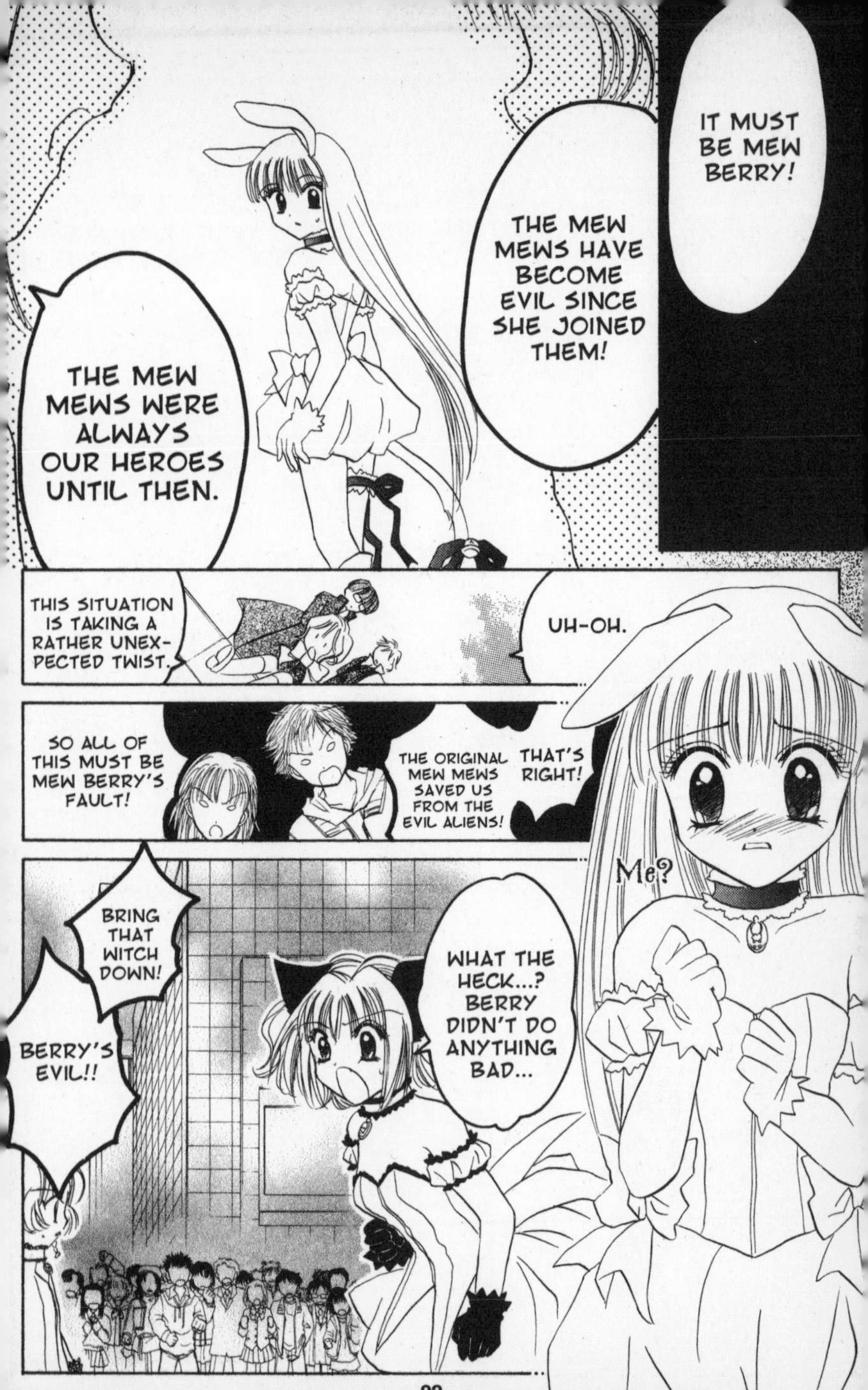
IT MUST BE MEW BERRY!
THE MEW MEWS HAVE BECOME EVIL SINCE SHE JOINED THEM!
THE MEW MEWS WERE ALWAYS OUR HEROES UNTIL THEN.
UH-OH.
THIS SITUATION IS TAKING A RATHER UNEXPECTED TWIST.
THAT'S RIGHT!
THE ORIGINAL MEW MEWS SAVED US FROM THE EVIL ALIENS!
SO ALL OF THIS MUST BE MEW BERRY'S FAULT!
Me?
WHAT THE HECK...? BERRY DIDN'T DO ANYTHING BAD...
BRING THAT WITCH DOWN!
BERRY'S EVIL!!

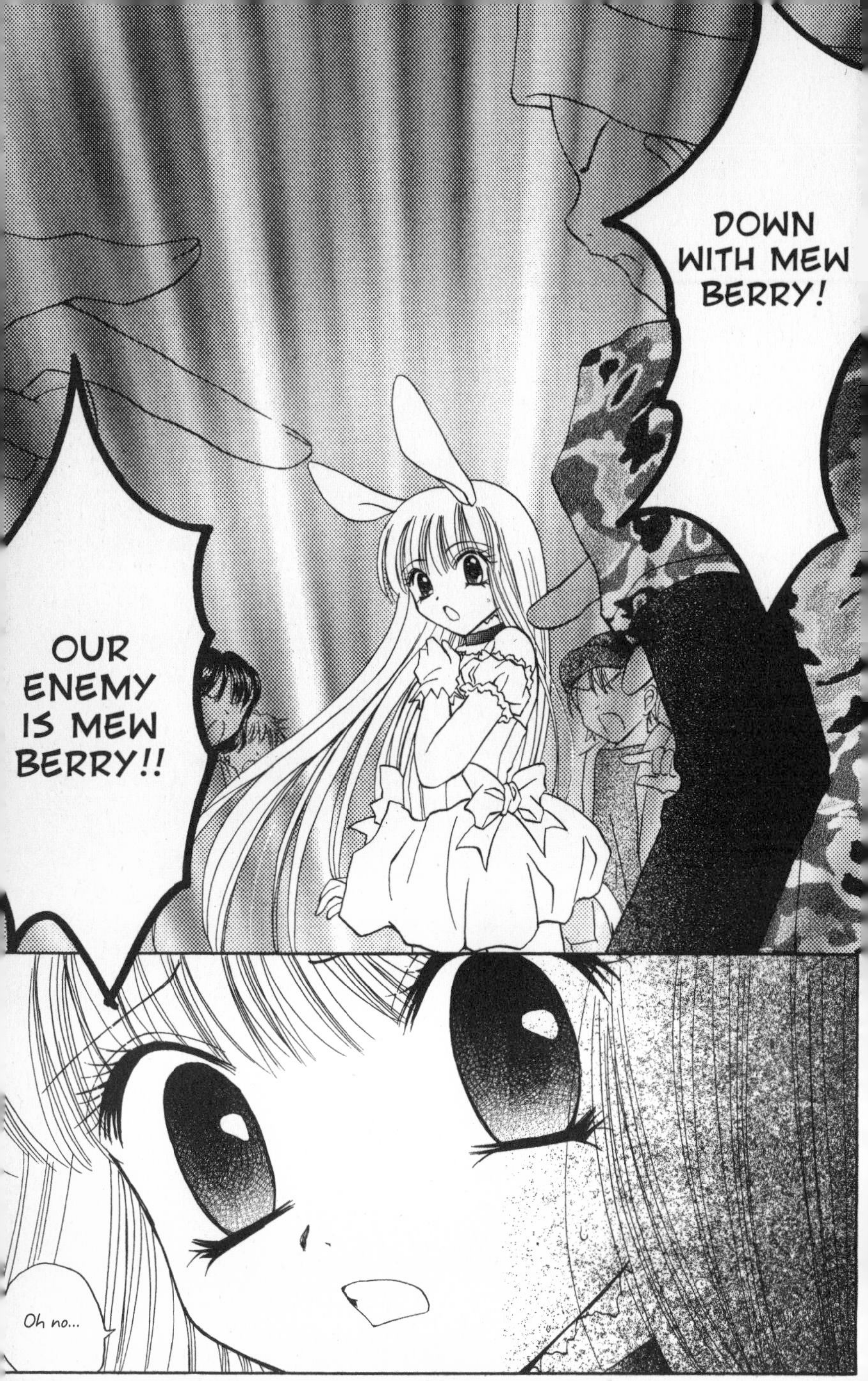
DOWN WITH MEW BERRY!
OUR ENEMY IS MEW BERRY!!
Oh no...

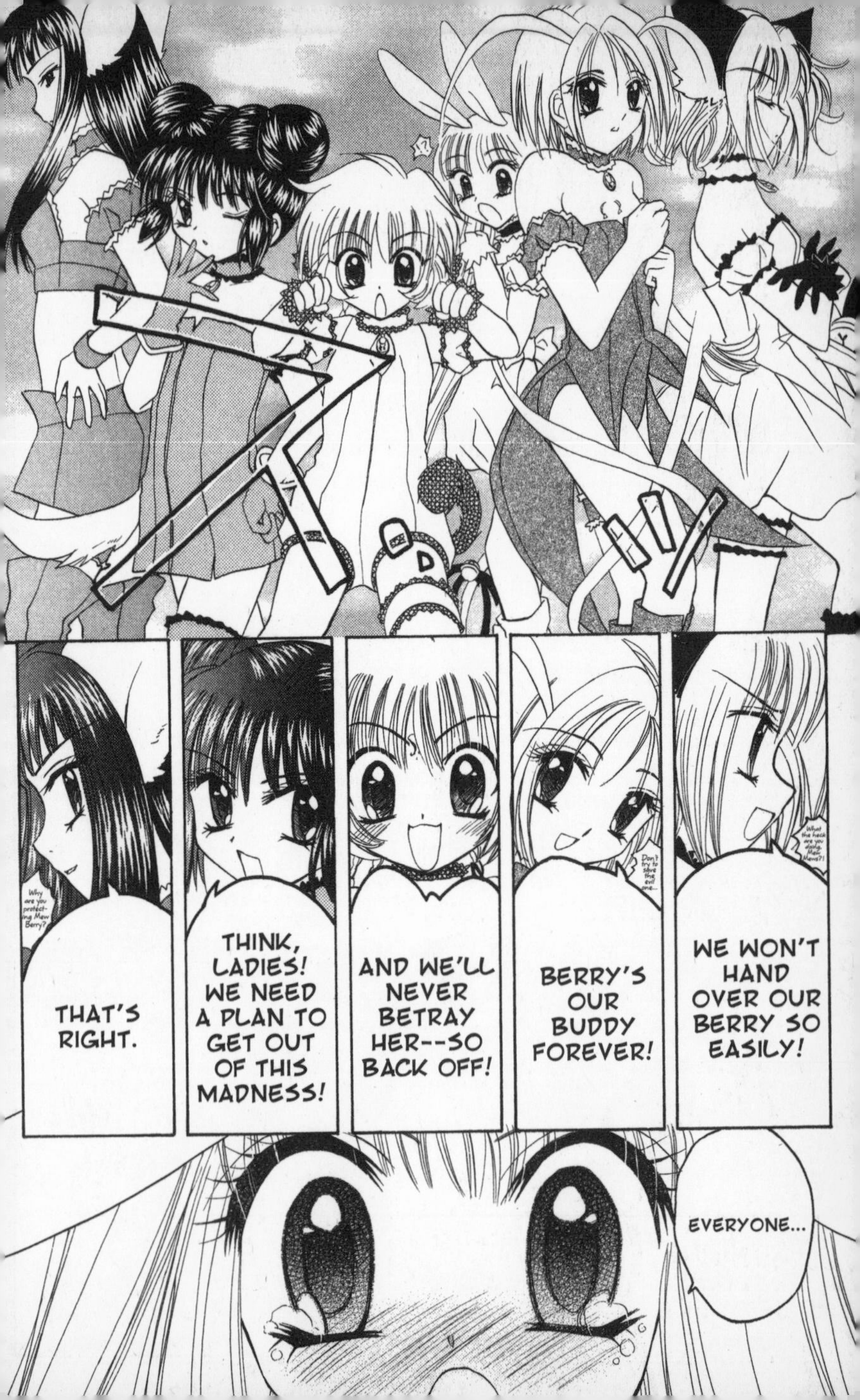
What the heck are you doing, Mew Mews?!
WE WON'T HAND OVER OUR BERRY SO EASILY!
Don't try to save the evil one...
BERRY'S OUR BUDDY FOREVER!
AND WE'LL NEVER BETRAY HER--SO BACK OFF!
THINK, LADIES! WE NEED A PLAN TO GET OUT OF THIS MADNESS!
Why are you protecting Mew Berry?
THAT'S RIGHT.
EVERYONE...

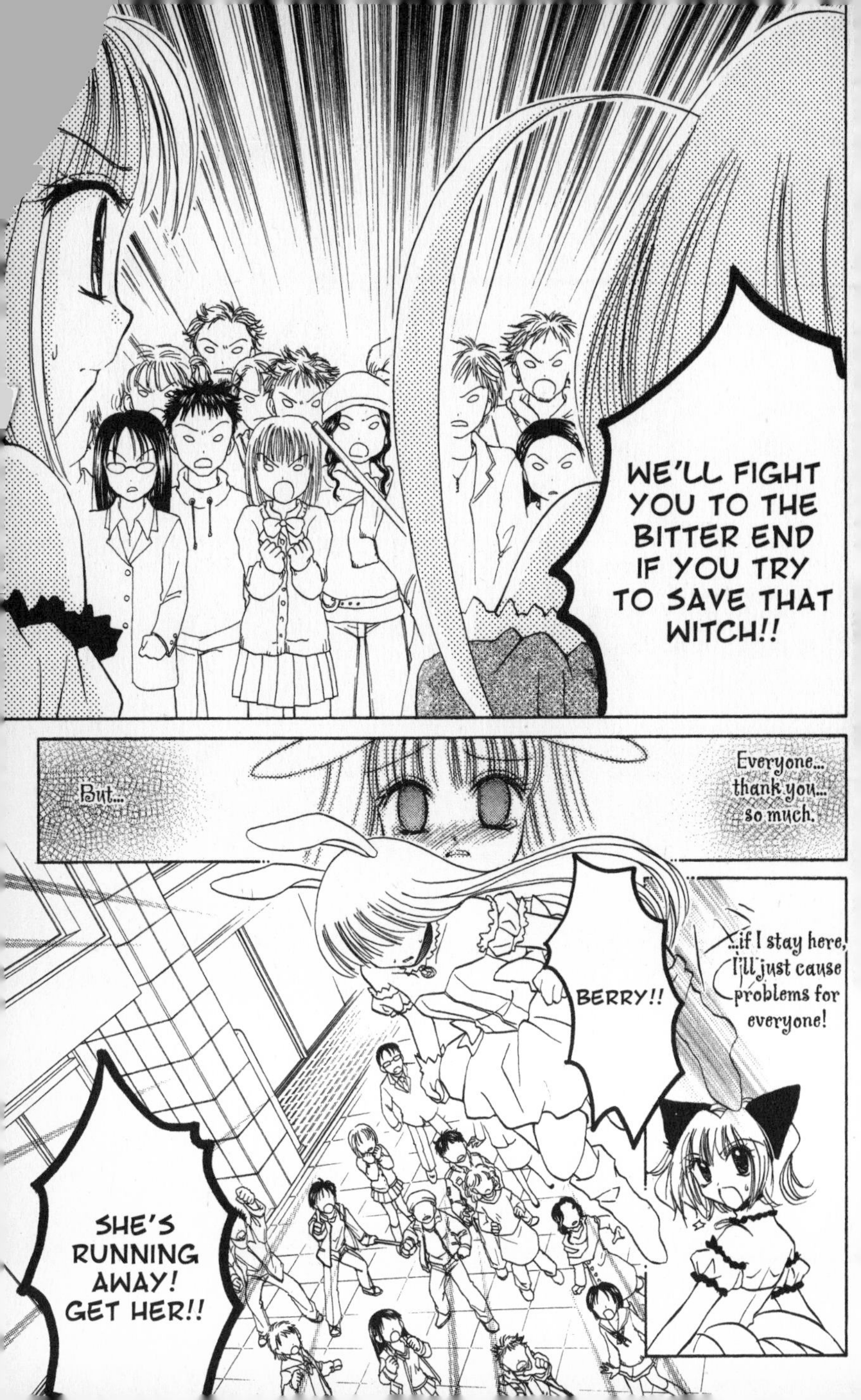
WE'LL FIGHT YOU TO THE BITTER END IF YOU TRY TO SAVE THAT WITCH!!
Everyone... thank you... so much.
But...
...if I stay here, I'll just cause problems for everyone!
BERRY!!
SHE'S RUNNING AWAY! GET HER!!

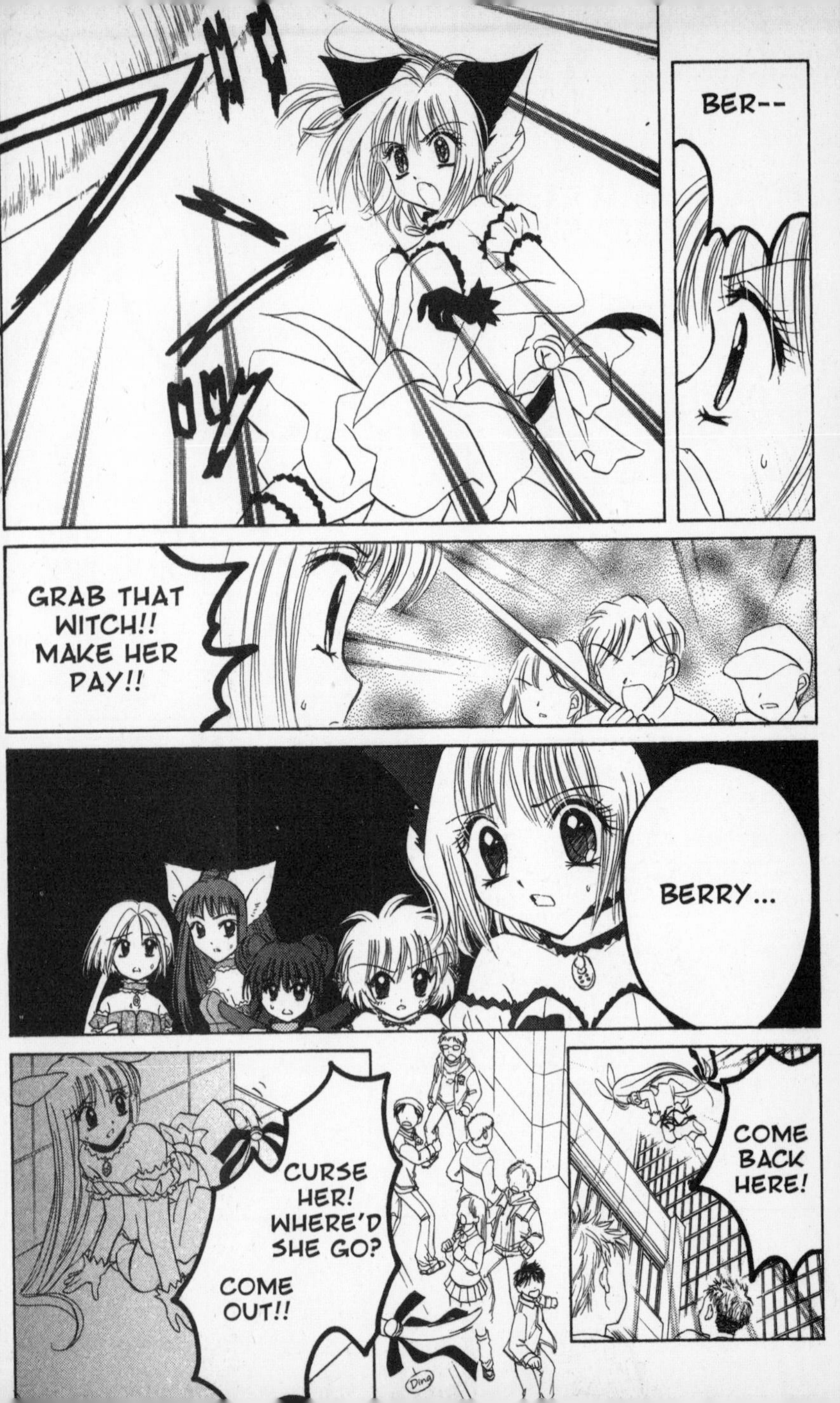
BER--
GRAB THAT WITCH!! MAKE HER PAY!!
BERRY...
COME BACK HERE!
CURSE HER! WHERE'D SHE GO?
COME OUT!!
Ding

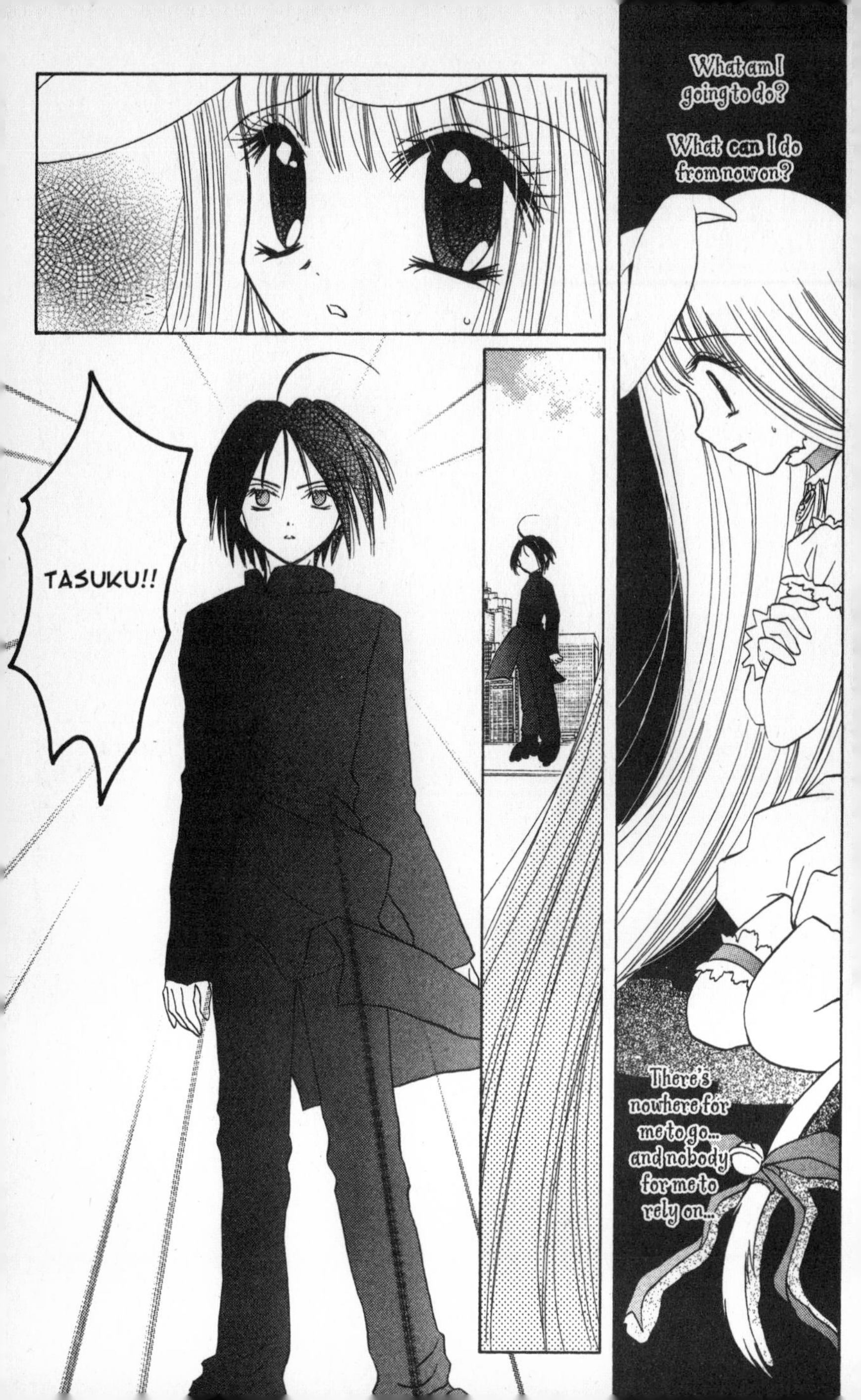
What am I going to do?
What can I do from now on?
There's nowhere for me to go... and nobody for me to rely on...
TASUKU!!

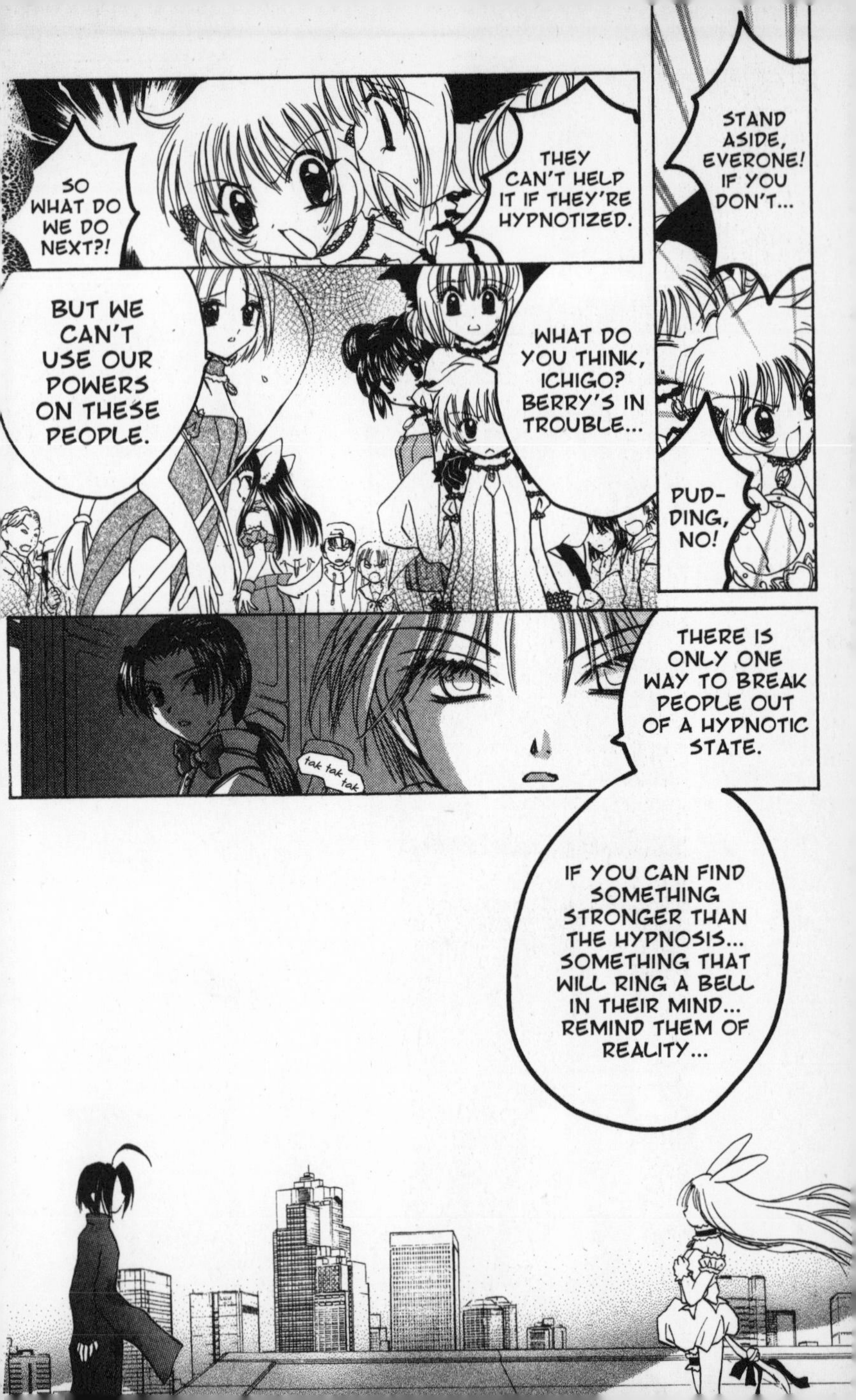
STAND ASIDE, EVERONE! IF YOU DON'T...
PUD-DING, NO!
THEY CAN'T HELP IT IF THEY'RE HYPNOTIZED.
SO WHAT DO WE DO NEXT?!
WHAT DO YOU THINK, ICHIGO? BERRY'S IN TROUBLE...
BUT WE CAN'T USE OUR POWERS ON THESE PEOPLE.
THERE IS ONLY ONE WAY TO BREAK PEOPLE OUT OF A HYPNOTIC STATE.
tak tak tak
IF YOU CAN FIND SOMETHING STRONGER THAN THE HYPNOSIS... SOMETHING THAT WILL RING A BELL IN THEIR MIND... REMIND THEM OF REALITY...

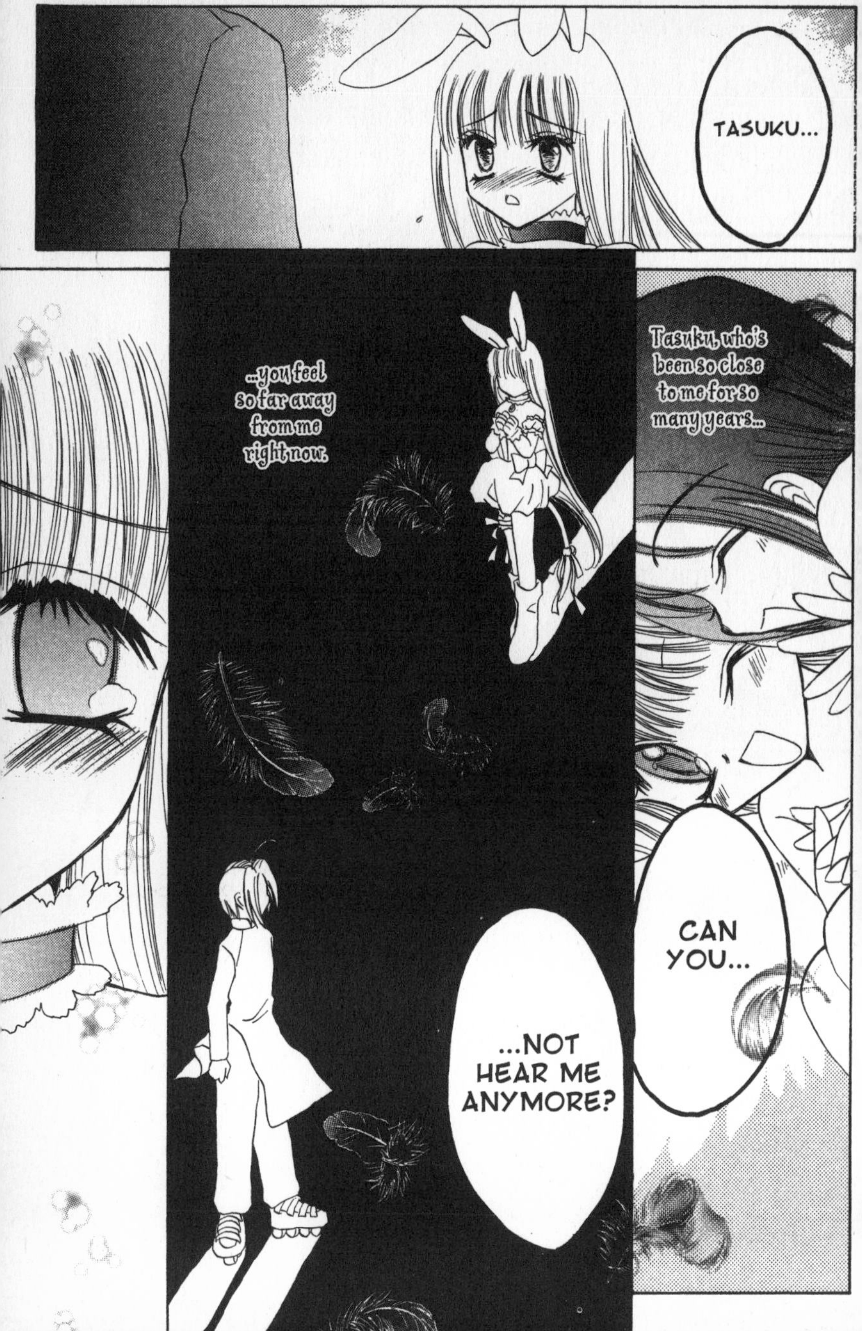
TASUKU...
Tasuku, who's been so close to me for so many years...
...you feel so far away from me right now.
CAN YOU...
...NOT HEAR ME ANYMORE?

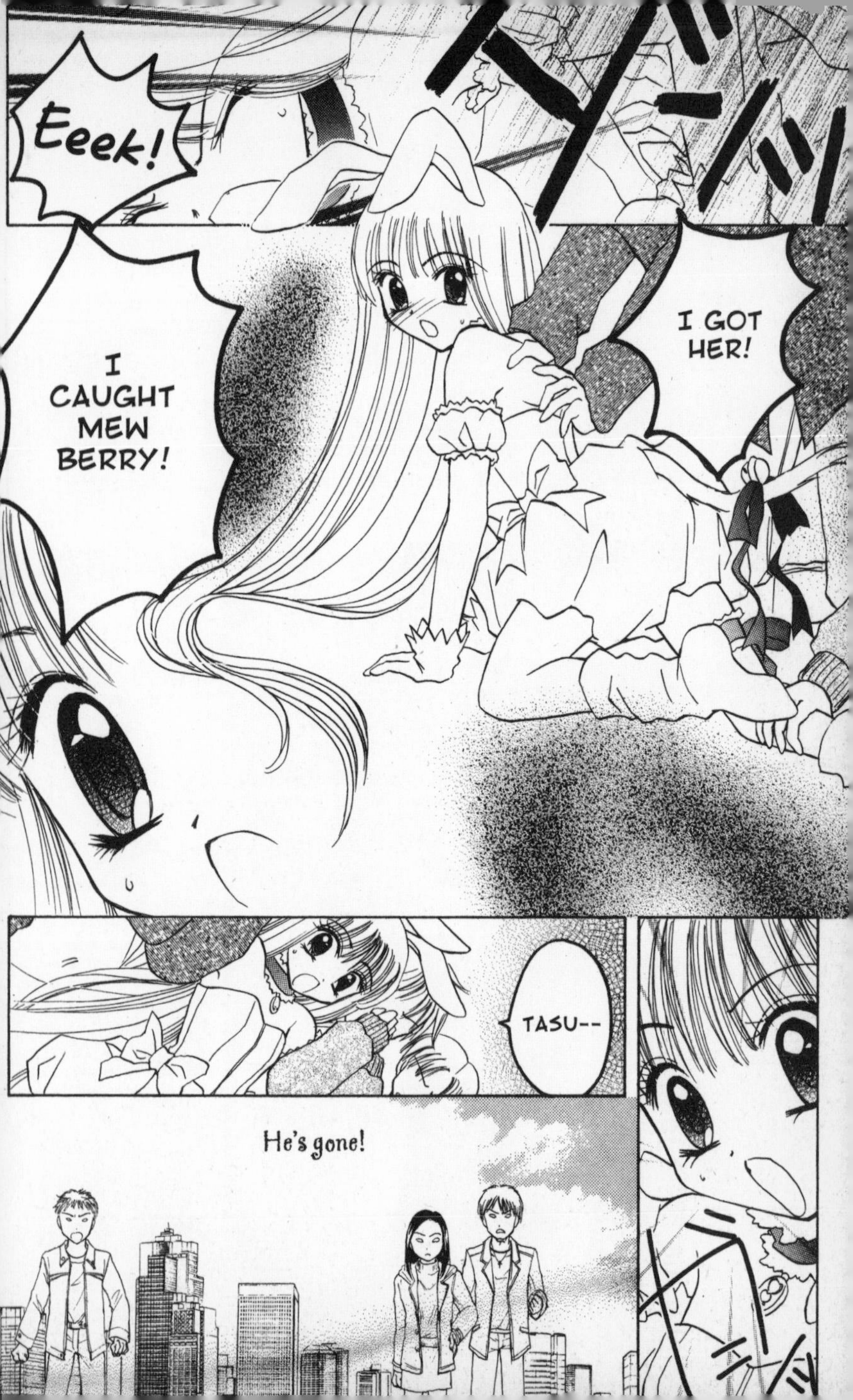
Eeek!
I GOT HER!
I CAUGHT MEW BERRY!
TASU--
He's gone!

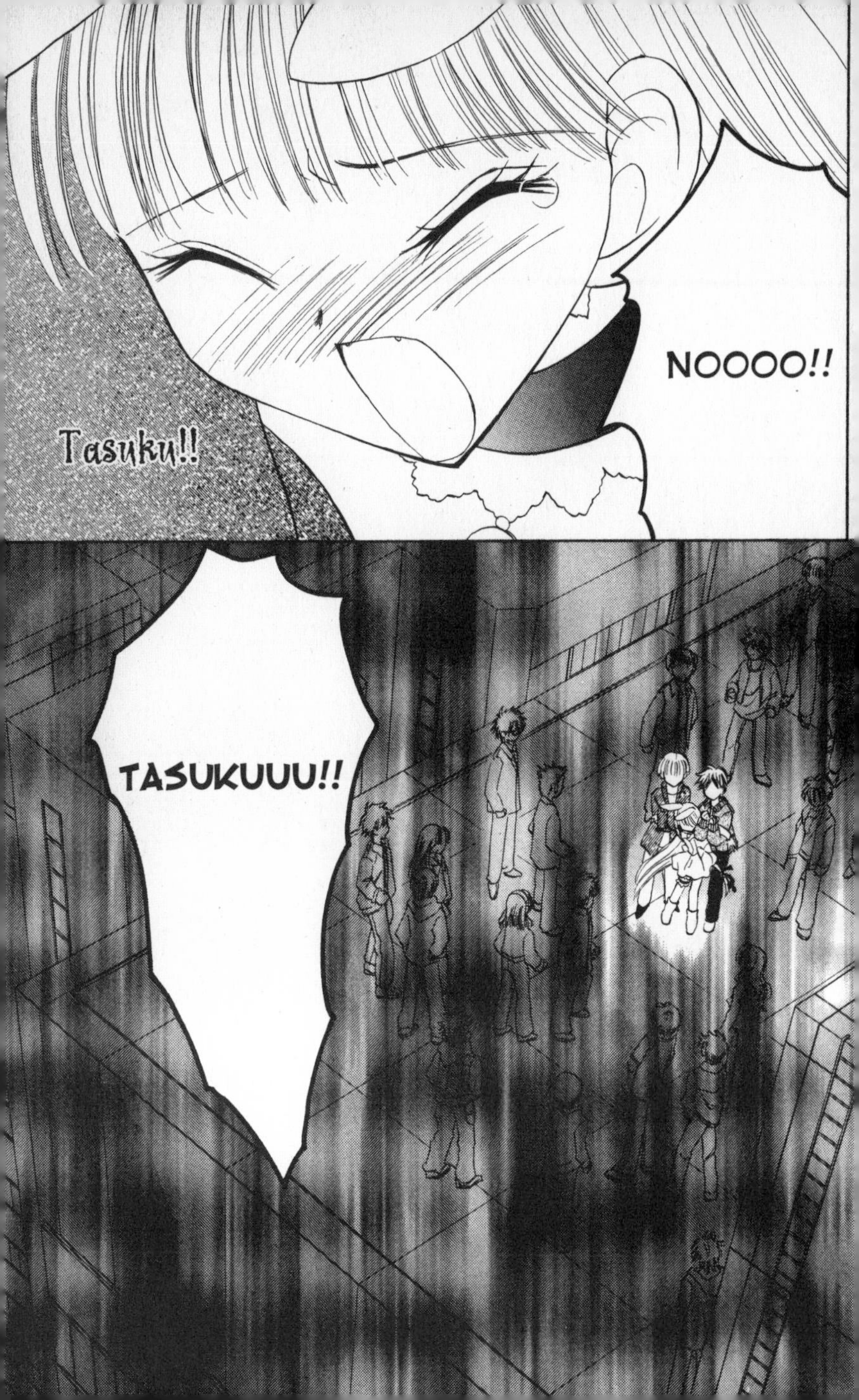
NOOOO!!
Tasuku!!
TASUKUUU!!

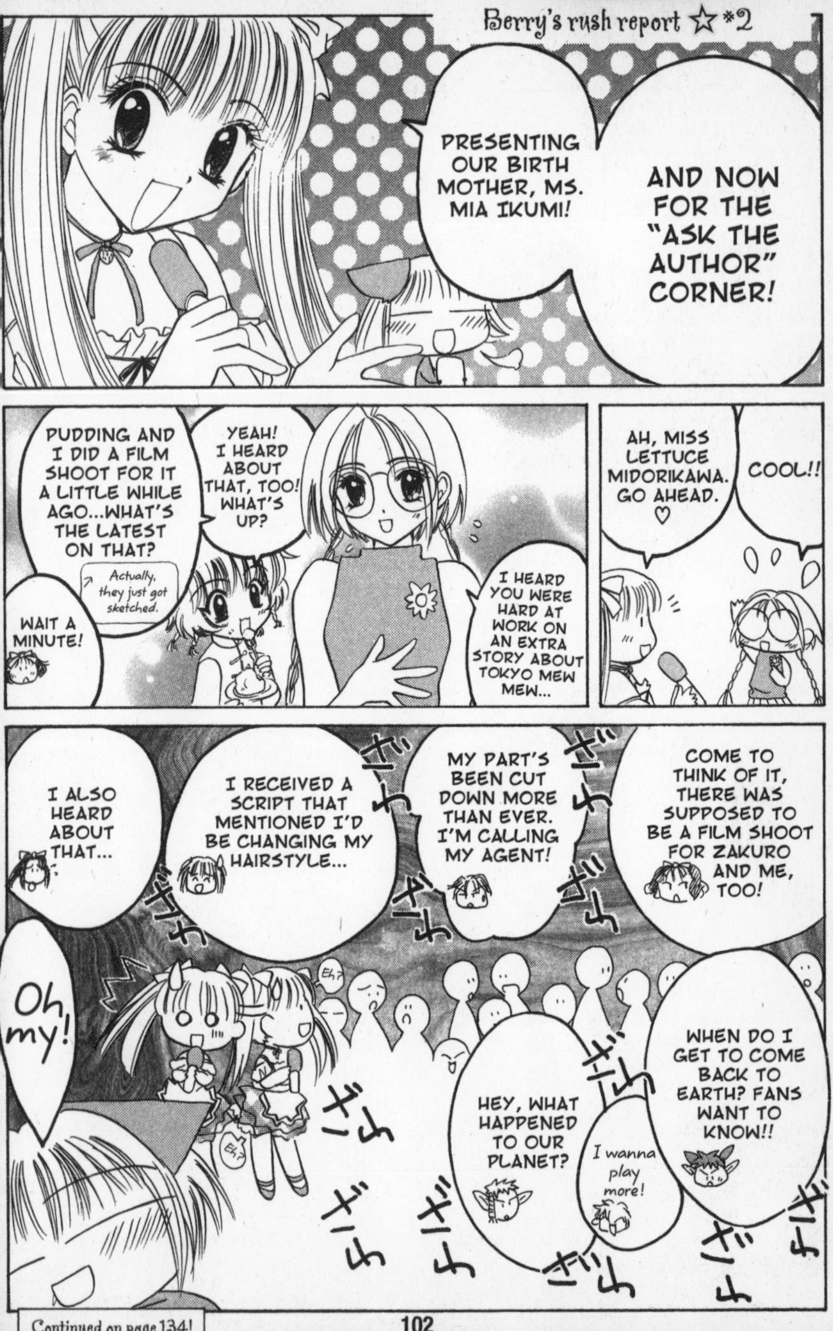
Berry's rush report ☆*2
AND NOW FOR THE "ASK THE AUTHOR" CORNER!
PRESENTING OUR BIRTH MOTHER, MS. MIA IKUMI!
COOL!!
AH, MISS LETTUCE MIDORIKAWA. GO AHEAD. ♡
I HEARD YOU WERE HARD AT WORK ON AN EXTRA STORY ABOUT TOKYO MEW MEW...
YEAH! I HEARD ABOUT THAT, TOO! WHAT'S UP?
PUDDING AND I DID A FILM SHOOT FOR IT A LITTLE WHILE AGO...WHAT'S THE LATEST ON THAT?
Actually, they just got sketched.
WAIT A MINUTE!
COME TO THINK OF IT, THERE WAS SUPPOSED TO BE A FILM SHOOT FOR ZAKURO AND ME, TOO!
MY PART'S BEEN CUT DOWN MORE THAN EVER. I'M CALLING MY AGENT!
I RECEIVED A SCRIPT THAT MENTIONED I'D BE CHANGING MY HAIRSTYLE...
I ALSO HEARD ABOUT THAT...
WHEN DO I GET TO COME BACK TO EARTH? FANS WANT TO KNOW!!
I wanna play more!
HEY, WHAT HAPPENED TO OUR PLANET?
Eh?
Eh?
Oh my!

Continued on page 134!

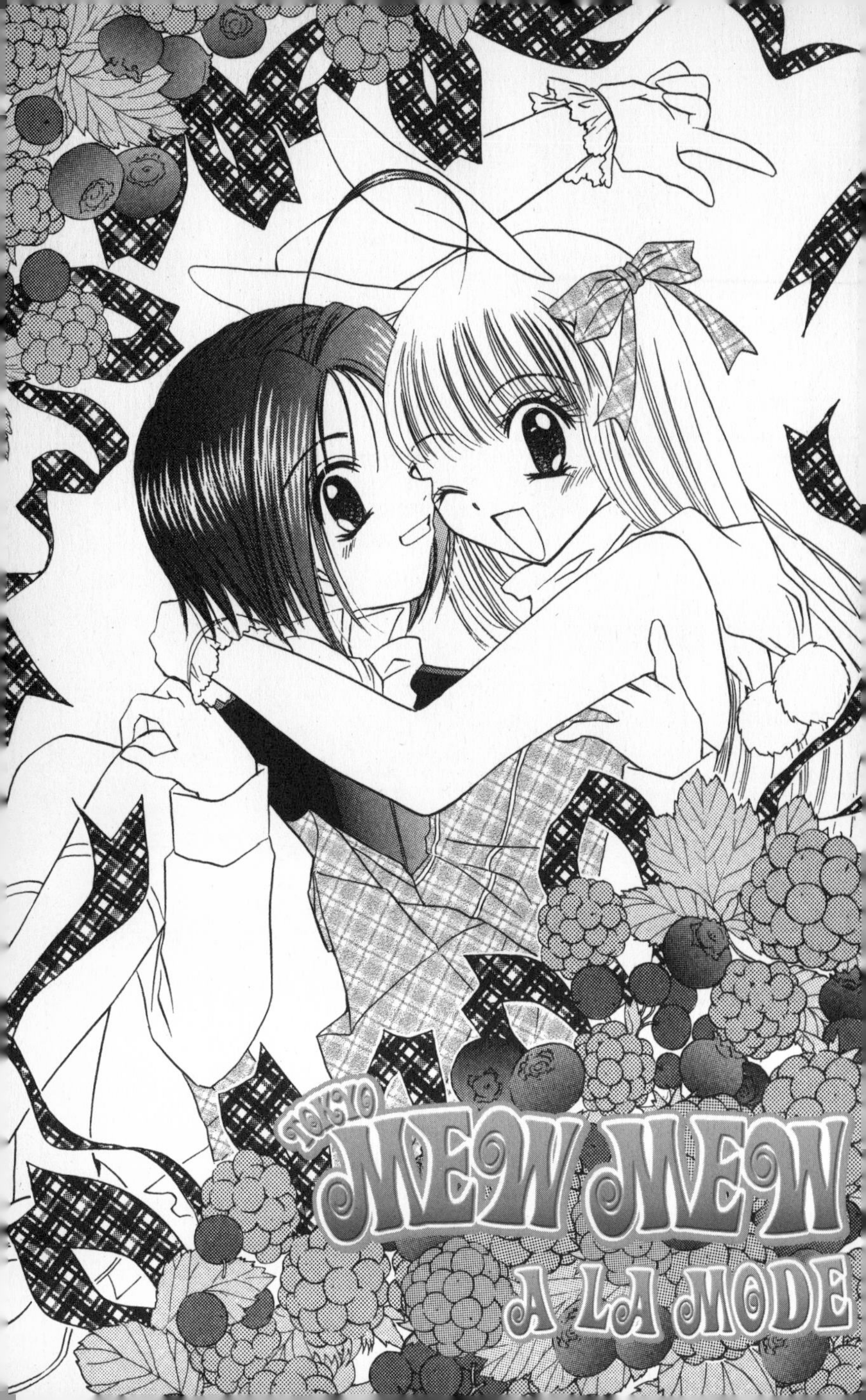
TOKYO
MEW MEW
A LA MODE

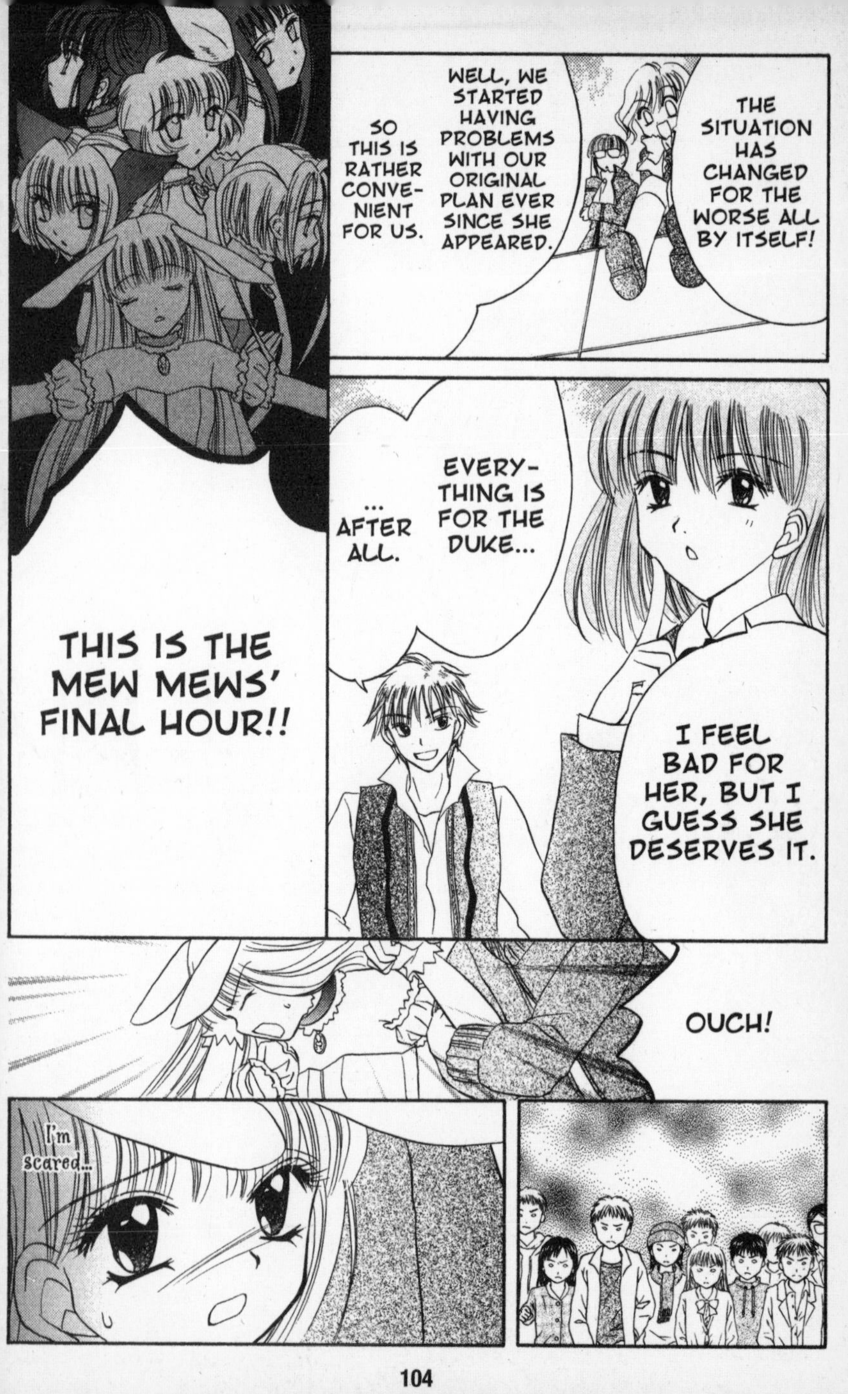
THE SITUATION HAS CHANGED FOR THE WORSE ALL BY ITSELF!
WELL, WE STARTED HAVING PROBLEMS WITH OUR ORIGINAL PLAN EVER SINCE SHE APPEARED.
SO THIS IS RATHER CONVE-NIENT FOR US.
THIS IS THE MEW MEWS' FINAL HOUR!!
I FEEL BAD FOR HER, BUT I GUESS SHE DESERVES IT.
EVERY-THING IS FOR THE DUKE...
... AFTER ALL.
OUCH!
I'm scared...

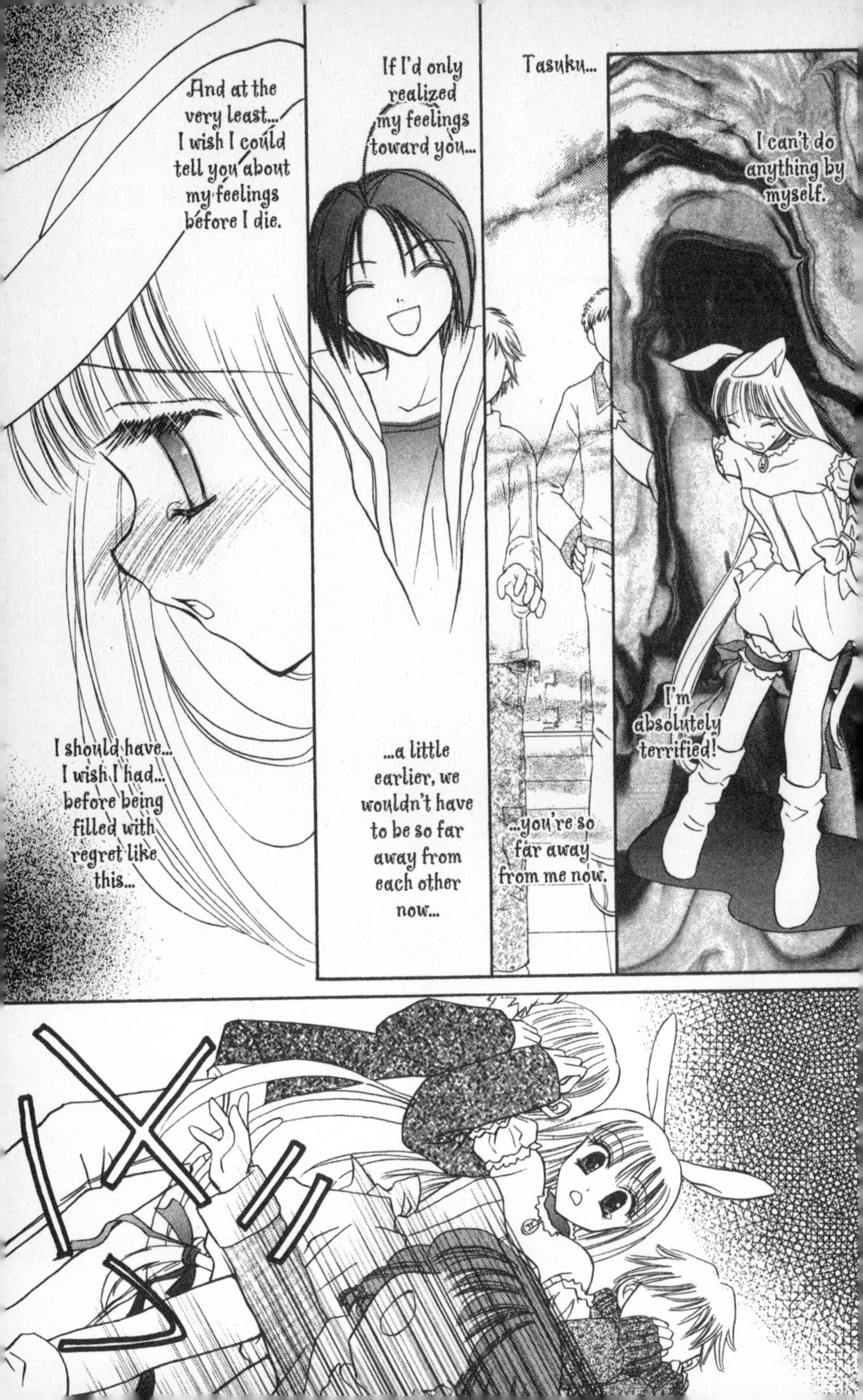
I can't do anything by myself.
I'm absolutely terrified!
Tasuku...
...you're so far away from me now.
If I'd only realized my feelings toward you...
...a little earlier, we wouldn't have to be so far away from each other now...
And at the very least... I wish I could tell you about my feelings before I die.
I should have... I wish I had... before being filled with regret like this...

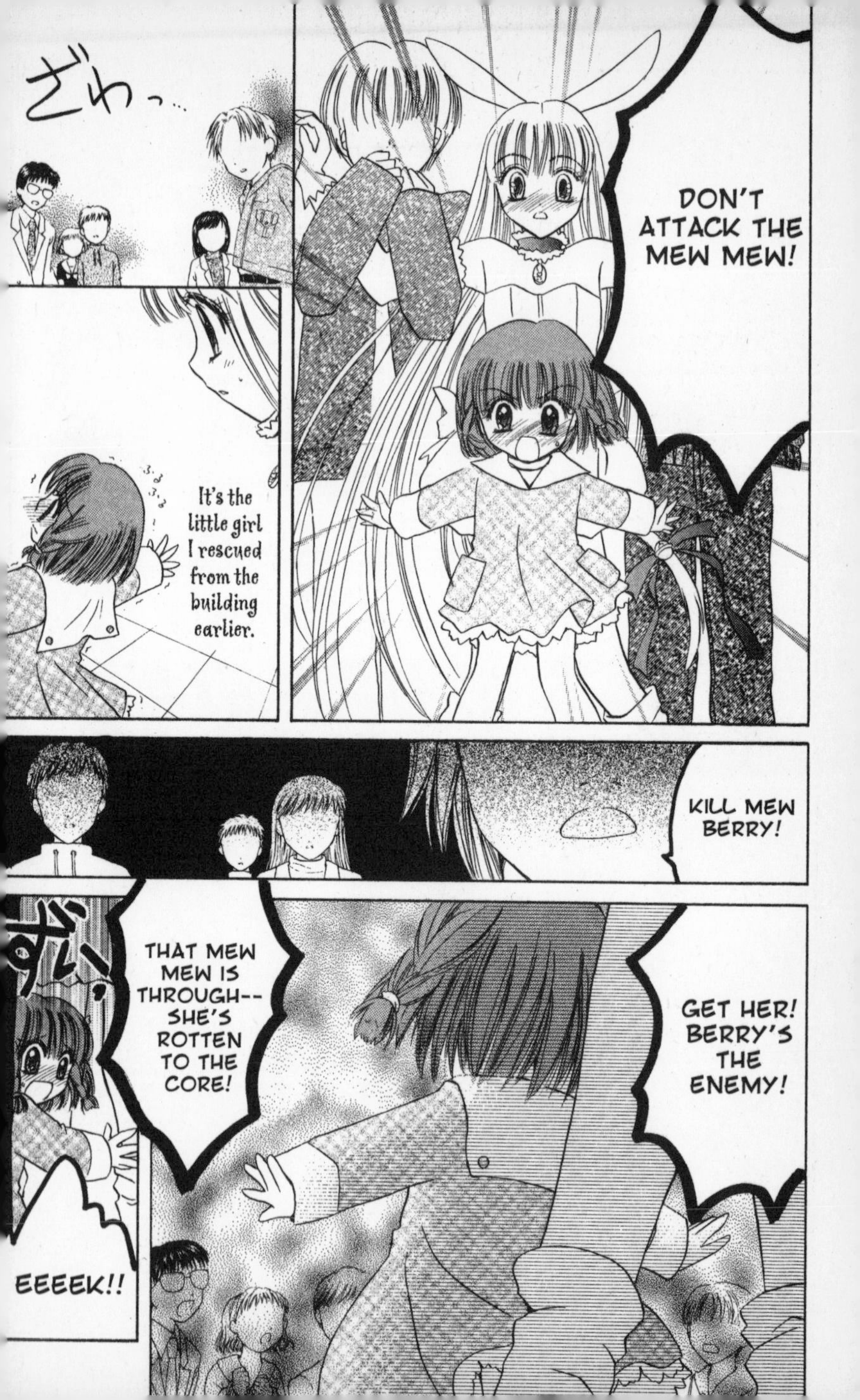
DON'T ATTACK THE MEW MEW!
ざわっ…
It's the little girl I rescued from the building earlier.
KILL MEW BERRY!
GET HER! BERRY'S THE ENEMY!
THAT MEW MEW IS THROUGH--SHE'S ROTTEN TO THE CORE!
EEEEK!!

SPECIALTHANKS!!

A.OKAWA

T.MATSUMOTO
M.OMORI

M.NAKAZAWA
K.TODA
A.SUZUKI

M.FUNAKAWA

M.SEKIYA
K.NAKAMA

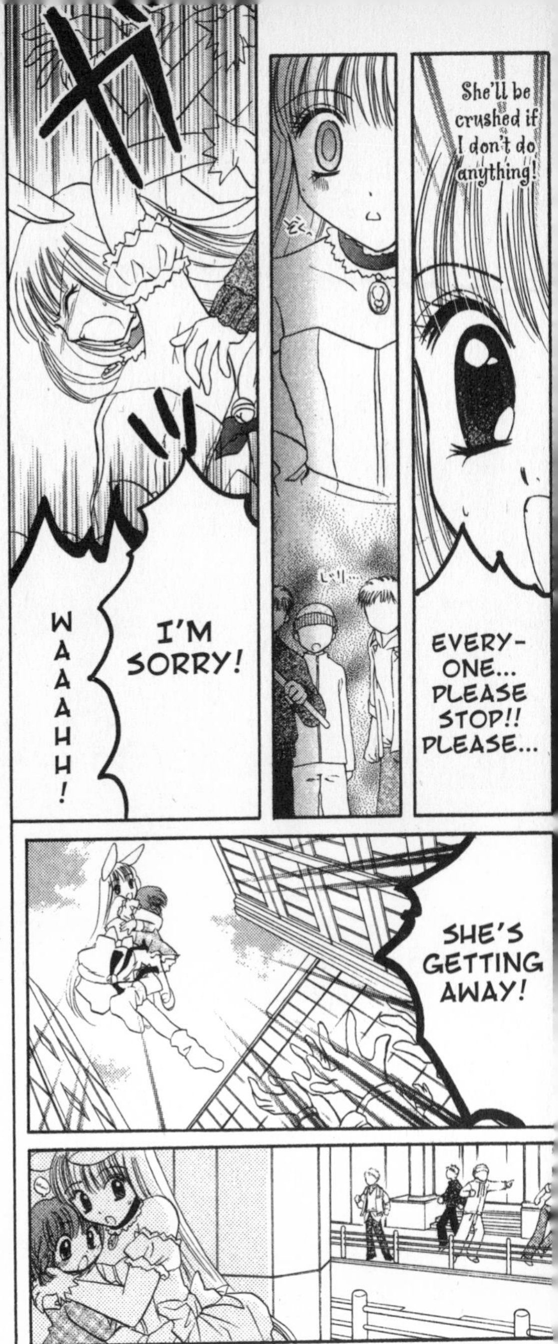
She'll be crushed if I don't do anything!
EVERY-ONE... PLEASE STOP!! PLEASE...
I'M SORRY!
WAAAAHH!
SHE'S GETTING AWAY!

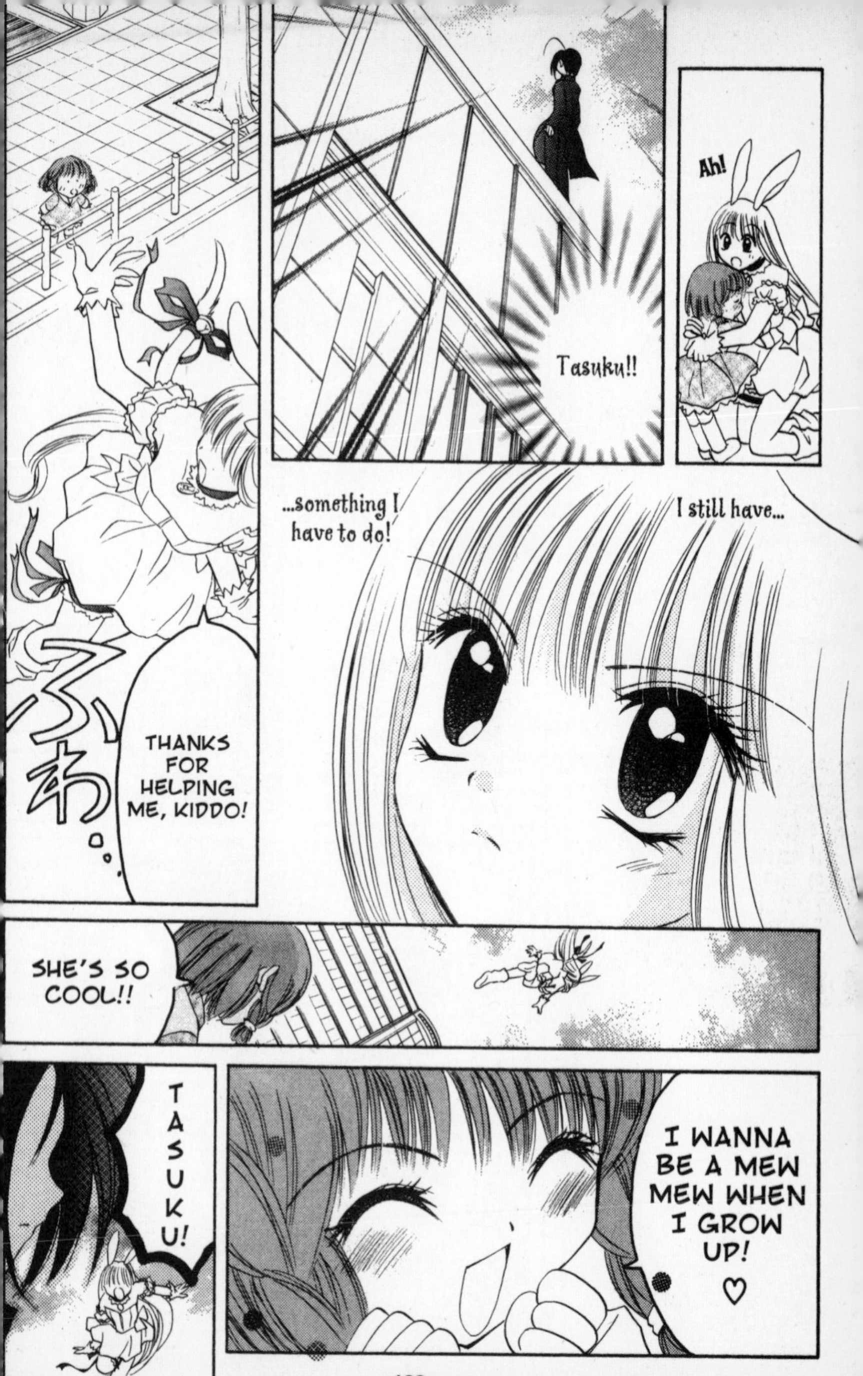
Ah!
Tasuku!!
I still have...
...something I have to do!
THANKS FOR HELPING ME, KIDDO!
ふわ。。
SHE'S SO COOL!!
I WANNA BE A MEW MEW WHEN I GROW UP! ♡
TASUKU!

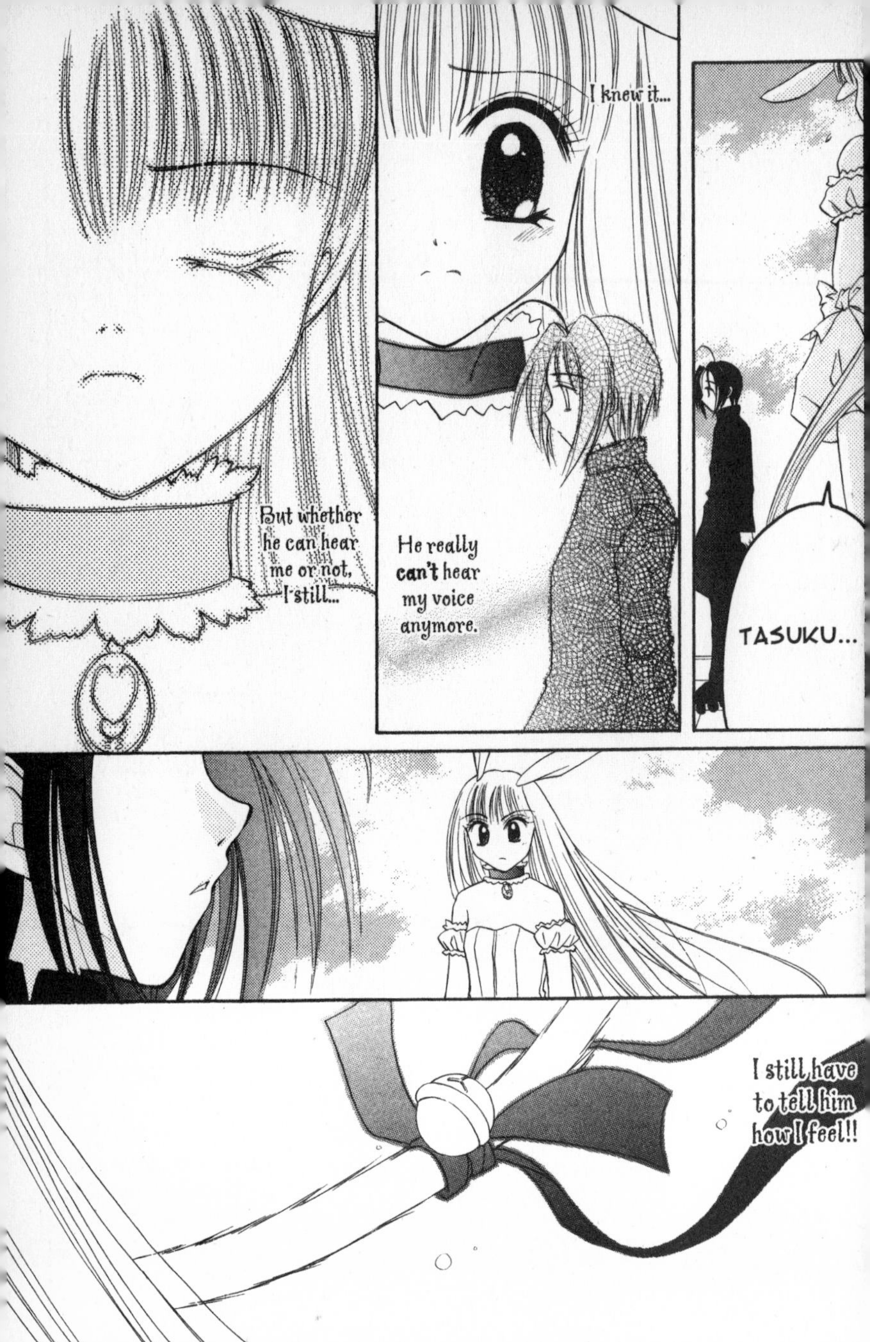
TASUKU...
I knew it...
He really can't hear my voice anymore.
But whether he can hear me or not, I still...
I still have to tell him how I feel!!

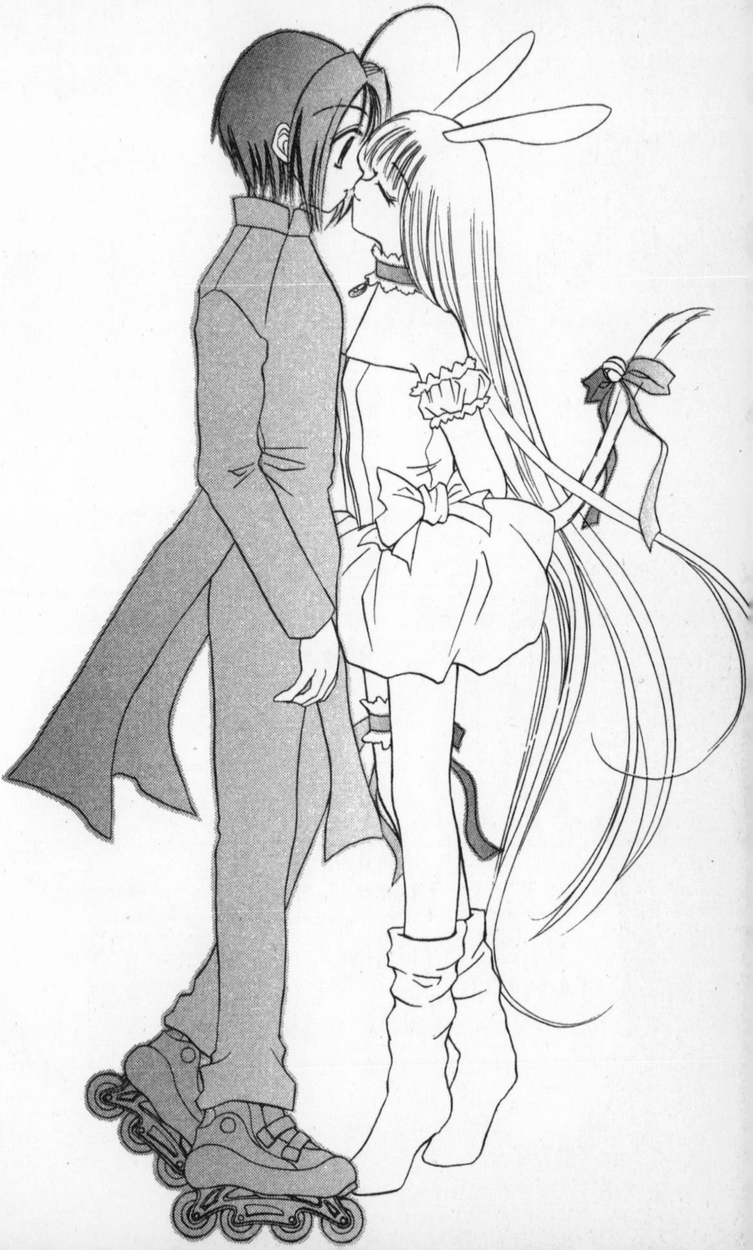

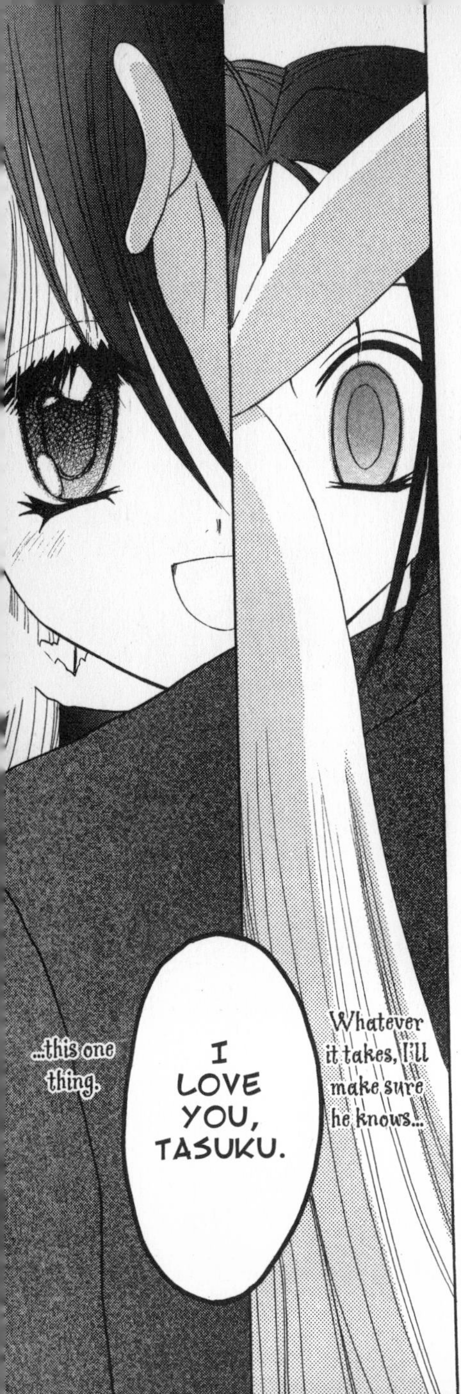
Whatever it takes, I'll make sure he knows...
I LOVE YOU, TASUKU.
...this one thing.

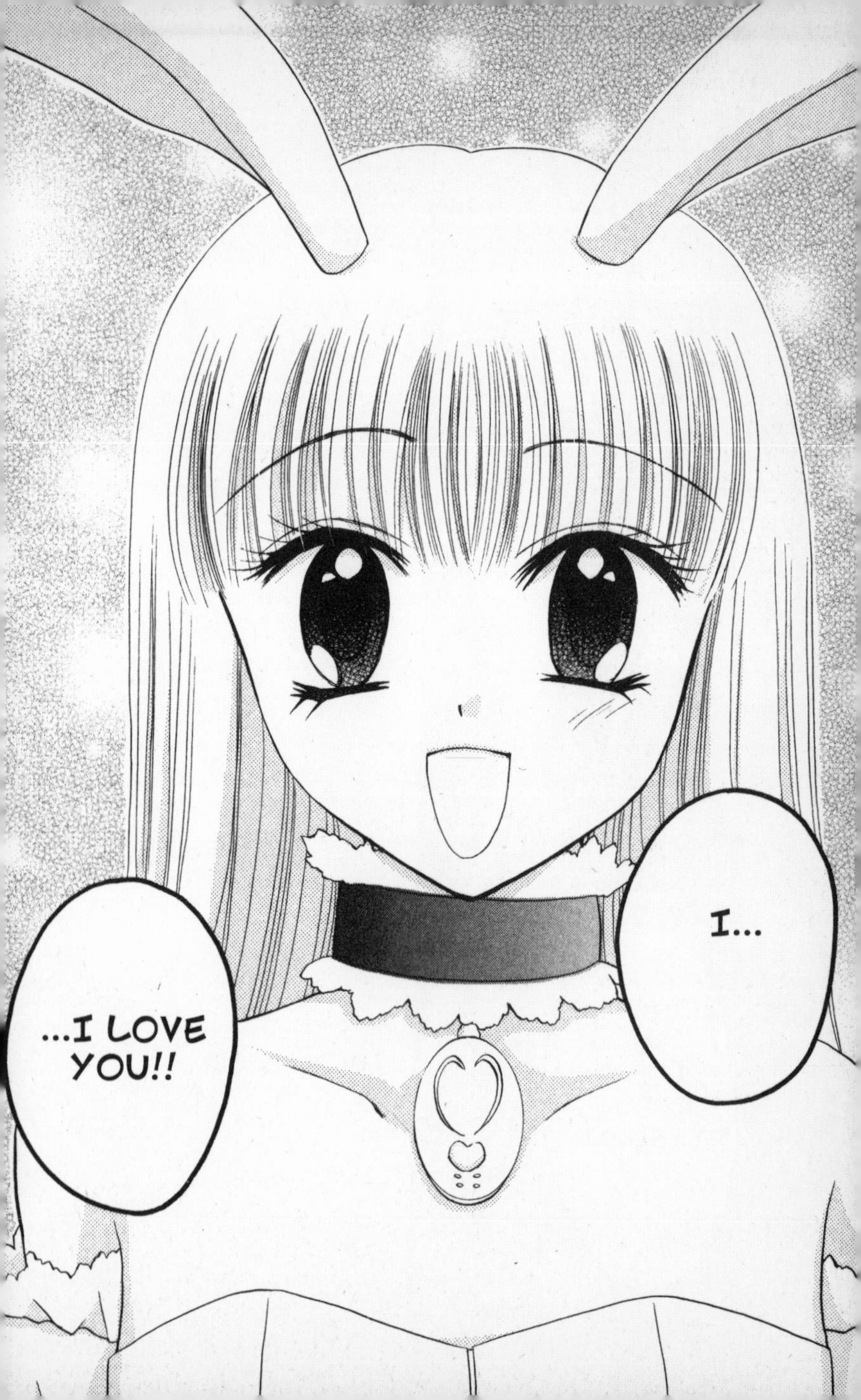
I...
...I LOVE YOU!!

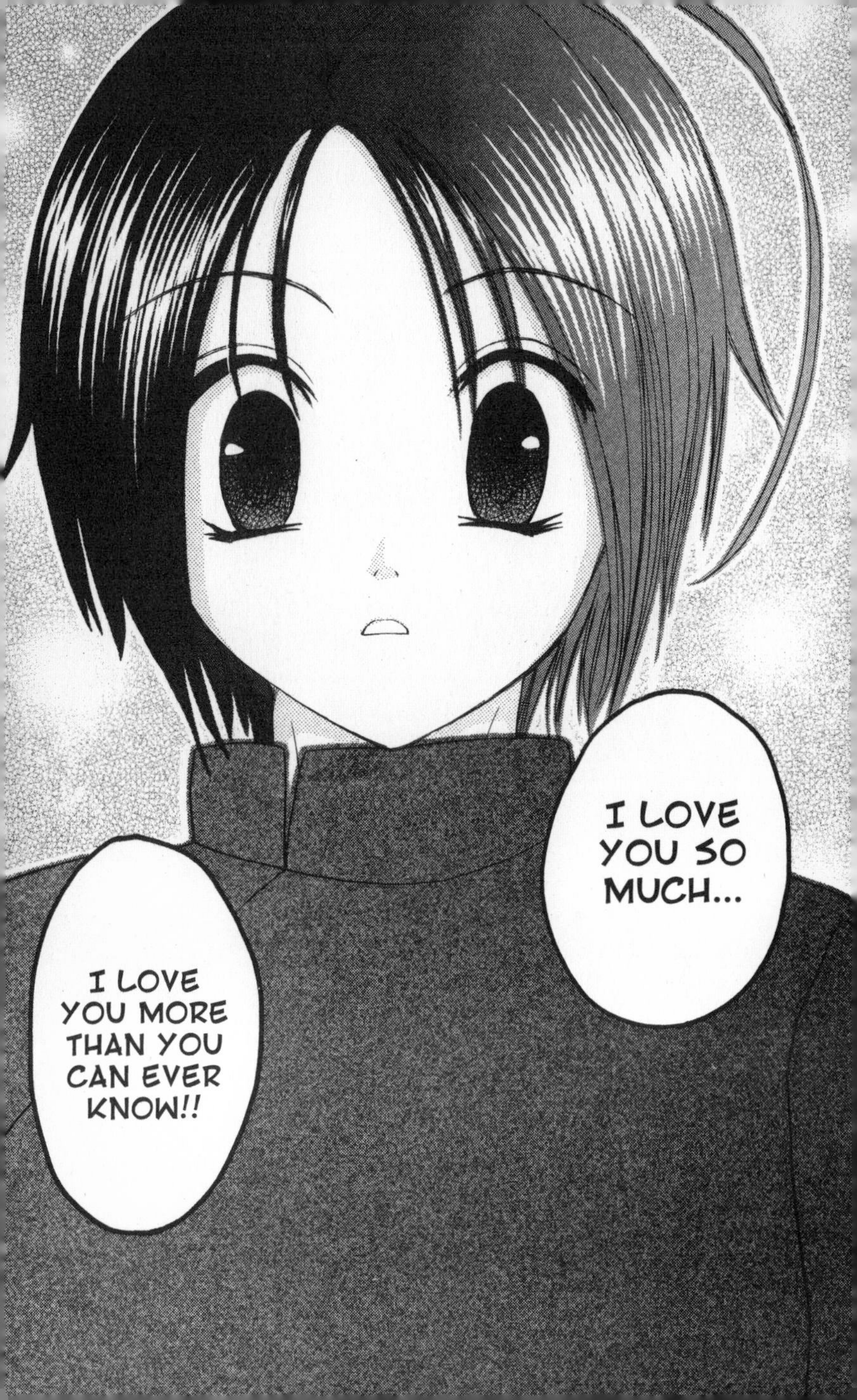
I LOVE YOU SO MUCH...
I LOVE YOU MORE THAN YOU CAN EVER KNOW!!

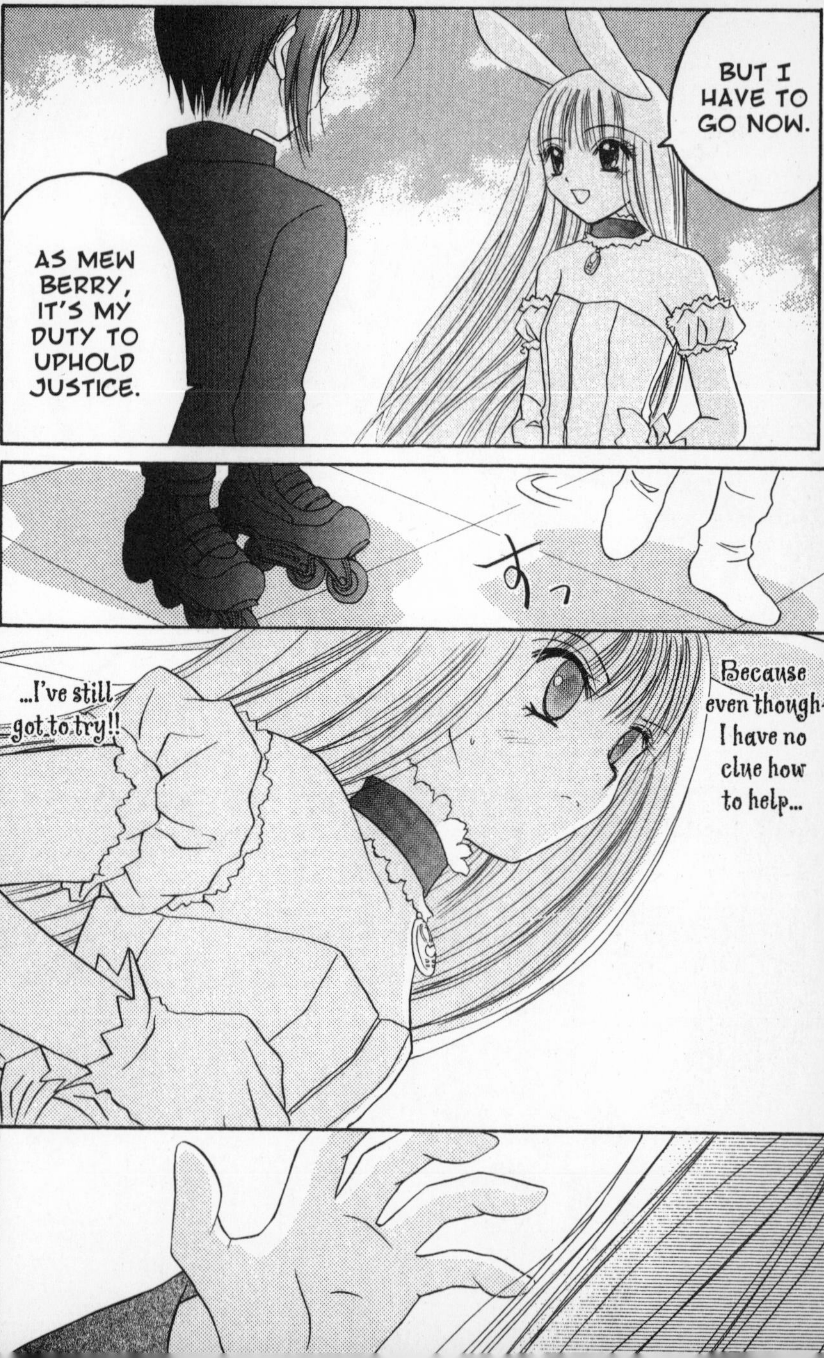
BUT I HAVE TO GO NOW.
AS MEW BERRY, IT'S MY DUTY TO UPHOLD JUSTICE.
すっ
Because even though I have no clue how to help...
...I've still got to try!!

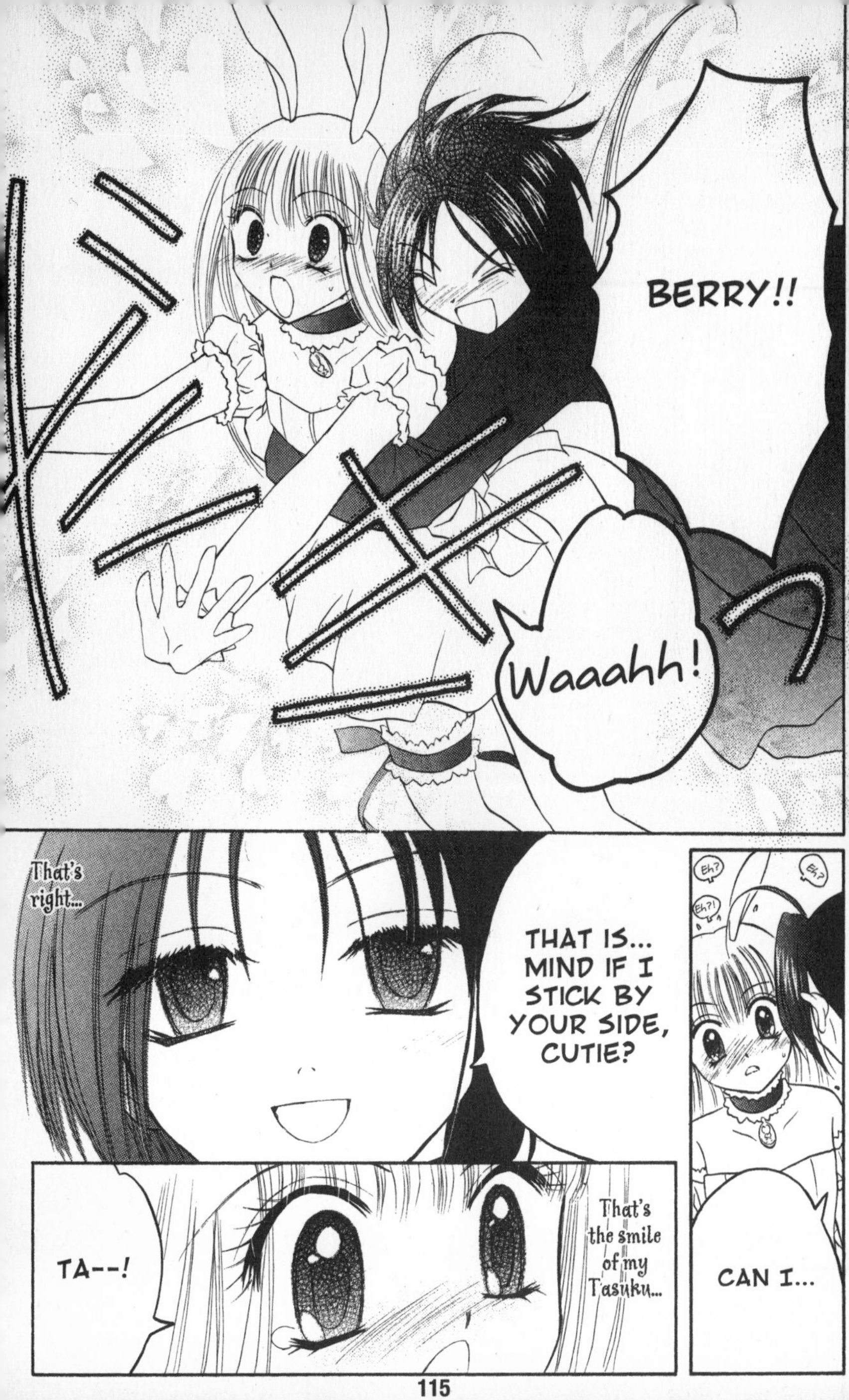
BERRY!!
Waaahh!
Eh?
Eh?
Eh?!
CAN I...
THAT IS... MIND IF I STICK BY YOUR SIDE, CUTIE?
That's right...
That's the smile of my Tasuku...
TA--!

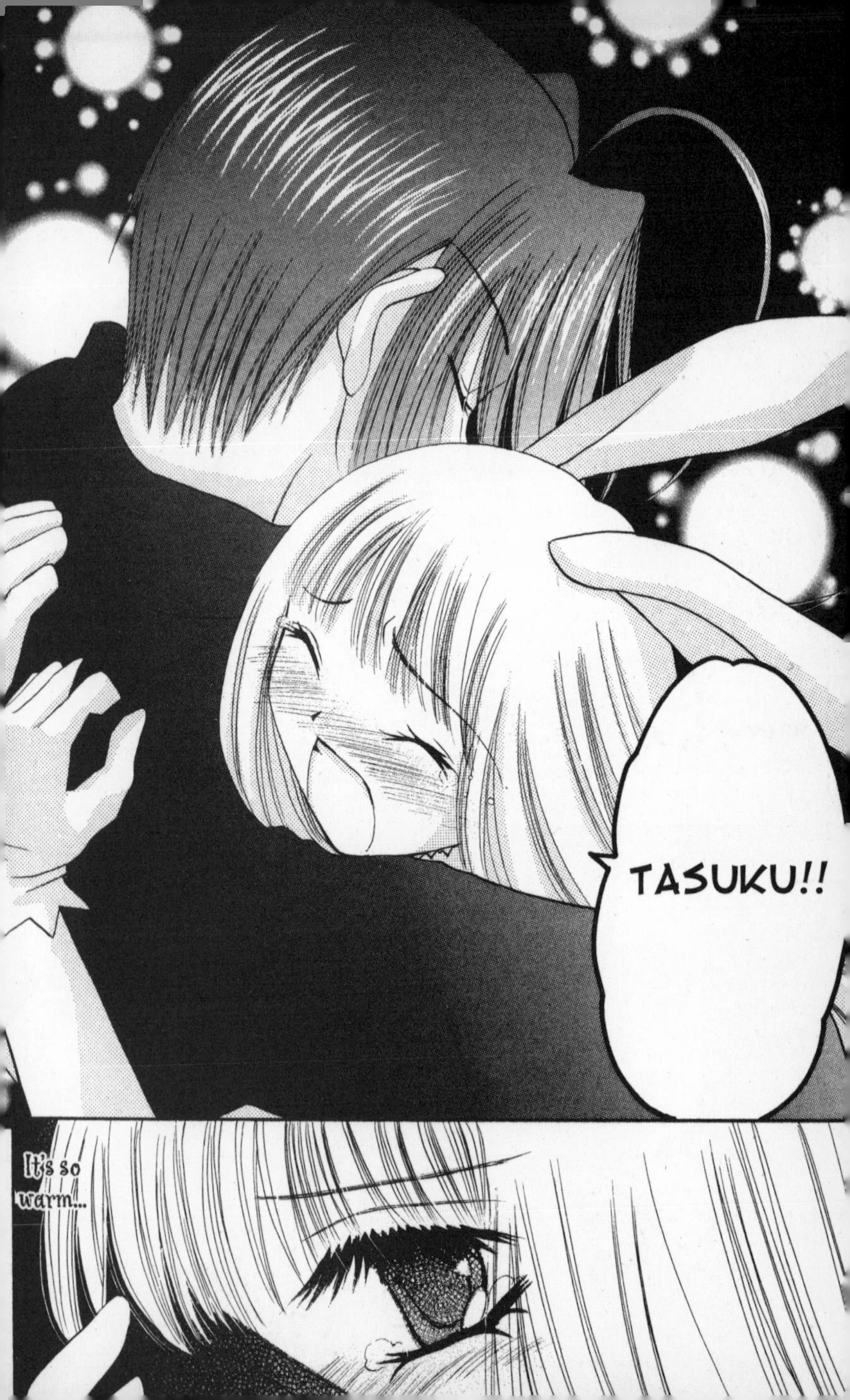
TASUKU!!
It's so warm...

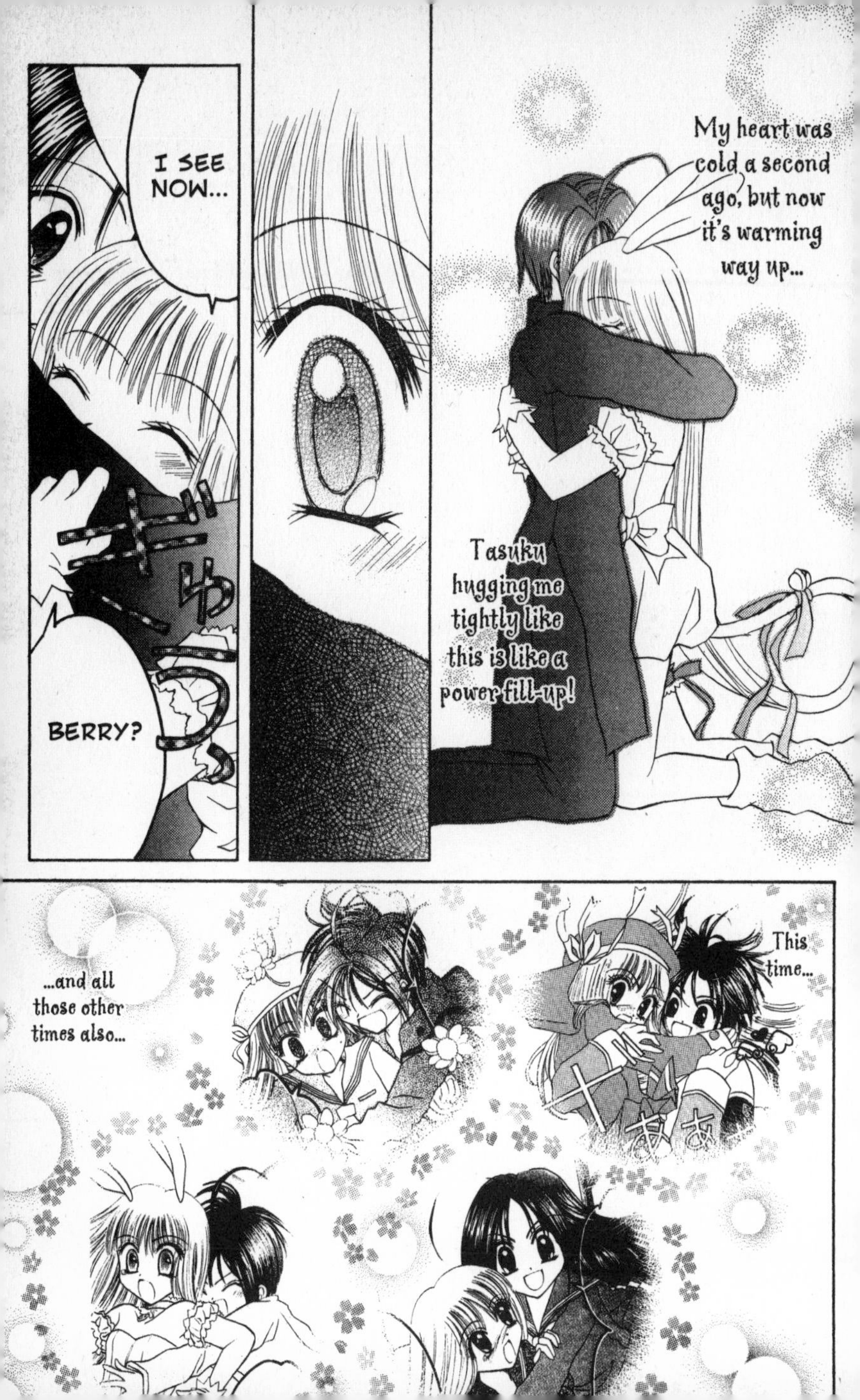
My heart was cold a second ago, but now it's warming way up...
Tasuku hugging me tightly like this is like a power fill-up!
I SEE NOW...
BERRY?
This time...
...and all those other times also...

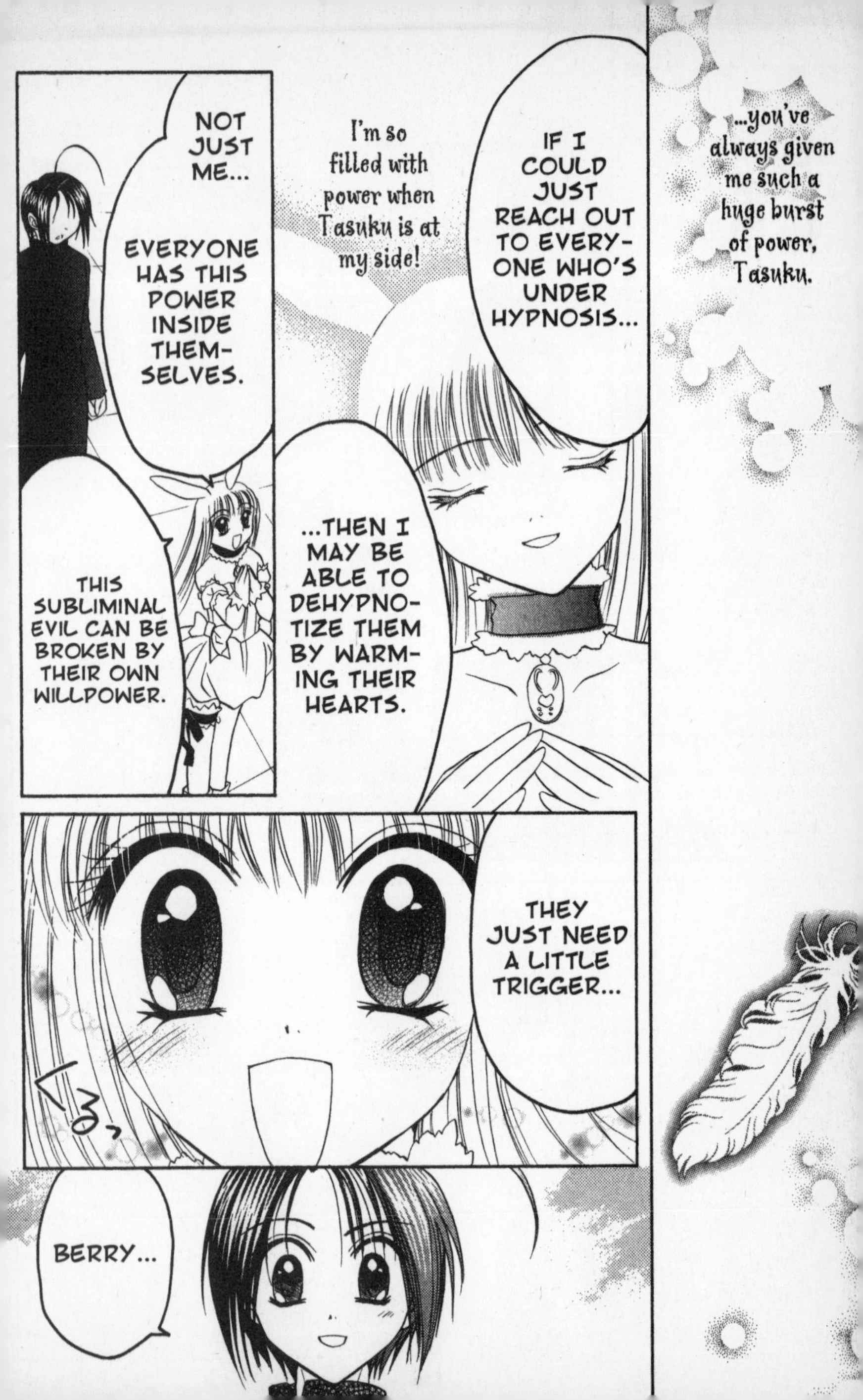
IF I COULD JUST REACH OUT TO EVERY-ONE WHO'S UNDER HYPNOSIS...
...THEN I MAY BE ABLE TO DEHYPNO-TIZE THEM BY WARM-ING THEIR HEARTS.
I'm so filled with power when Tasuku is at my side!
...you've always given me such a huge burst of power, Tasuku.
NOT JUST ME...
EVERYONE HAS THIS POWER INSIDE THEM-SELVES.
THIS SUBLIMINAL EVIL CAN BE BROKEN BY THEIR OWN WILLPOWER.
THEY JUST NEED A LITTLE TRIGGER...
くるっ
BERRY...

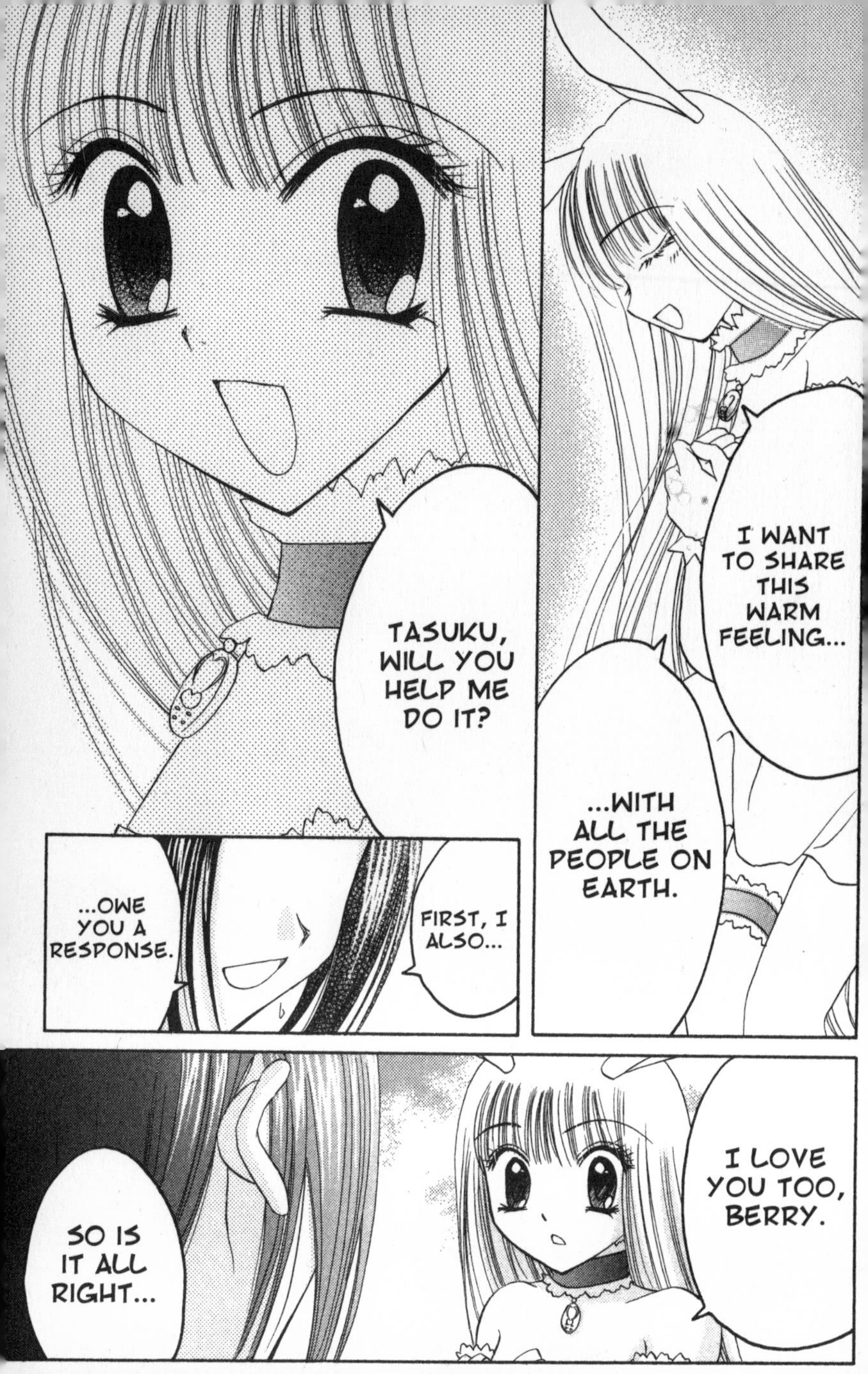
I WANT TO SHARE THIS WARM FEELING...
...WITH ALL THE PEOPLE ON EARTH.
TASUKU, WILL YOU HELP ME DO IT?
FIRST, I ALSO...
...OWE YOU A RESPONSE.
I LOVE YOU TOO, BERRY.
SO IS IT ALL RIGHT...

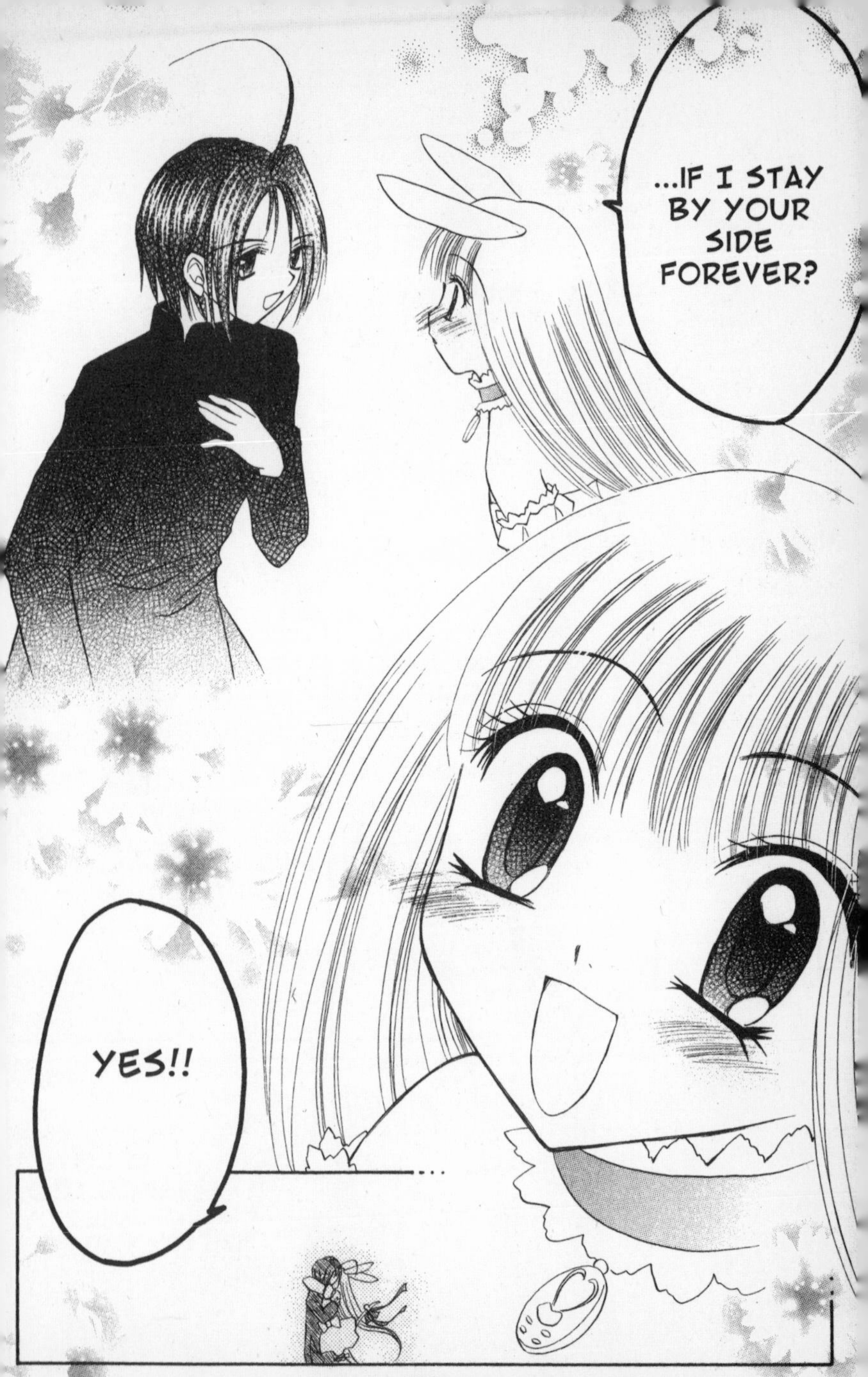
...IF I STAY BY YOUR SIDE FOREVER?
YES!!

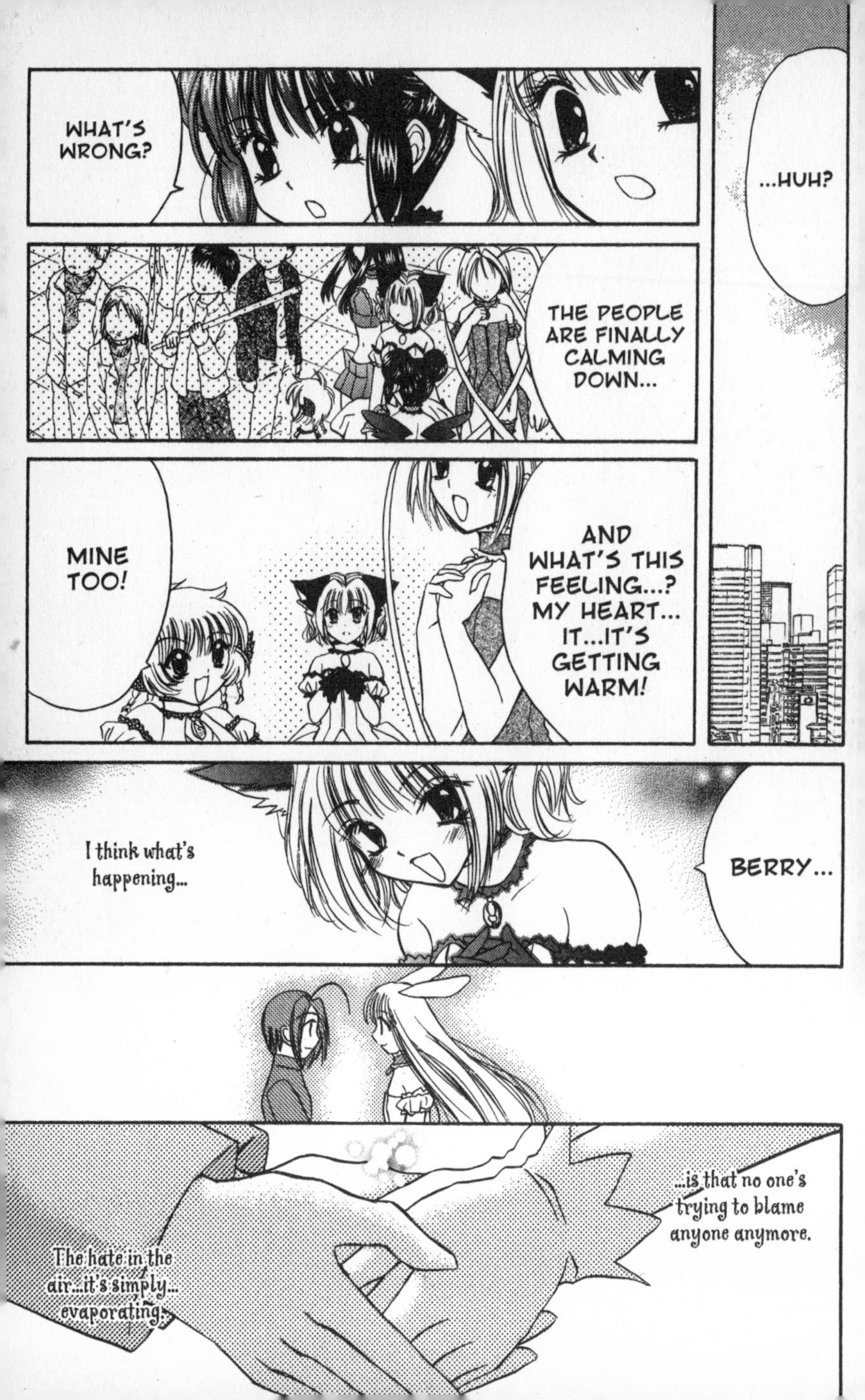
...HUH?
WHAT'S WRONG?
THE PEOPLE ARE FINALLY CALMING DOWN...
AND WHAT'S THIS FEELING...? MY HEART... IT...IT'S GETTING WARM!
MINE TOO!
BERRY...
I think what's happening...
...is that no one's trying to blame anyone anymore.
The hate in the air...it's simply... evaporating.

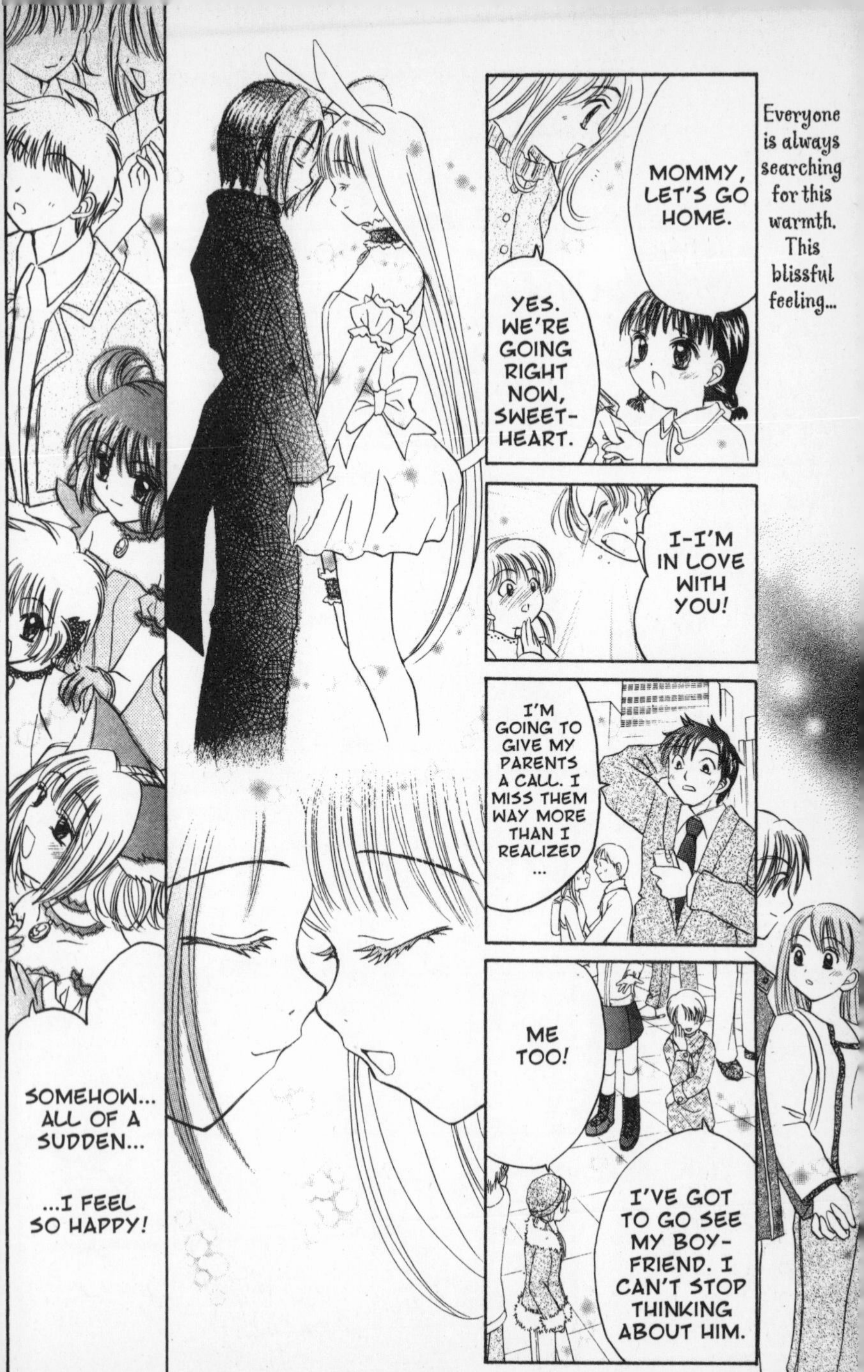
Everyone is always searching for this warmth. This blissful feeling...
MOMMY, LET'S GO HOME.
YES. WE'RE GOING RIGHT NOW, SWEET-HEART.
I-I'M IN LOVE WITH YOU!
I'M GOING TO GIVE MY PARENTS A CALL. I MISS THEM WAY MORE THAN I REALIZED ...
ME TOO!
I'VE GOT TO GO SEE MY BOY-FRIEND. I CAN'T STOP THINKING ABOUT HIM.
SOMEHOW... ALL OF A SUDDEN...
...I FEEL SO HAPPY!

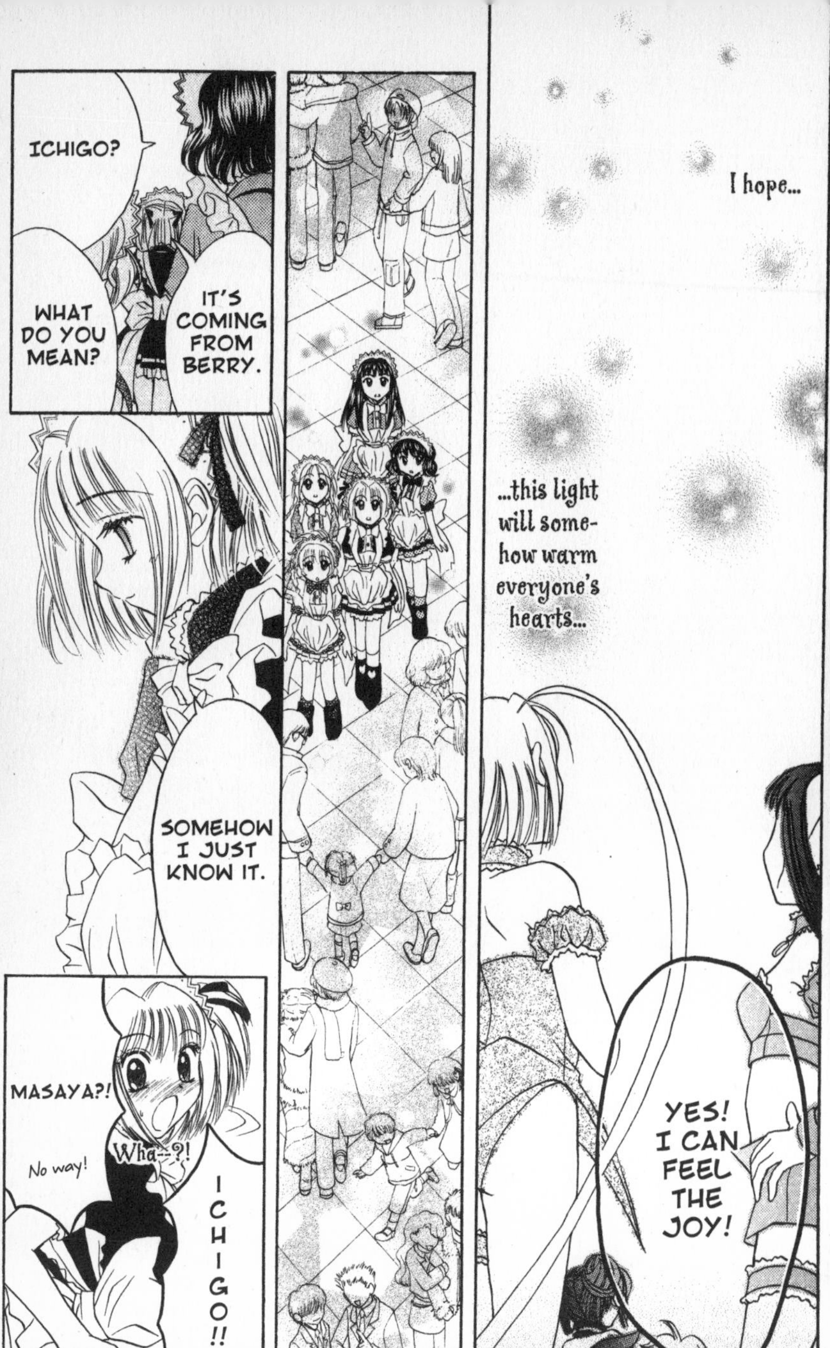
I hope...
...this light will somehow warm everyone's hearts...
YES! I CAN FEEL THE JOY!
ICHIGO?
IT'S COMING FROM BERRY.
WHAT DO YOU MEAN?
SOMEHOW I JUST KNOW IT.
ICHIGO!!
MASAYA?!
Wha--?!
No way!

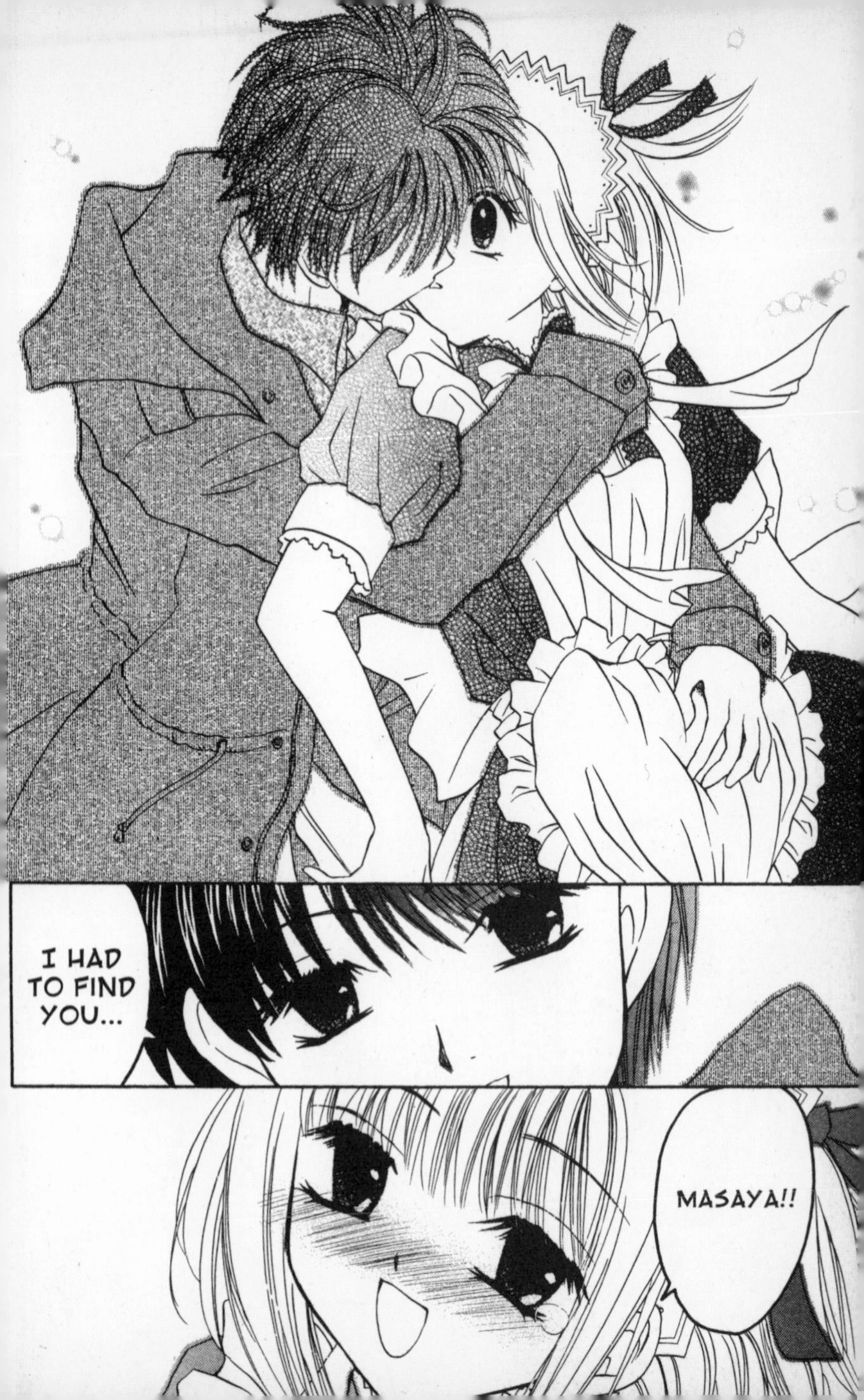
I HAD TO FIND YOU...
MASAYA!!

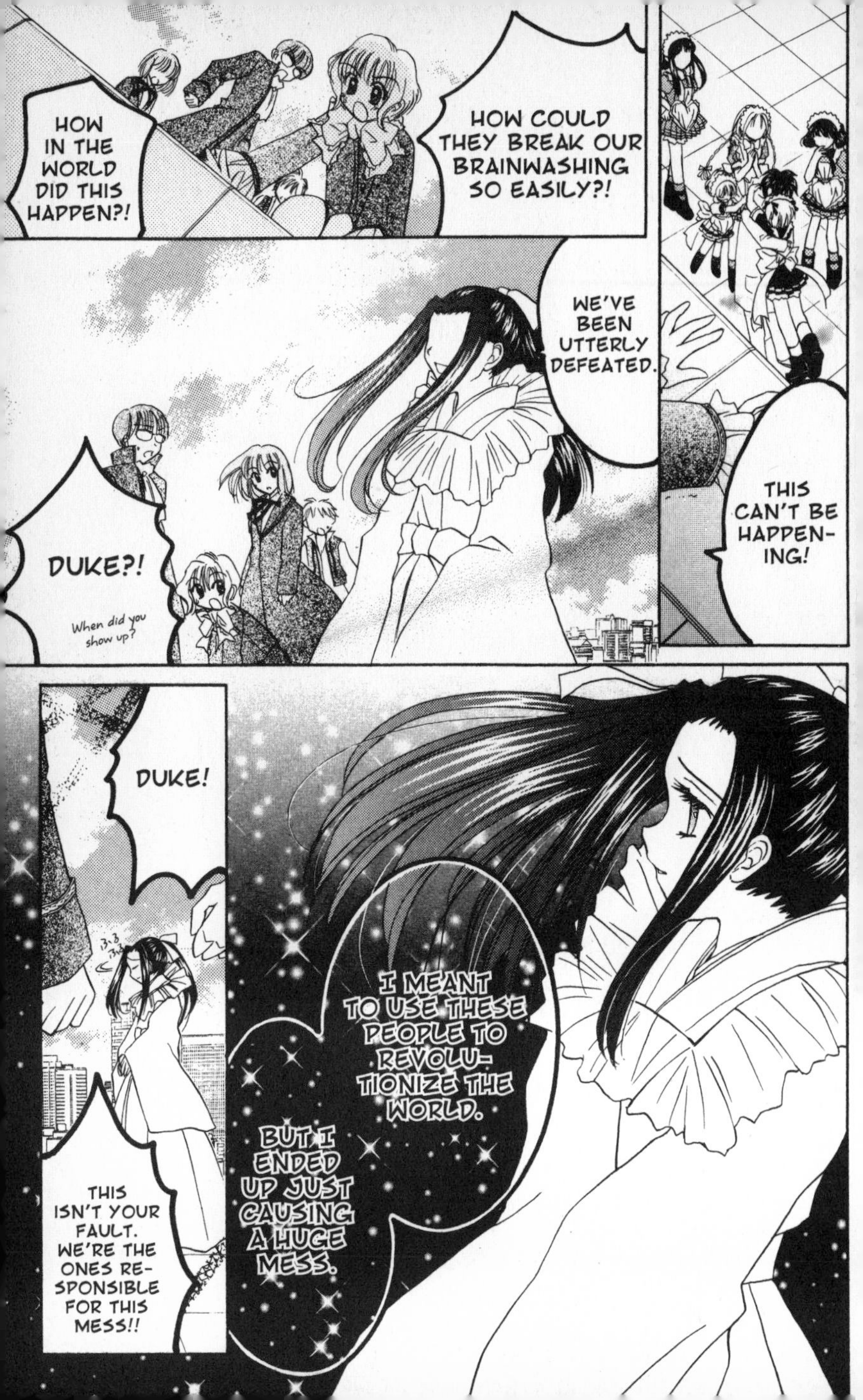

HOW COULD THEY BREAK OUR BRAINWASHING SO EASILY?!
HOW IN THE WORLD DID THIS HAPPEN?!
THIS CAN'T BE HAPPEN-ING!
WE'VE BEEN UTTERLY DEFEATED.
DUKE?!
When did you show up?
I MEANT TO USE THESE PEOPLE TO REVOLU-TIONIZE THE WORLD.
BUT I ENDED UP JUST CAUSING A HUGE MESS.
DUKE!
THIS ISN'T YOUR FAULT. WE'RE THE ONES RE-SPONSIBLE FOR THIS MESS!!

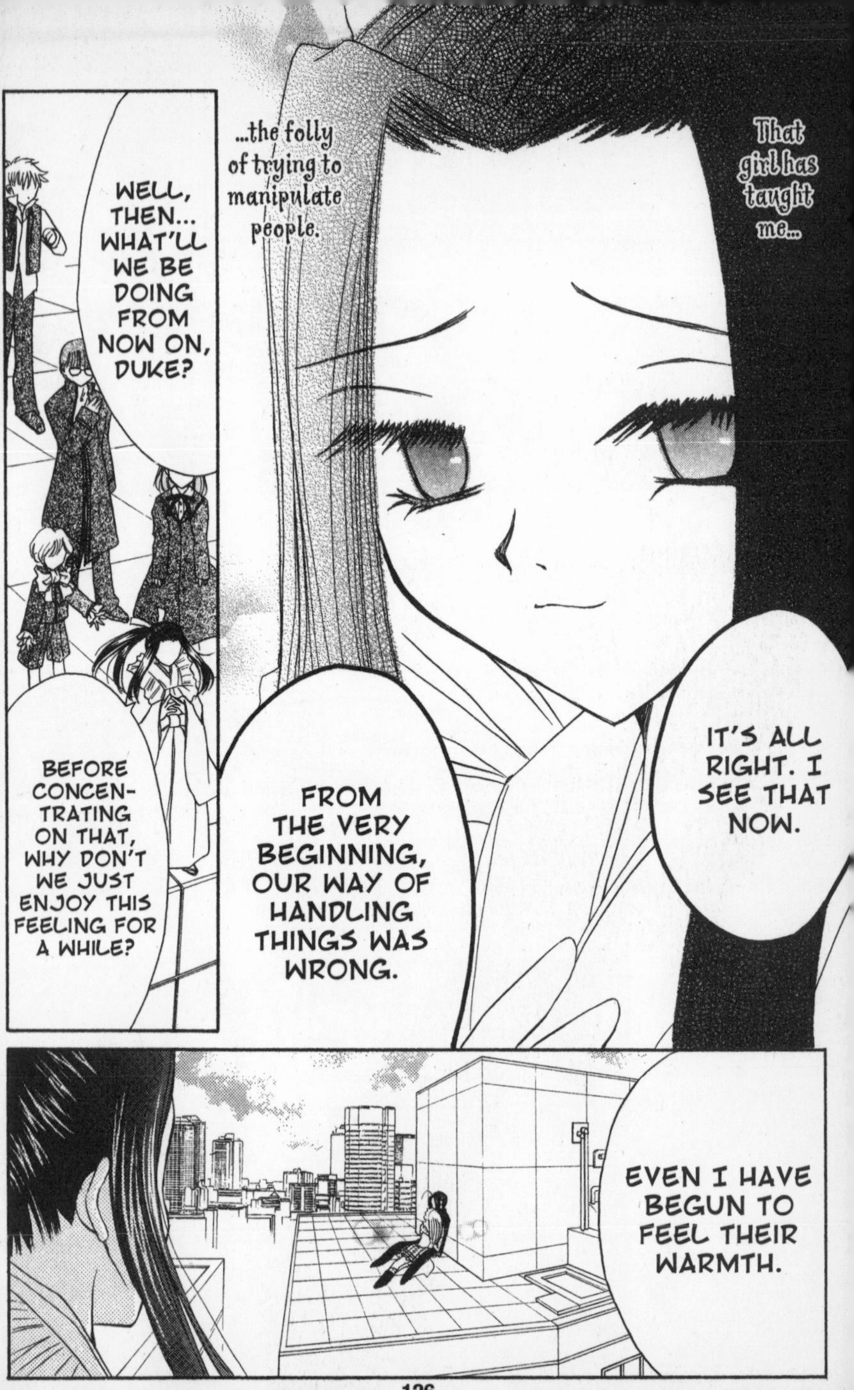
That girl has taught me...
...the folly of trying to manipulate people.
IT'S ALL RIGHT. I SEE THAT NOW.
FROM THE VERY BEGINNING, OUR WAY OF HANDLING THINGS WAS WRONG.
WELL, THEN... WHAT'LL WE BE DOING FROM NOW ON, DUKE?
BEFORE CONCENTRATING ON THAT, WHY DON'T WE JUST ENJOY THIS FEELING FOR A WHILE?
EVEN I HAVE BEGUN TO FEEL THEIR WARMTH.

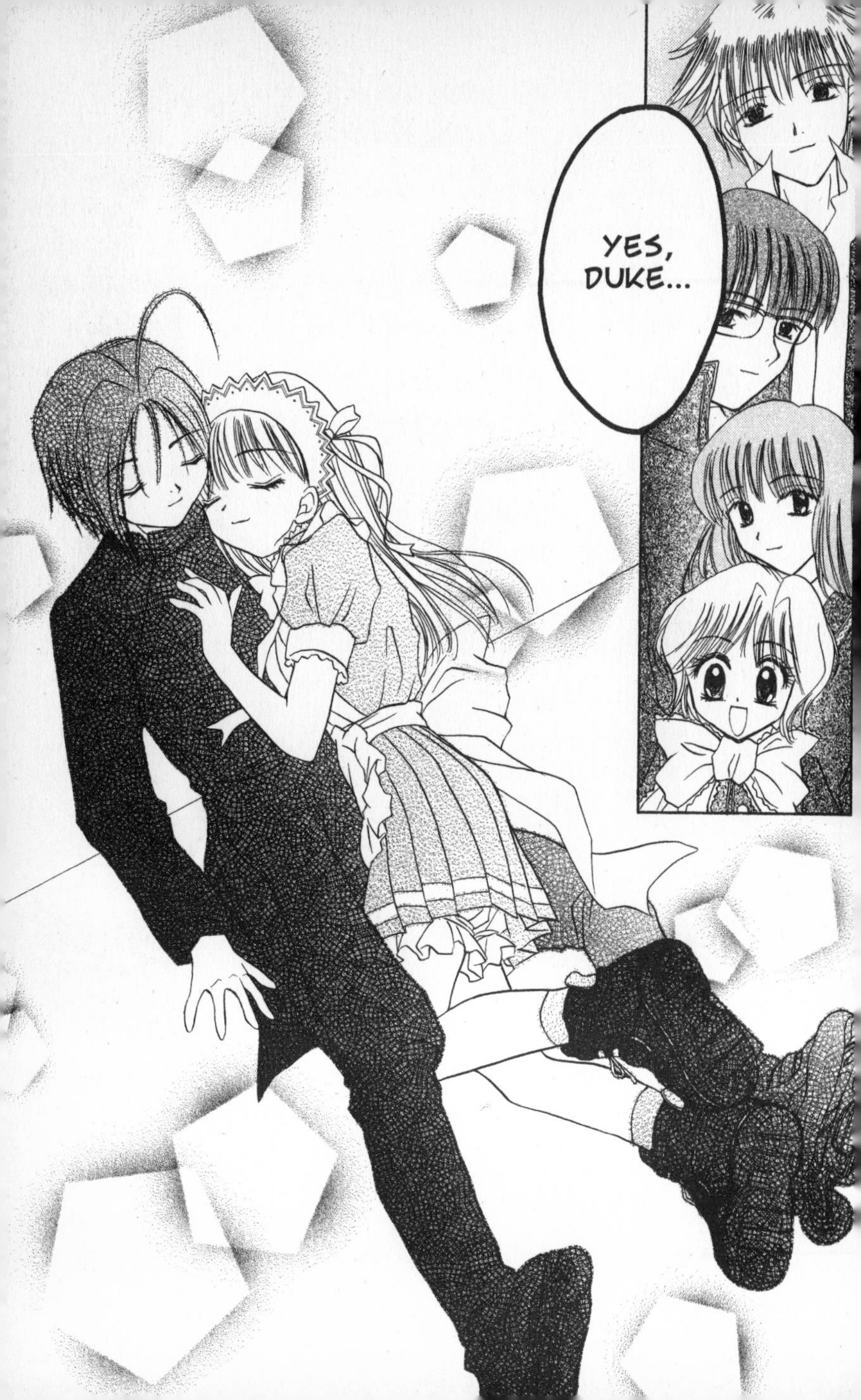
YES, DUKE...

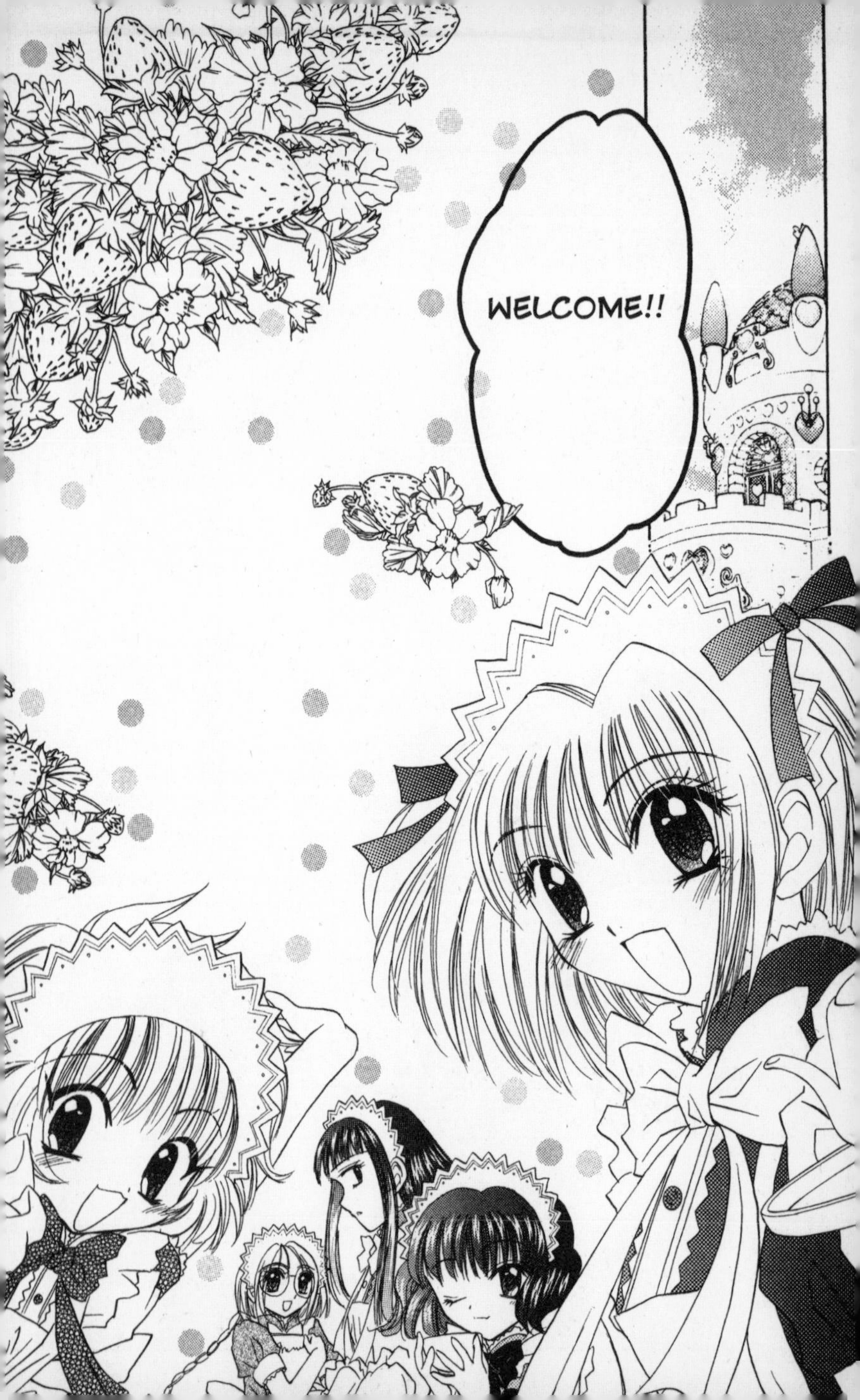
WELCOME!!

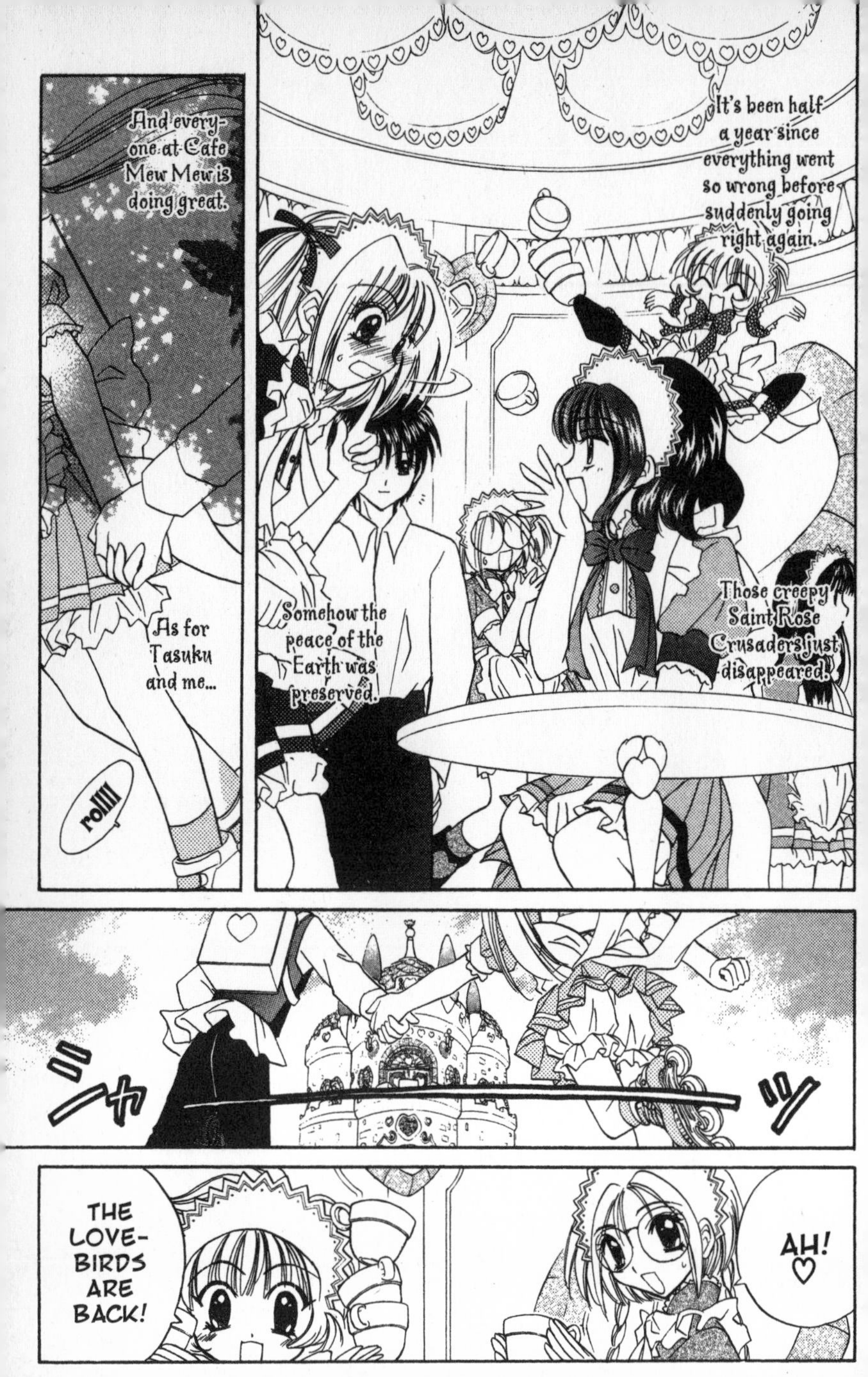
It's been half a year since everything went so wrong before suddenly going right again.
And every-one at Cafe Mew Mew is doing great.
Those creepy Saint Rose Crusaders just disappeared!
Somehow the peace of the Earth was preserved.
As for Tasuku and me...
rolll
AH! ♡
THE LOVE-BIRDS ARE BACK!

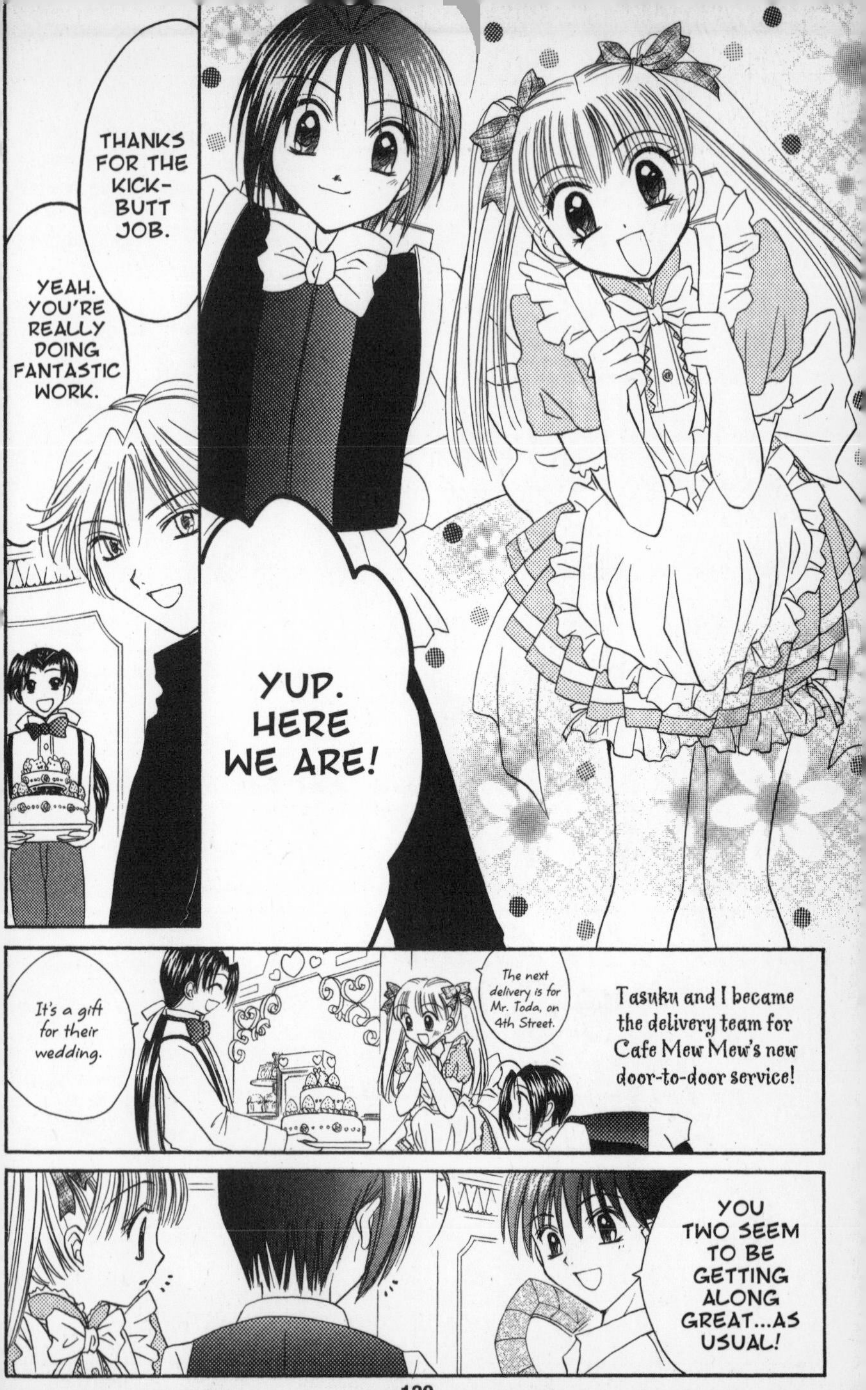
YUP. HERE WE ARE!
THANKS FOR THE KICK-BUTT JOB.
YEAH. YOU'RE REALLY DOING FANTASTIC WORK.
Tasuku and I became the delivery team for Cafe Mew Mew's new door-to-door service!
The next delivery is for Mr. Toda, on 4th Street.
It's a gift for their wedding.
YOU TWO SEEM TO BE GETTING ALONG GREAT...AS USUAL!

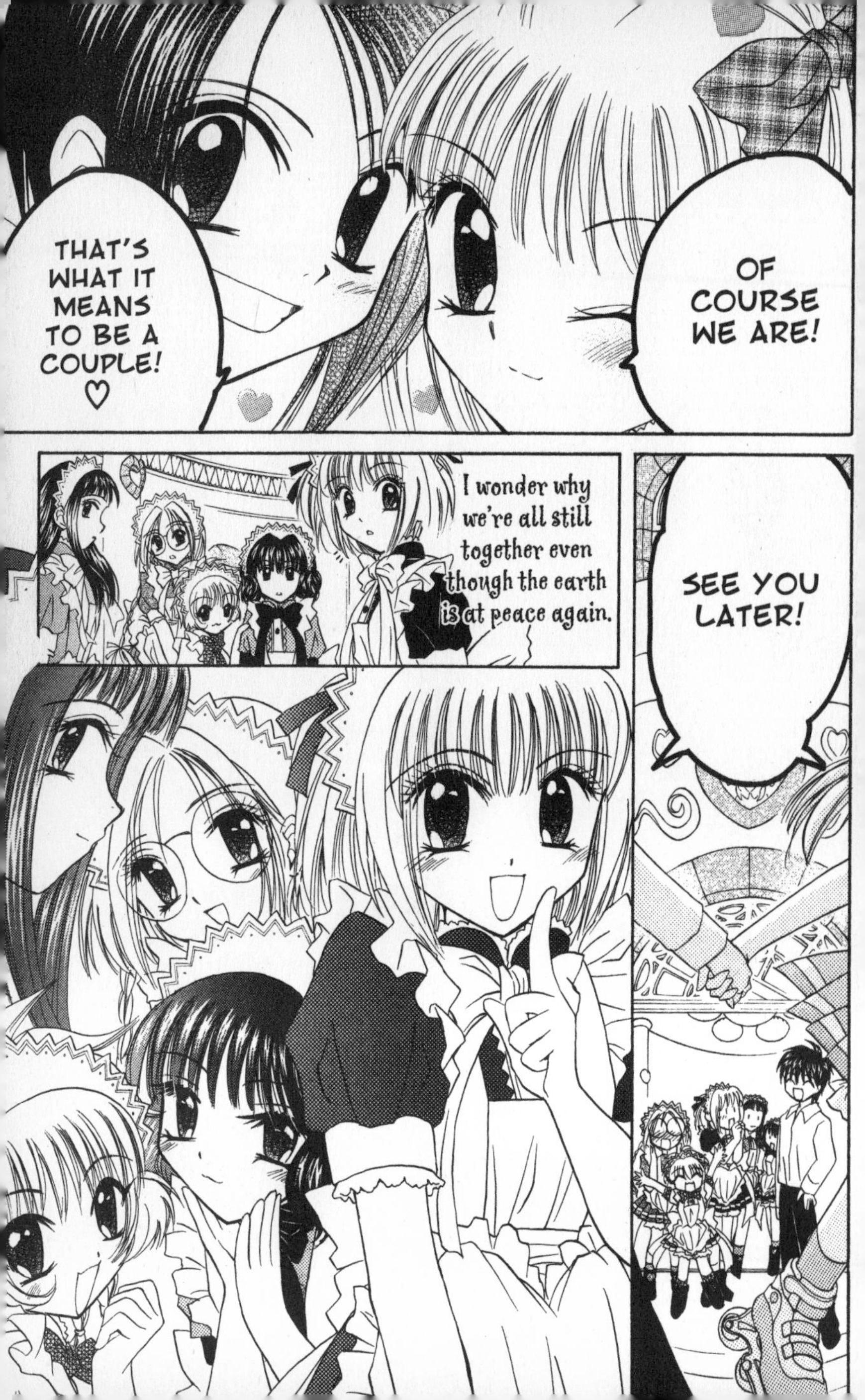
OF COURSE WE ARE!
THAT'S WHAT IT MEANS TO BE A COUPLE! ♡
SEE YOU LATER!
I wonder why we're all still together even though the earth is at peace again.

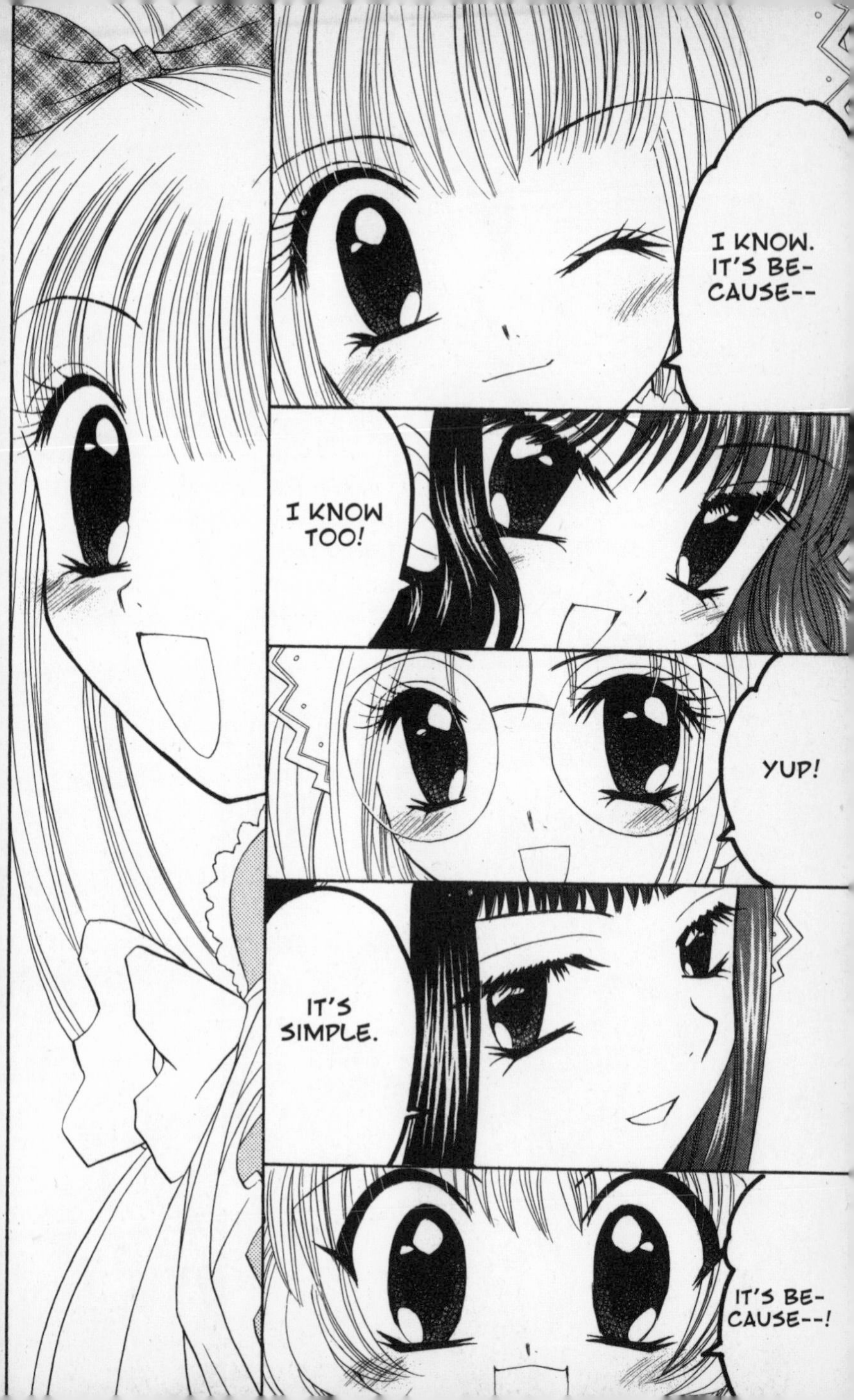
I KNOW. IT'S BE- CAUSE--
I KNOW TOO!
YUP!
IT'S SIMPLE.
IT'S BE- CAUSE--!

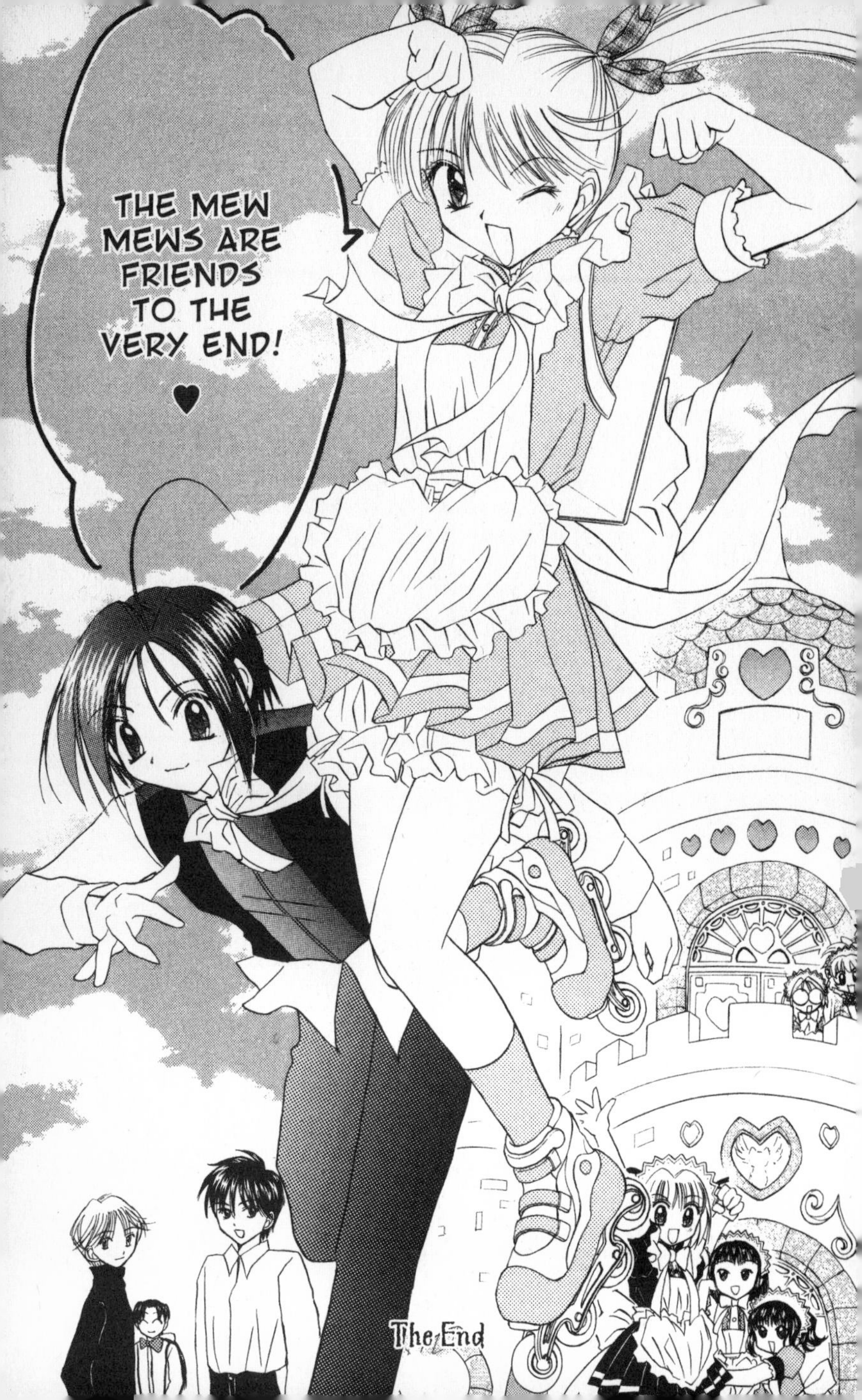
THE MEW MEWS ARE FRIENDS TO THE VERY END! ♥
The End

Special manga extra!

Berry's Rush Report ☆*3

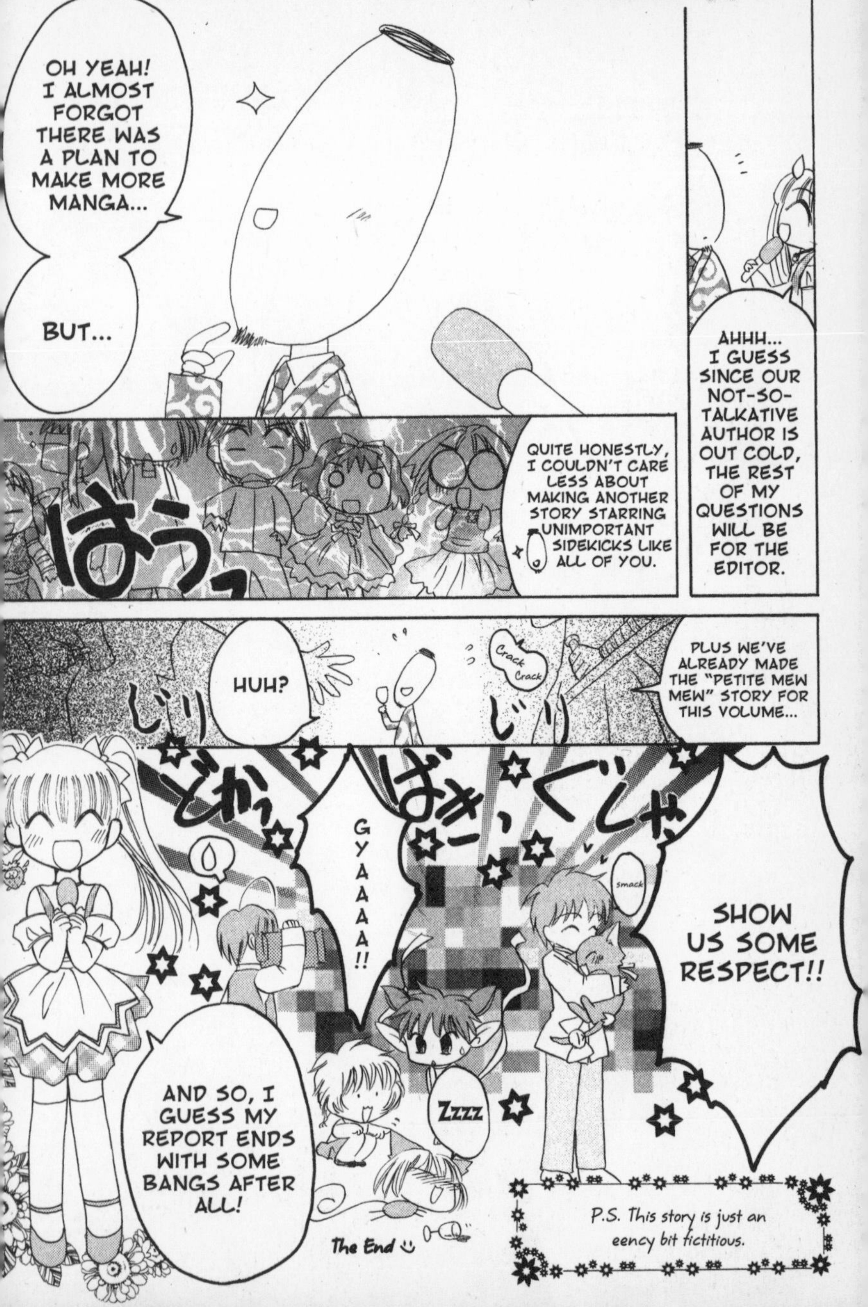

AHHH... I GUESS SINCE OUR NOT-SO-TALKATIVE AUTHOR IS OUT COLD, THE REST OF MY QUESTIONS WILL BE FOR THE EDITOR.
OH YEAH! I ALMOST FORGOT THERE WAS A PLAN TO MAKE MORE MANGA...
BUT...
QUITE HONESTLY, I COULDN'T CARE LESS ABOUT MAKING ANOTHER STORY STARRING UNIMPORTANT SIDEKICKS LIKE ALL OF YOU.
はうっ
PLUS WE'VE ALREADY MADE THE "PETITE MEW MEW" STORY FOR THIS VOLUME...
Crack Crack
じりじり
HUH?
SHOW US SOME RESPECT!!
smack
ばきっ、ぐしゃ
GYAAAAA!!
どかっ
Zzzz
AND SO, I GUESS MY REPORT ENDS WITH SOME BANGS AFTER ALL!
The End
P.S. This story is just an eency bit fictitious.

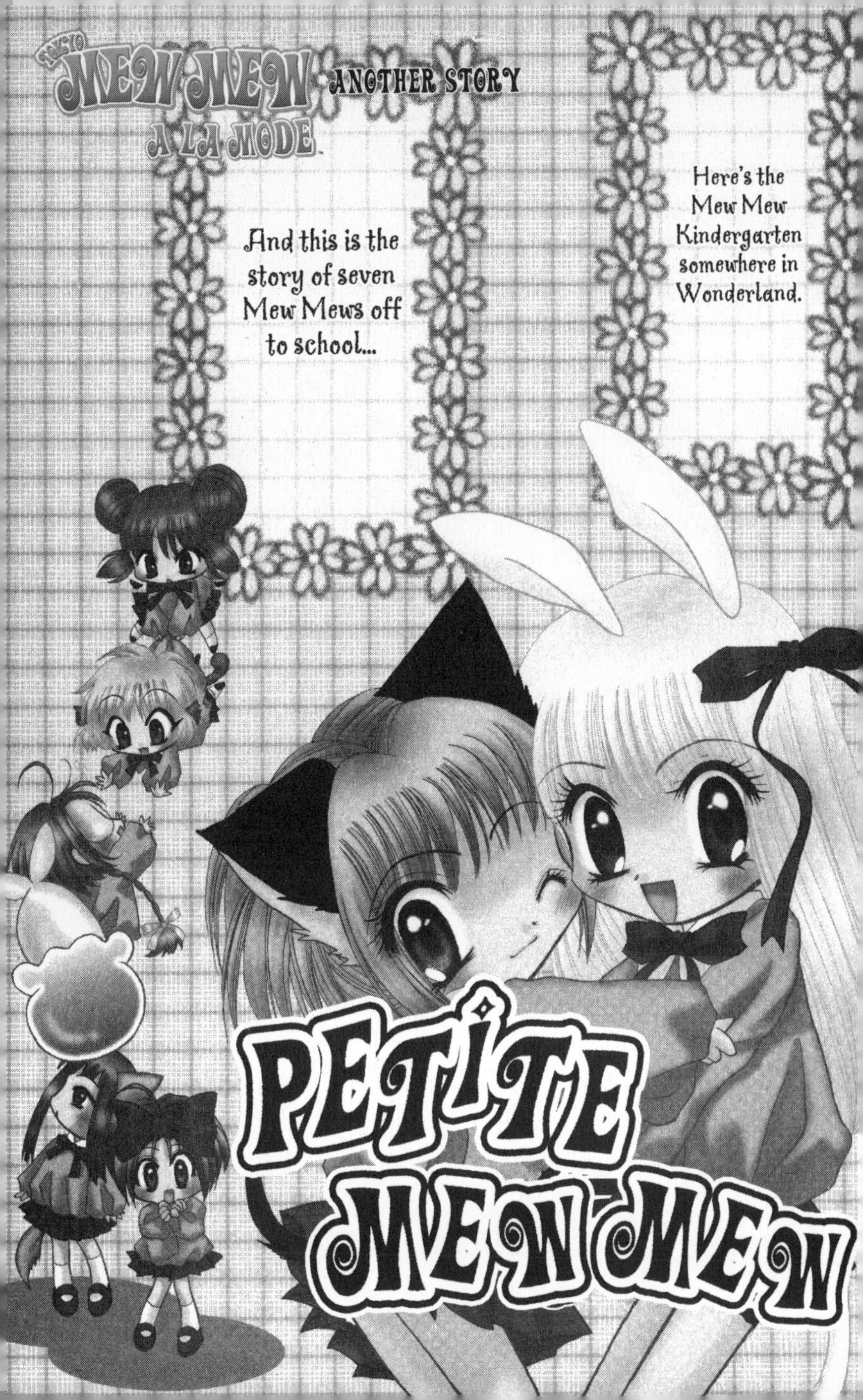
TOKYO MEW MEW A LA MODE
ANOTHER STORY
Here's the Mew Mew Kindergarten somewhere in Wonderland.
And this is the story of seven Mew Mews off to school...
PETITE MEW MEW

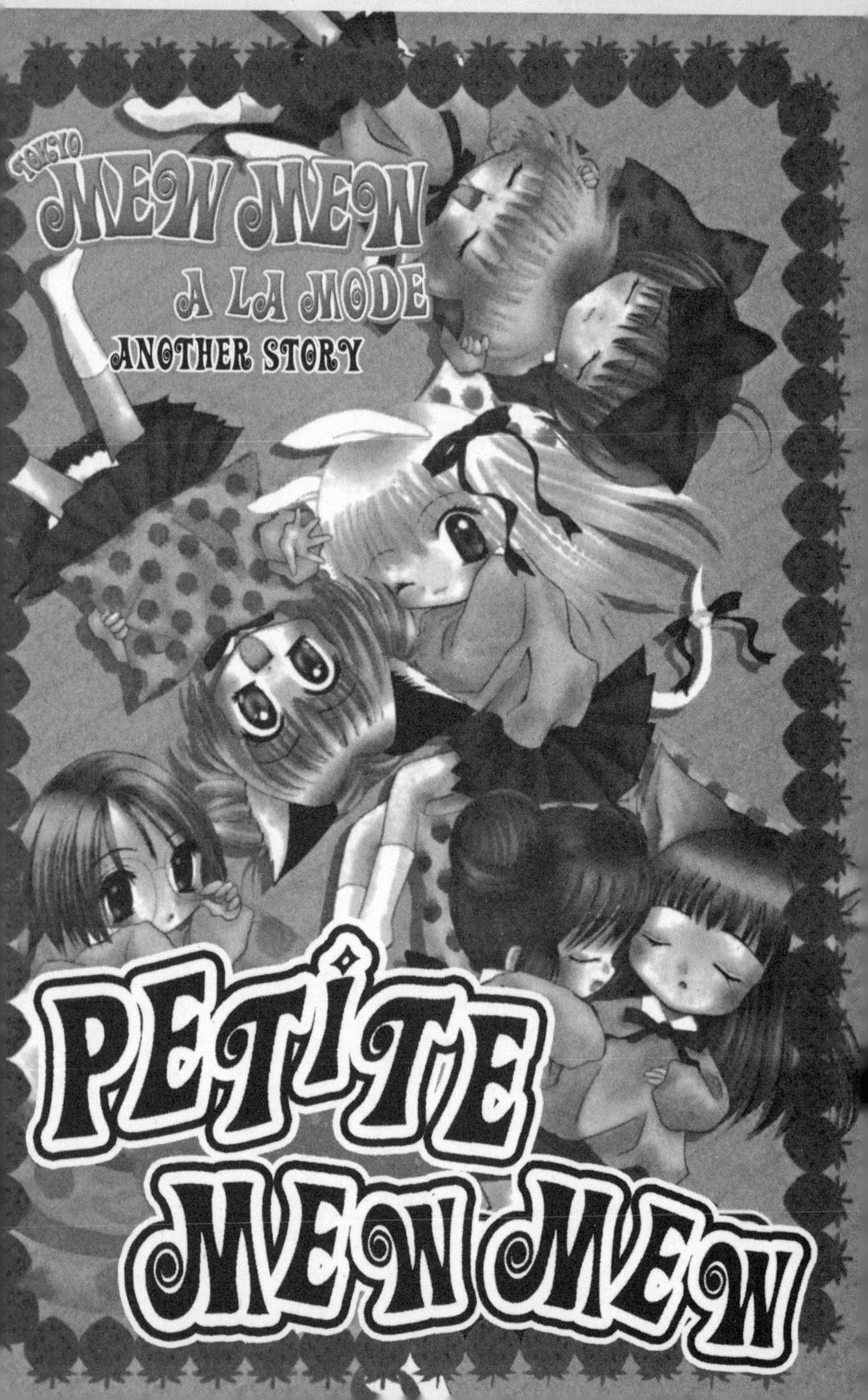
TOKYO
MEW MEW
A LA MODE
ANOTHER STORY
PETITE
MEW MEW

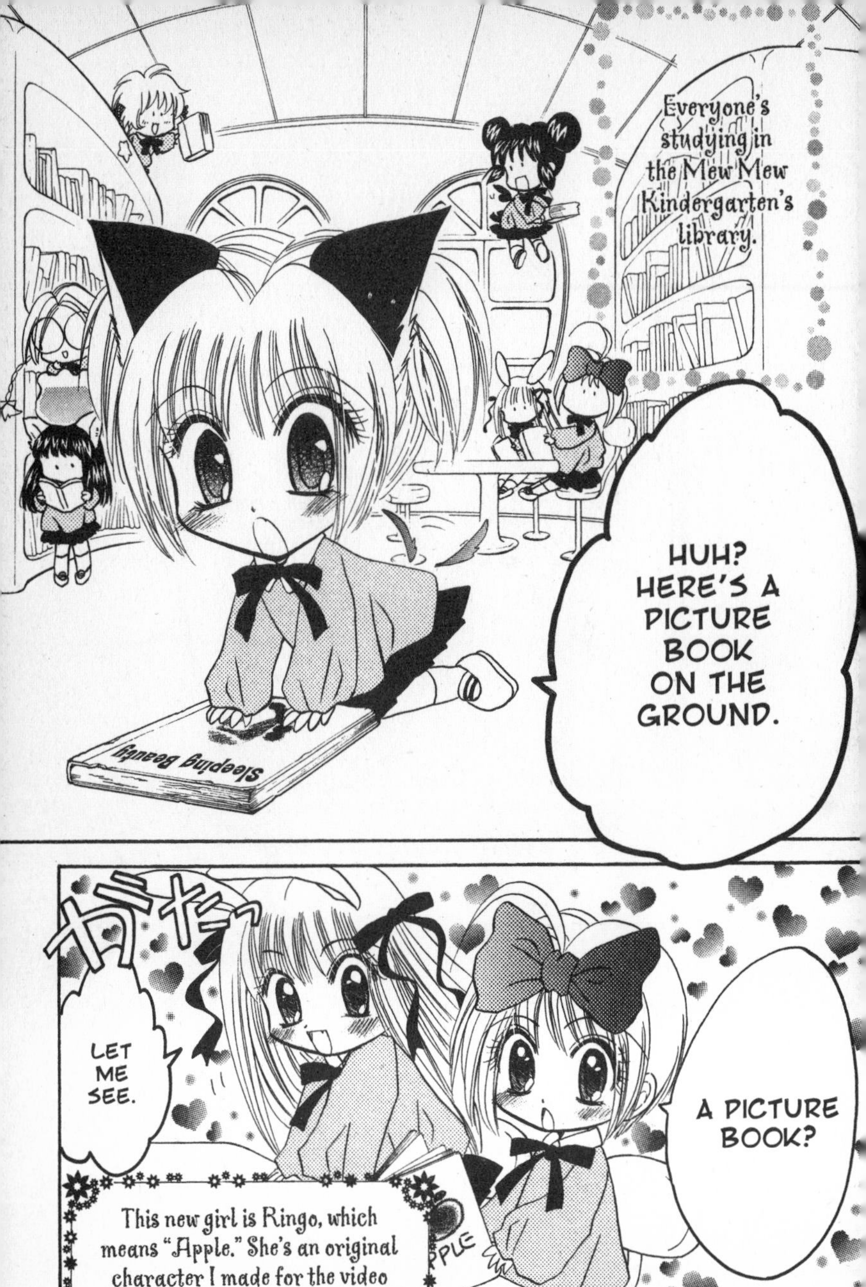
Everyone's studying in the Mew Mew Kindergarten's library.
HUH? HERE'S A PICTURE BOOK ON THE GROUND.
Sleeping Beauty
A PICTURE BOOK?
LET ME SEE.
This new girl is Ringo, which means "Apple." She's an original character I made for the video game. Isn't she totally cute? ♡

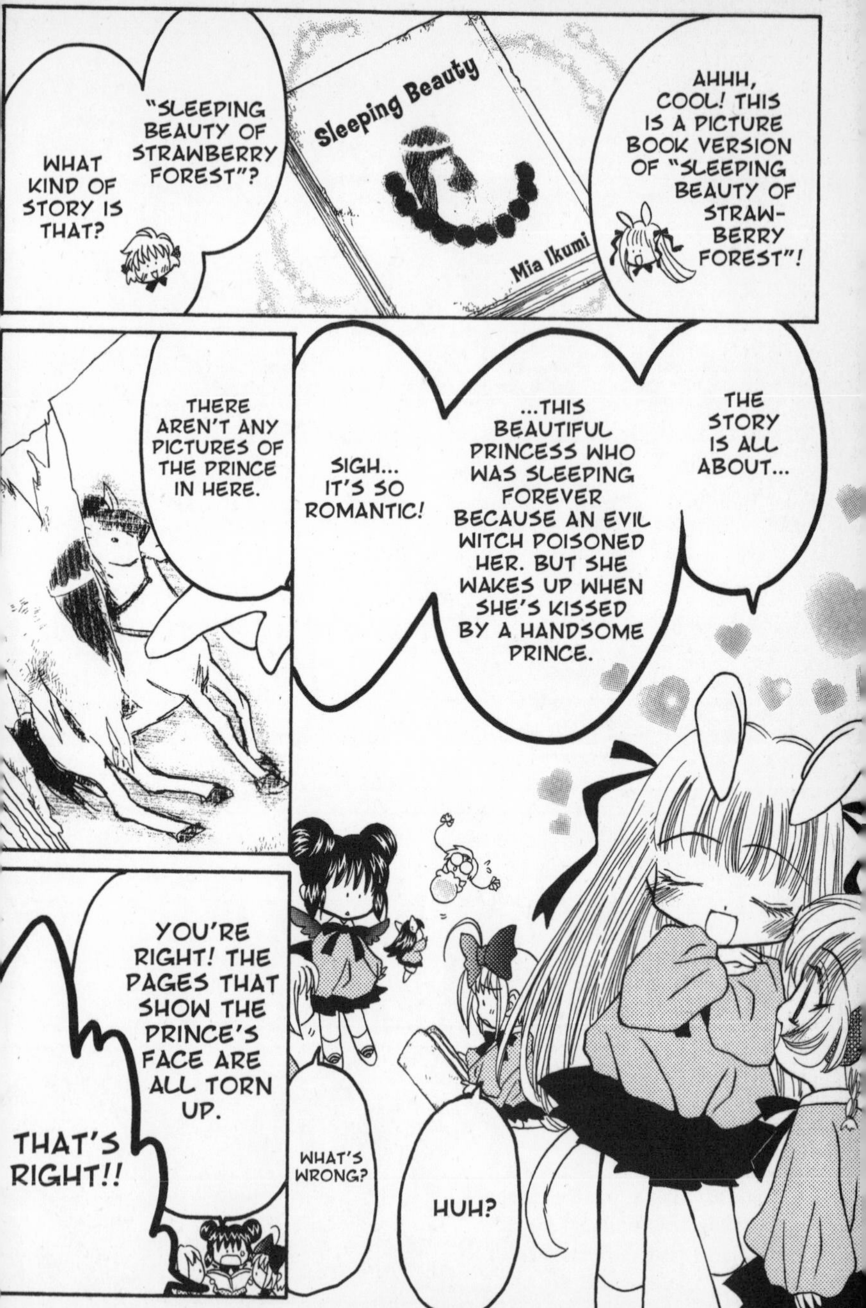

AHHH, COOL! THIS IS A PICTURE BOOK VERSION OF "SLEEPING BEAUTY OF STRAW-BERRY FOREST"!
Sleeping Beauty
Mia Ikumi
"SLEEPING BEAUTY OF STRAWBERRY FOREST"?
WHAT KIND OF STORY IS THAT?
THE STORY IS ALL ABOUT...
...THIS BEAUTIFUL PRINCESS WHO WAS SLEEPING FOREVER BECAUSE AN EVIL WITCH POISONED HER. BUT SHE WAKES UP WHEN SHE'S KISSED BY A HANDSOME PRINCE.
SIGH... IT'S SO ROMANTIC!
THERE AREN'T ANY PICTURES OF THE PRINCE IN HERE.
HUH?
WHAT'S WRONG?
YOU'RE RIGHT! THE PAGES THAT SHOW THE PRINCE'S FACE ARE ALL TORN UP.
THAT'S RIGHT!!

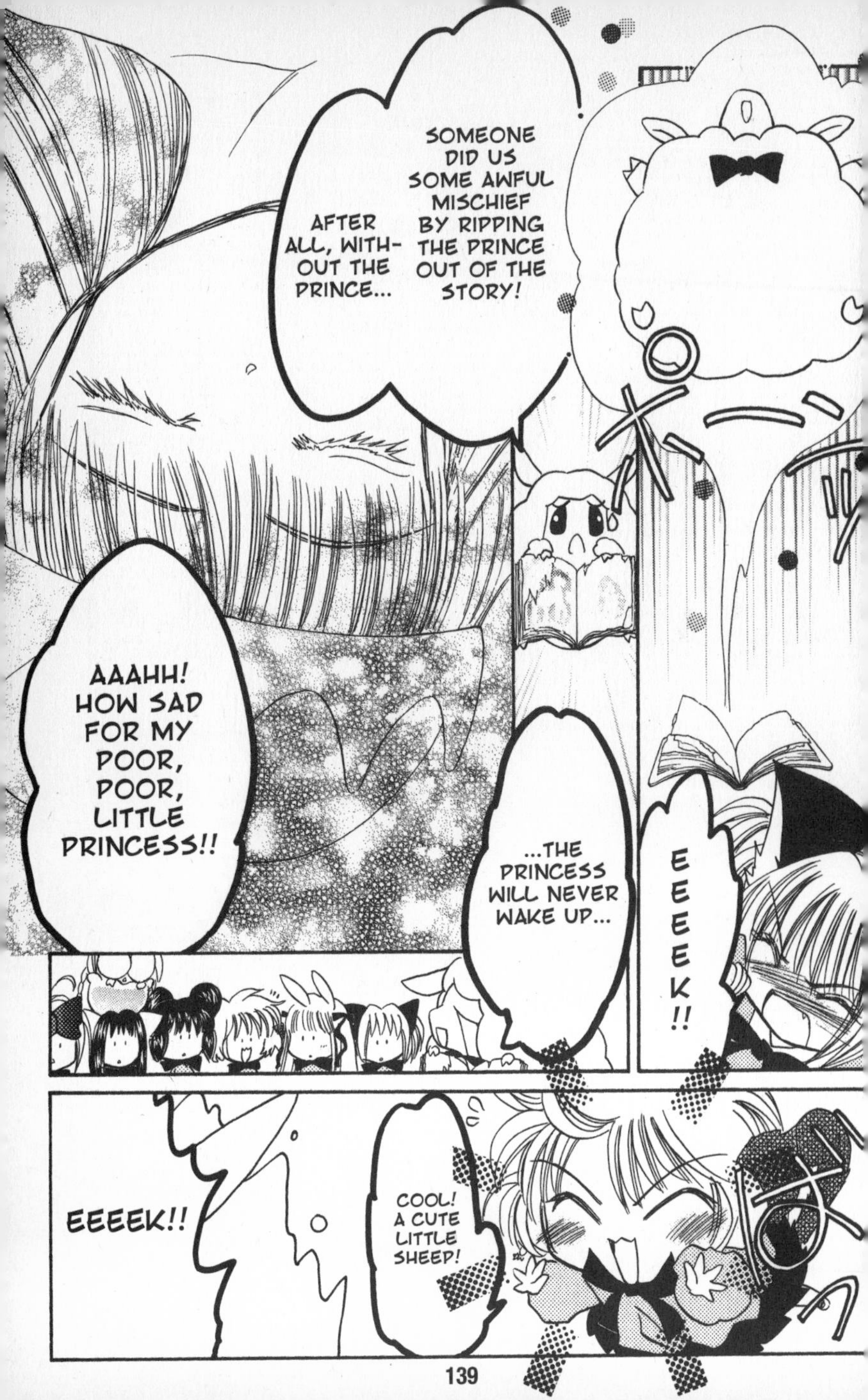
SOMEONE DID US SOME AWFUL MISCHIEF BY RIPPING THE PRINCE OUT OF THE STORY!
AFTER ALL, WITH-OUT THE PRINCE...
...THE PRINCESS WILL NEVER WAKE UP...
EEEEEK!!
AAAHH! HOW SAD FOR MY POOR, POOR, LITTLE PRINCESS!!
COOL! A CUTE LITTLE SHEEP!
EEEEK!!

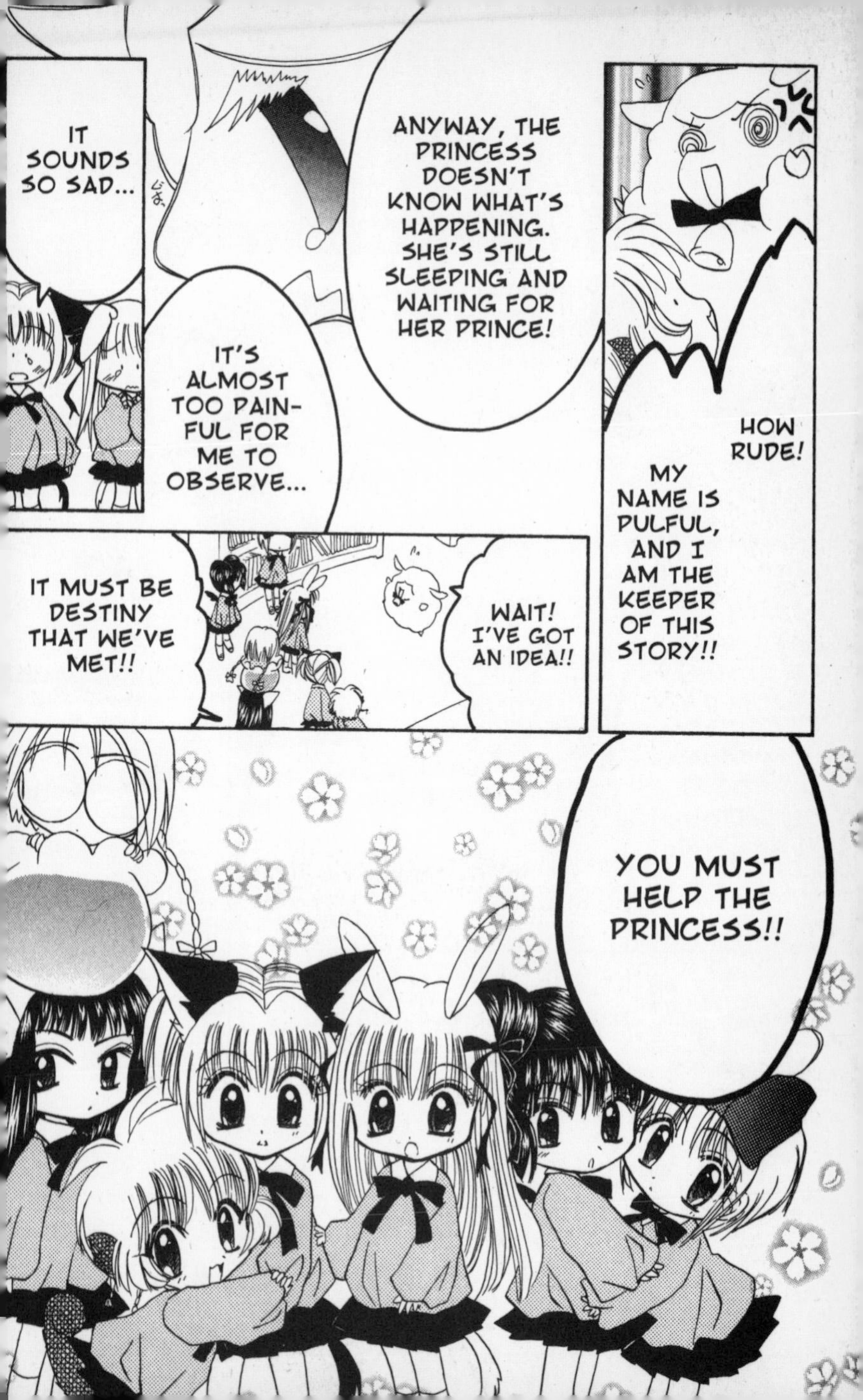
HOW RUDE!
MY NAME IS PULFUL, AND I AM THE KEEPER OF THIS STORY!!
ANYWAY, THE PRINCESS DOESN'T KNOW WHAT'S HAPPENING. SHE'S STILL SLEEPING AND WAITING FOR HER PRINCE!
IT SOUNDS SO SAD...
IT'S ALMOST TOO PAIN-FUL FOR ME TO OBSERVE...
WAIT! I'VE GOT AN IDEA!!
IT MUST BE DESTINY THAT WE'VE MET!!
YOU MUST HELP THE PRINCESS!!

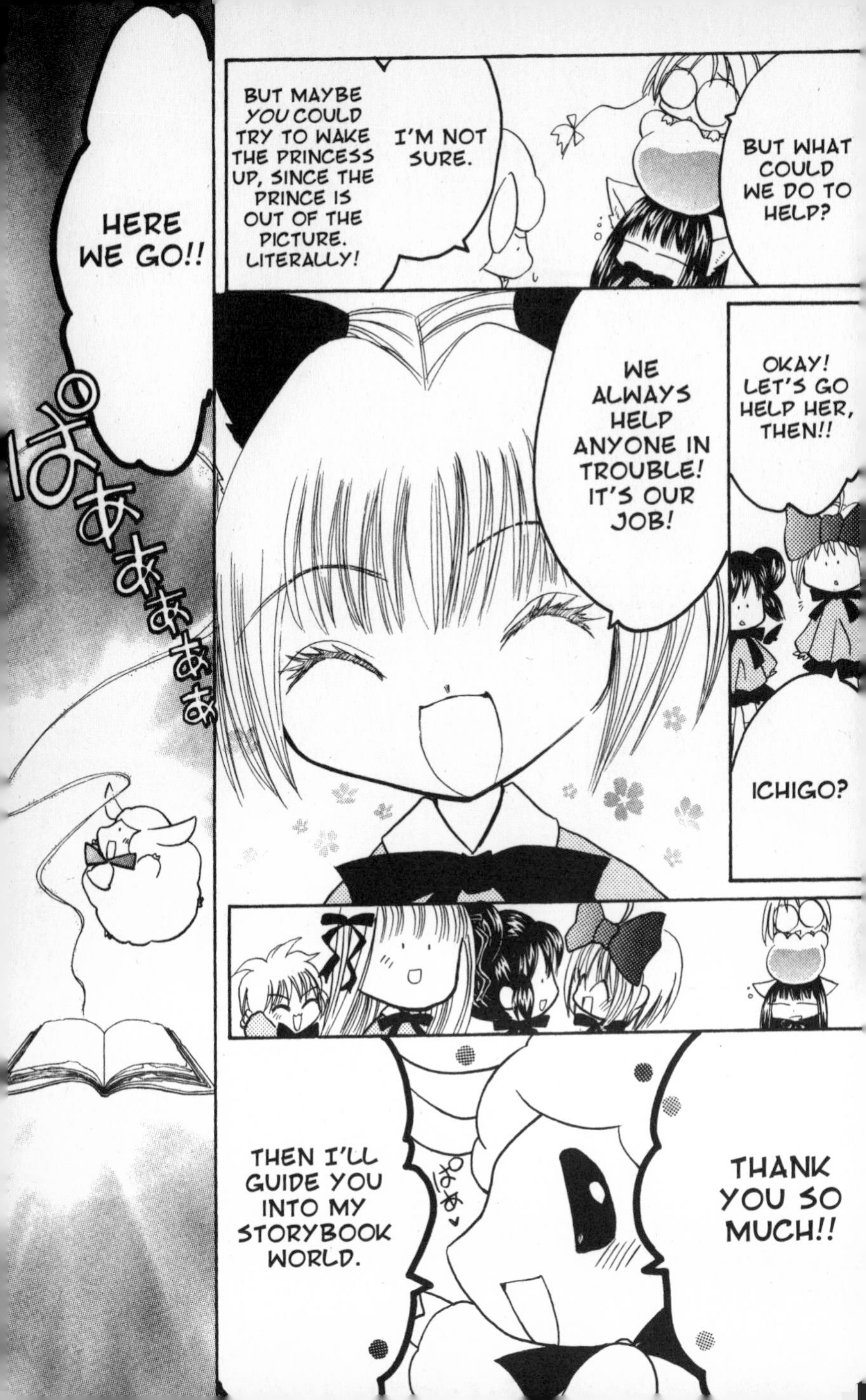
BUT WHAT COULD WE DO TO HELP?
I'M NOT SURE.
BUT MAYBE *YOU* COULD TRY TO WAKE THE PRINCESS UP, SINCE THE PRINCE IS OUT OF THE PICTURE. LITERALLY!
OKAY! LET'S GO HELP HER, THEN!!
WE ALWAYS HELP ANYONE IN TROUBLE! IT'S OUR JOB!
ICHIGO?
THANK YOU SO MUCH!!
ぱあ♥
THEN I'LL GUIDE YOU INTO MY STORYBOOK WORLD.
HERE WE GO!!
ぱあああああ

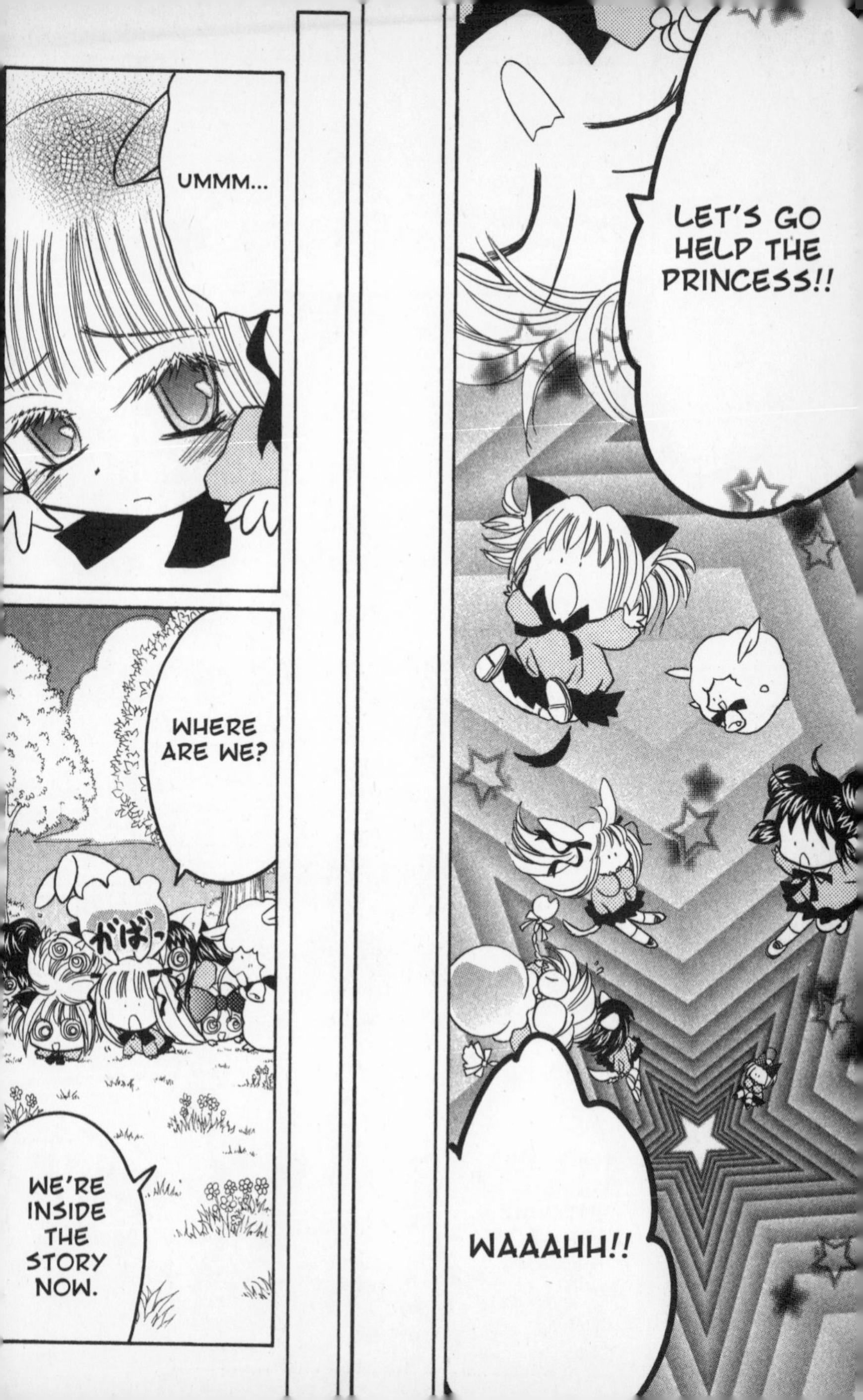
LET'S GO HELP THE PRINCESS!!
WAAAHH!!
UMMM...
WHERE ARE WE?
がばっ
WE'RE INSIDE THE STORY NOW.

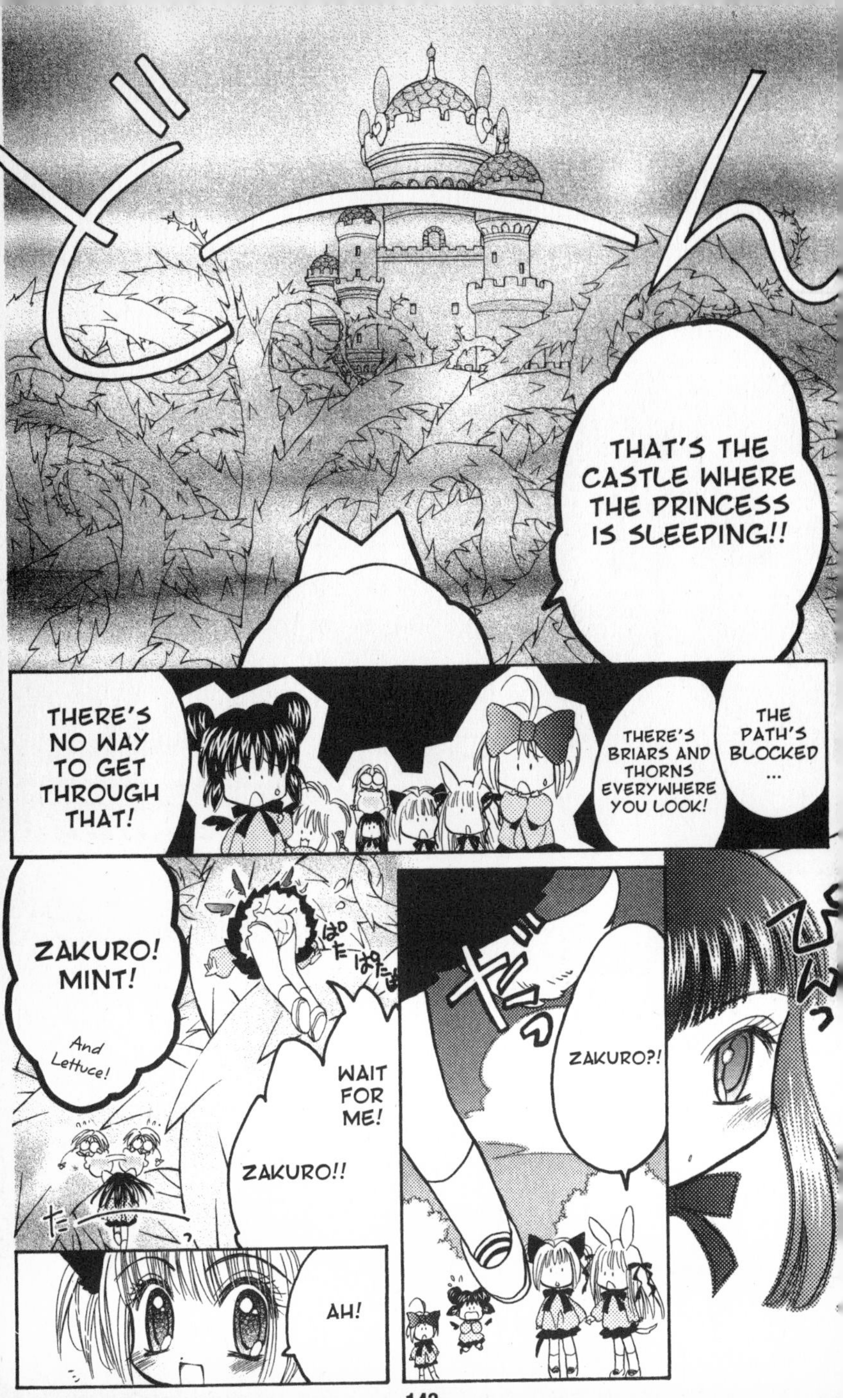

THAT'S THE CASTLE WHERE THE PRINCESS IS SLEEPING!!
THE PATH'S BLOCKED ...
THERE'S BRIARS AND THORNS EVERYWHERE YOU LOOK!
THERE'S NO WAY TO GET THROUGH THAT!
ZAKURO?!
WAIT FOR ME!
ZAKURO!!
ZAKURO! MINT!
And Lettuce!
AH!

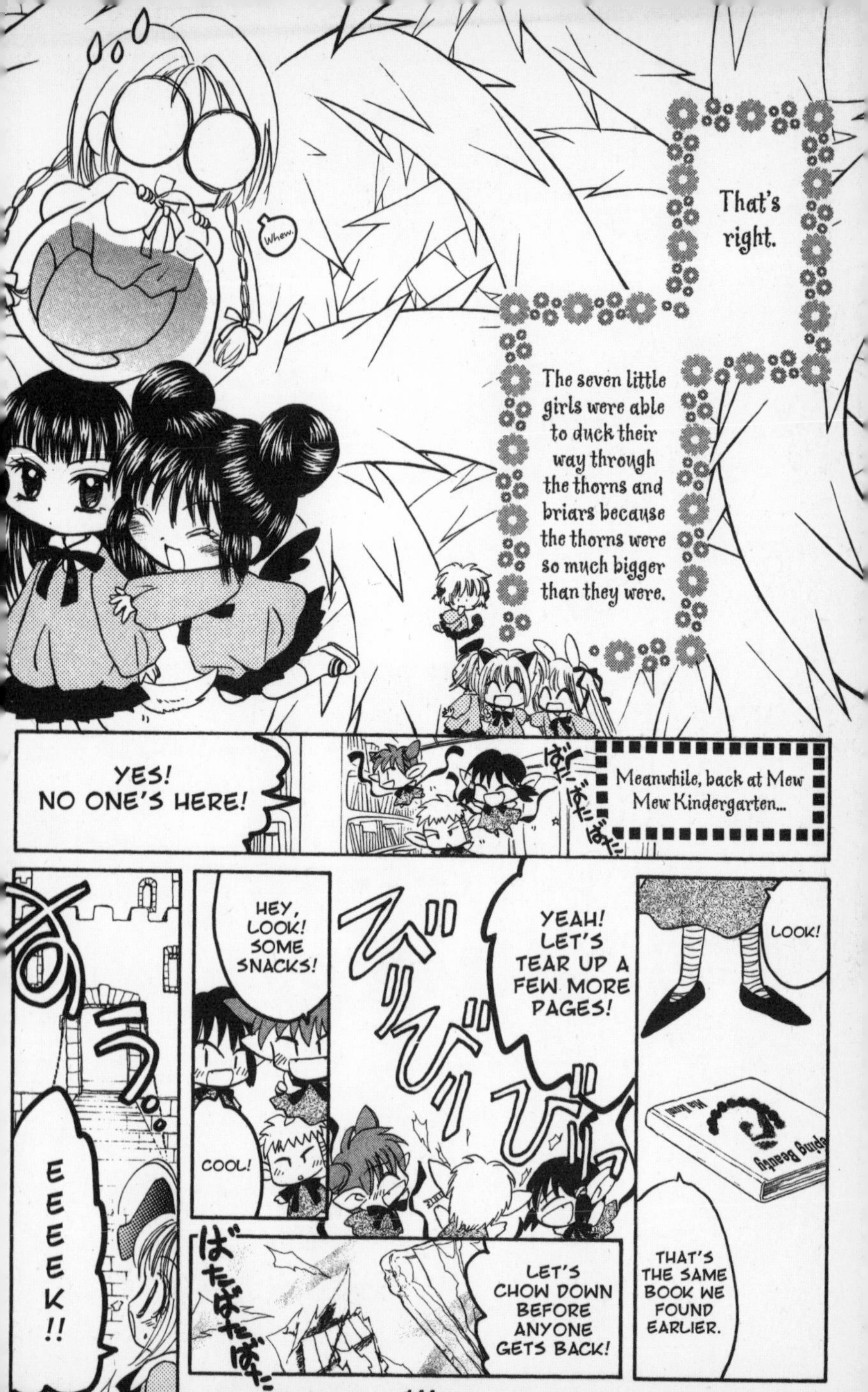
That's right.
The seven little girls were able to duck their way through the thorns and briars because the thorns were so much bigger than they were.
Whew.
Meanwhile, back at Mew Mew Kindergarten...
YES! NO ONE'S HERE!
LOOK!
THAT'S THE SAME BOOK WE FOUND EARLIER.
YEAH! LET'S TEAR UP A FEW MORE PAGES!
HEY, LOOK! SOME SNACKS!
COOL!
LET'S CHOW DOWN BEFORE ANYONE GETS BACK!
EEEEEK!!

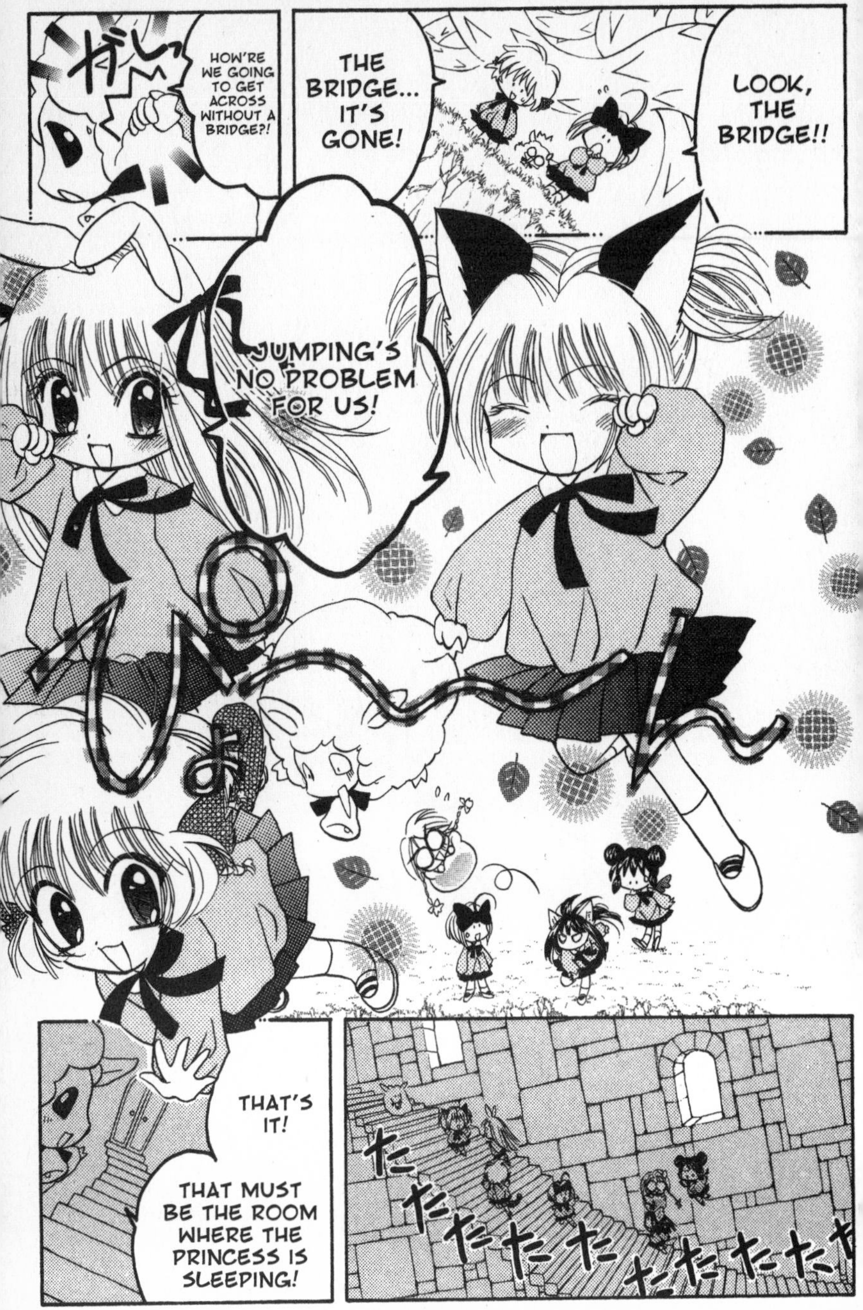
LOOK, THE BRIDGE!!
THE BRIDGE... IT'S GONE!
HOW'RE WE GOING TO GET ACROSS WITHOUT A BRIDGE?!
JUMPING'S NO PROBLEM FOR US!
THAT'S IT!
THAT MUST BE THE ROOM WHERE THE PRINCESS IS SLEEPING!

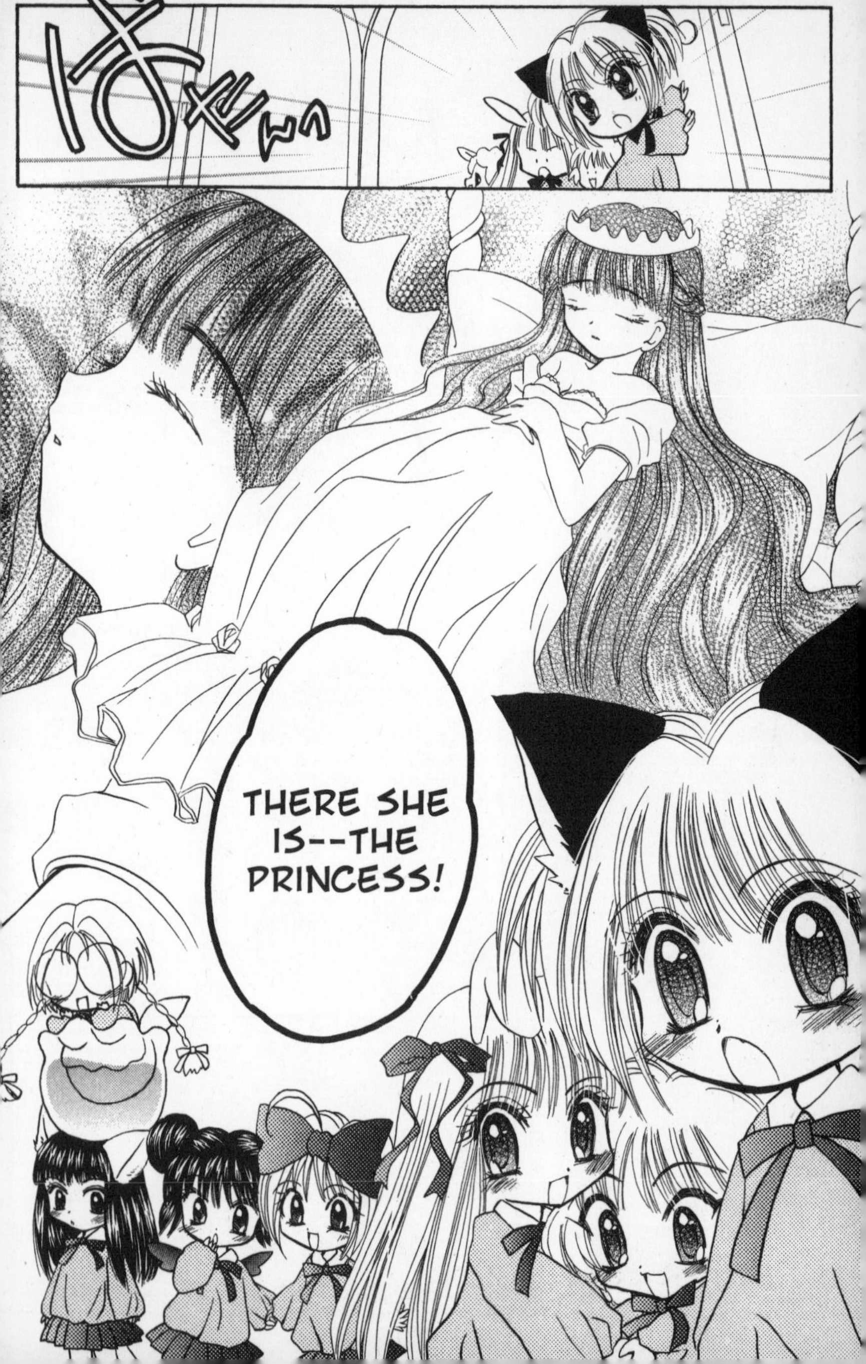
THERE SHE IS--THE PRINCESS!

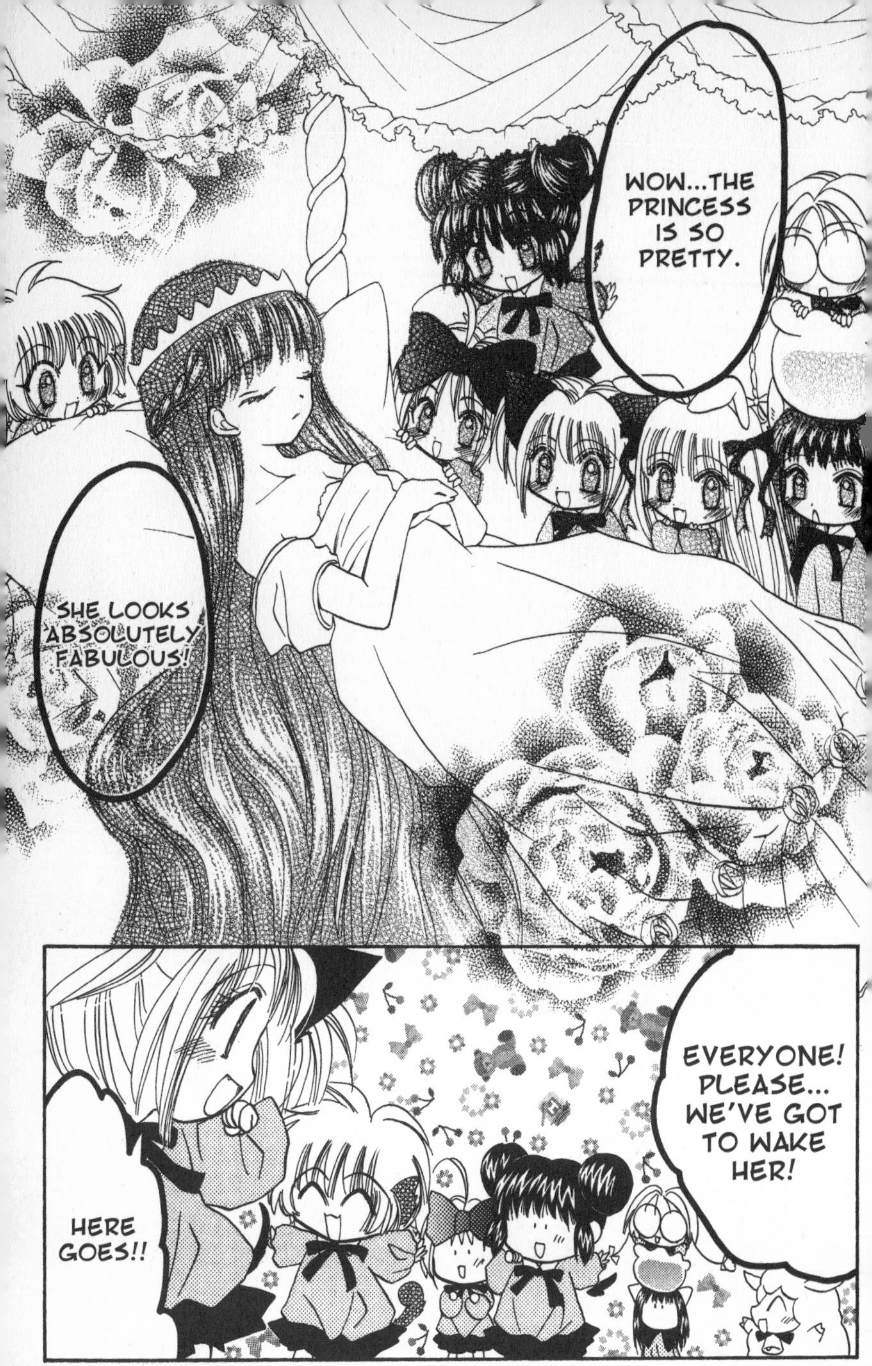
WOW...THE PRINCESS IS SO PRETTY.
SHE LOOKS ABSOLUTELY FABULOUS!
EVERYONE! PLEASE... WE'VE GOT TO WAKE HER!
HERE GOES!!

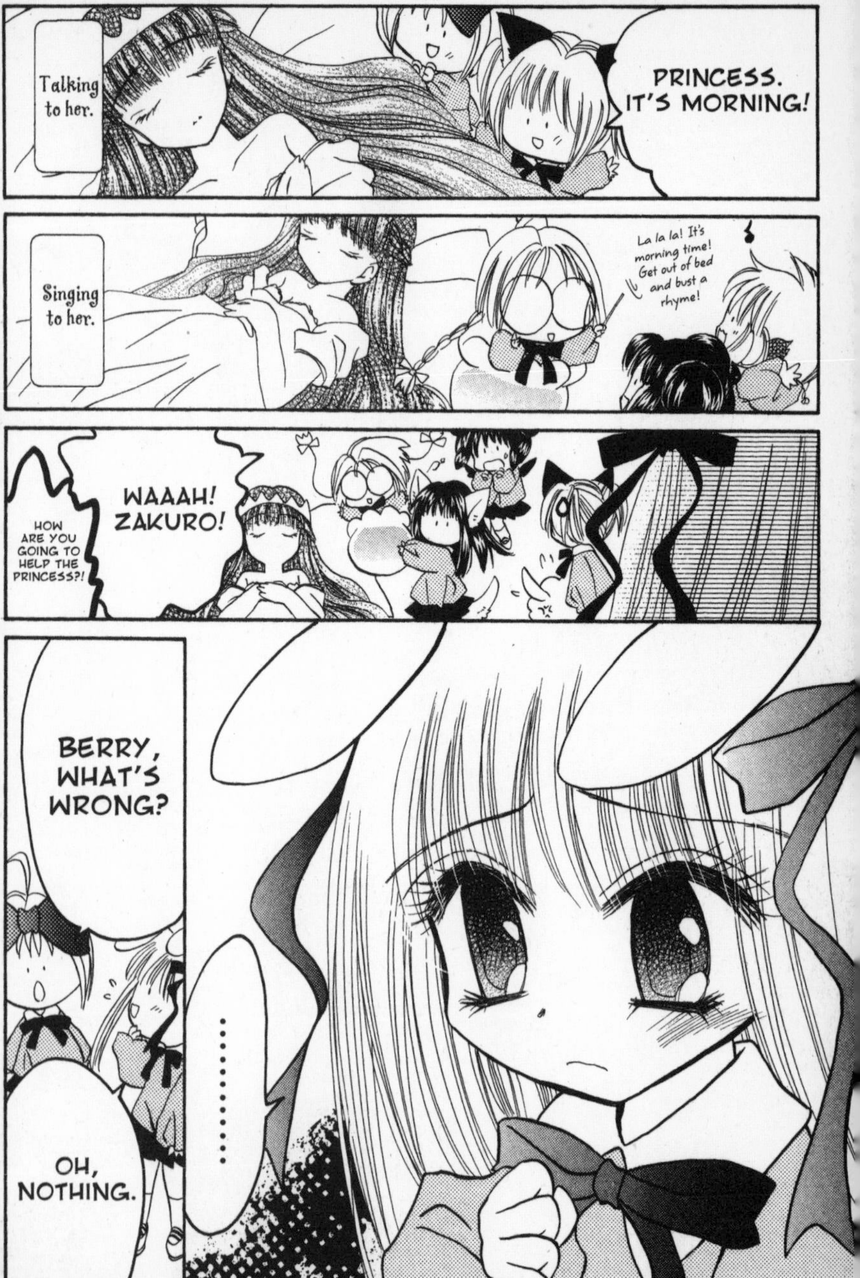
PRINCESS. IT'S MORNING!
Talking to her.
La la la! It's morning time! Get out of bed and bust a rhyme!
Singing to her.
WAAAH! ZAKURO!
HOW ARE YOU GOING TO HELP THE PRINCESS?!
......
BERRY, WHAT'S WRONG?
OH, NOTHING.

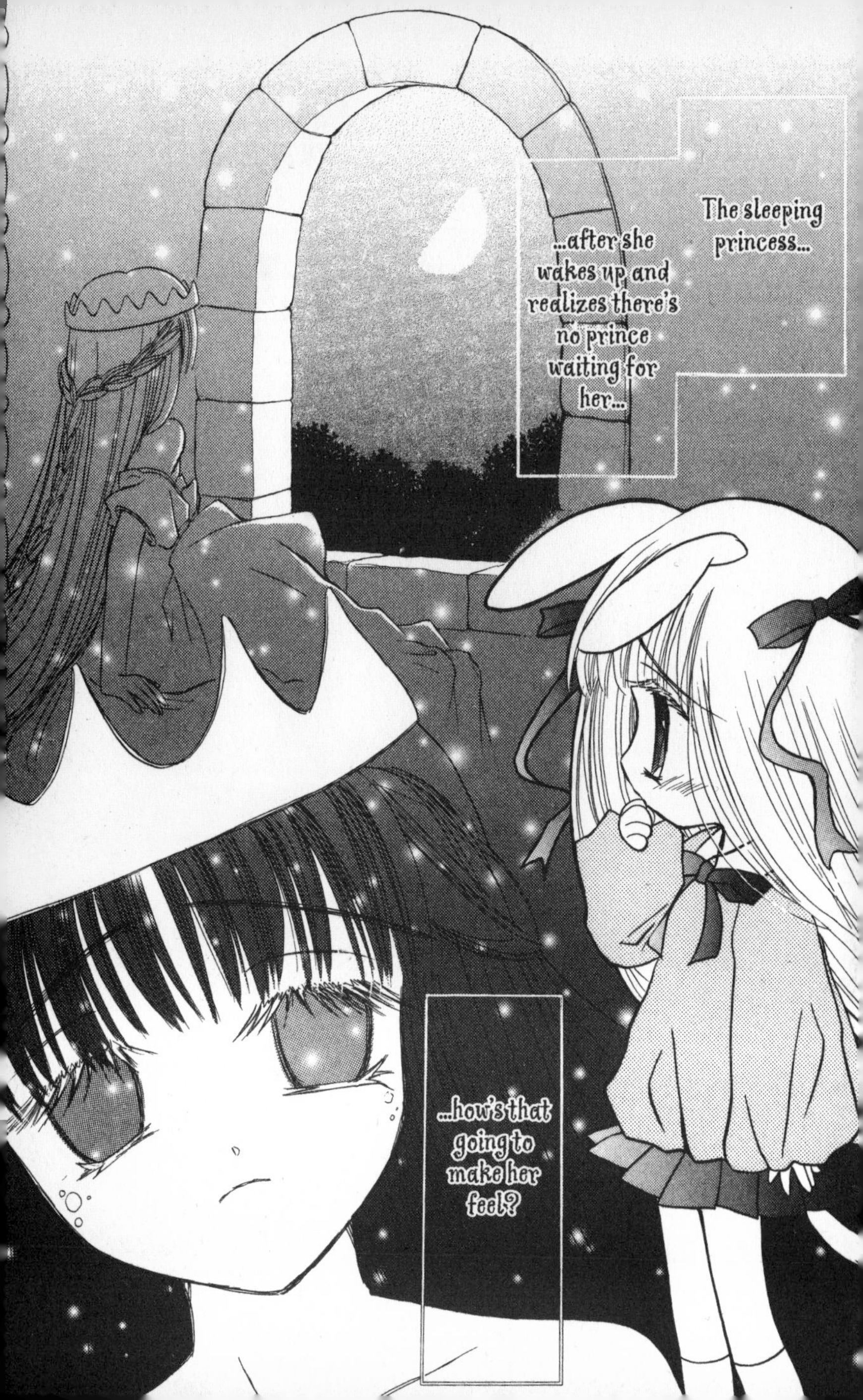
The sleeping princess...
...after she wakes up and realizes there's no prince waiting for her...
...how's that going to make her feel?

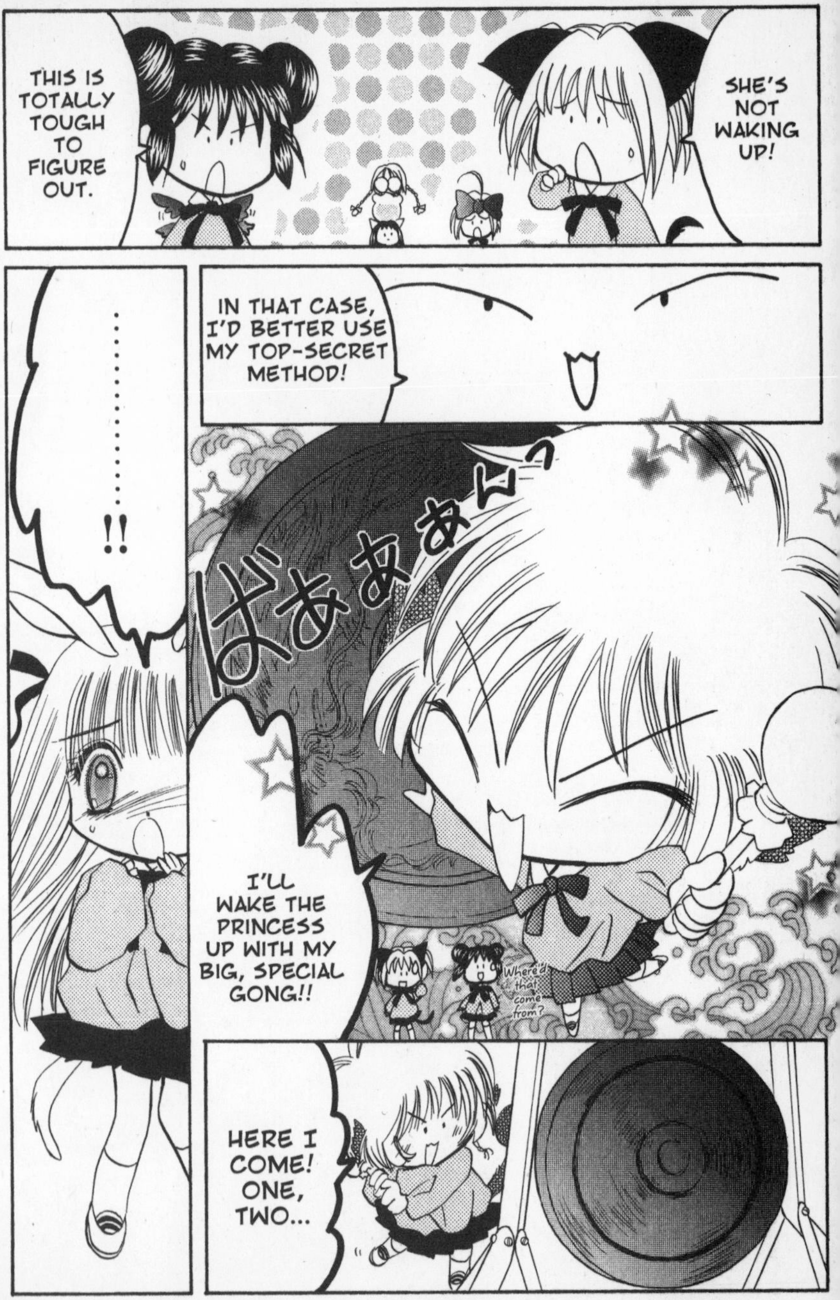
SHE'S NOT WAKING UP!
THIS IS TOTALLY TOUGH TO FIGURE OUT.
IN THAT CASE, I'D BETTER USE MY TOP-SECRET METHOD!
ばぁぁぁあんっ
I'LL WAKE THE PRINCESS UP WITH MY BIG, SPECIAL GONG!!
Where'd that come from?
......!!
HERE I COME! ONE, TWO...

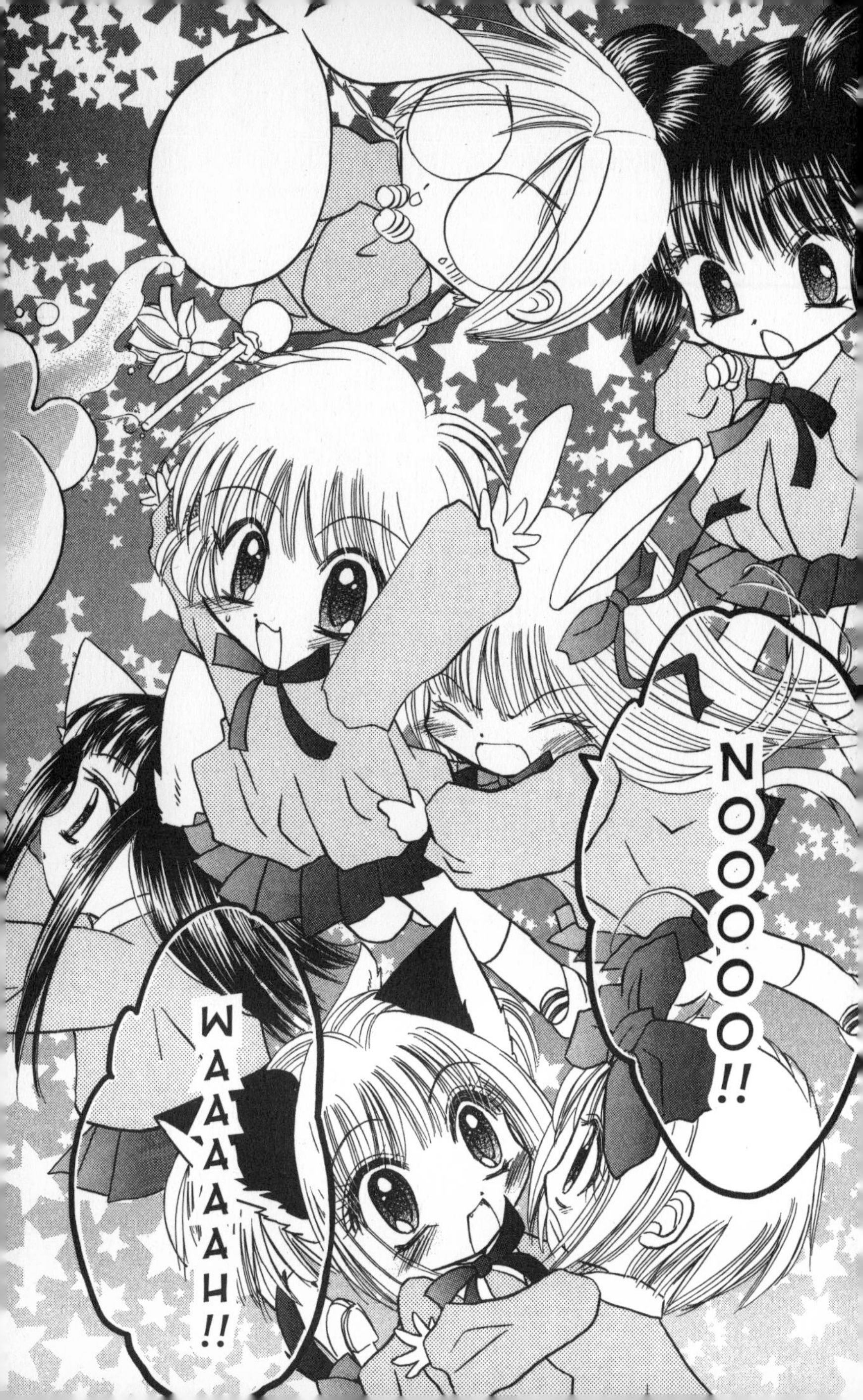
NOOOOOO!!
WAAAAAAH!!

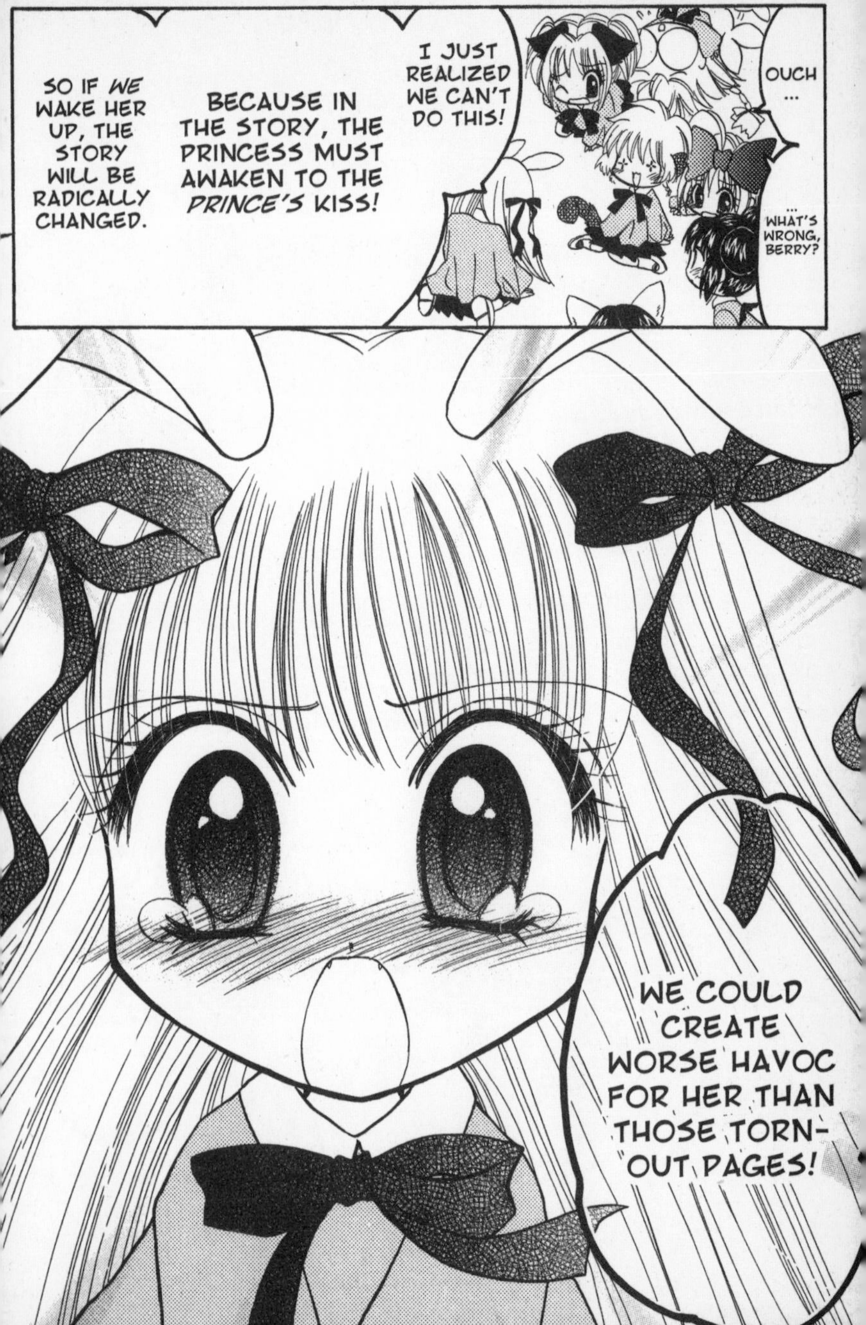
OUCH ...
... WHAT'S WRONG, BERRY?
I JUST REALIZED WE CAN'T DO THIS!
BECAUSE IN THE STORY, THE PRINCESS MUST AWAKEN TO THE *PRINCE'S* KISS!
SO IF *WE* WAKE HER UP, THE STORY WILL BE RADICALLY CHANGED.
WE COULD CREATE WORSE HAVOC FOR HER THAN THOSE TORN-OUT PAGES!

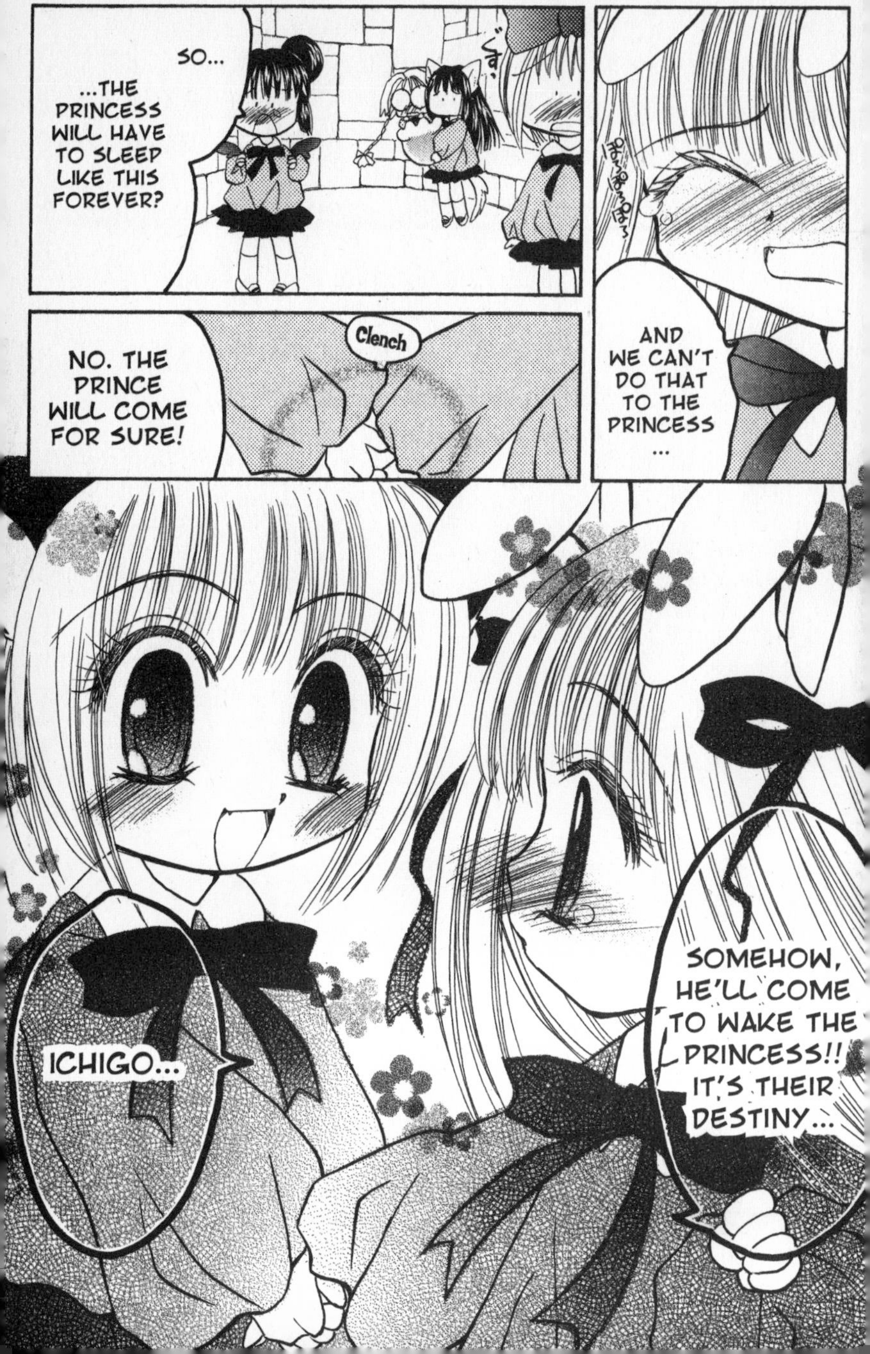
SO...
...THE PRINCESS WILL HAVE TO SLEEP LIKE THIS FOREVER?
AND WE CAN'T DO THAT TO THE PRINCESS ...
Clench
NO. THE PRINCE WILL COME FOR SURE!
SOMEHOW, HE'LL COME TO WAKE THE PRINCESS!! IT'S THEIR DESTINY...
ICHIGO...

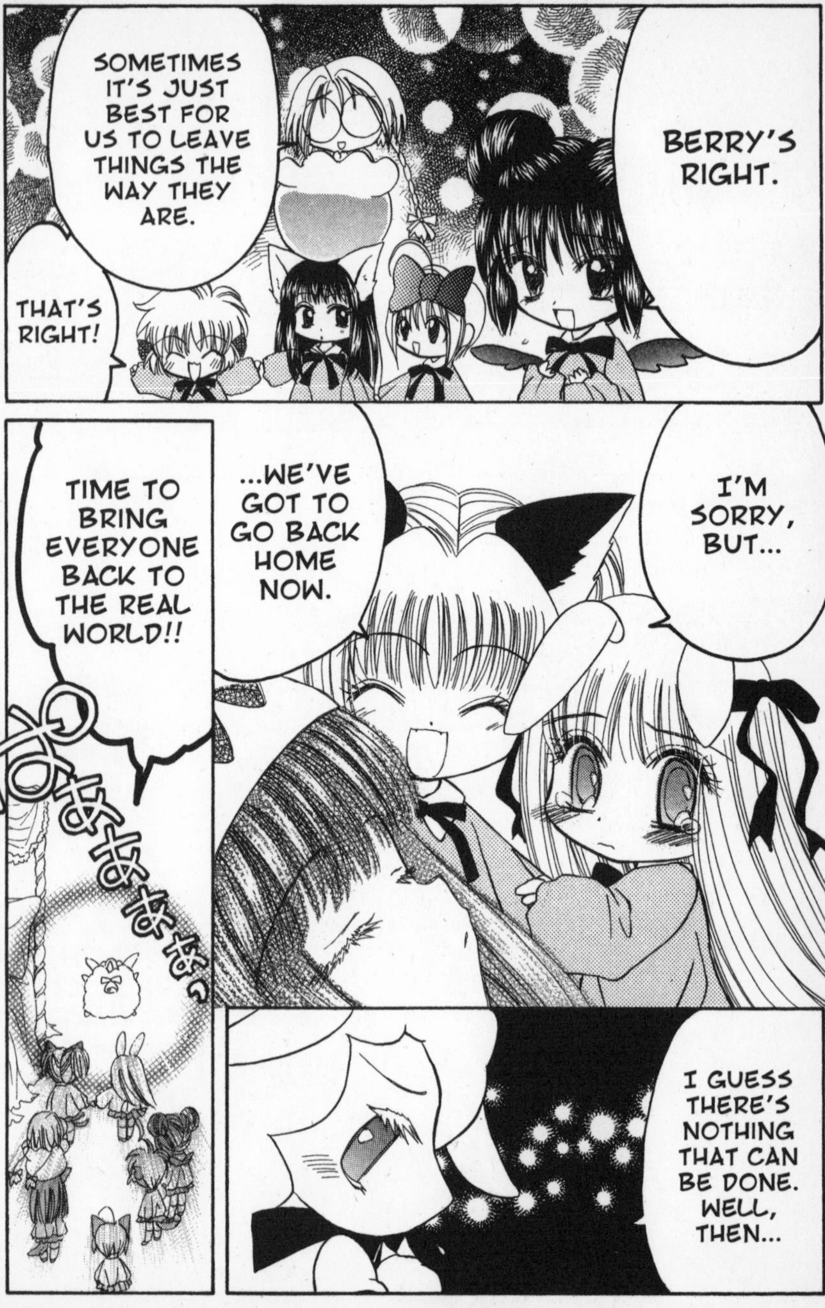
BERRY'S RIGHT.
SOMETIMES IT'S JUST BEST FOR US TO LEAVE THINGS THE WAY THEY ARE.
THAT'S RIGHT!
I'M SORRY, BUT...
...WE'VE GOT TO GO BACK HOME NOW.
I GUESS THERE'S NOTHING THAT CAN BE DONE. WELL, THEN...
TIME TO BRING EVERYONE BACK TO THE REAL WORLD!!

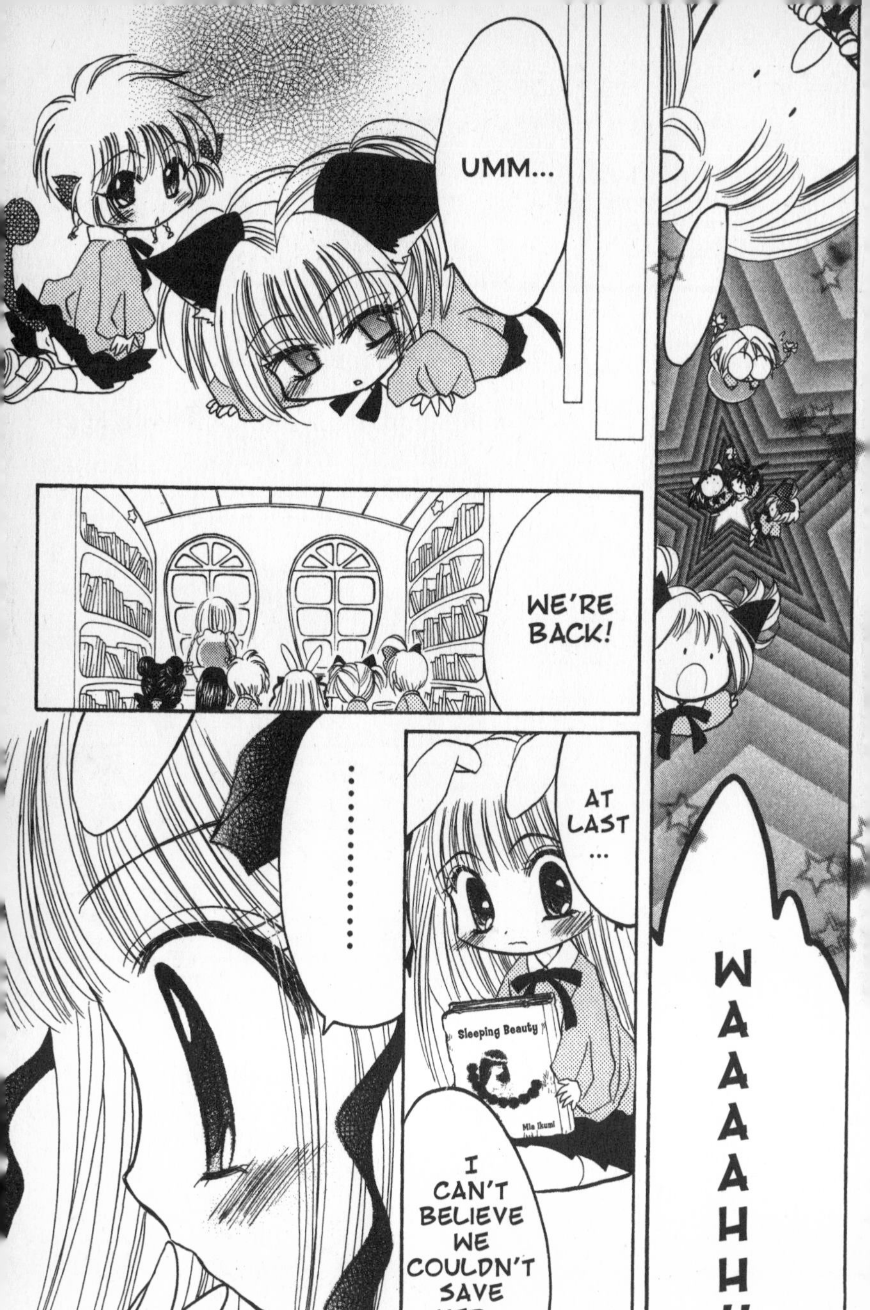
UMM...
WE'RE BACK!
AT LAST ...
I CAN'T BELIEVE WE COULDN'T SAVE HER...
Sleeping Beauty
Mia Ikumi
....
WAAAAAHH!!

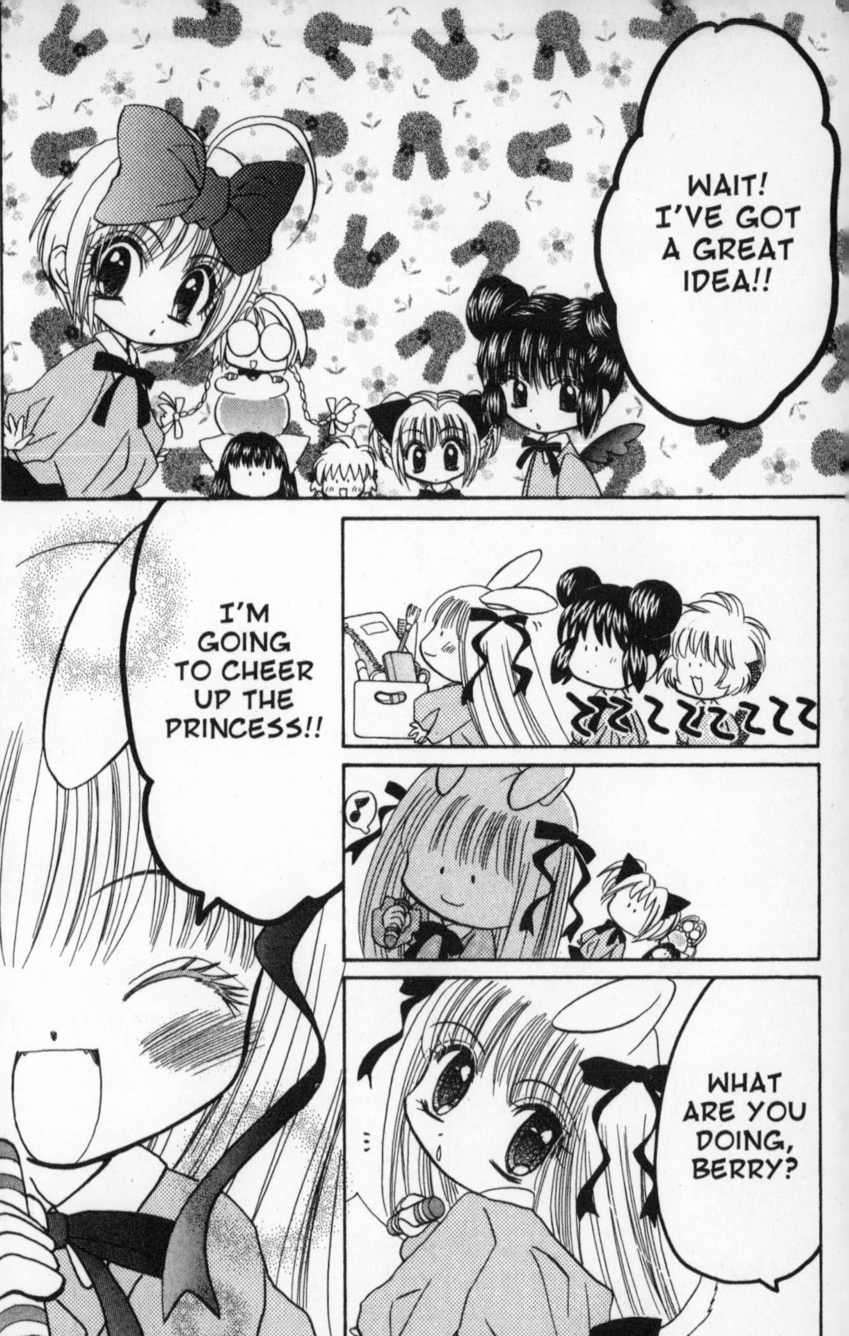
WAIT! I'VE GOT A GREAT IDEA!!
I'M GOING TO CHEER UP THE PRINCESS!!
WHAT ARE YOU DOING, BERRY?

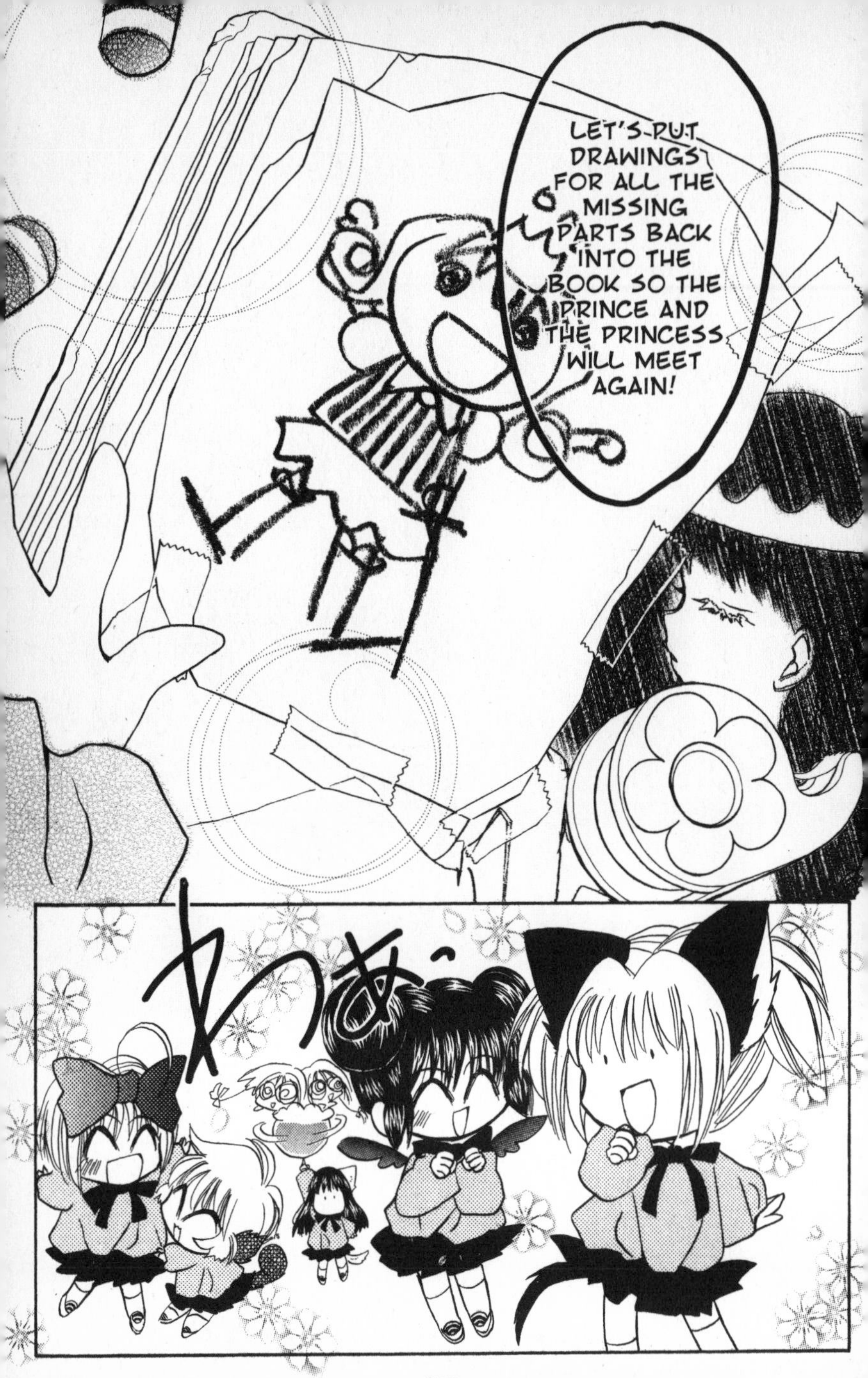
LET'S PUT DRAWINGS FOR ALL THE MISSING PARTS BACK INTO THE BOOK SO THE PRINCE AND THE PRINCESS WILL MEET AGAIN!
わぁ～

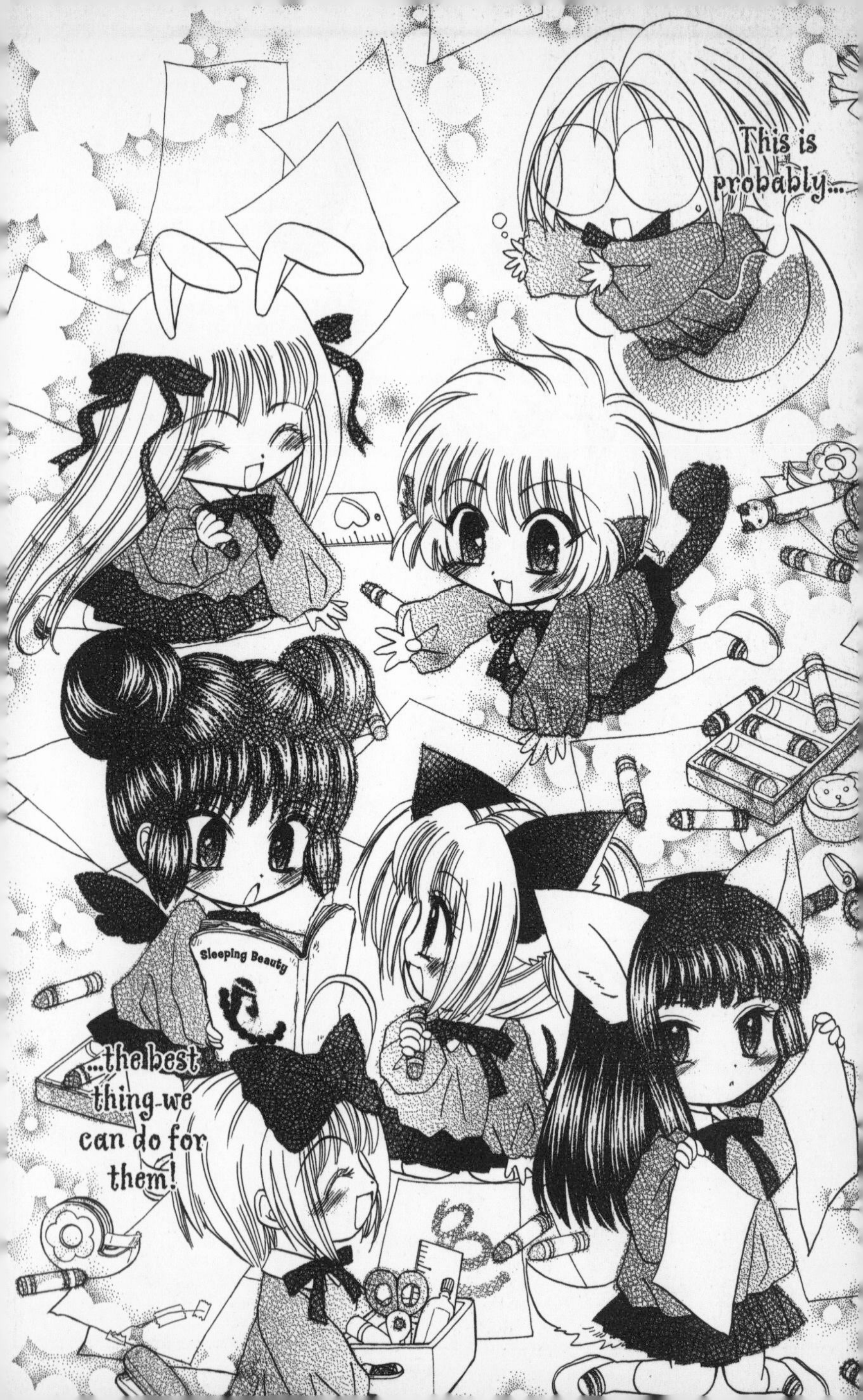
This is probably...
Sleeping Beauty
...the best thing we can do for them!

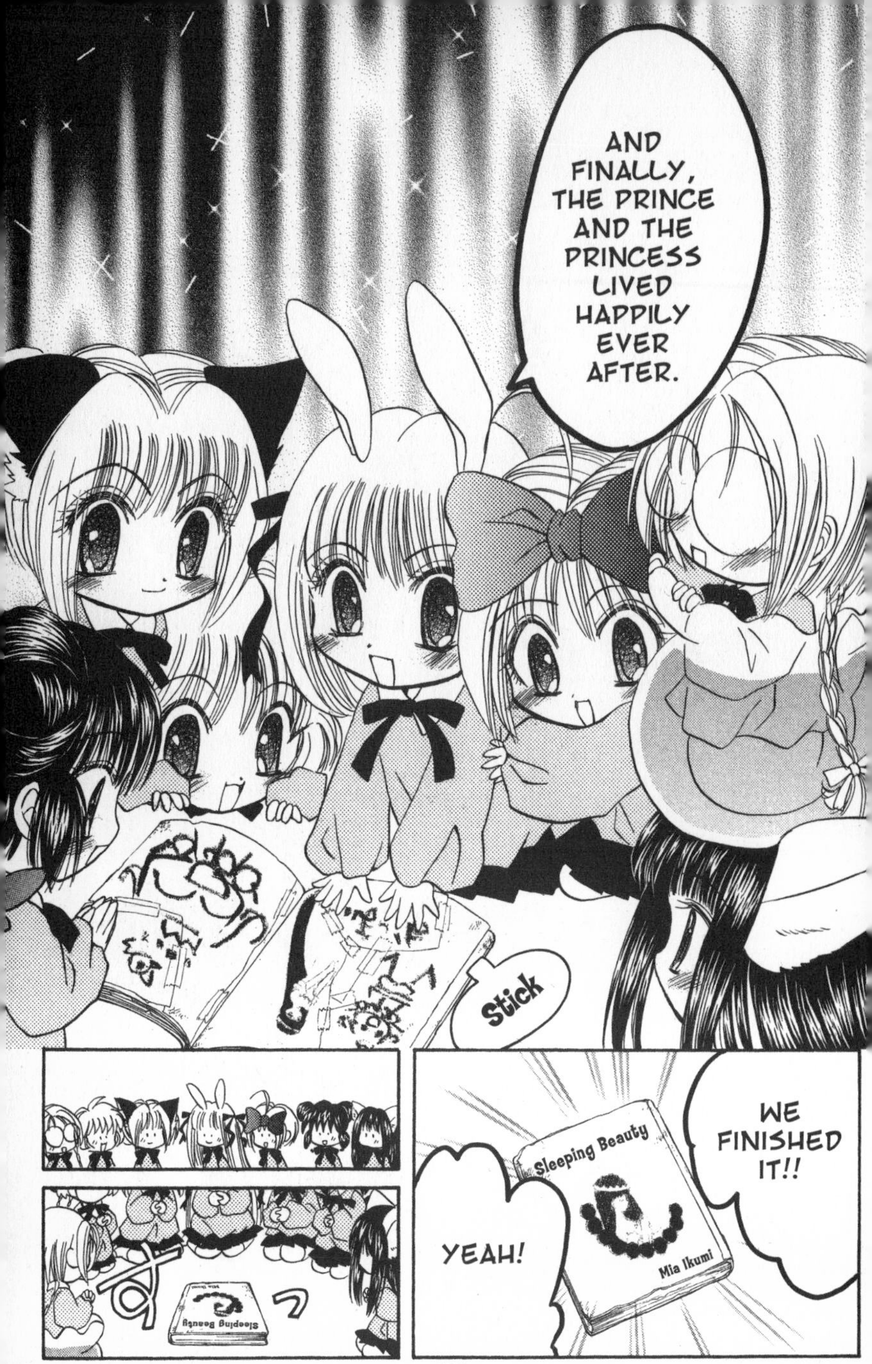
AND FINALLY, THE PRINCE AND THE PRINCESS LIVED HAPPILY EVER AFTER.
Stick
Sleeping Beauty
Sleeping Beauty
Mia Ikumi
WE FINISHED IT!!
YEAH!

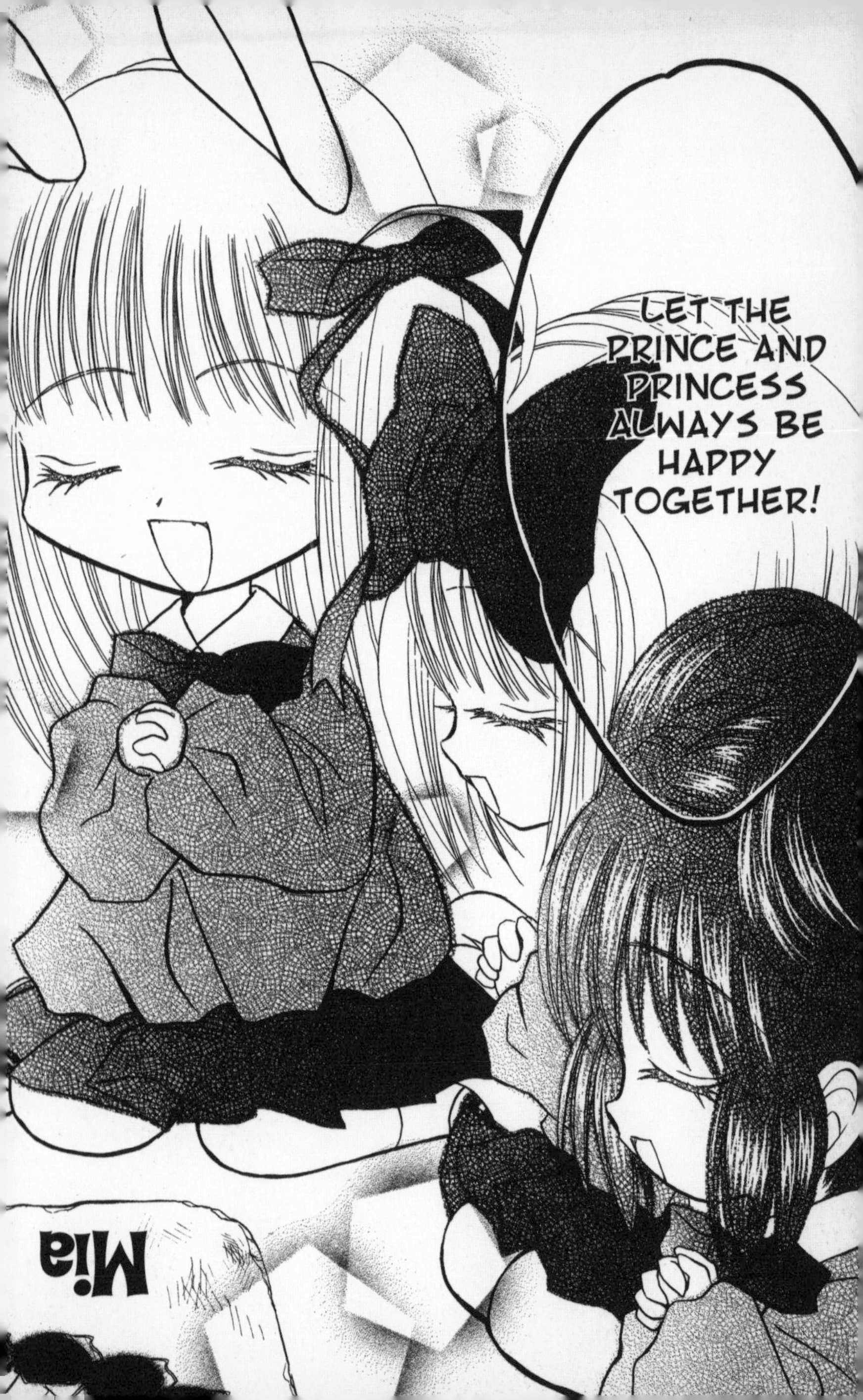
LET THE PRINCE AND PRINCESS ALWAYS BE HAPPY TOGETHER!
Mia

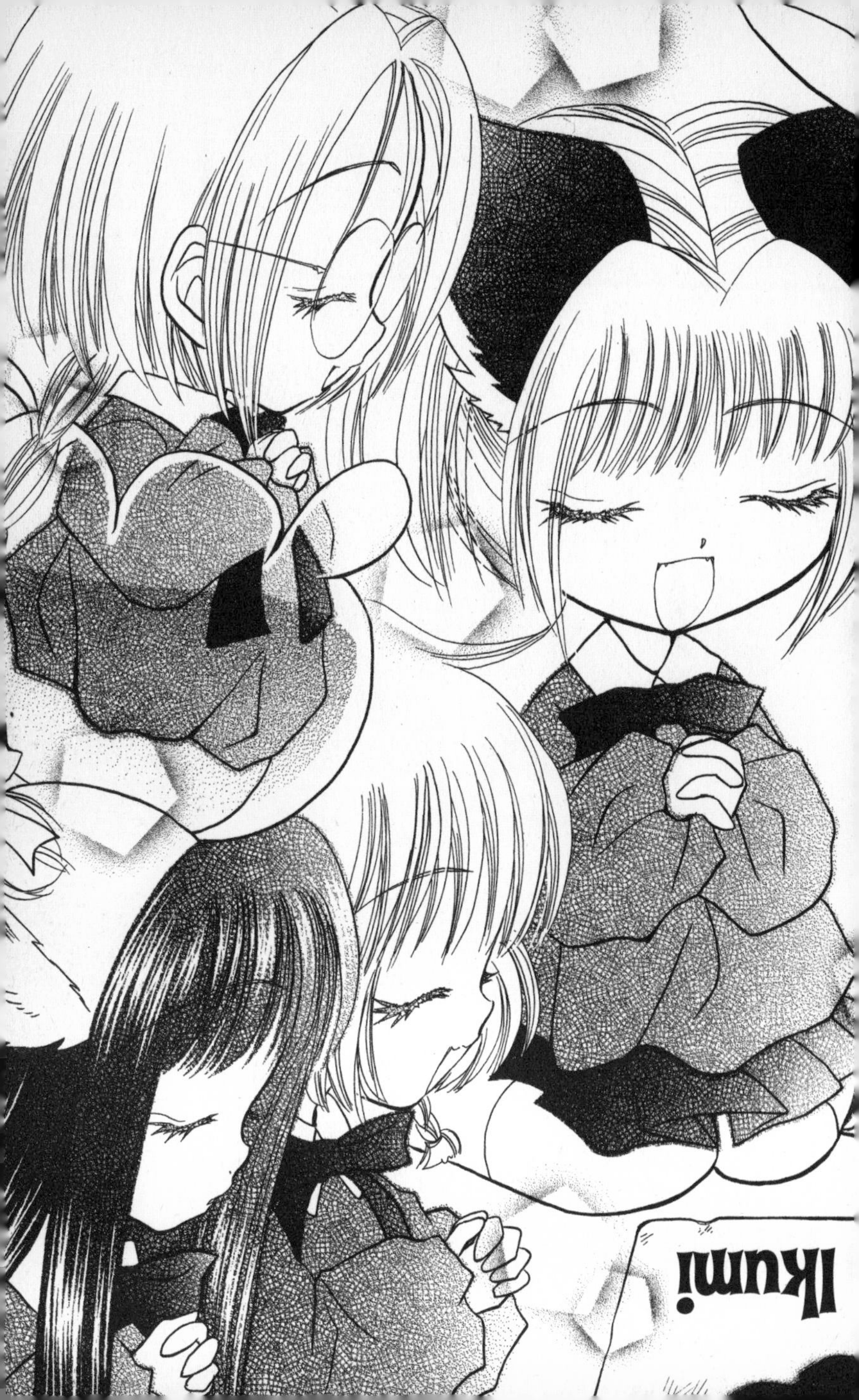
Ikumi

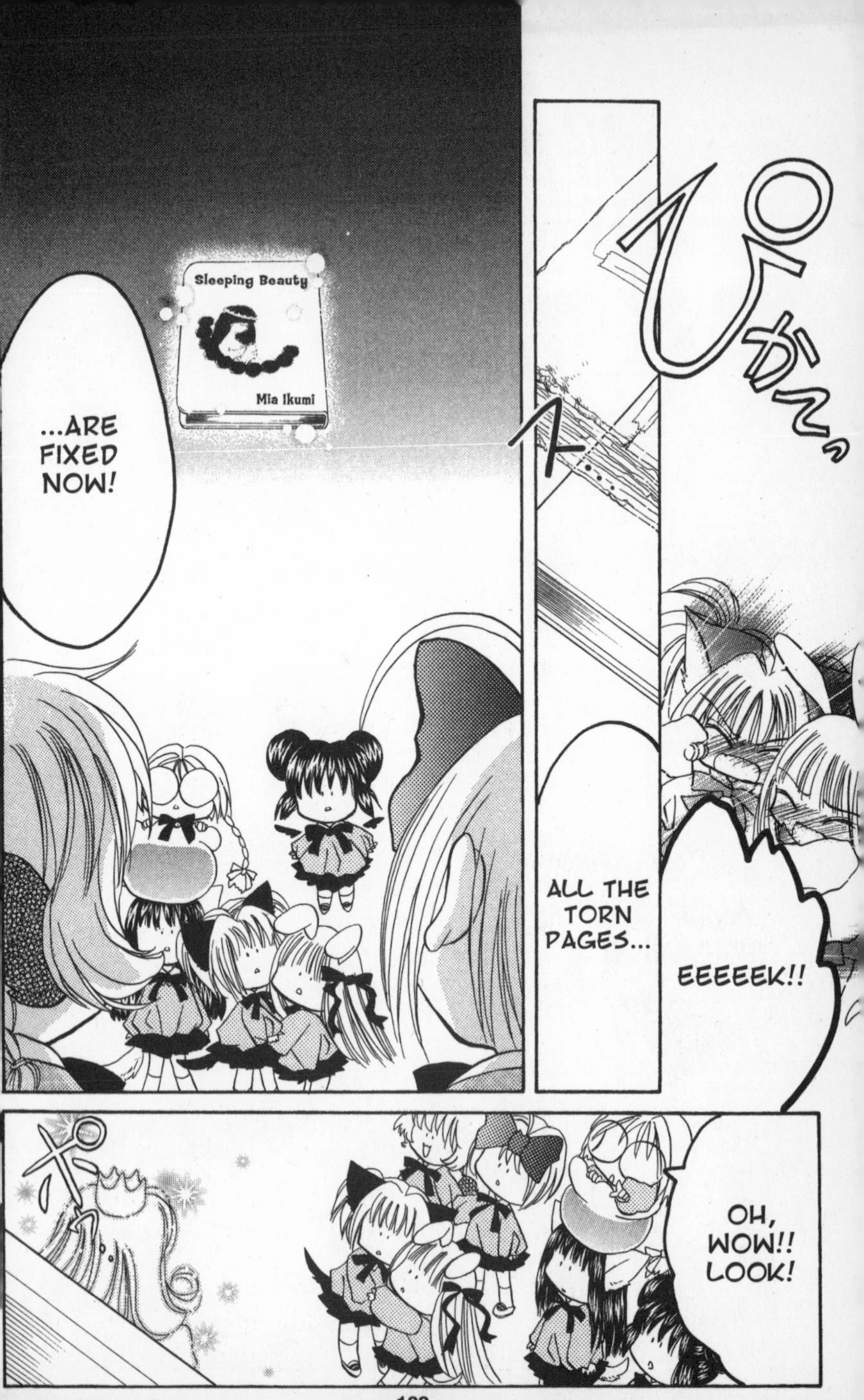
EEEEEK!!
ALL THE TORN PAGES...
...ARE FIXED NOW!
Sleeping Beauty
Mia Ikumi
OH, WOW!! LOOK!

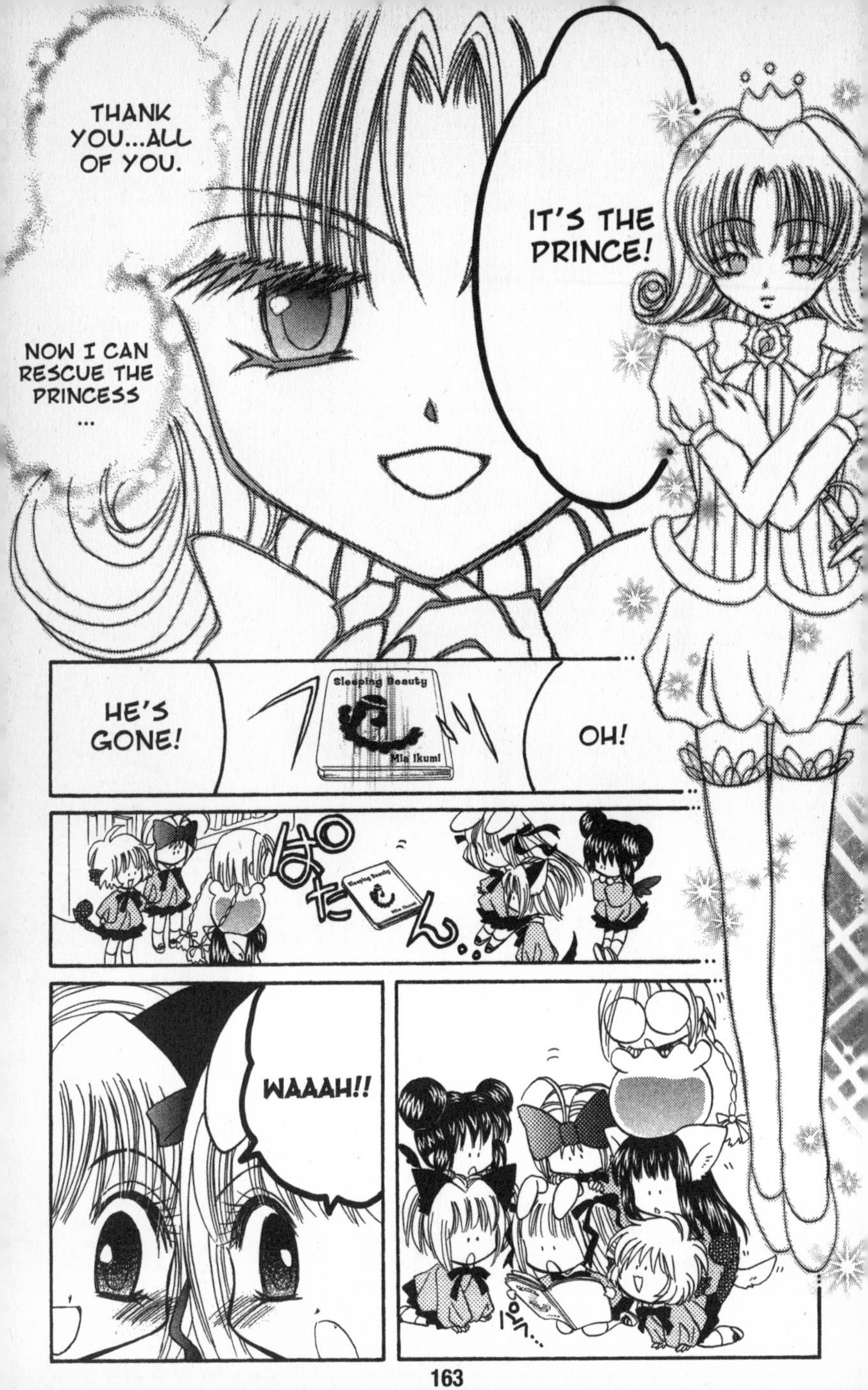
IT'S THE PRINCE!
THANK YOU...ALL OF YOU.
NOW I CAN RESCUE THE PRINCESS ...
OH!
Sleeping Beauty
Mia Ikumi
HE'S GONE!
ぱたん
WAAAH!!

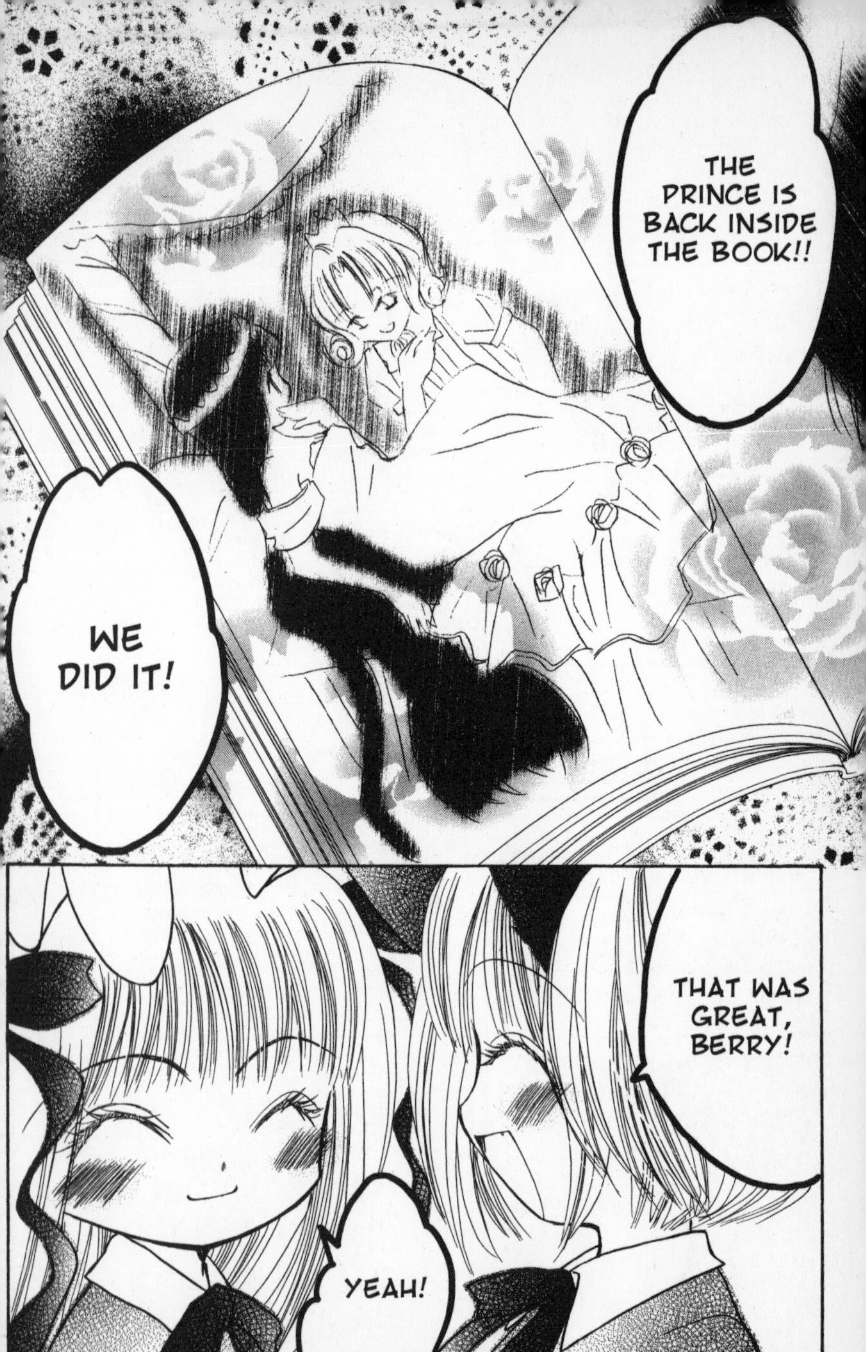
THE PRINCE IS BACK INSIDE THE BOOK!!
WE DID IT!
THAT WAS GREAT, BERRY!
YEAH!

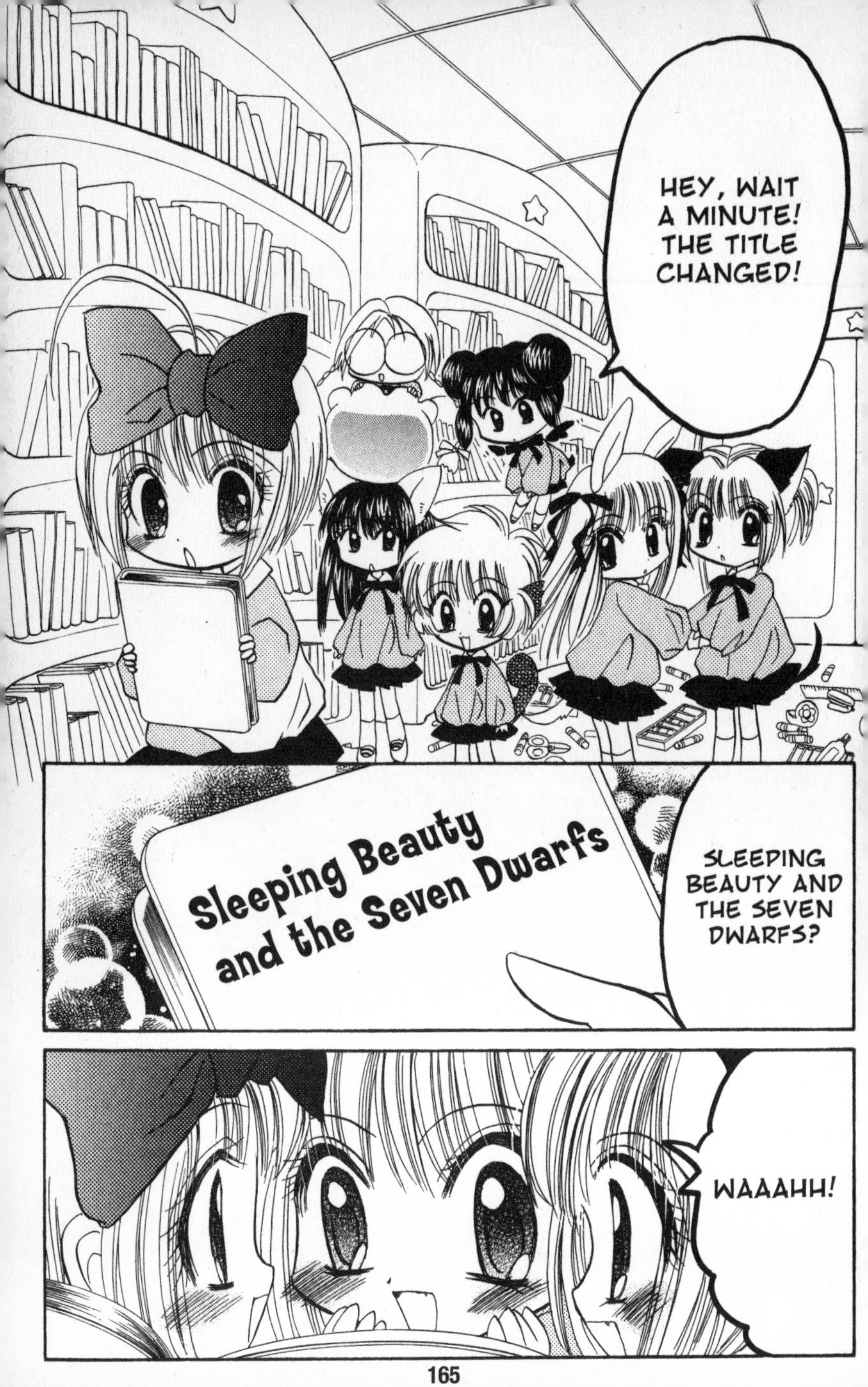
HEY, WAIT A MINUTE! THE TITLE CHANGED!
Sleeping Beauty and the Seven Dwarfs
SLEEPING BEAUTY AND THE SEVEN DWARFS?
WAAAHH!

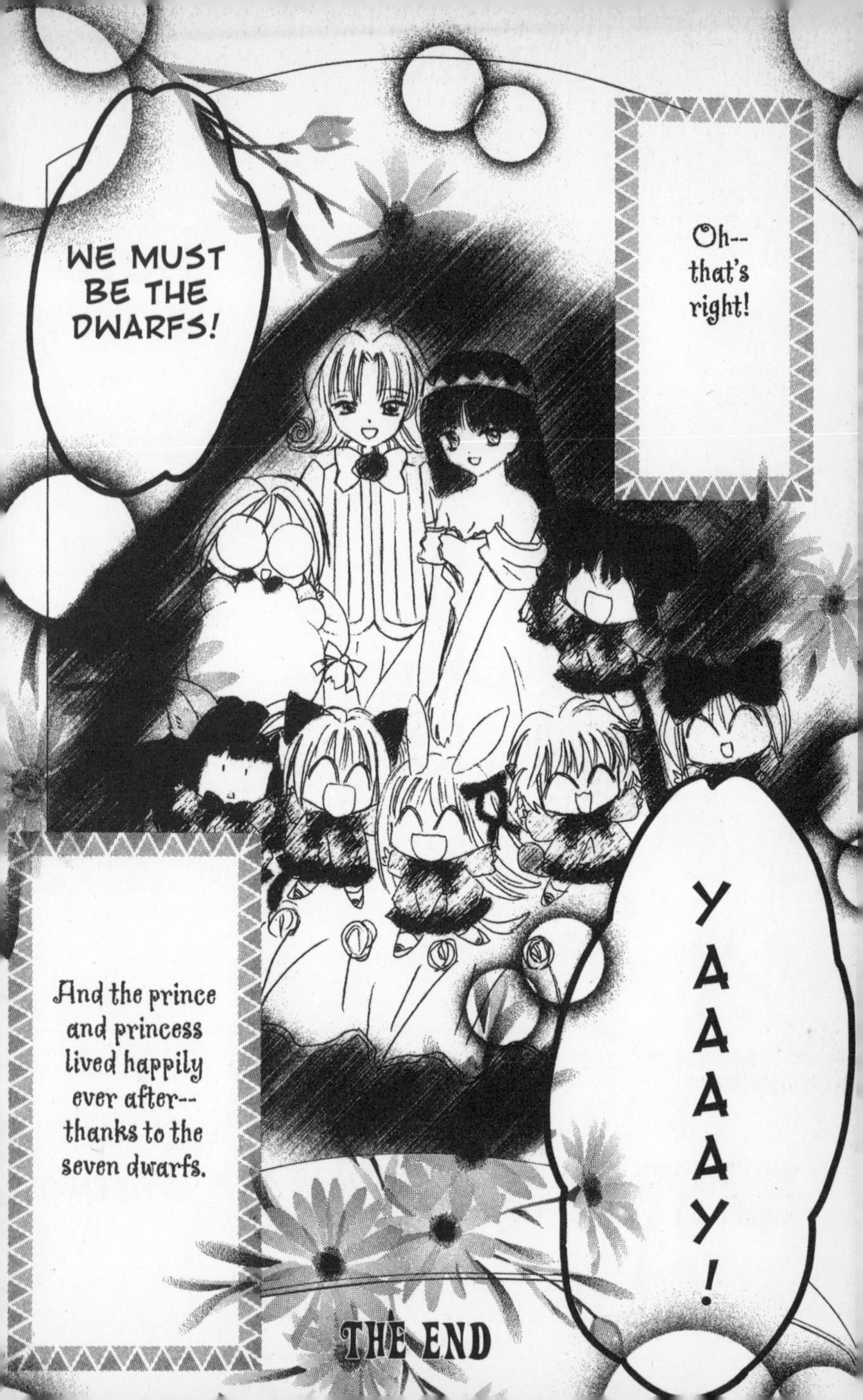
Oh--
that's
right!
WE MUST
BE THE
DWARFS!
And the prince
and princess
lived happily
ever after--
thanks to the
seven dwarfs.
YAAAAY!
THE END

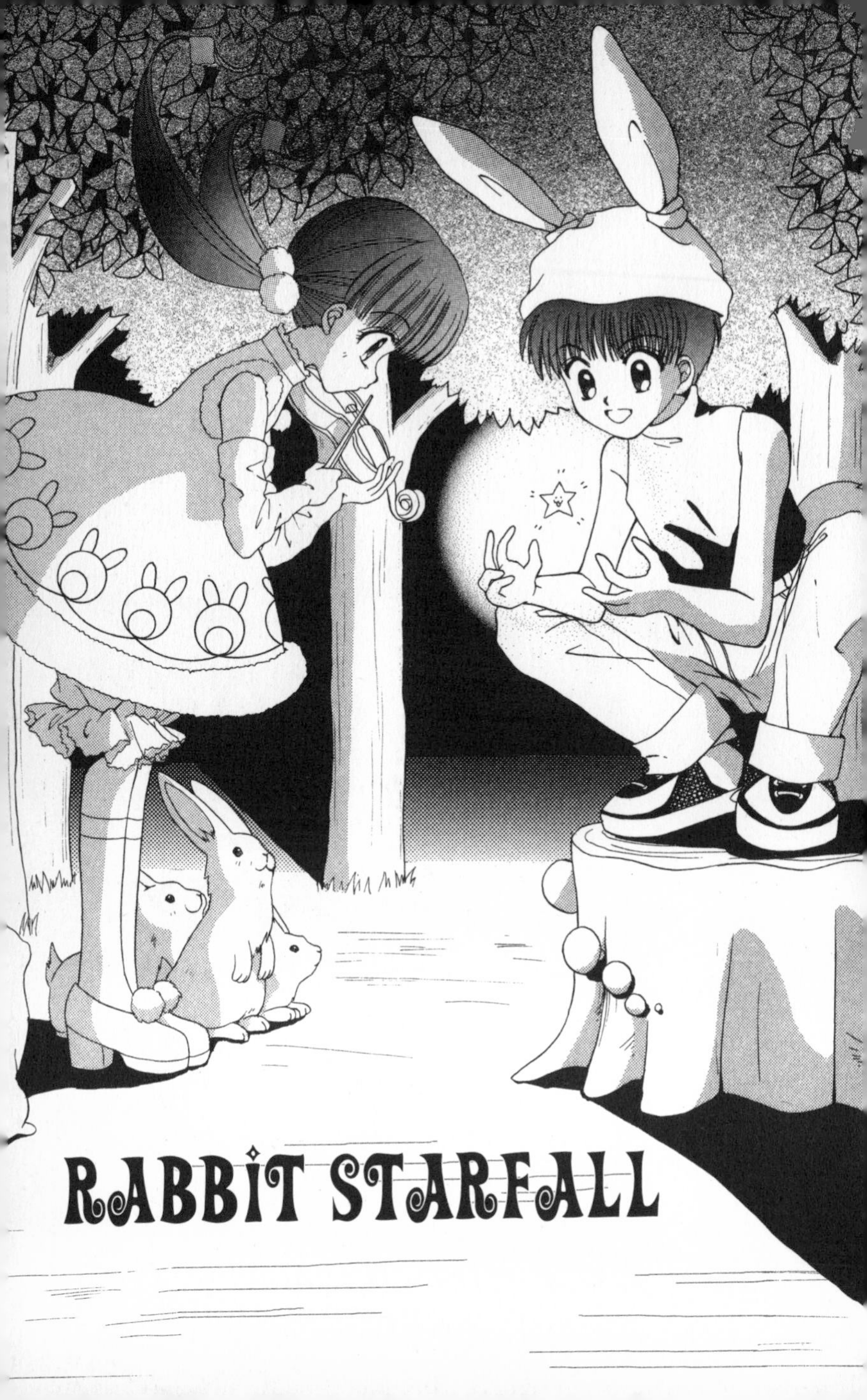
RABBIT STARFALL

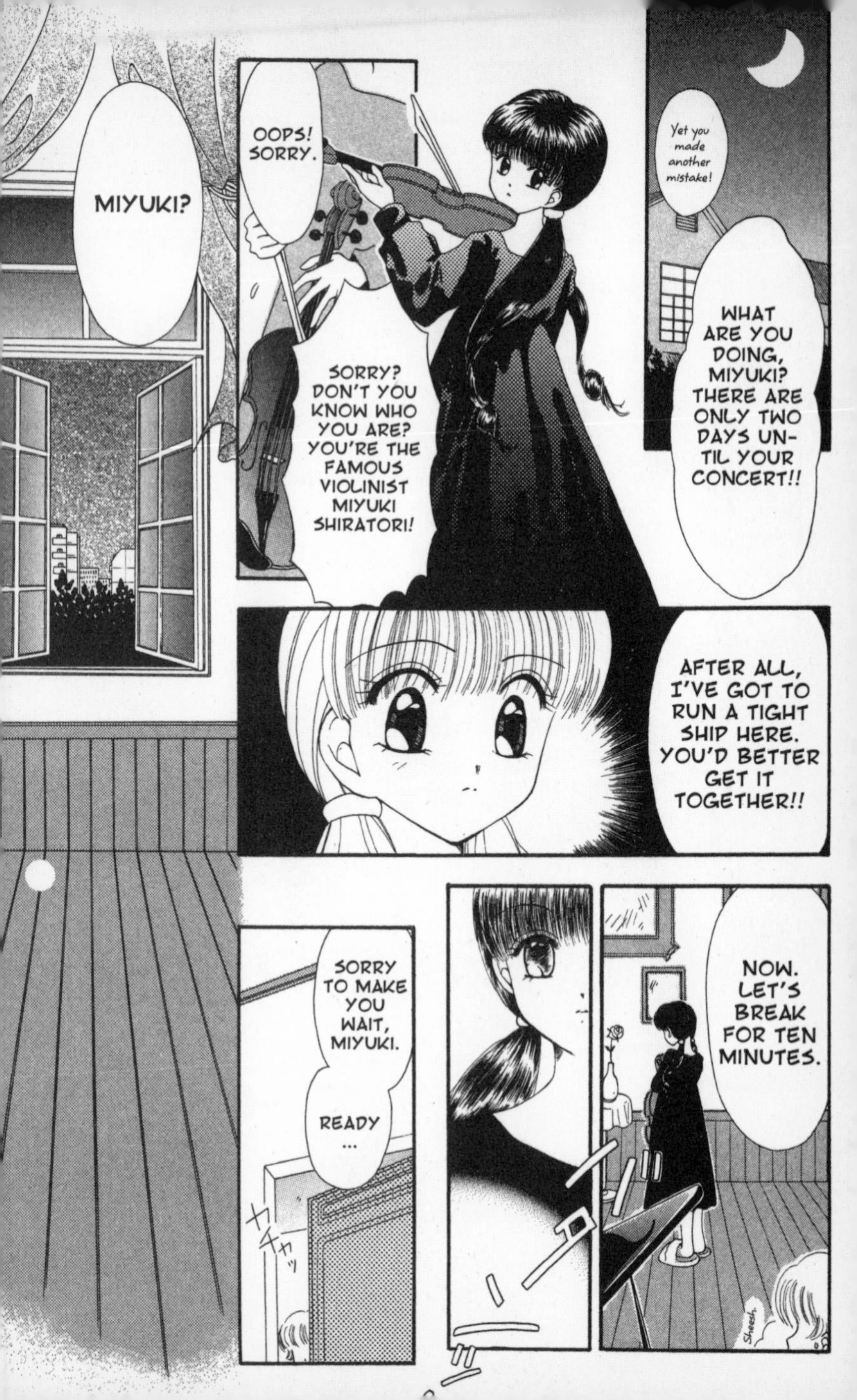
Yet you made another mistake!
WHAT ARE YOU DOING, MIYUKI? THERE ARE ONLY TWO DAYS UN-TIL YOUR CONCERT!!
OOPS! SORRY.
SORRY? DON'T YOU KNOW WHO YOU ARE? YOU'RE THE FAMOUS VIOLINIST MIYUKI SHIRATORI!
AFTER ALL, I'VE GOT TO RUN A TIGHT SHIP HERE. YOU'D BETTER GET IT TOGETHER!!
MIYUKI?
NOW. LET'S BREAK FOR TEN MINUTES.
Sheesh.
SORRY TO MAKE YOU WAIT, MIYUKI.
READY ...

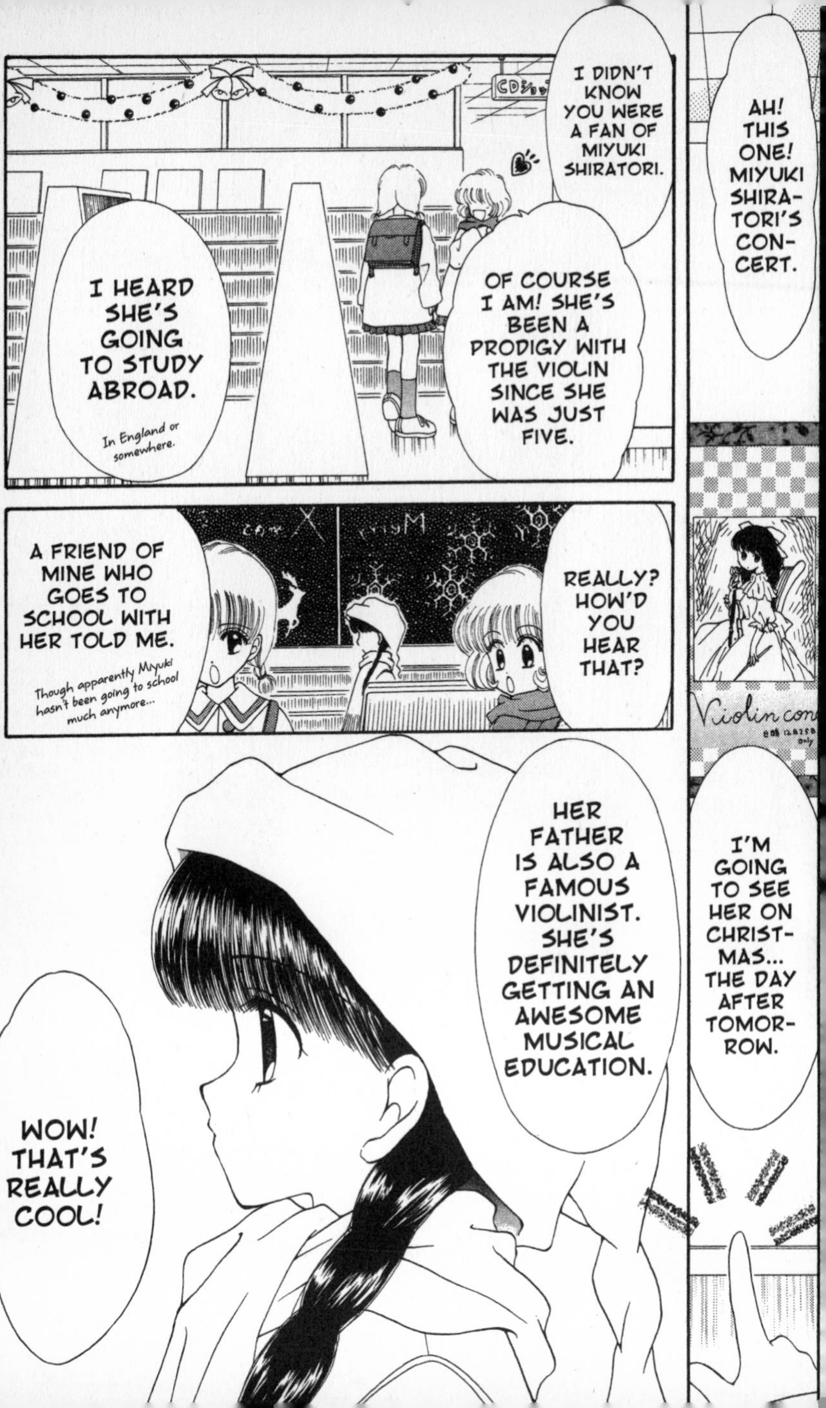
AH! THIS ONE! MIYUKI SHIRA-TORI'S CON-CERT.
I'M GOING TO SEE HER ON CHRIST-MAS... THE DAY AFTER TOMOR-ROW.
I DIDN'T KNOW YOU WERE A FAN OF MIYUKI SHIRATORI.
OF COURSE I AM! SHE'S BEEN A PRODIGY WITH THE VIOLIN SINCE SHE WAS JUST FIVE.
I HEARD SHE'S GOING TO STUDY ABROAD.
In England or somewhere.
REALLY? HOW'D YOU HEAR THAT?
A FRIEND OF MINE WHO GOES TO SCHOOL WITH HER TOLD ME.
Though apparently Miyuki hasn't been going to school much anymore...
HER FATHER IS ALSO A FAMOUS VIOLINIST. SHE'S DEFINITELY GETTING AN AWESOME MUSICAL EDUCATION.
WOW! THAT'S REALLY COOL!

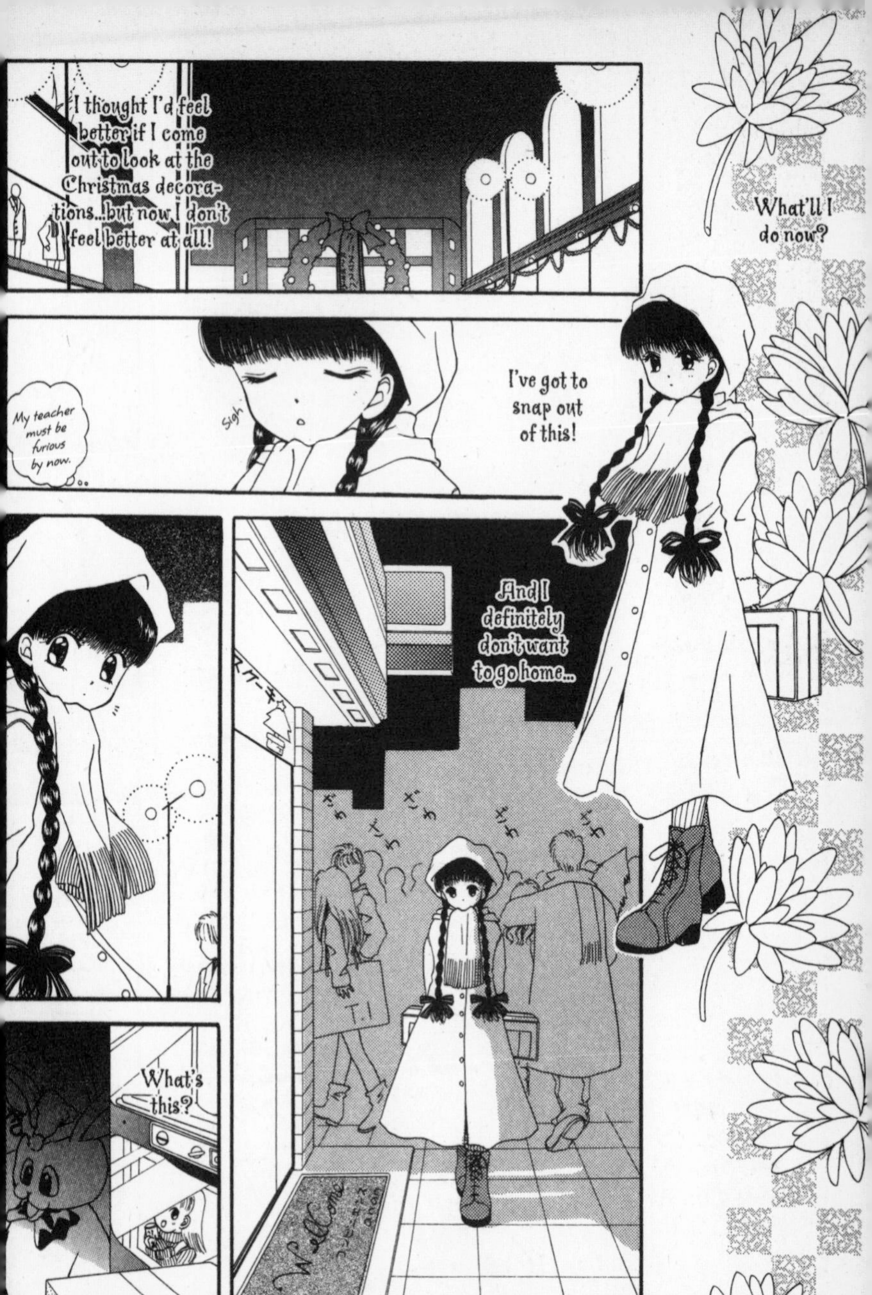
I thought I'd feel better if I come out to look at the Christmas decorations...but now I don't feel better at all!
What'll I do now?
I've got to snap out of this!
Sigh
My teacher must be furious by now.
And I definitely don't want to go home...
What's this?

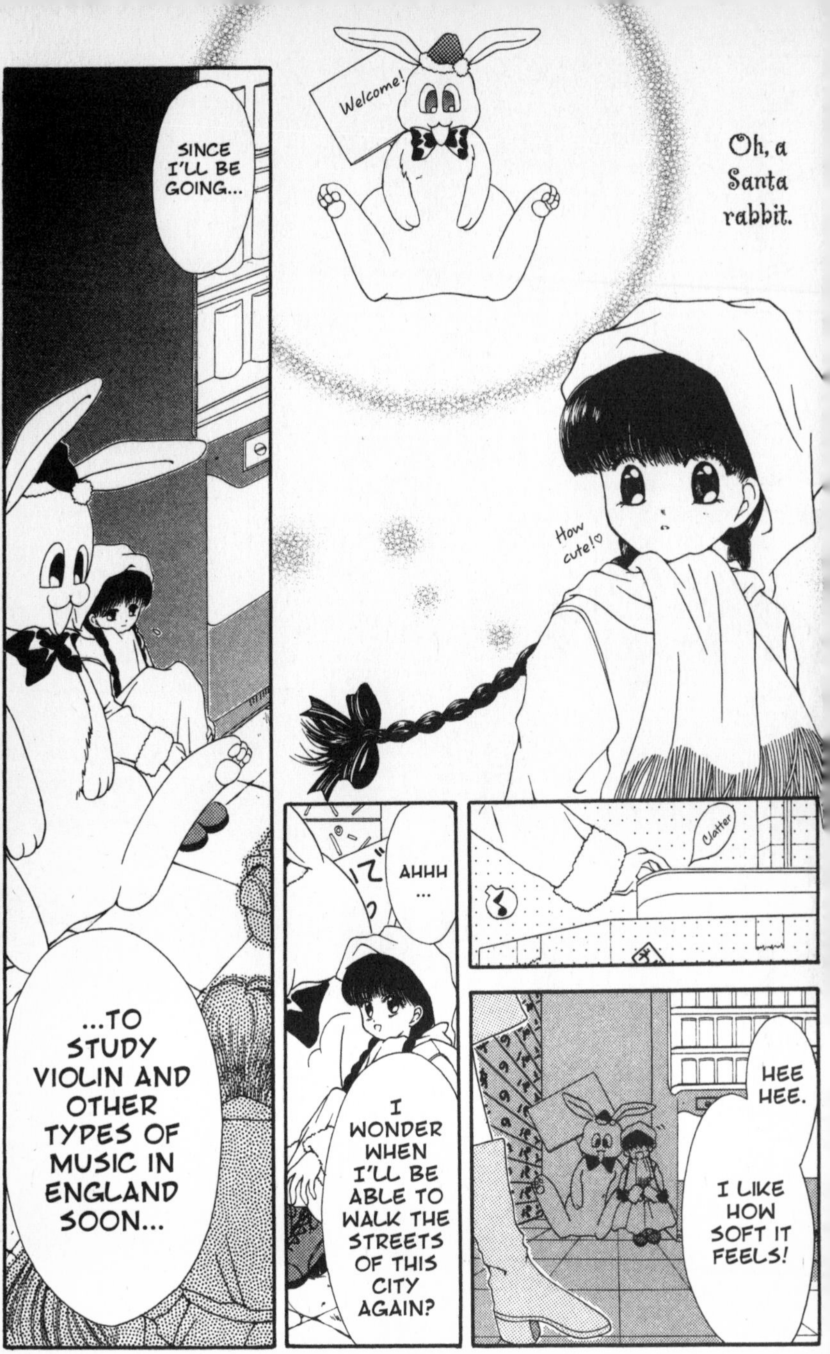

Welcome!
Oh, a Santa rabbit.
How cute!♡
Clatter
HEE HEE.
I LIKE HOW SOFT IT FEELS!
AHHH...
I WONDER WHEN I'LL BE ABLE TO WALK THE STREETS OF THIS CITY AGAIN?
SINCE I'LL BE GOING...
...TO STUDY VIOLIN AND OTHER TYPES OF MUSIC IN ENGLAND SOON...

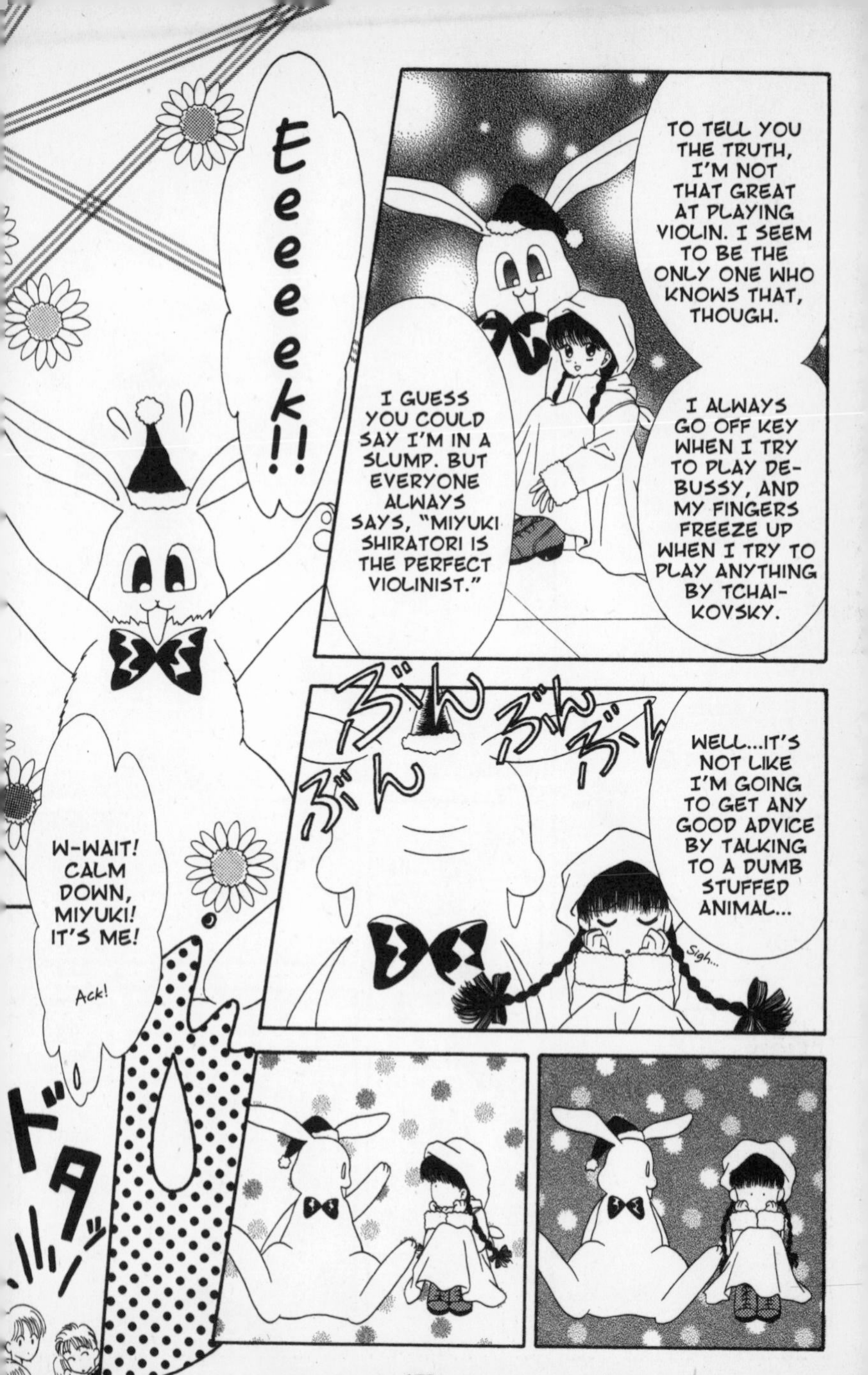
TO TELL YOU THE TRUTH, I'M NOT THAT GREAT AT PLAYING VIOLIN. I SEEM TO BE THE ONLY ONE WHO KNOWS THAT, THOUGH.
I ALWAYS GO OFF KEY WHEN I TRY TO PLAY DE-BUSSY, AND MY FINGERS FREEZE UP WHEN I TRY TO PLAY ANYTHING BY TCHAI-KOVSKY.
I GUESS YOU COULD SAY I'M IN A SLUMP. BUT EVERYONE ALWAYS SAYS, "MIYUKI SHIRATORI IS THE PERFECT VIOLINIST."
ぶんぶん
ぶんぶん
ぶんぶ
WELL...IT'S NOT LIKE I'M GOING TO GET ANY GOOD ADVICE BY TALKING TO A DUMB STUFFED ANIMAL...
Sigh...
Eeeeek!!
W-WAIT! CALM DOWN, MIYUKI! IT'S ME!
Ack!
ドタッ

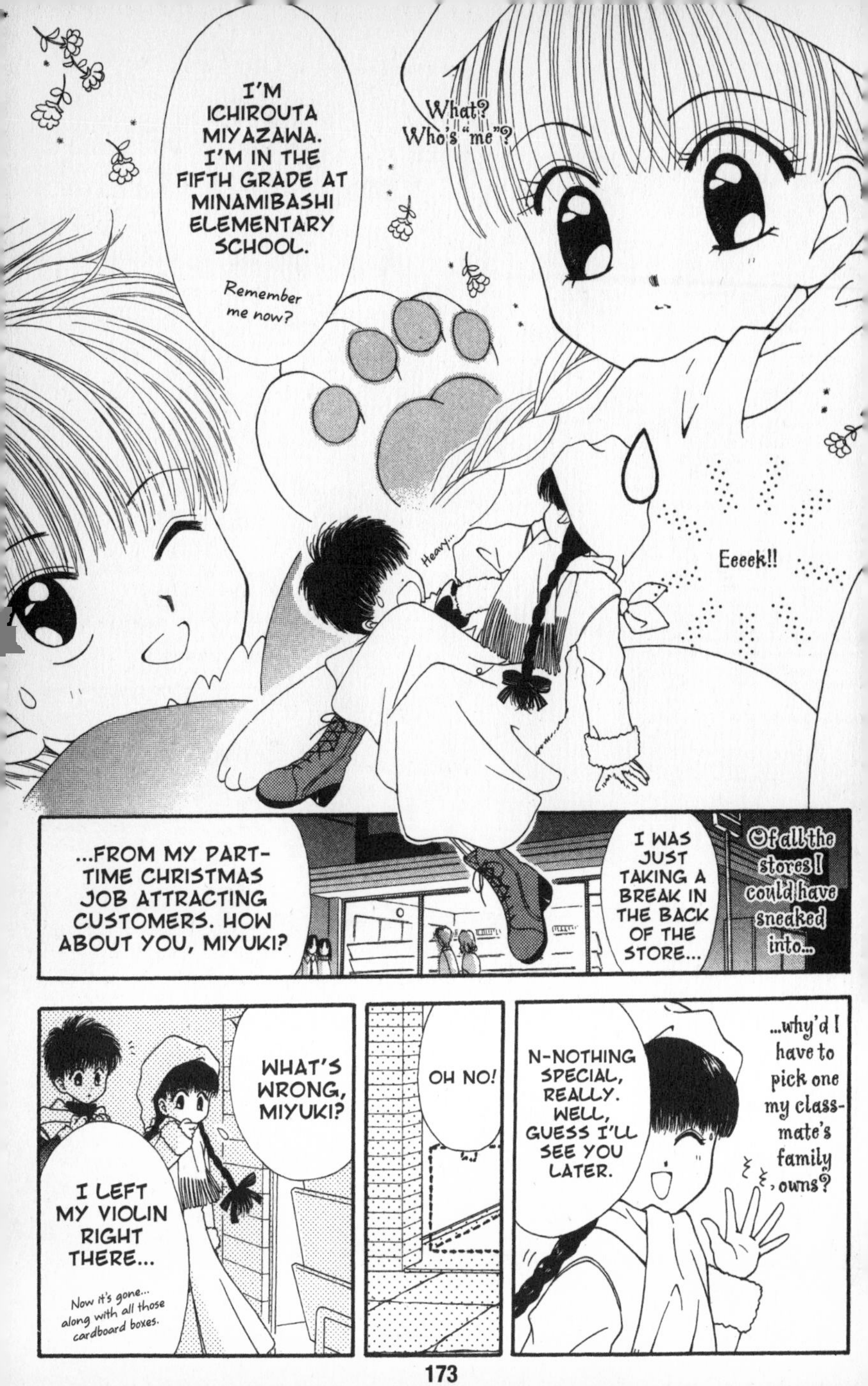
What? Who's "me"?
I'M ICHIROUTA MIYAZAWA. I'M IN THE FIFTH GRADE AT MINAMIBASHI ELEMENTARY SCHOOL.
Remember me now?
Eeeek!!
Heavy...
Of all the stores I could have sneaked into...
I WAS JUST TAKING A BREAK IN THE BACK OF THE STORE...
...FROM MY PART-TIME CHRISTMAS JOB ATTRACTING CUSTOMERS. HOW ABOUT YOU, MIYUKI?
N-NOTHING SPECIAL, REALLY. WELL, GUESS I'LL SEE YOU LATER.
...why'd I have to pick one my classmate's family owns?
OH NO!
WHAT'S WRONG, MIYUKI?
I LEFT MY VIOLIN RIGHT THERE...
Now it's gone... along with all those cardboard boxes.

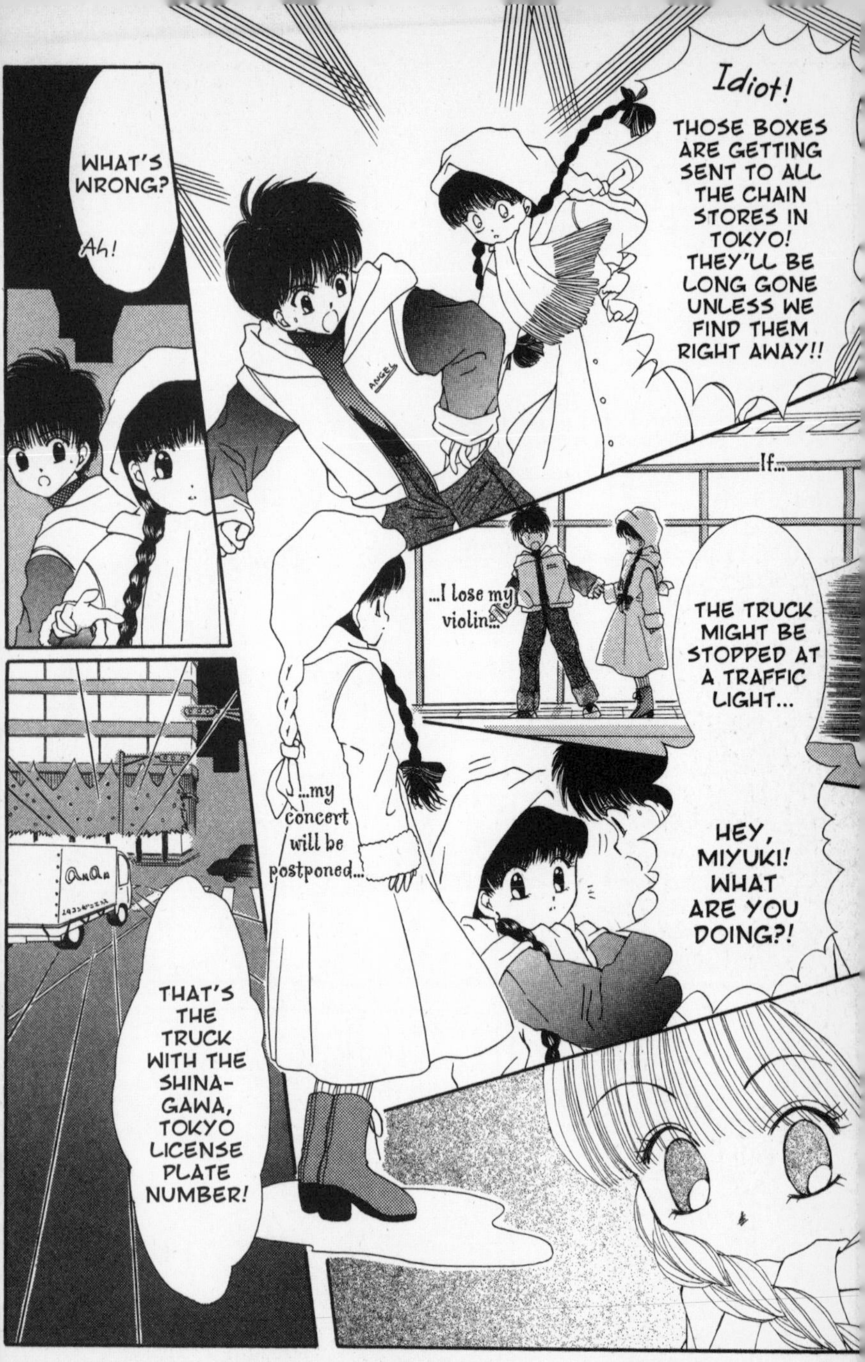
Idiot!
THOSE BOXES ARE GETTING SENT TO ALL THE CHAIN STORES IN TOKYO! THEY'LL BE LONG GONE UNLESS WE FIND THEM RIGHT AWAY!!
WHAT'S WRONG?
Ah!
THAT'S THE TRUCK WITH THE SHINA-GAWA, TOKYO LICENSE PLATE NUMBER!
If...
...I lose my violin...
...my concert will be postponed...
THE TRUCK MIGHT BE STOPPED AT A TRAFFIC LIGHT...
HEY, MIYUKI! WHAT ARE YOU DOING?!

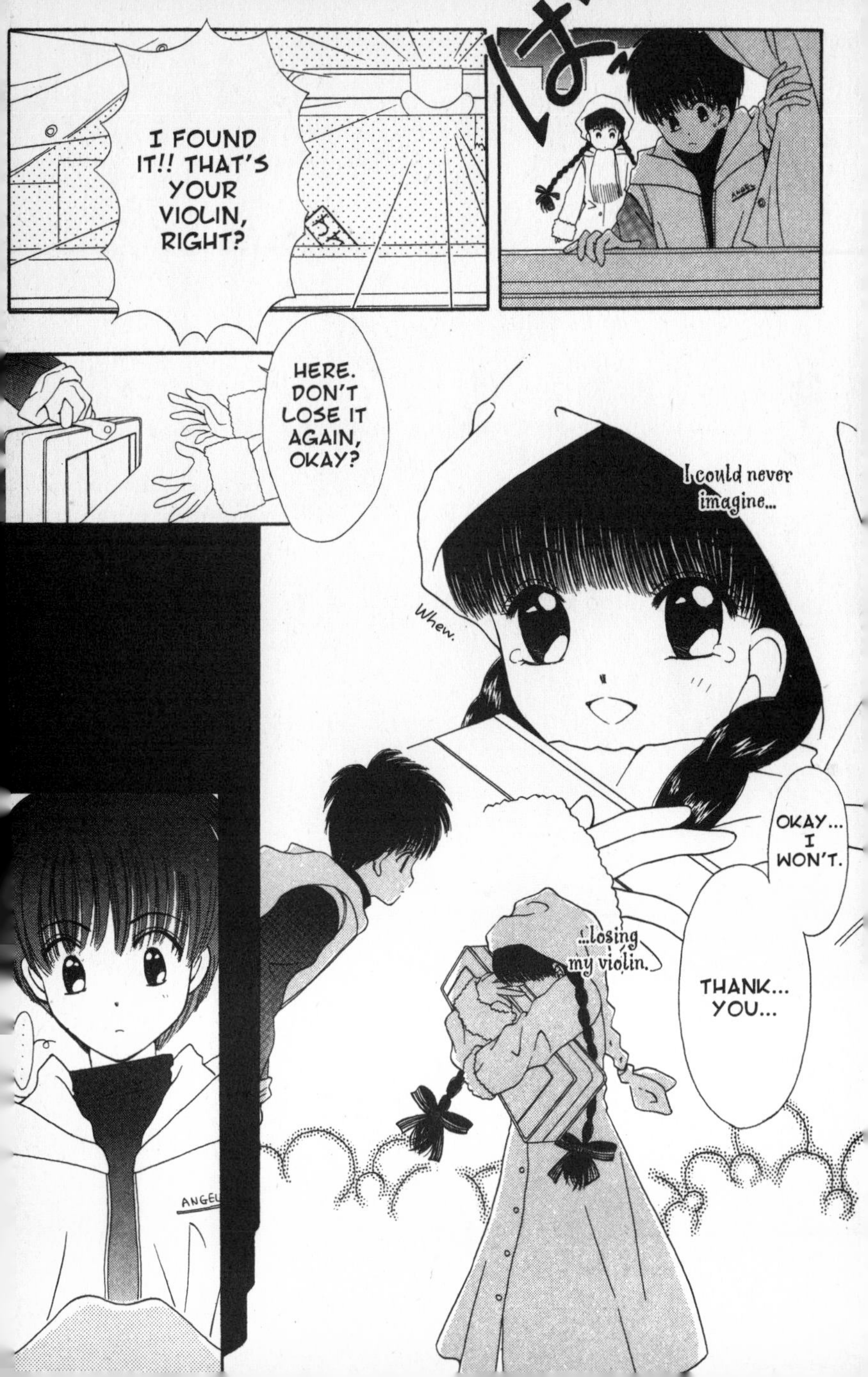
I FOUND IT!! THAT'S YOUR VIOLIN, RIGHT?
HERE. DON'T LOSE IT AGAIN, OKAY?
I could never imagine...
Whew.
OKAY... I WON'T.
THANK... YOU...
...losing my violin.
ANGEL

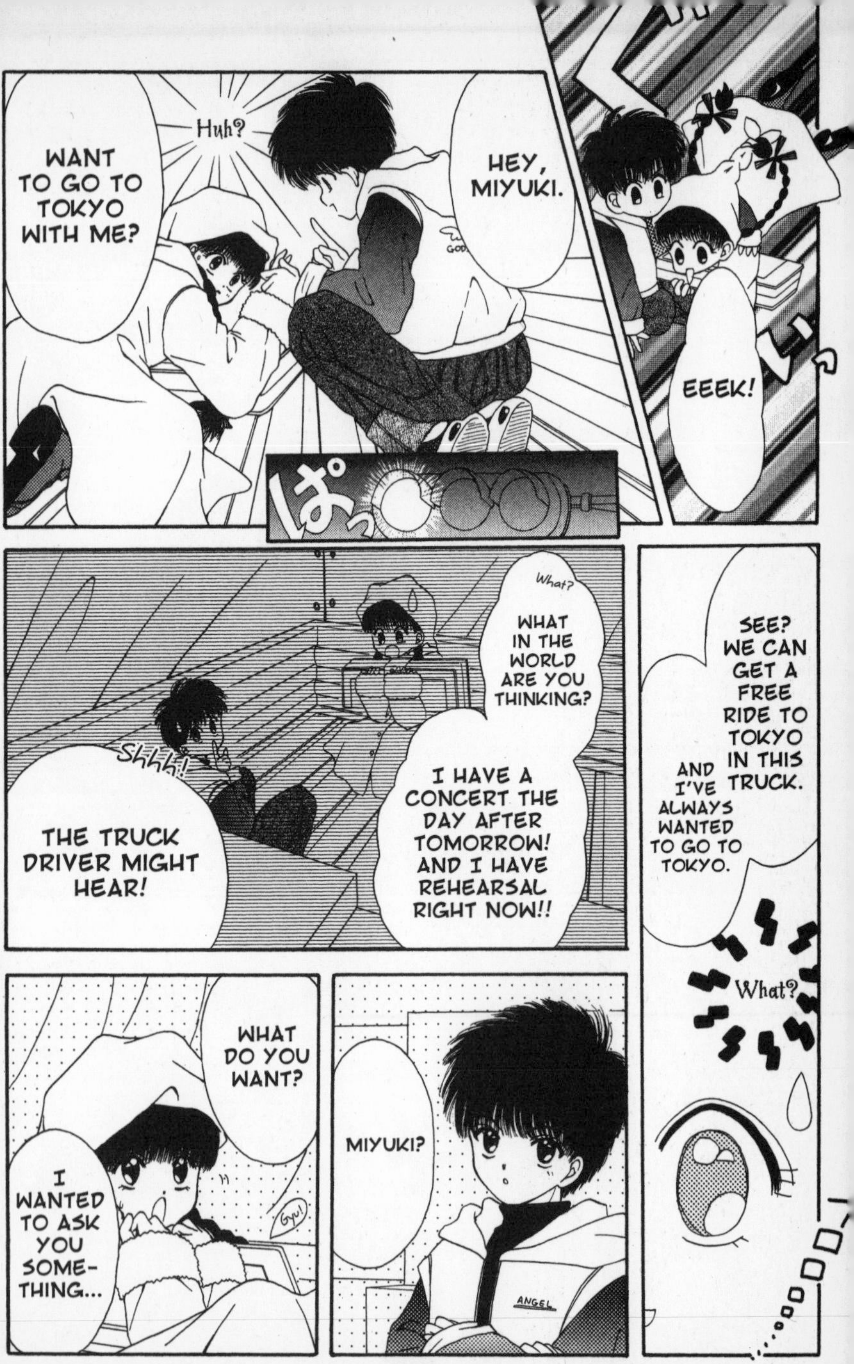
HEY, MIYUKI.
Huh?
WANT TO GO TO TOKYO WITH ME?
EEEK!
ぱっ
SEE? WE CAN GET A FREE RIDE TO TOKYO IN THIS TRUCK.
AND I'VE ALWAYS WANTED TO GO TO TOKYO.
What?
What?
WHAT IN THE WORLD ARE YOU THINKING?
I HAVE A CONCERT THE DAY AFTER TOMORROW! AND I HAVE REHEARSAL RIGHT NOW!!
Shhh!
THE TRUCK DRIVER MIGHT HEAR!
MIYUKI?
WHAT DO YOU WANT?
Gyu!
I WANTED TO ASK YOU SOME-THING...

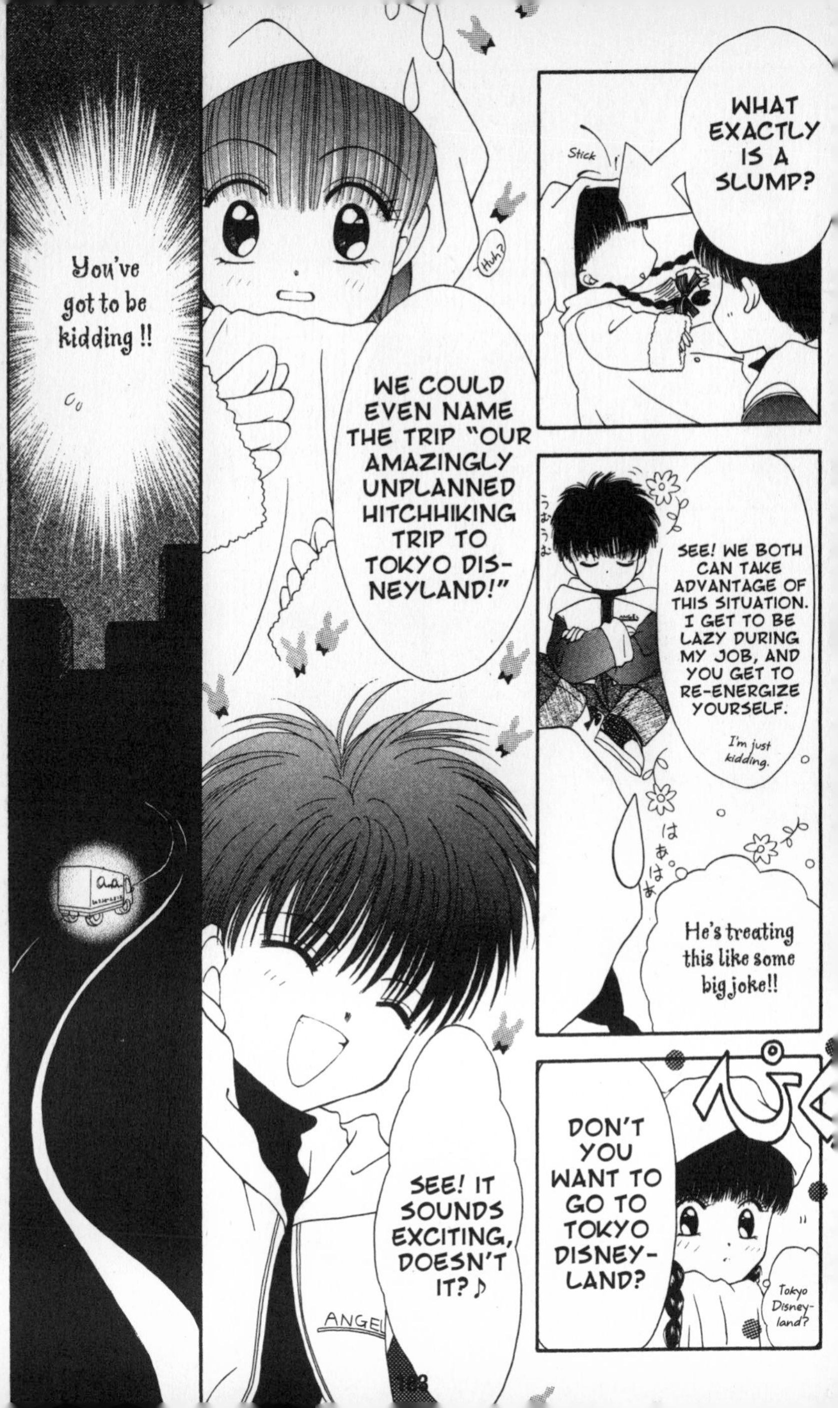
Stick
WHAT EXACTLY IS A SLUMP?
Huh?
WE COULD EVEN NAME THE TRIP "OUR AMAZINGLY UNPLANNED HITCHHIKING TRIP TO TOKYO DIS-NEYLAND!"
うむうむ
SEE! WE BOTH CAN TAKE ADVANTAGE OF THIS SITUATION. I GET TO BE LAZY DURING MY JOB, AND YOU GET TO RE-ENERGIZE YOURSELF.
I'm just kidding.
はあはあ
He's treating this like some big joke!!
DON'T YOU WANT TO GO TO TOKYO DISNEY-LAND?
Tokyo Disney-land?
SEE! IT SOUNDS EXCITING, DOESN'T IT?♪
ANGEL
You've got to be kidding!!

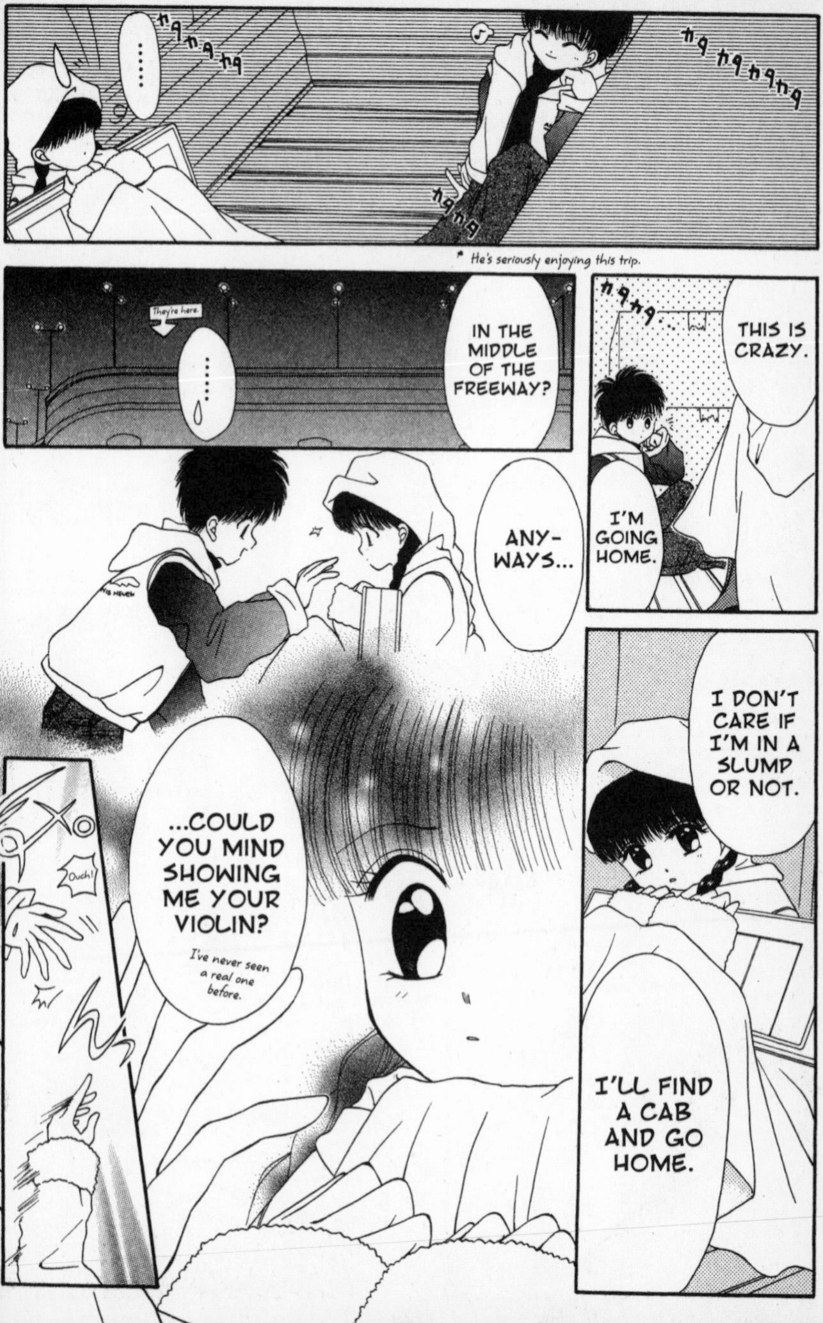
......
He's seriously enjoying this trip.
THIS IS CRAZY.
I'M GOING HOME.
IN THE MIDDLE OF THE FREEWAY?
They're here.
......
ANY-WAYS...
I DON'T CARE IF I'M IN A SLUMP OR NOT.
I'LL FIND A CAB AND GO HOME.
...COULD YOU MIND SHOWING ME YOUR VIOLIN?
I've never seen a real one before.
Ouch!

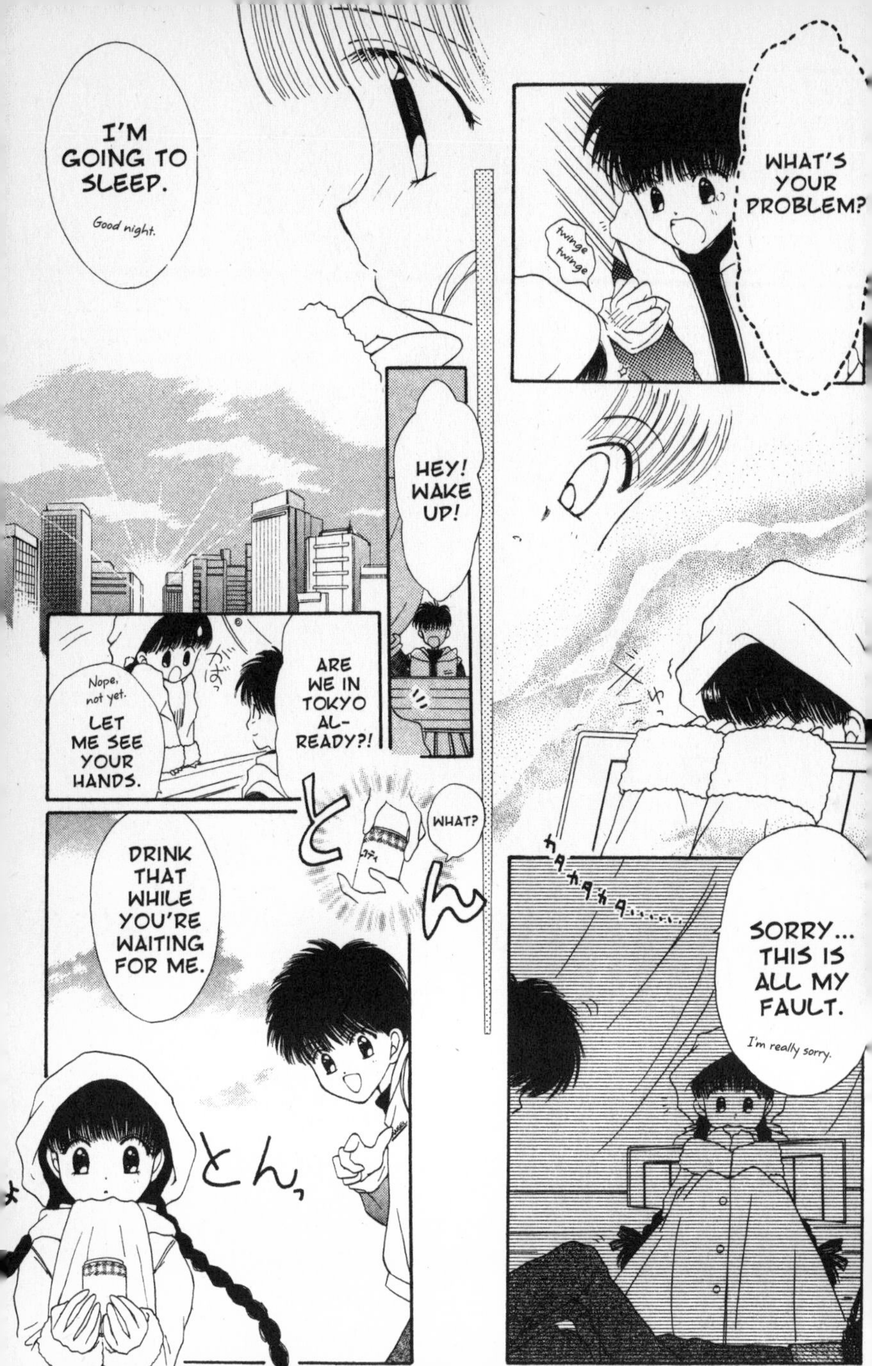
WHAT'S YOUR PROBLEM?
twinge twinge
SORRY... THIS IS ALL MY FAULT.
I'm really sorry.
I'M GOING TO SLEEP.
Good night.
HEY! WAKE UP!
ARE WE IN TOKYO AL-READY?!
Nope, not yet.
LET ME SEE YOUR HANDS.
WHAT?
とん
DRINK THAT WHILE YOU'RE WAITING FOR ME.
とん

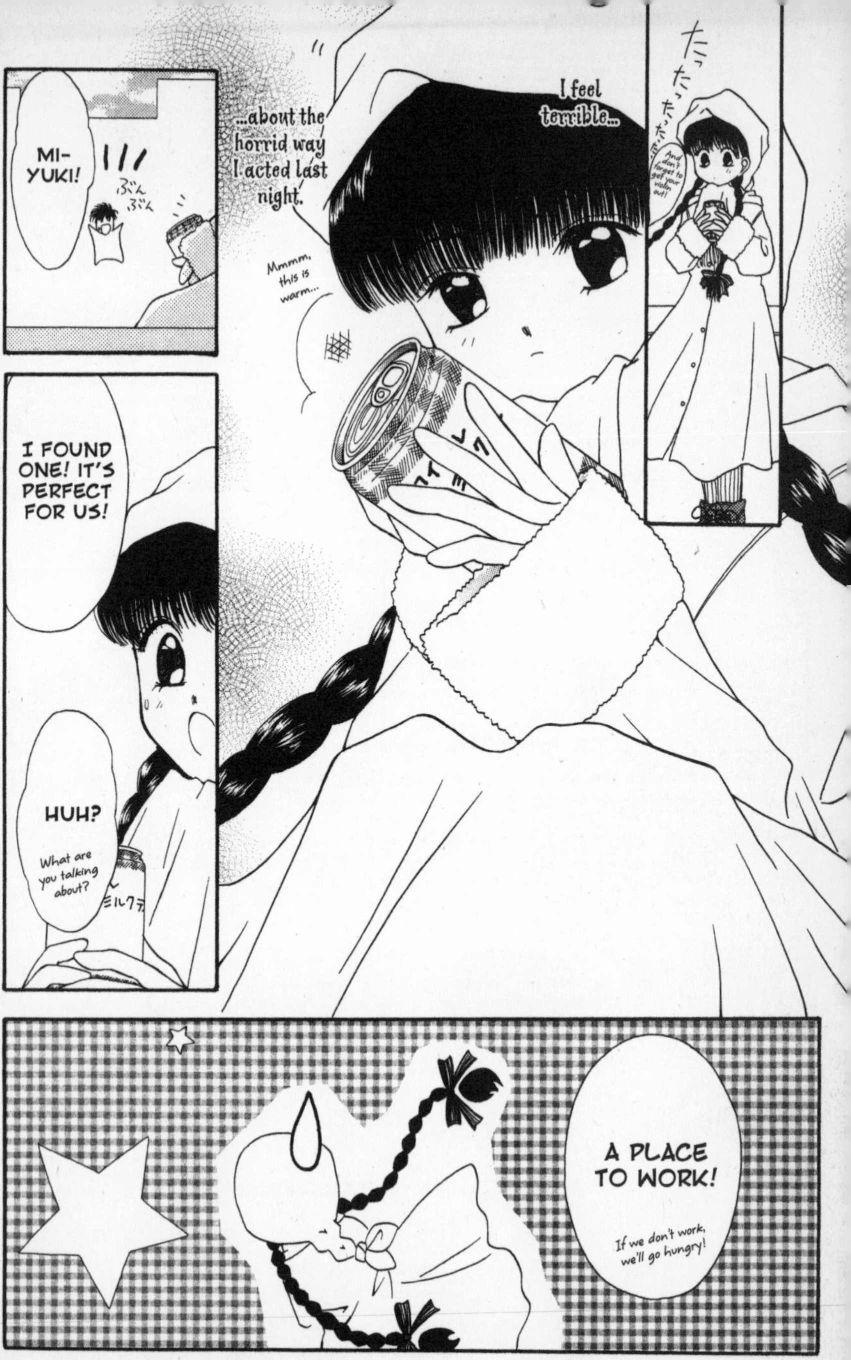
たったったっ
And don't forget to get your violin out!
I feel terrible...
...about the horrid way I acted last night.
Mmmm, this is warm...
MI-YUKI!
ぶん ぶん
I FOUND ONE! IT'S PERFECT FOR US!
HUH?
What are you talking about?
A PLACE TO WORK!
If we don't work, we'll go hungry!

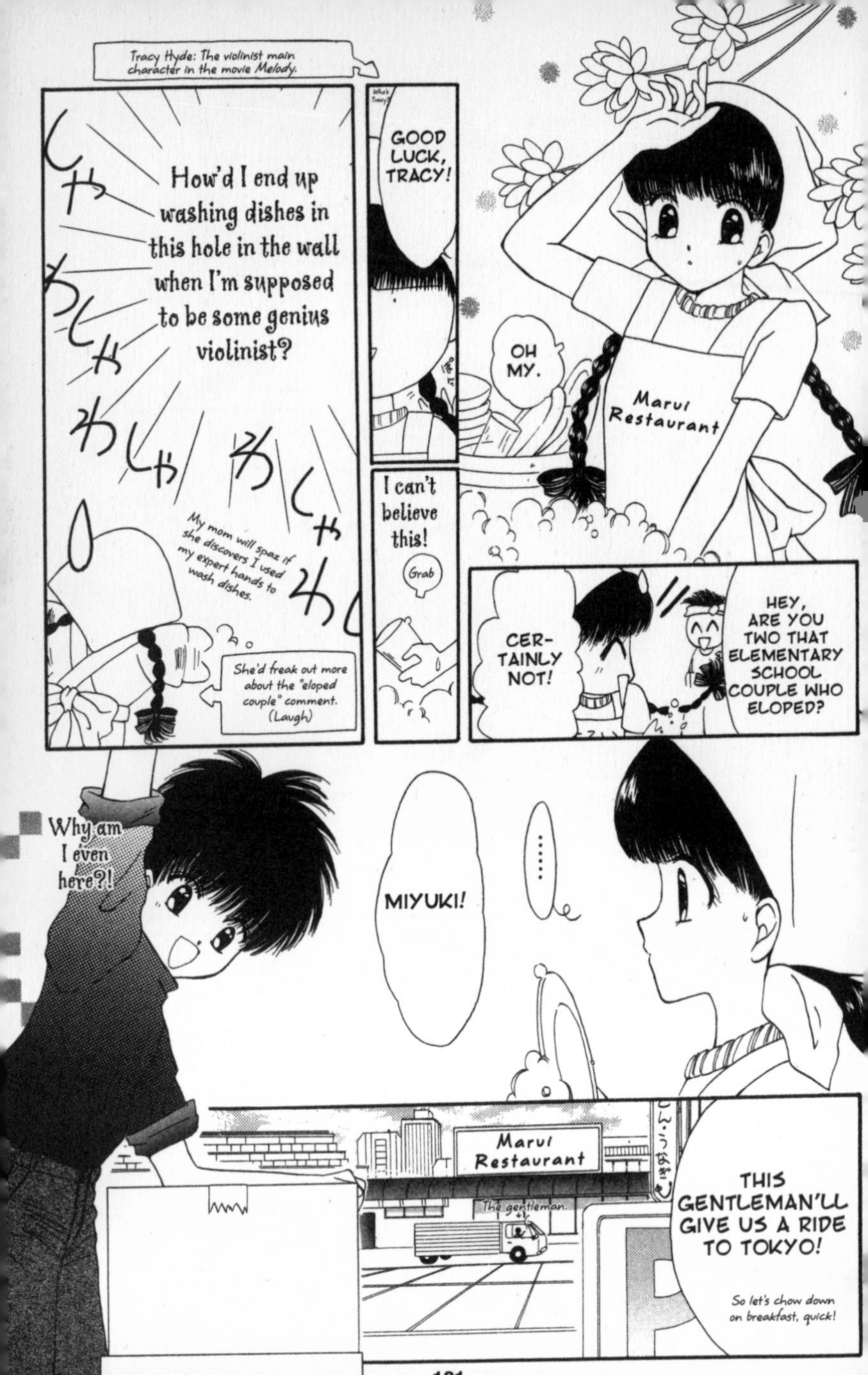

OH MY.
Marui Restaurant
Who's Tracy?
GOOD LUCK, TRACY!
Tracy Hyde: The violinist main character in the movie Melody.
How'd I end up washing dishes in this hole in the wall when I'm supposed to be some genius violinist?
My mom will spaz if she discovers I used my expert hands to wash dishes.
She'd freak out more about the "eloped couple" comment. (Laugh)
HEY, ARE YOU TWO THAT ELEMENTARY SCHOOL COUPLE WHO ELOPED?
CERTAINLY NOT!
I can't believe this!
Grab
MIYUKI!
......
Why am I even here?!
THIS GENTLEMAN'LL GIVE US A RIDE TO TOKYO!
So let's chow down on breakfast, quick!
Marui Restaurant
The gentleman.

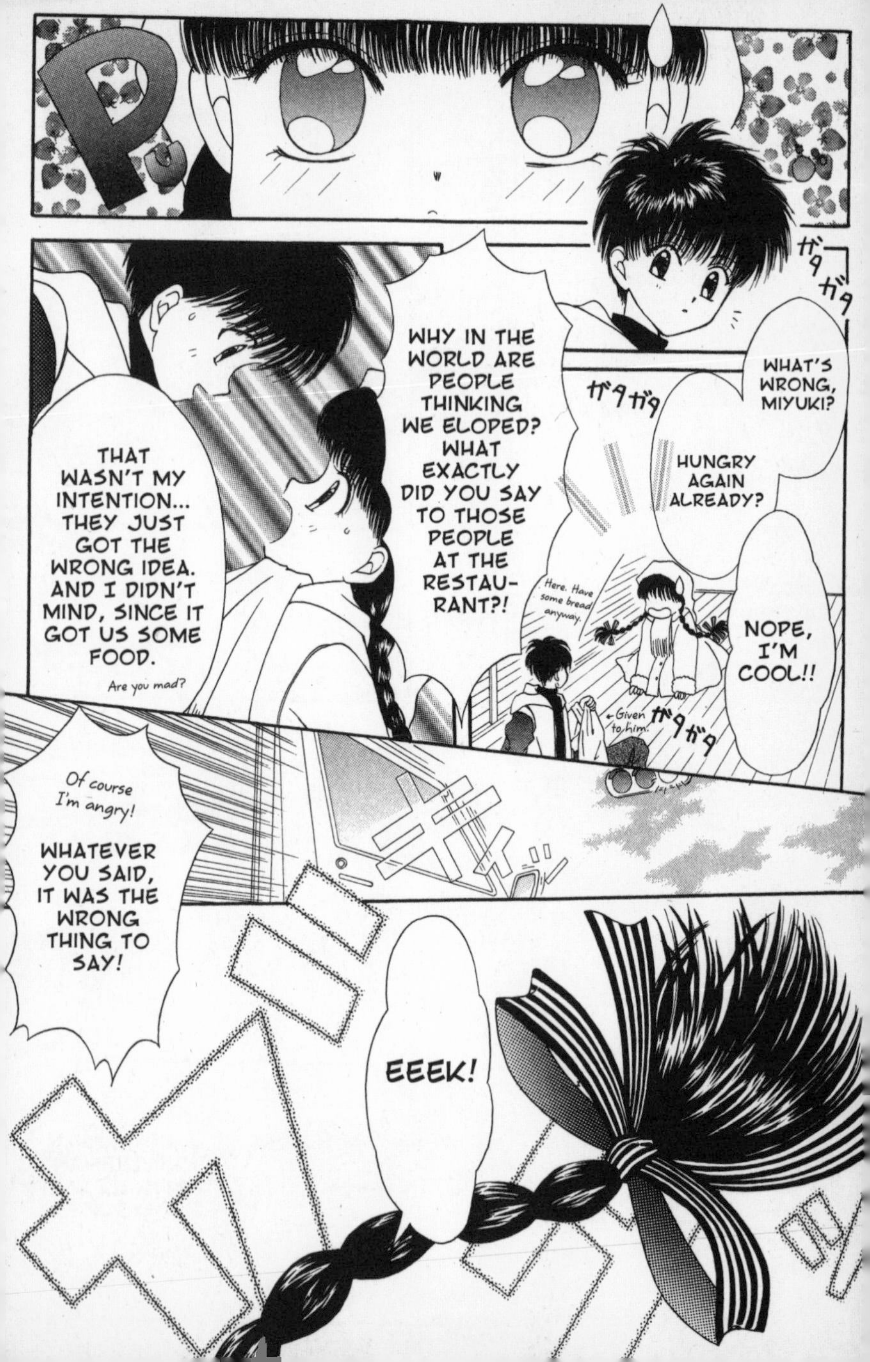
ガタガタ
WHAT'S WRONG, MIYUKI?
HUNGRY AGAIN ALREADY?
NOPE, I'M COOL!!
Here. Have some bread anyway.
Given to him.
ガタガタ
WHY IN THE WORLD ARE PEOPLE THINKING WE ELOPED? WHAT EXACTLY DID YOU SAY TO THOSE PEOPLE AT THE RESTAURANT?!
THAT WASN'T MY INTENTION... THEY JUST GOT THE WRONG IDEA. AND I DIDN'T MIND, SINCE IT GOT US SOME FOOD.
Are you mad?
Of course I'm angry!
WHATEVER YOU SAID, IT WAS THE WRONG THING TO SAY!
EEEK!

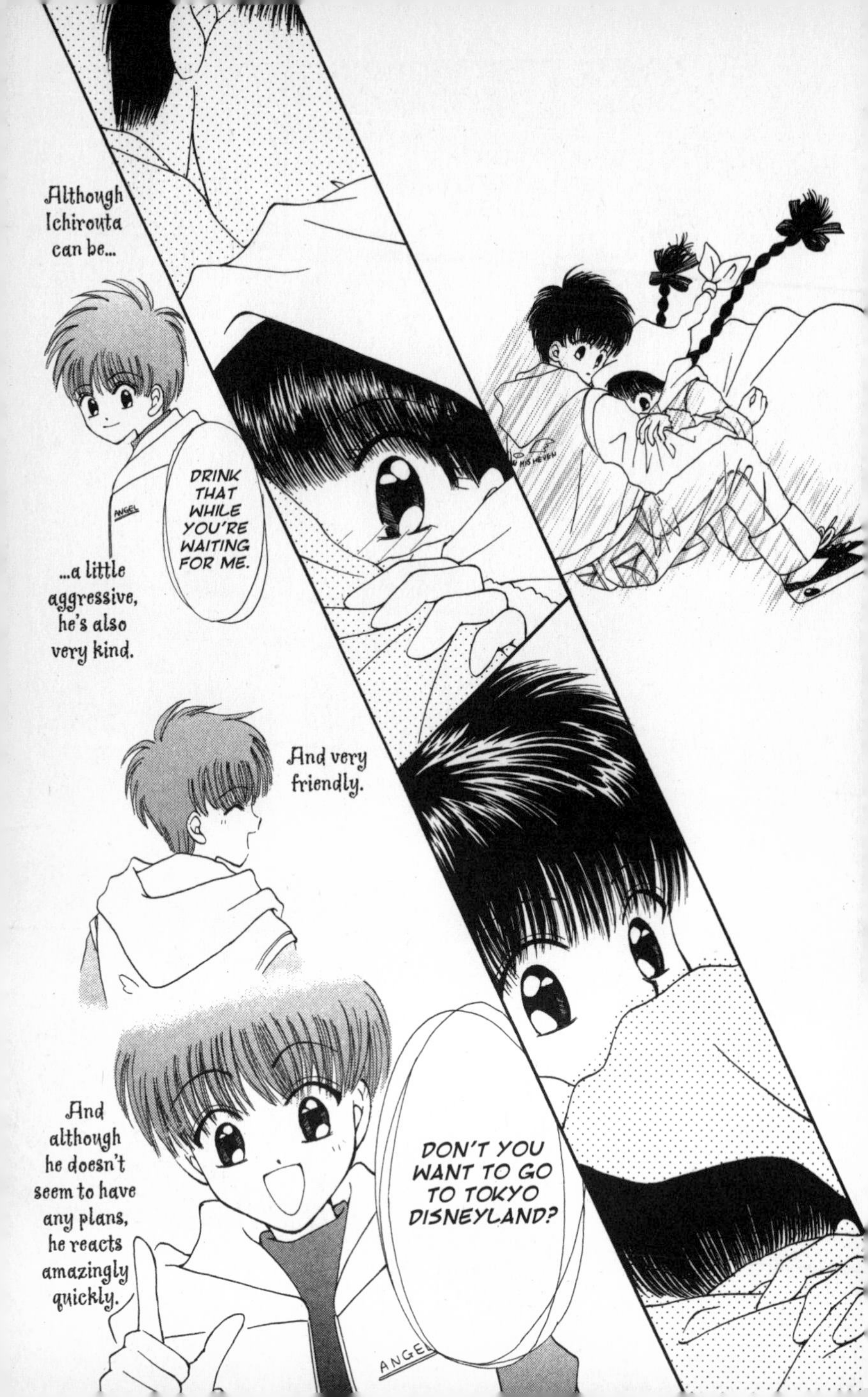

Although Ichirouta can be...
DRINK THAT WHILE YOU'RE WAITING FOR ME.
...a little aggressive, he's also very kind.
And very friendly.
And although he doesn't seem to have any plans, he reacts amazingly quickly.
DON'T YOU WANT TO GO TO TOKYO DISNEYLAND?

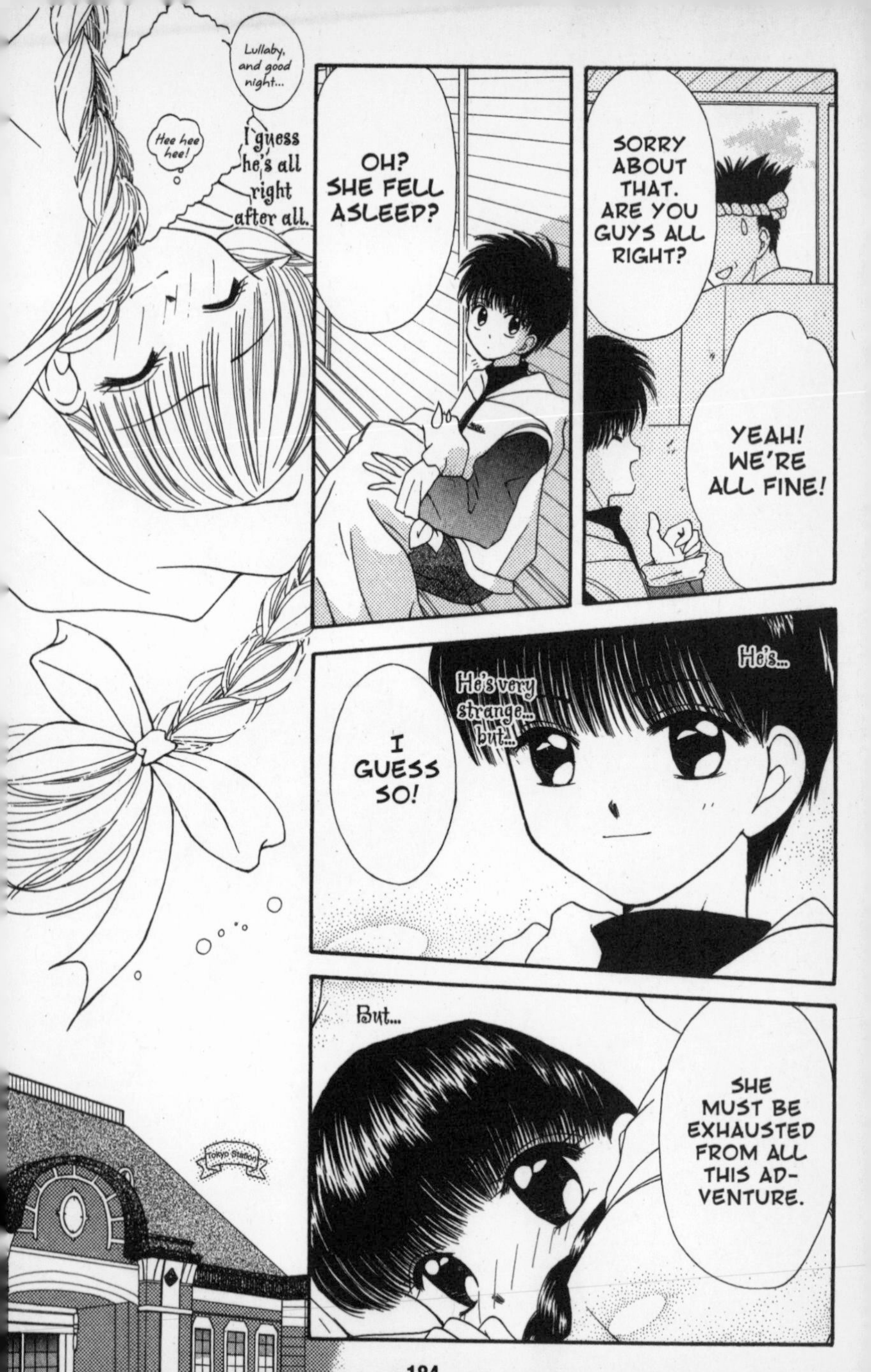
SORRY ABOUT THAT. ARE YOU GUYS ALL RIGHT?
YEAH! WE'RE ALL FINE!
OH? SHE FELL ASLEEP?
Lullaby, and good night...
Hee hee hee!
I guess he's all right after all.
He's...
He's very strange... but...
I GUESS SO!
But...
SHE MUST BE EXHAUSTED FROM ALL THIS AD-VENTURE.
Tokyo Station

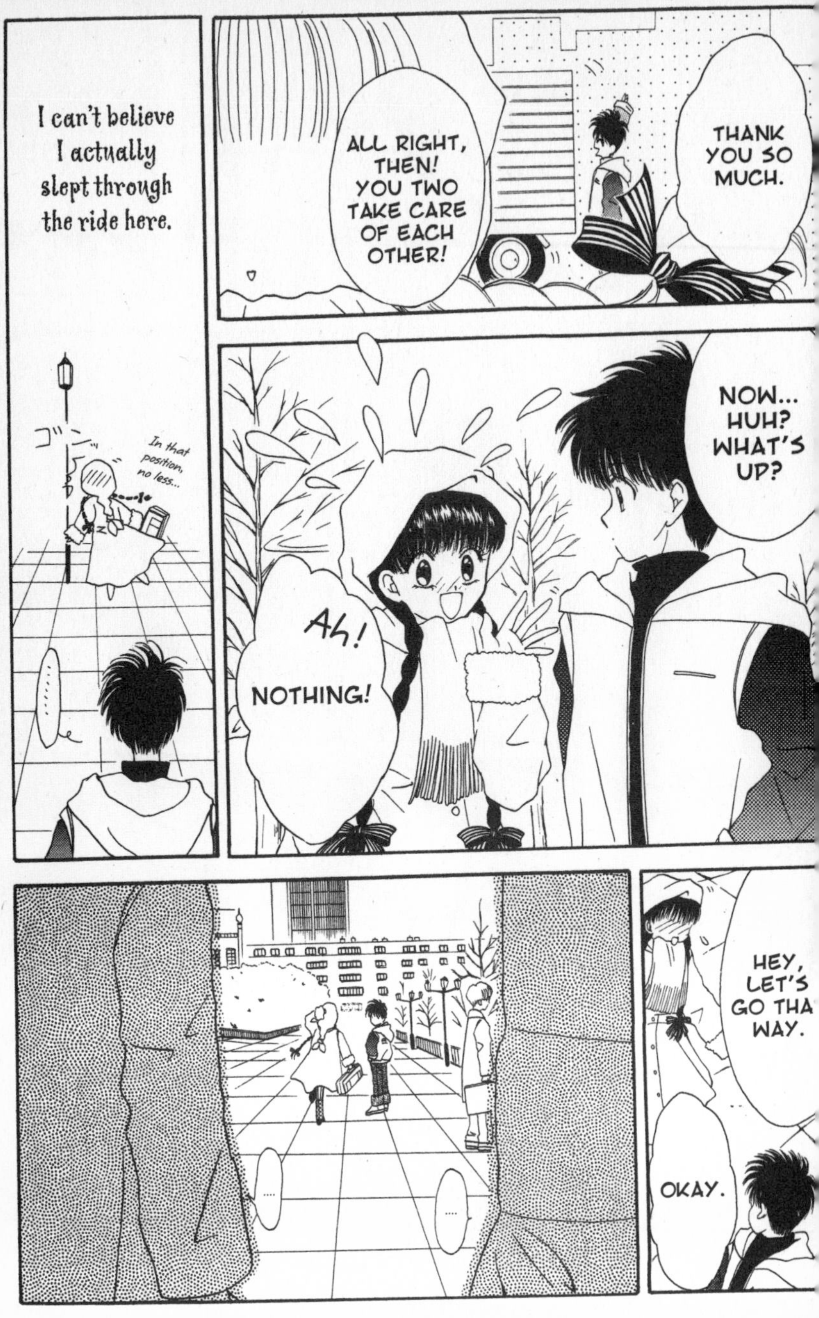
THANK YOU SO MUCH.
ALL RIGHT, THEN! YOU TWO TAKE CARE OF EACH OTHER!
NOW... HUH? WHAT'S UP?
Ah! NOTHING!
I can't believe I actually slept through the ride here.
In that position, no less...
HEY, LET'S GO THA WAY.
OKAY.

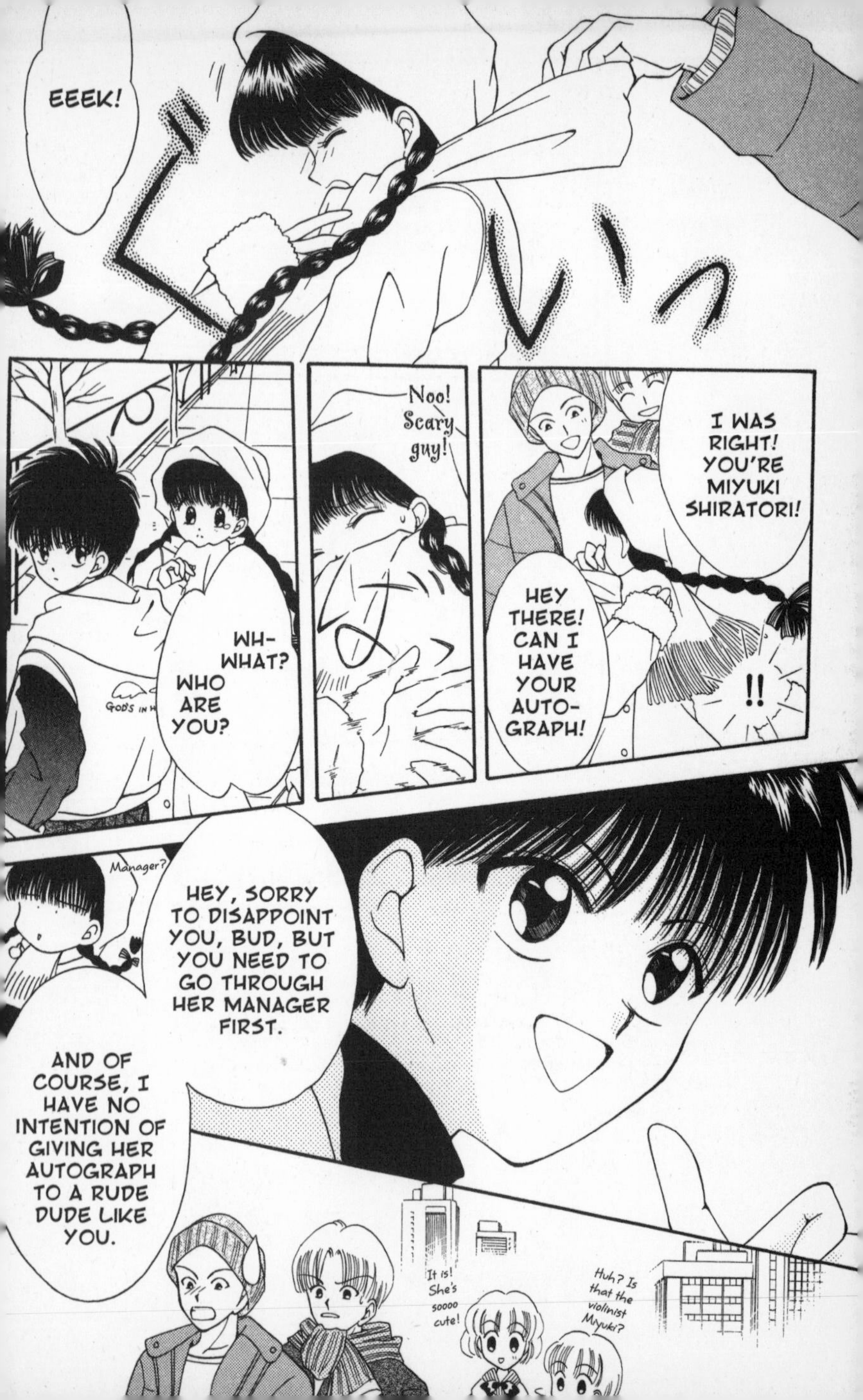
EEEK!
I WAS RIGHT! YOU'RE MIYUKI SHIRATORI!
HEY THERE! CAN I HAVE YOUR AUTO-GRAPH!
!!
Noo! Scary guy!
WH-WHAT? WHO ARE YOU?
GOD'S IN H
HEY, SORRY TO DISAPPOINT YOU, BUD, BUT YOU NEED TO GO THROUGH HER MANAGER FIRST.
Manager?
AND OF COURSE, I HAVE NO INTENTION OF GIVING HER AUTOGRAPH TO A RUDE DUDE LIKE YOU.
Huh? Is that the violinist Miyuki?
It is! She's soooo cute!

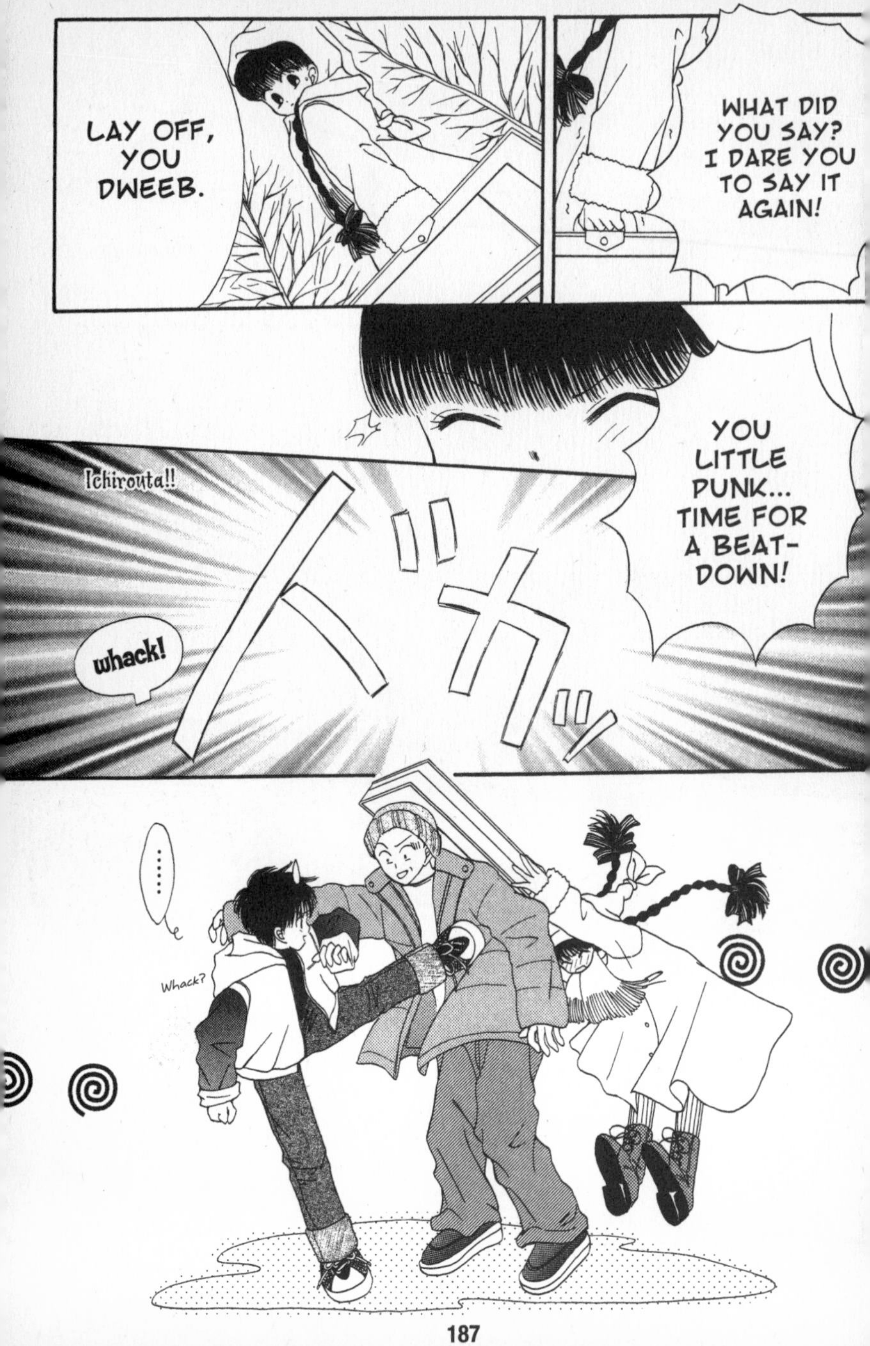

WHAT DID YOU SAY? I DARE YOU TO SAY IT AGAIN!
LAY OFF, YOU DWEEB.
YOU LITTLE PUNK... TIME FOR A BEAT-DOWN!
Ichirouta!!
whack!
......
Whack?

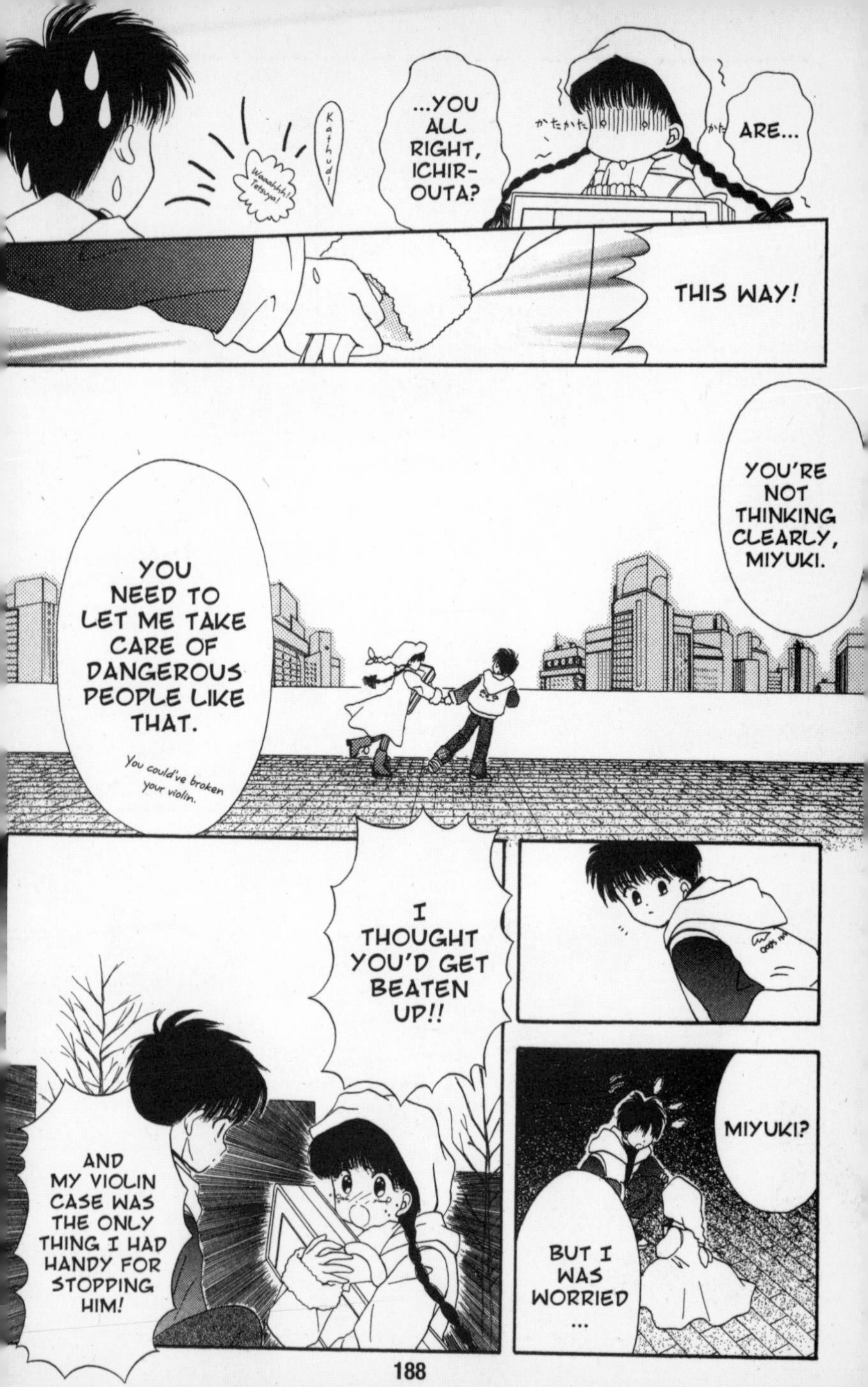
ARE...
かたかた
かた
...YOU ALL RIGHT, ICHIROUTA?
Kathud!
Waaahhh!! Tetsuya!
THIS WAY!
YOU'RE NOT THINKING CLEARLY, MIYUKI.
YOU NEED TO LET ME TAKE CARE OF DANGEROUS PEOPLE LIKE THAT.
You could've broken your violin.
I THOUGHT YOU'D GET BEATEN UP!!
AND MY VIOLIN CASE WAS THE ONLY THING I HAD HANDY FOR STOPPING HIM!
MIYUKI?
BUT I WAS WORRIED ...

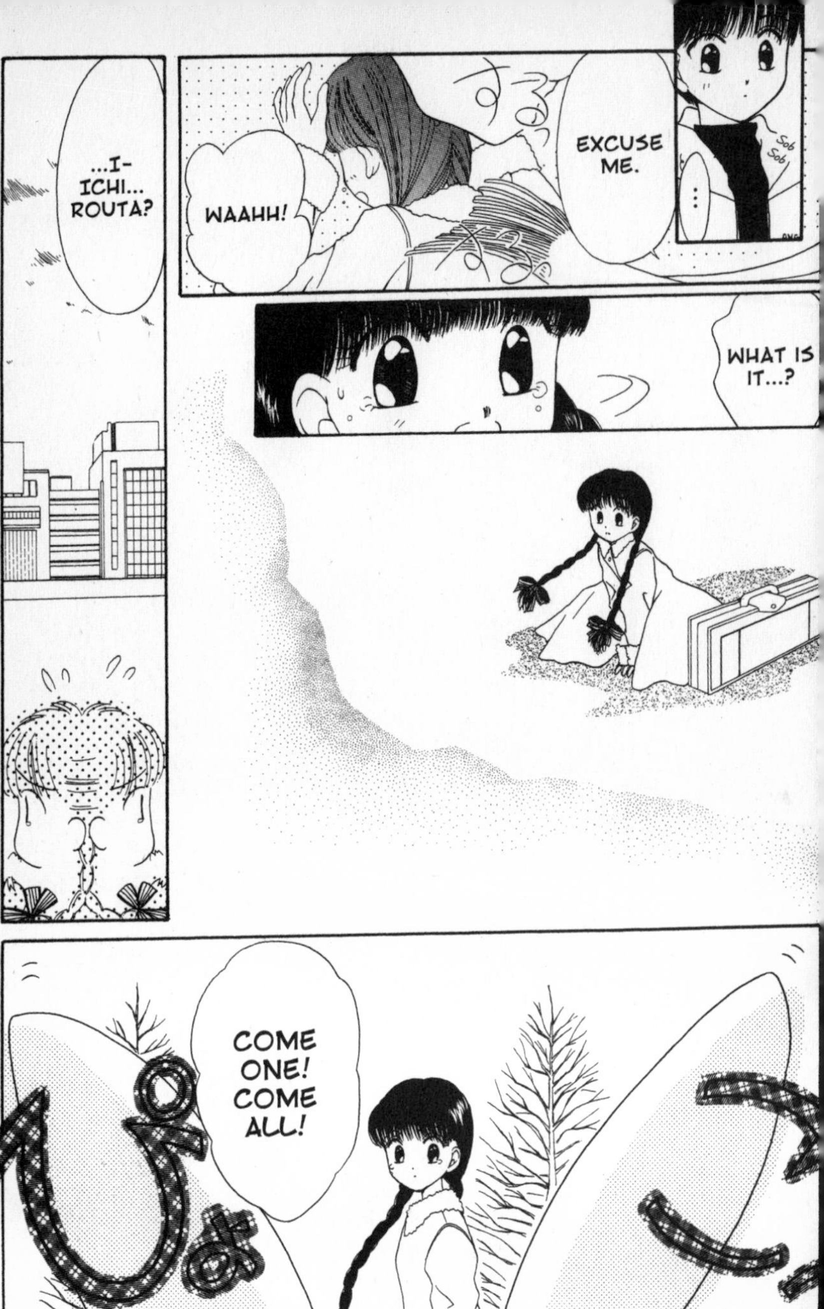
Sob
Sob
...
EXCUSE ME.
WAAHH!
WHAT IS IT...?
...I-ICHI... ROUTA?
COME ONE! COME ALL!

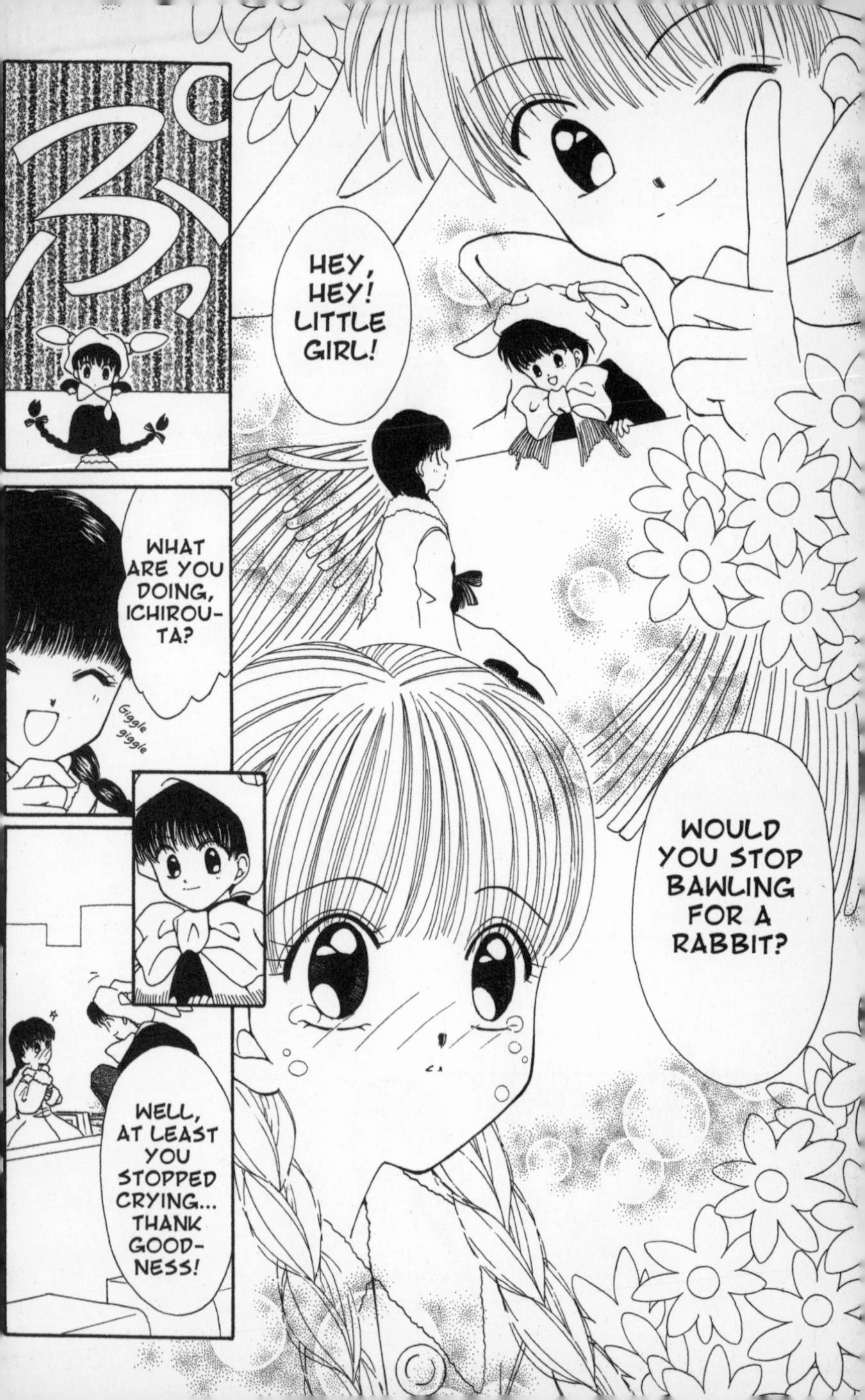
HEY, HEY! LITTLE GIRL!
WOULD YOU STOP BAWLING FOR A RABBIT?
ぷっ
WHAT ARE YOU DOING, ICHIROU-TA?
Giggle giggle
WELL, AT LEAST YOU STOPPED CRYING... THANK GOOD-NESS!

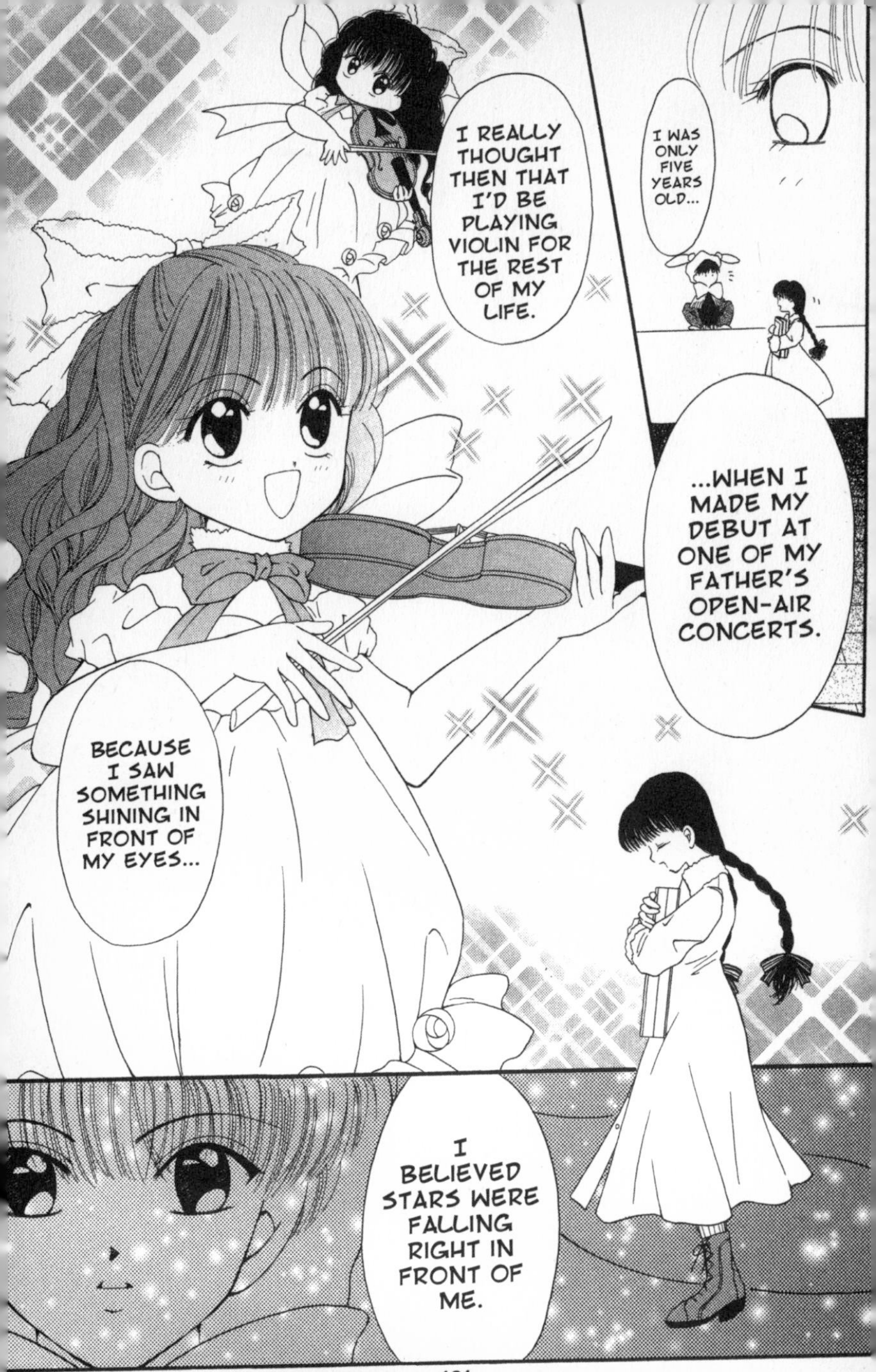
I WAS ONLY FIVE YEARS OLD...
...WHEN I MADE MY DEBUT AT ONE OF MY FATHER'S OPEN-AIR CONCERTS.
I REALLY THOUGHT THEN THAT I'D BE PLAYING VIOLIN FOR THE REST OF MY LIFE.
BECAUSE I SAW SOMETHING SHINING IN FRONT OF MY EYES...
I BELIEVED STARS WERE FALLING RIGHT IN FRONT OF ME.

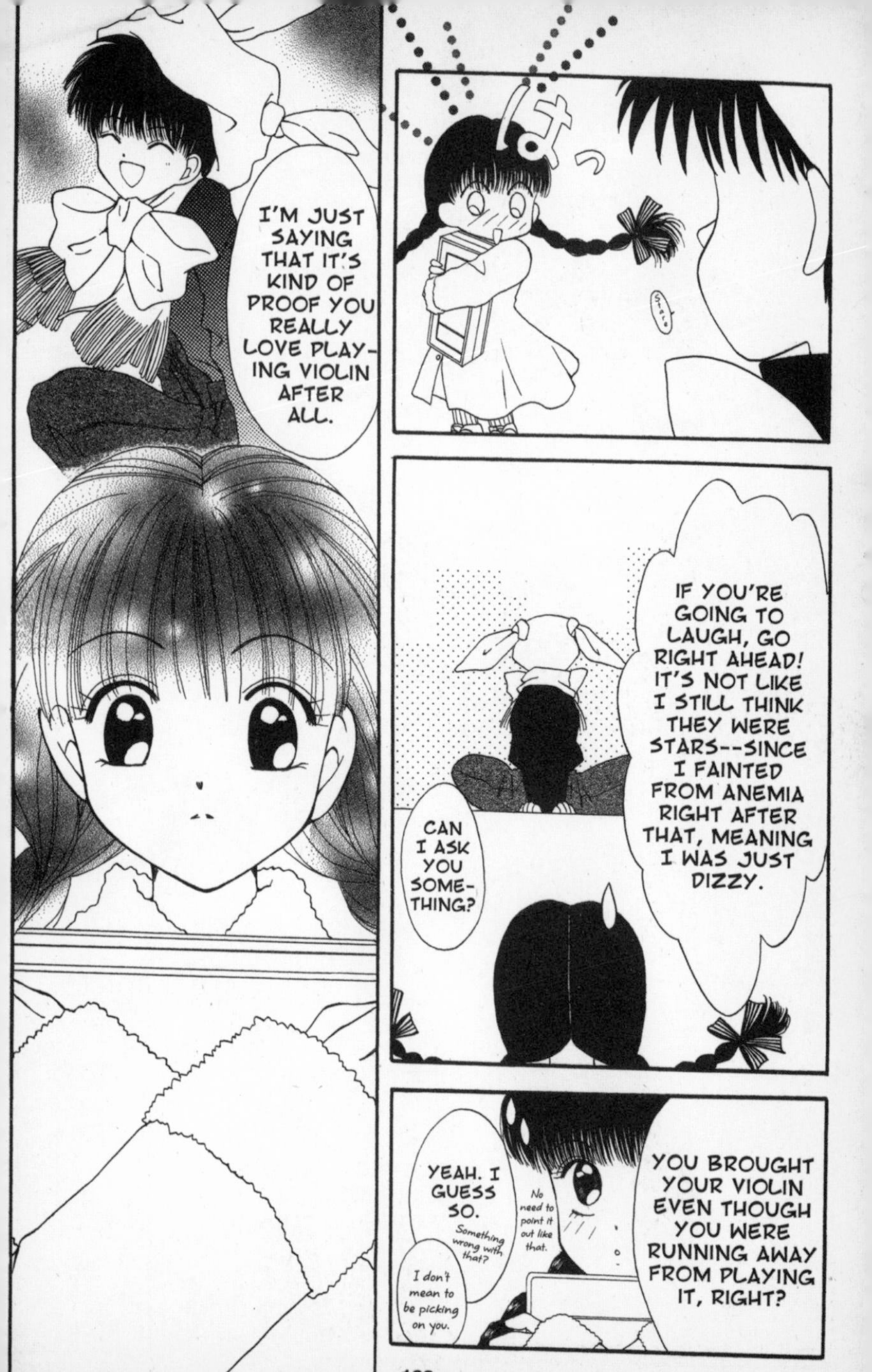
はっ
Stare
IF YOU'RE GOING TO LAUGH, GO RIGHT AHEAD! IT'S NOT LIKE I STILL THINK THEY WERE STARS--SINCE I FAINTED FROM ANEMIA RIGHT AFTER THAT, MEANING I WAS JUST DIZZY.
CAN I ASK YOU SOMETHING?
YOU BROUGHT YOUR VIOLIN EVEN THOUGH YOU WERE RUNNING AWAY FROM PLAYING IT, RIGHT?
No need to point it out like that.
YEAH. I GUESS SO.
Something wrong with that?
I don't mean to be picking on you.
I'M JUST SAYING THAT IT'S KIND OF PROOF YOU REALLY LOVE PLAYING VIOLIN AFTER ALL.

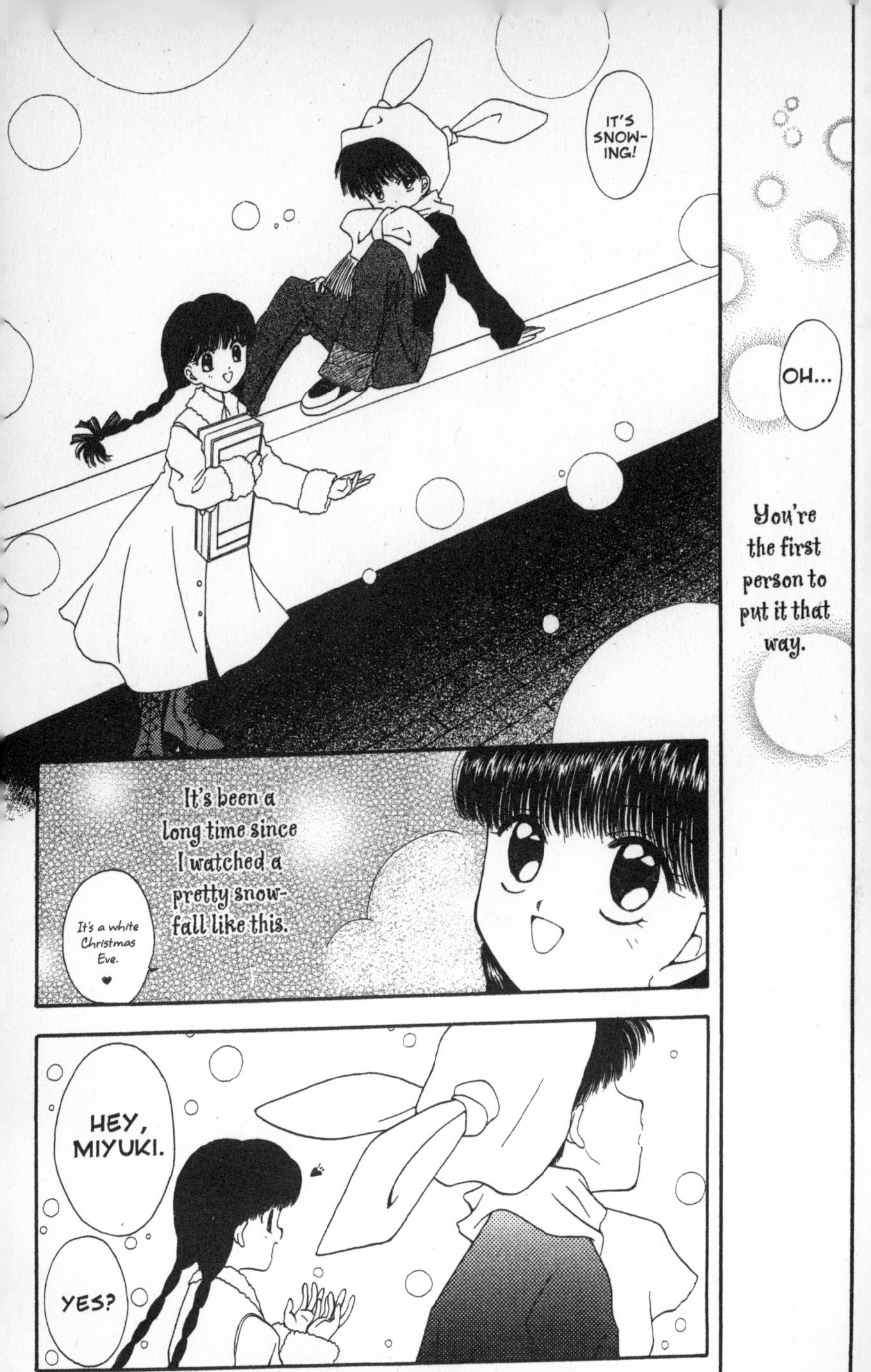

IT'S SNOWING!
OH...
You're the first person to put it that way.
It's been a long time since I watched a pretty snowfall like this.
It's a white Christmas Eve.
HEY, MIYUKI.
YES?

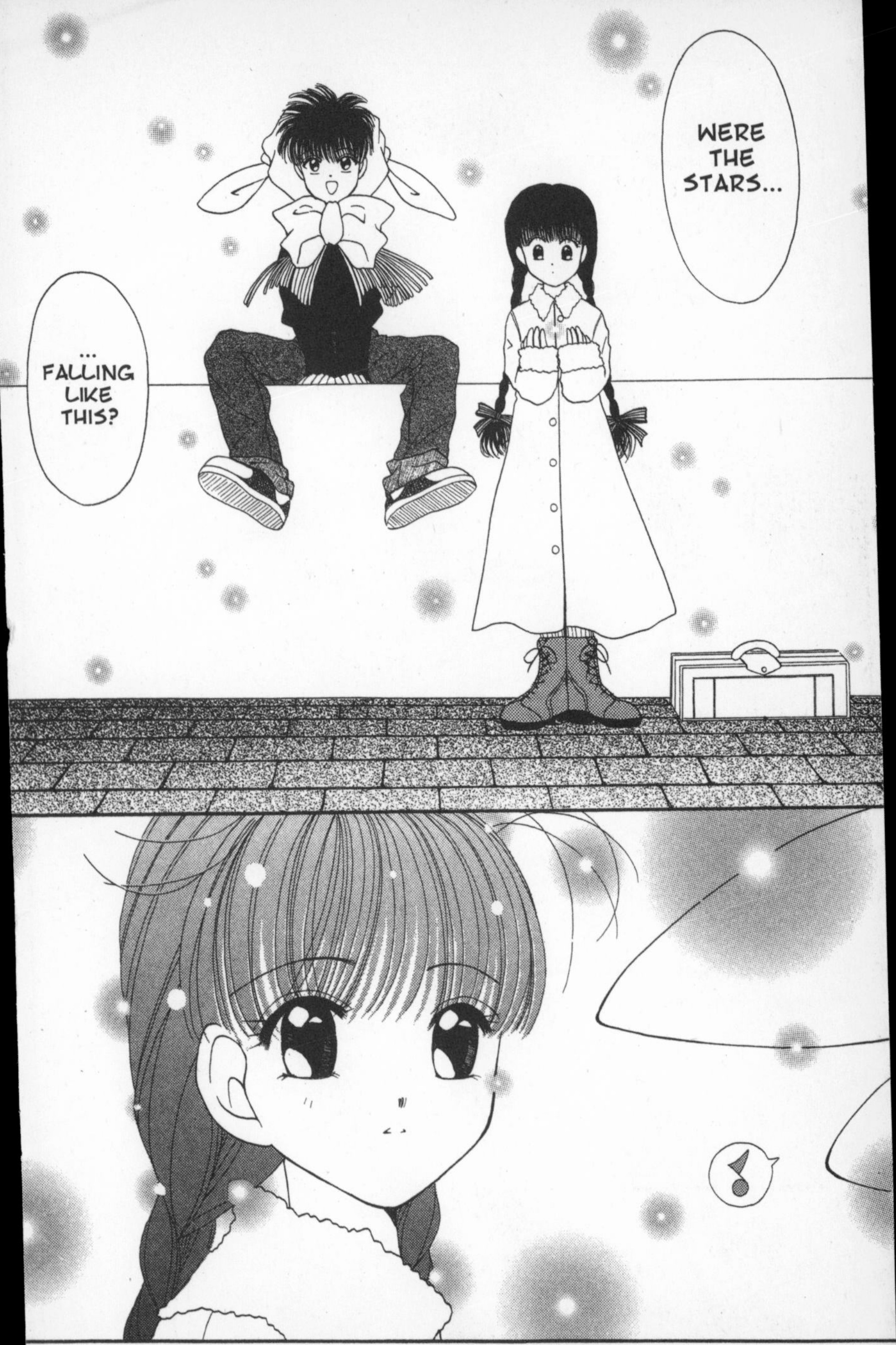
WERE THE STARS...
... FALLING LIKE THIS?

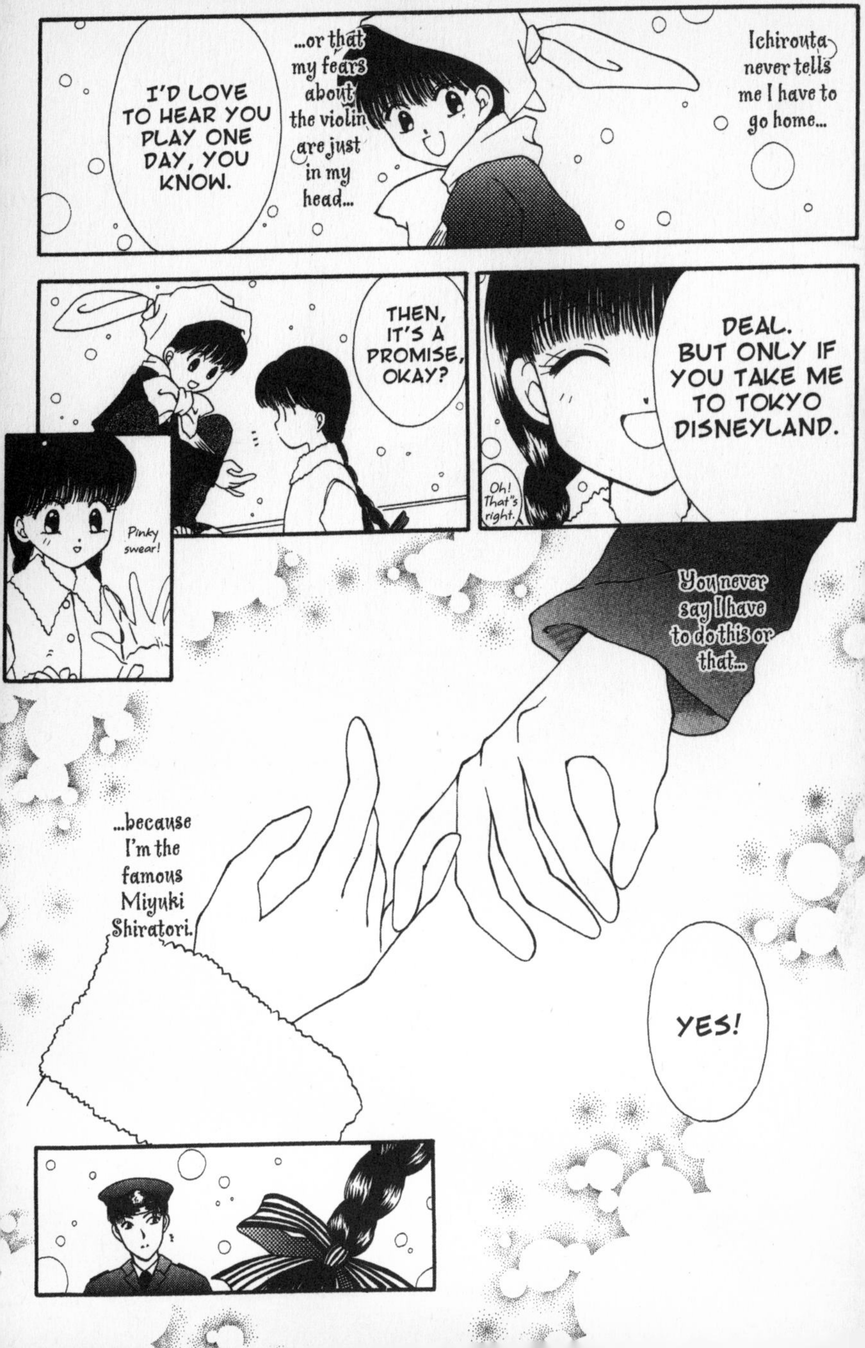
Ichirouta never tells me I have to go home...
...or that my fears about the violin are just in my head...
I'D LOVE TO HEAR YOU PLAY ONE DAY, YOU KNOW.
DEAL. BUT ONLY IF YOU TAKE ME TO TOKYO DISNEYLAND.
Oh! That's right.
THEN, IT'S A PROMISE, OKAY?
Pinky swear!
You never say I have to do this or that...
...because I'm the famous Miyuki Shiratori.
YES!

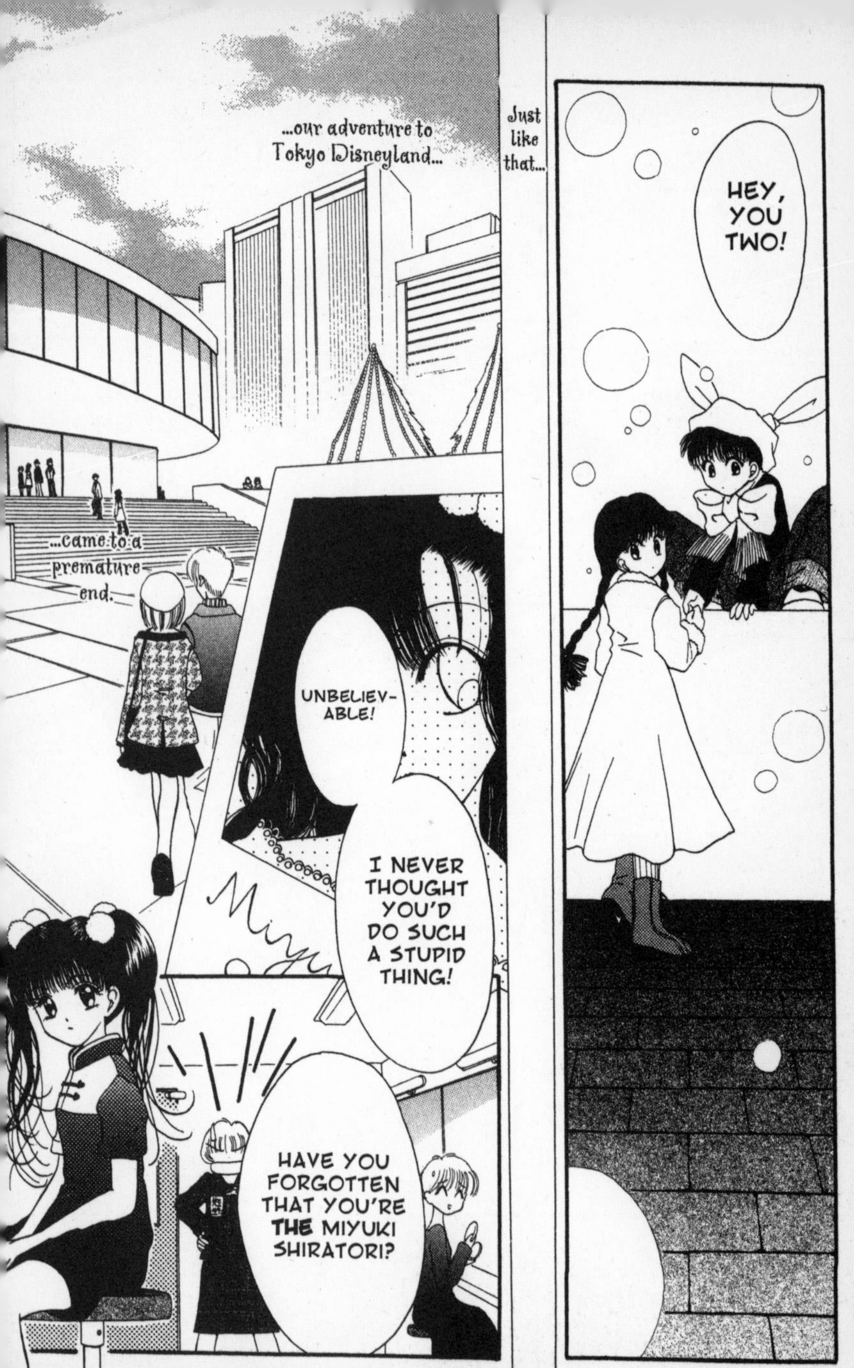
HEY, YOU TWO!
Just like that...
...our adventure to Tokyo Disneyland...
...came to a premature end.
UNBELIEV-ABLE!
I NEVER THOUGHT YOU'D DO SUCH A STUPID THING!
HAVE YOU FORGOTTEN THAT YOU'RE THE MIYUKI SHIRATORI?

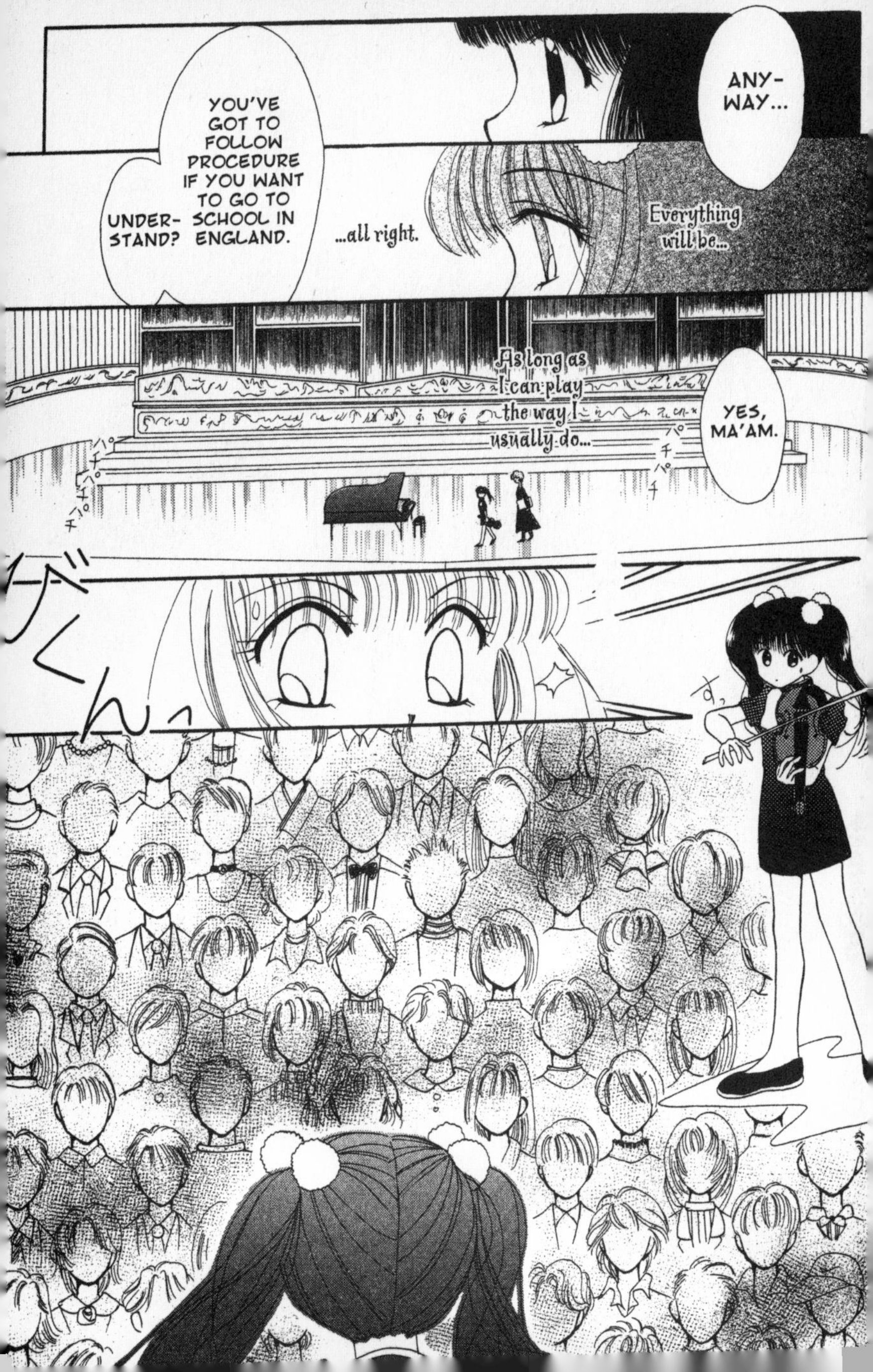
ANY-WAY...
YOU'VE GOT TO FOLLOW PROCEDURE IF YOU WANT TO GO TO SCHOOL IN ENGLAND.
UNDER-STAND?
Everything will be...
...all right.
YES, MA'AM.
As long as I can play the way I usually do...

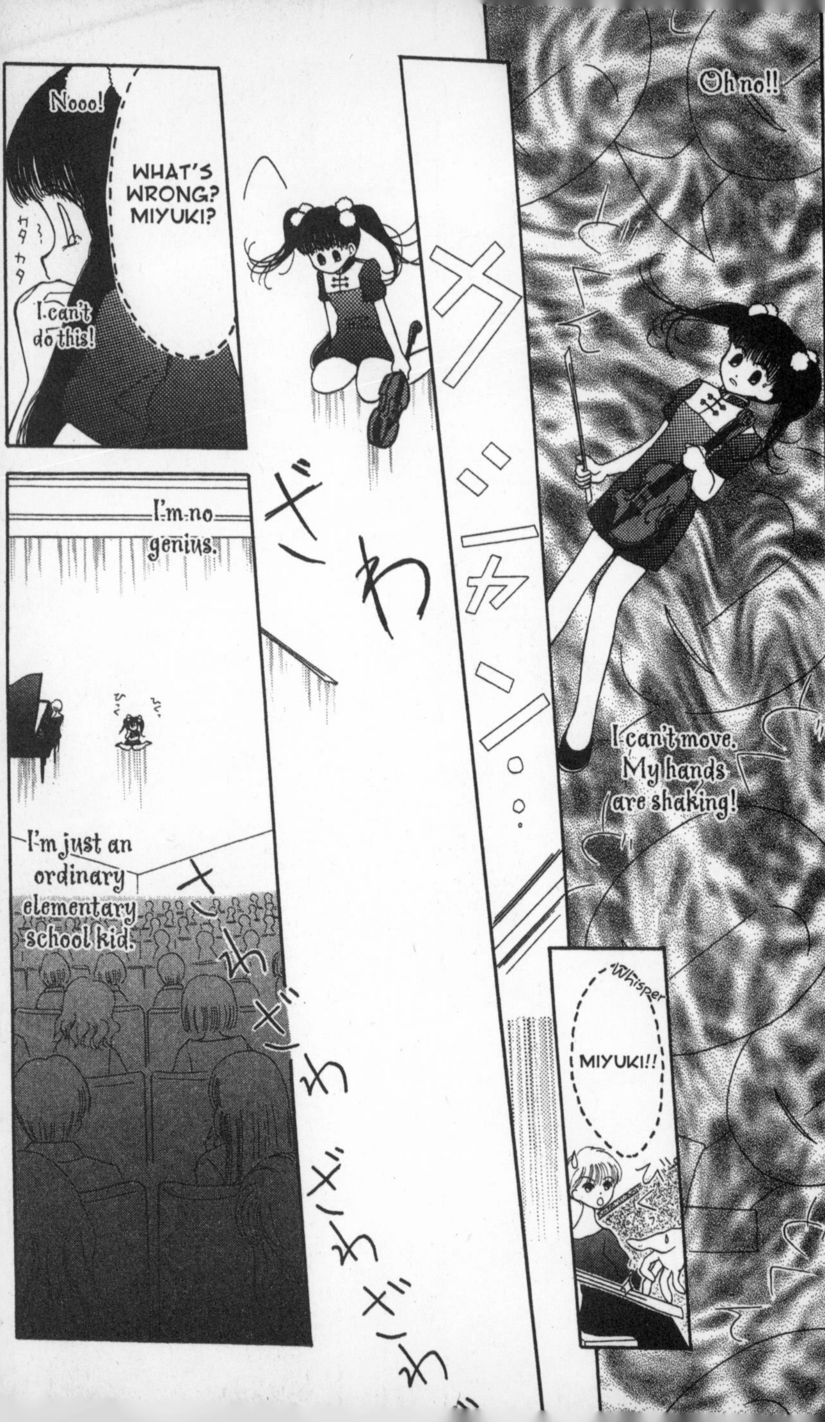

Oh no!!
I can't move. My hands are shaking!
Whisper
MIYUKI!!
カシャン
ざわ
ざわざわざわ
Nooo!
WHAT'S WRONG? MIYUKI?
カタカタ
I can't do this!
I'm no genius.
I'm just an ordinary elementary school kid.

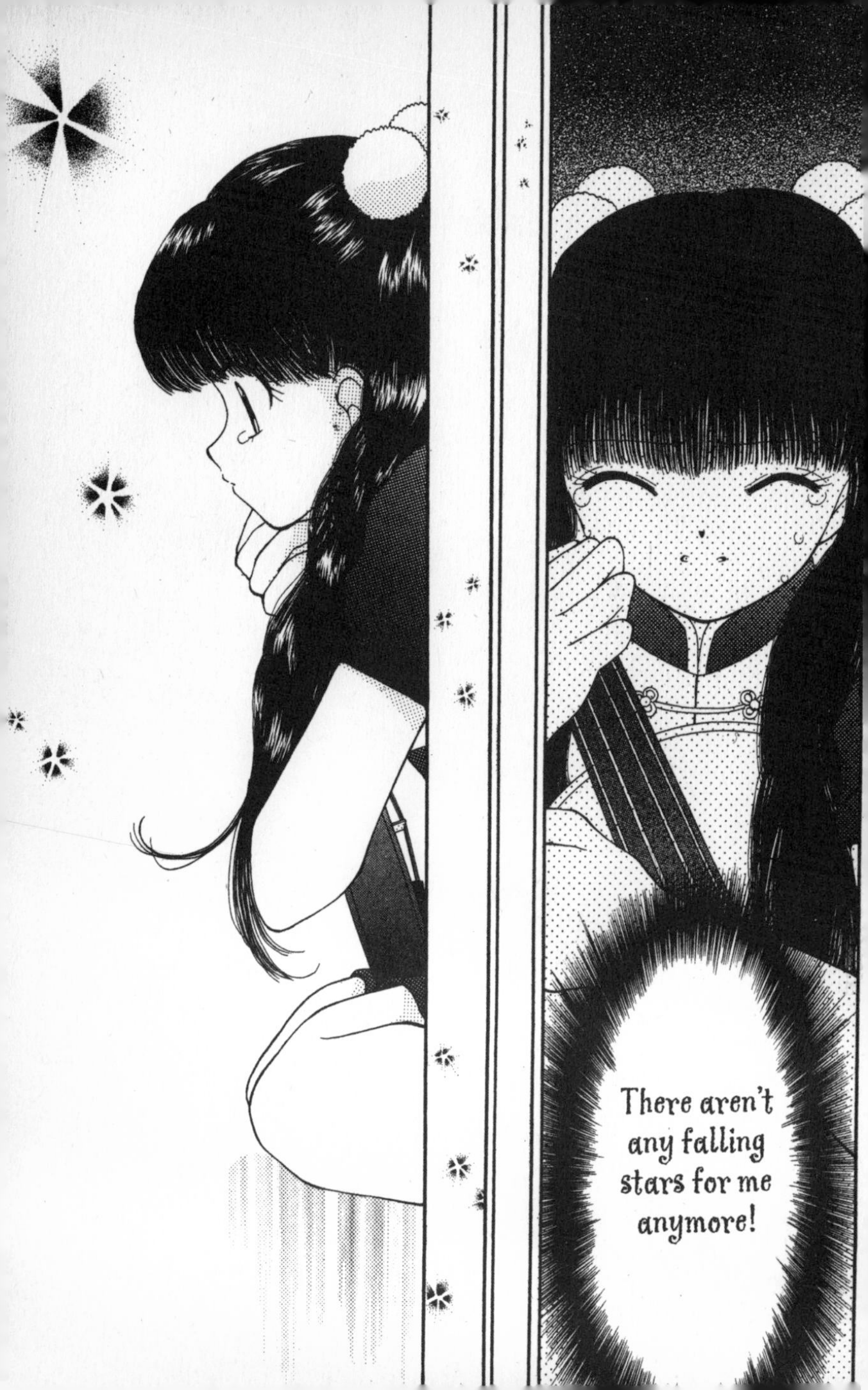
There aren't any falling stars for me anymore!

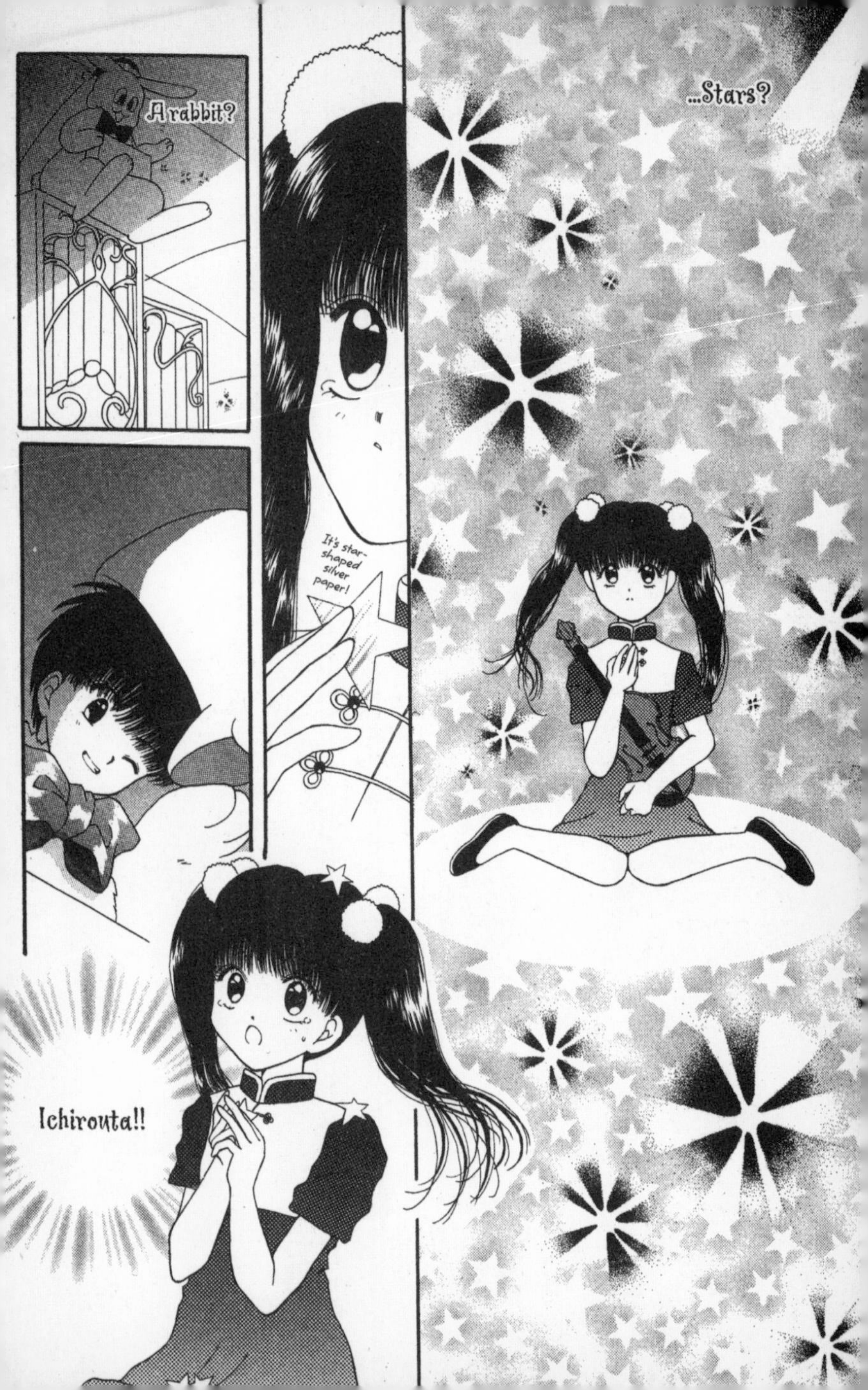
...Stars?
It's star-shaped silver paper!
A rabbit?
Ichirouta!!

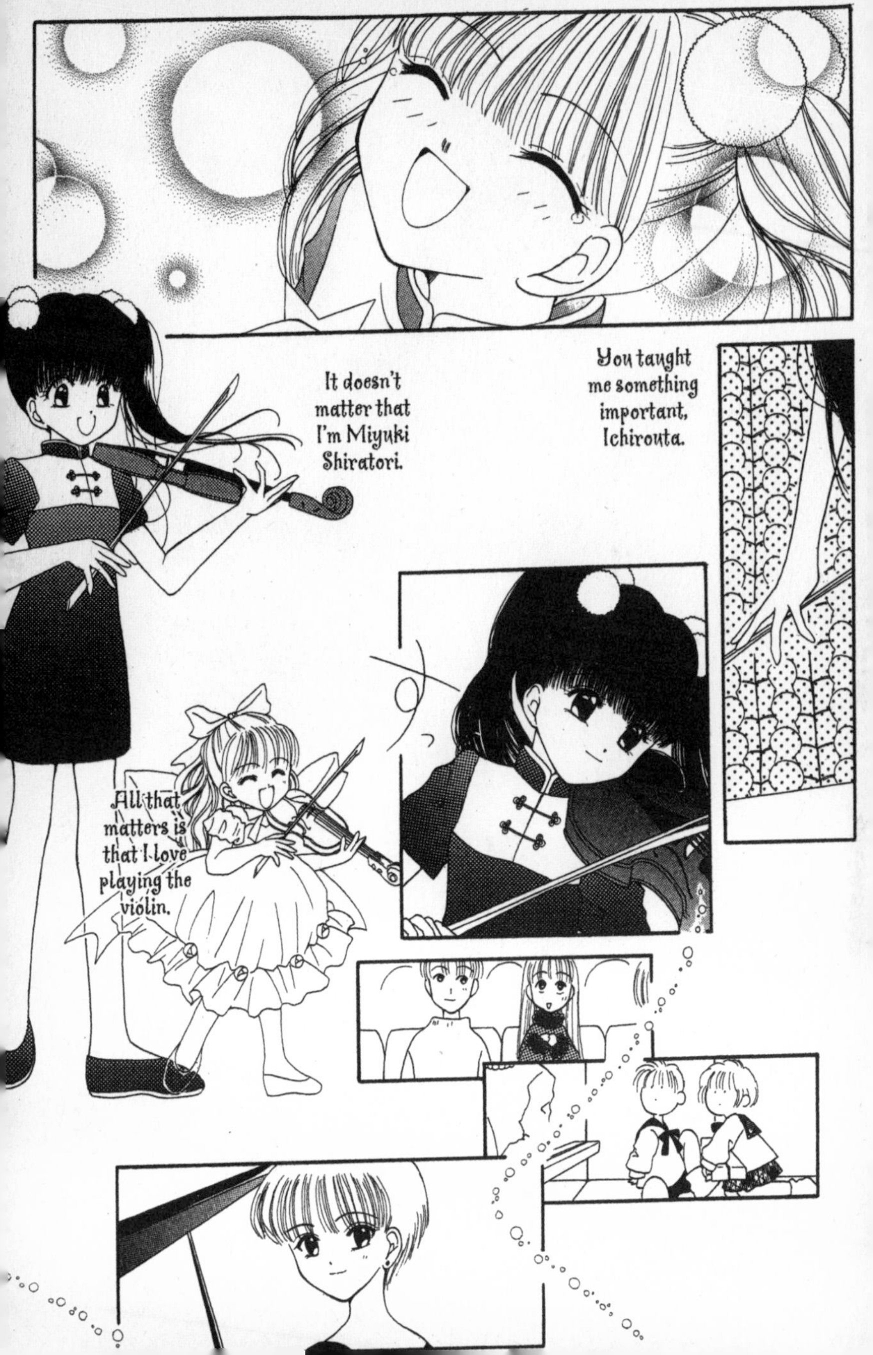
You taught me something important, Ichirouta.
It doesn't matter that I'm Miyuki Shiratori.
All that matters is that I love playing the violin.

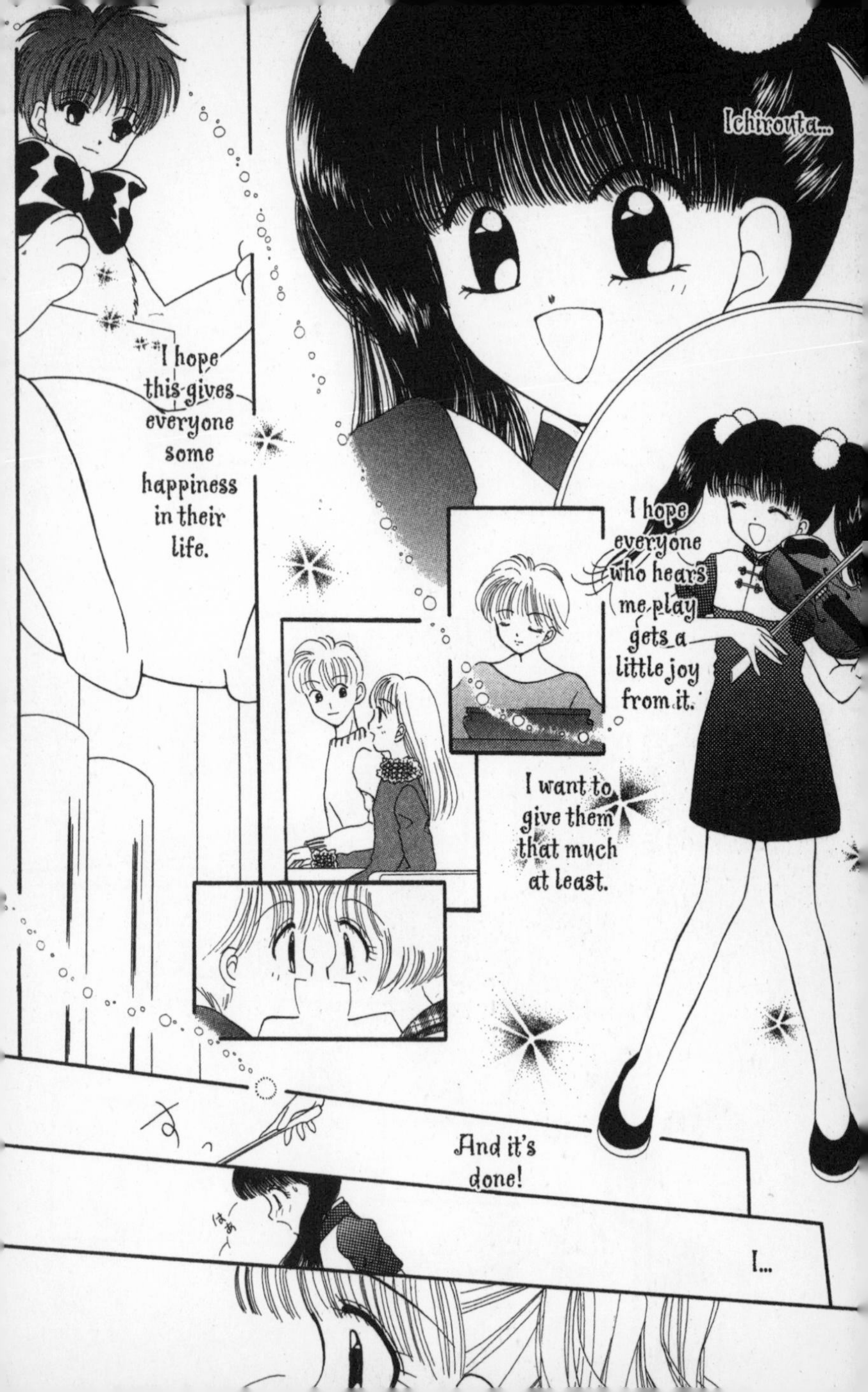
Ichirouta...
I hope this gives everyone some happiness in their life.
I hope everyone who hears me play gets a little joy from it.
I want to give them that much at least.
And it's done!
I...

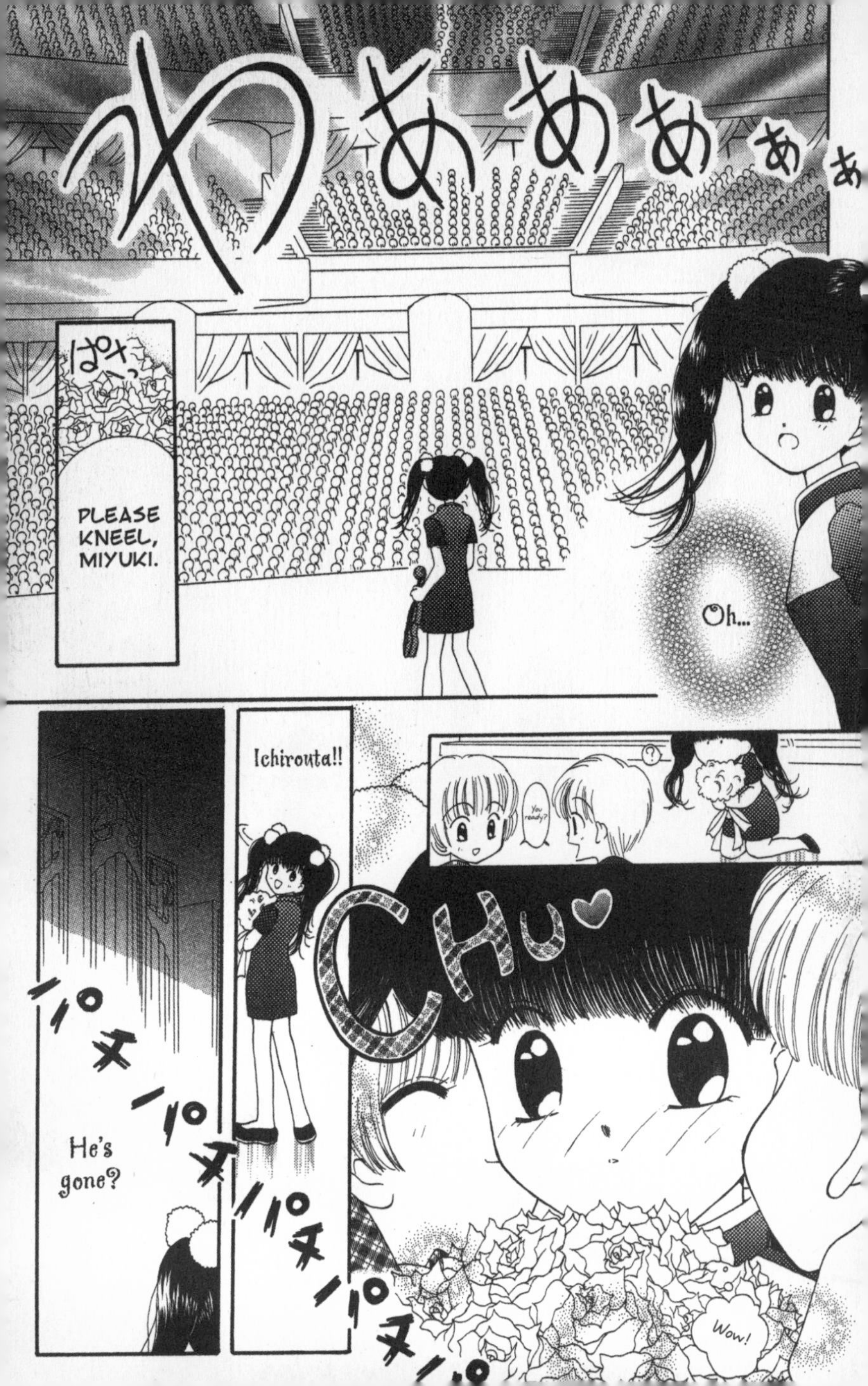
Oh...
PLEASE KNEEL, MIYUKI.
You ready?
CHU♥
Wow!
Ichirouta!!
He's gone?

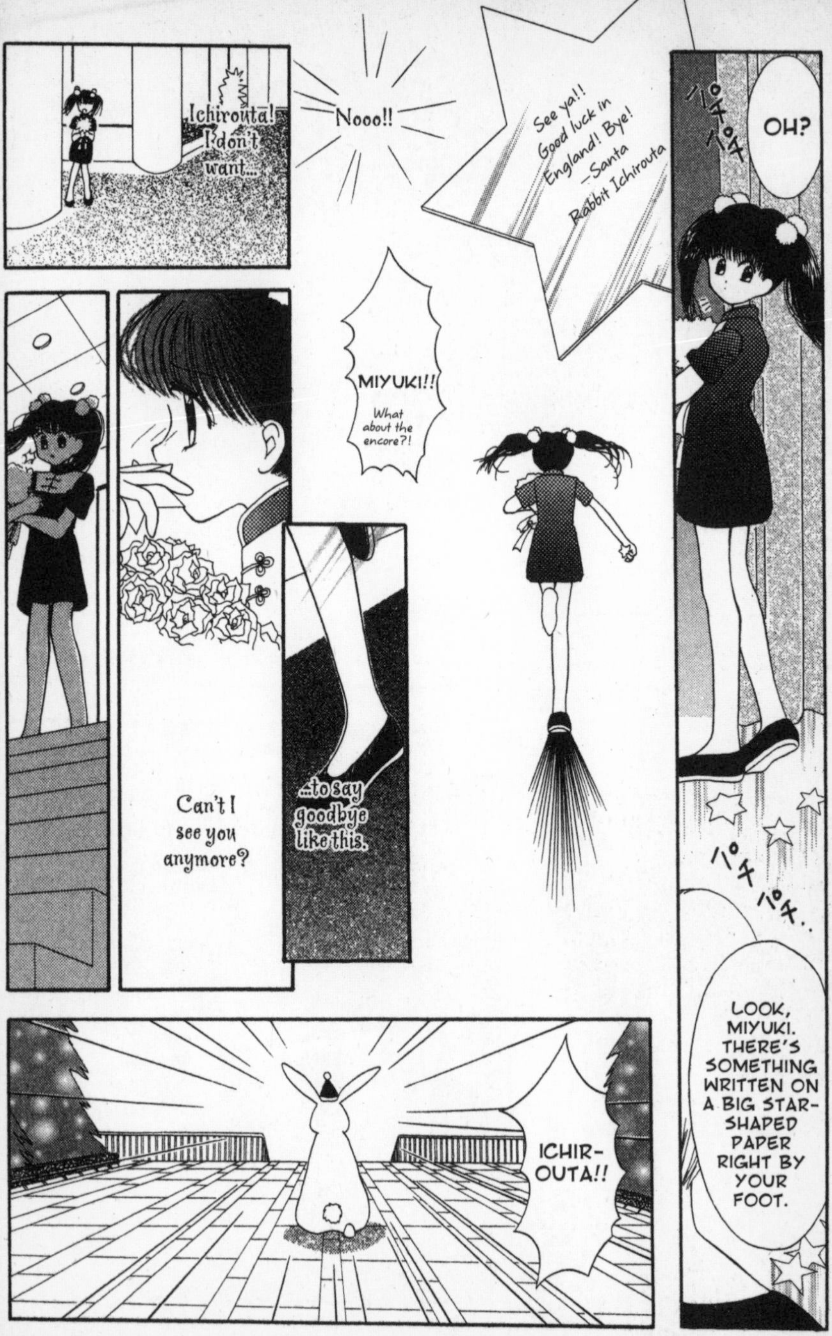
パチパチ
OH?
See ya!! Good luck in England! Bye! -Santa Rabbit Ichirouta
Nooo!!
Ichirouta! I don't want...
MIYUKI!!
What about the encore?!
...to say goodbye like this.
Can't I see you anymore?
パチパチ..
LOOK, MIYUKI. THERE'S SOMETHING WRITTEN ON A BIG STAR-SHAPED PAPER RIGHT BY YOUR FOOT.
ICHIR-OUTA!!

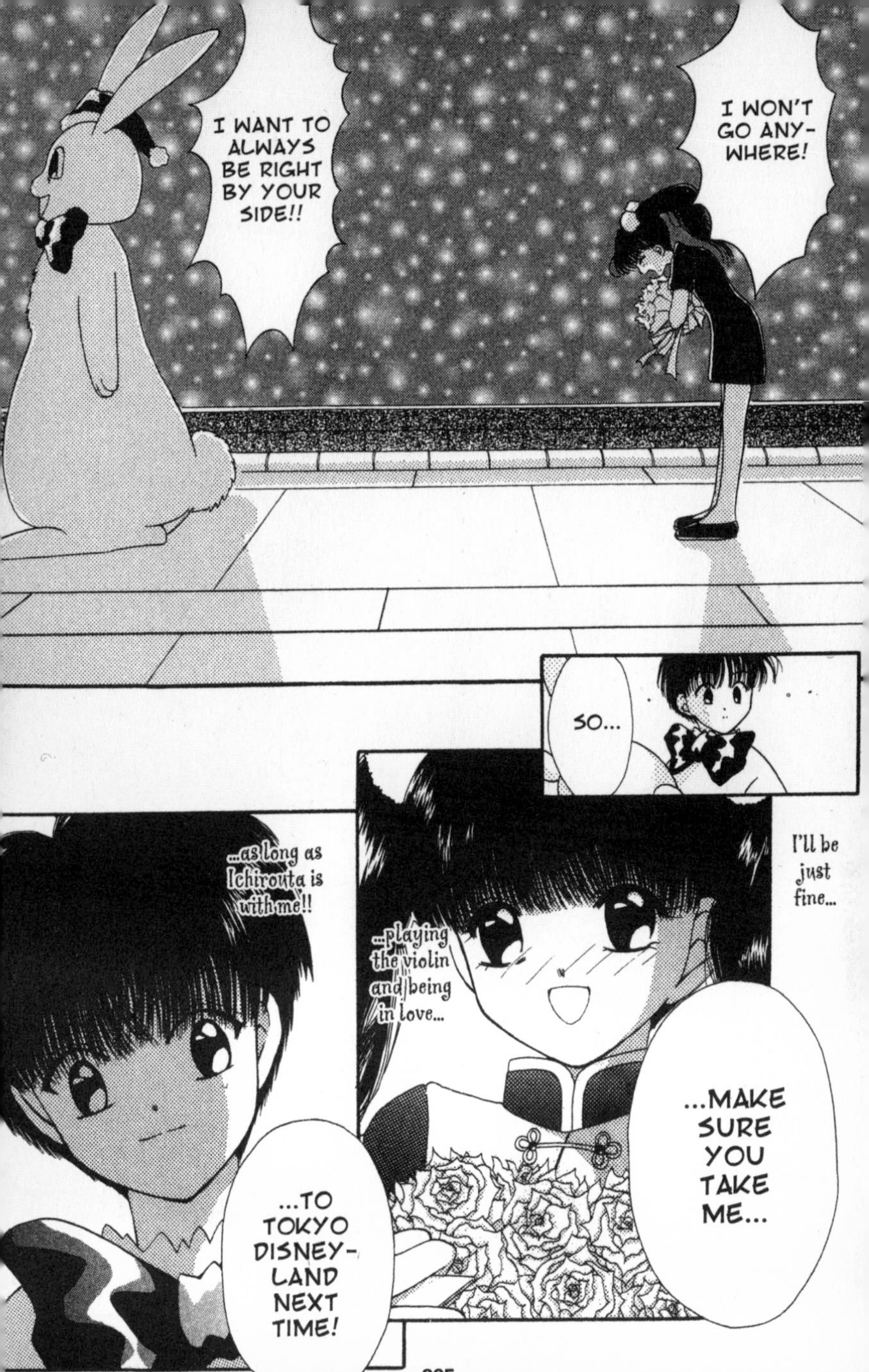
I WON'T GO ANY-WHERE!
I WANT TO ALWAYS BE RIGHT BY YOUR SIDE!!
SO...
I'll be just fine...
...playing the violin and being in love...
...as long as Ichirouta is with me!!
...MAKE SURE YOU TAKE ME...
...TO TOKYO DISNEY-LAND NEXT TIME!

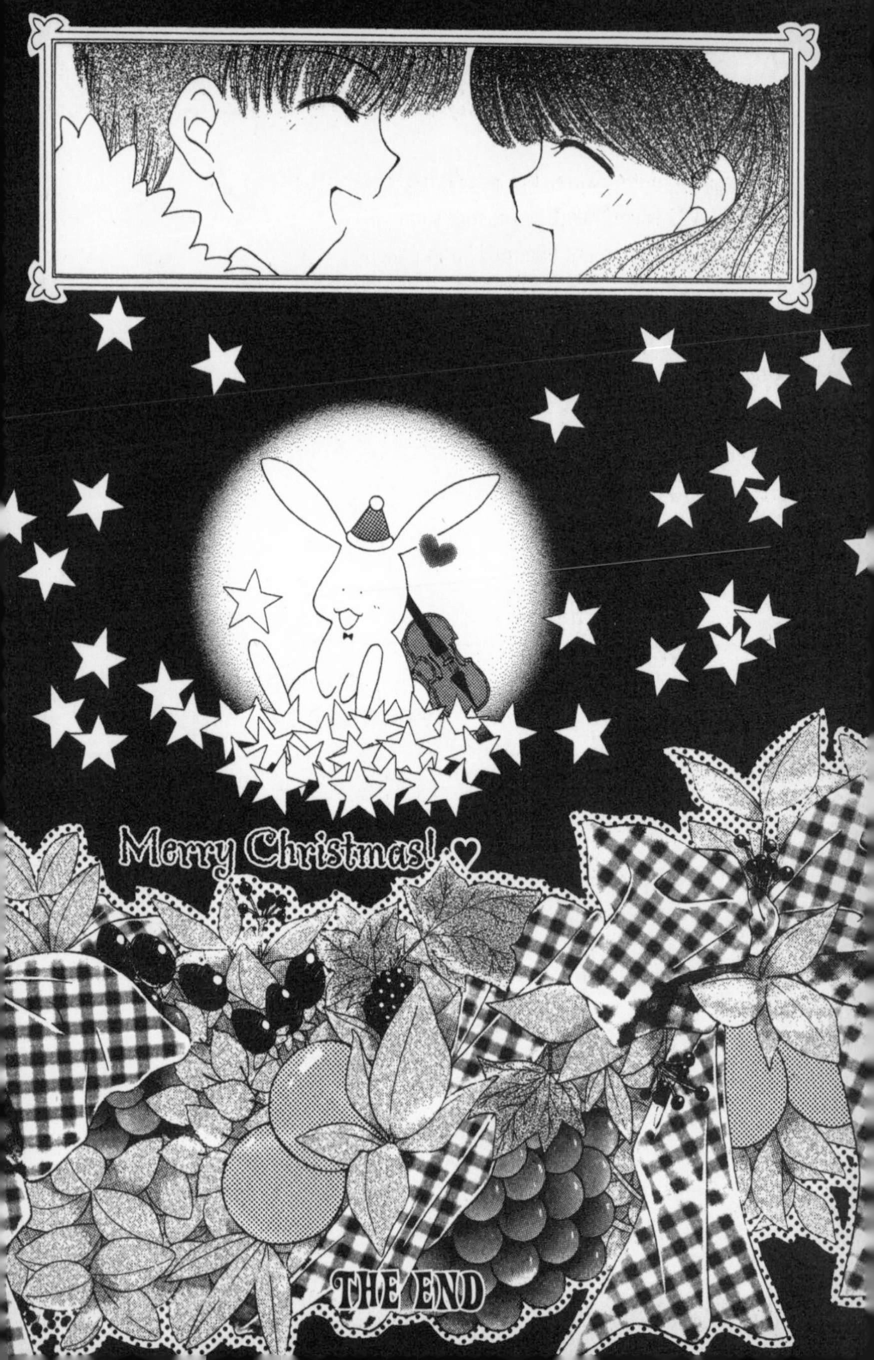
Merry Christmas! ♡
THE END

Rabbit Starfall

This was my debut work. It was originally 48 pages, but I had to cut it down to 40 when I realized it was too long. I had just been too nervous to fully check it over like I should have. I guess I'll give it another read when it comes out in the manga! (Laugh)

Meanwhile, I need to tell you about a mistake I made in *Tokyo Mew Mew A La Mode* volume one. It's in the "Special Thanks!!" feature where I usually list the names of my staff... "S. Hanazawa" should be "S. Nakazawa." And another mistake was that I completely forgot to list one person's name.

I'd like to take this opportunity to apologize for each and every mistake!! If possible, I want you to write "A. Okawa" in any blank space on that page. It's the name of my staff member who worked the longest hours over the past year. As always, thank you for your work.

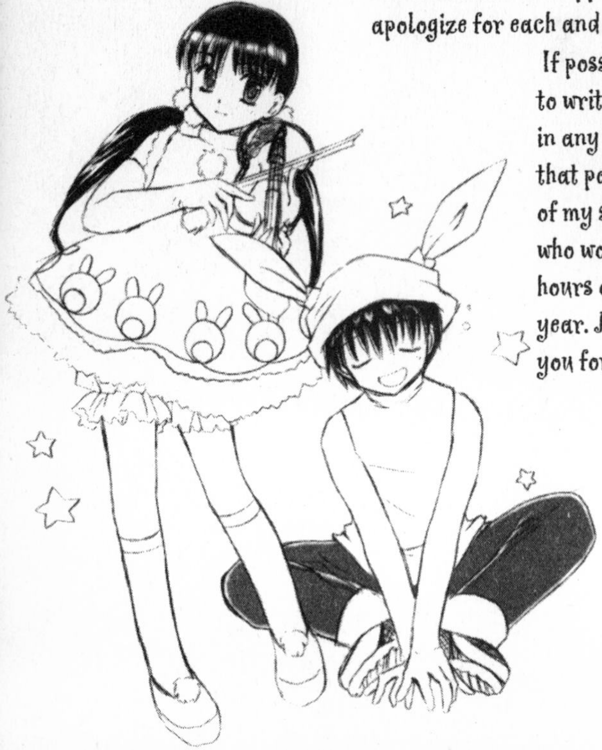

Postscript ☆

I'm currently working on a Mia Ikumi web page!
http://www.ikumimi.com/
Right now I've only got a placeholder up. And it might never be completed since my computer literacy kind of sucks. But I'm trying my best, so please come visit it! I may be able to add something new! ♡

Well, this is it... Usually I leave messages for my fans in the final pages of my comics. But this time I'd like to use the free space to record my feelings. I want to feel a bit of closure after working on this story for so many years. So please indulge me...

At the end...
To everyone who created this with me...
To everyone who got involved...
To everyone who read this work...
I'm overwhelmed with gratitude!

Oh yeah--and one thing for myself!

Good job, Mia! You did well!
2/9/2004 6:00 P.M. Mia Ikumi

Fruits Basket

Life in the Sohma household can be a real zoo!

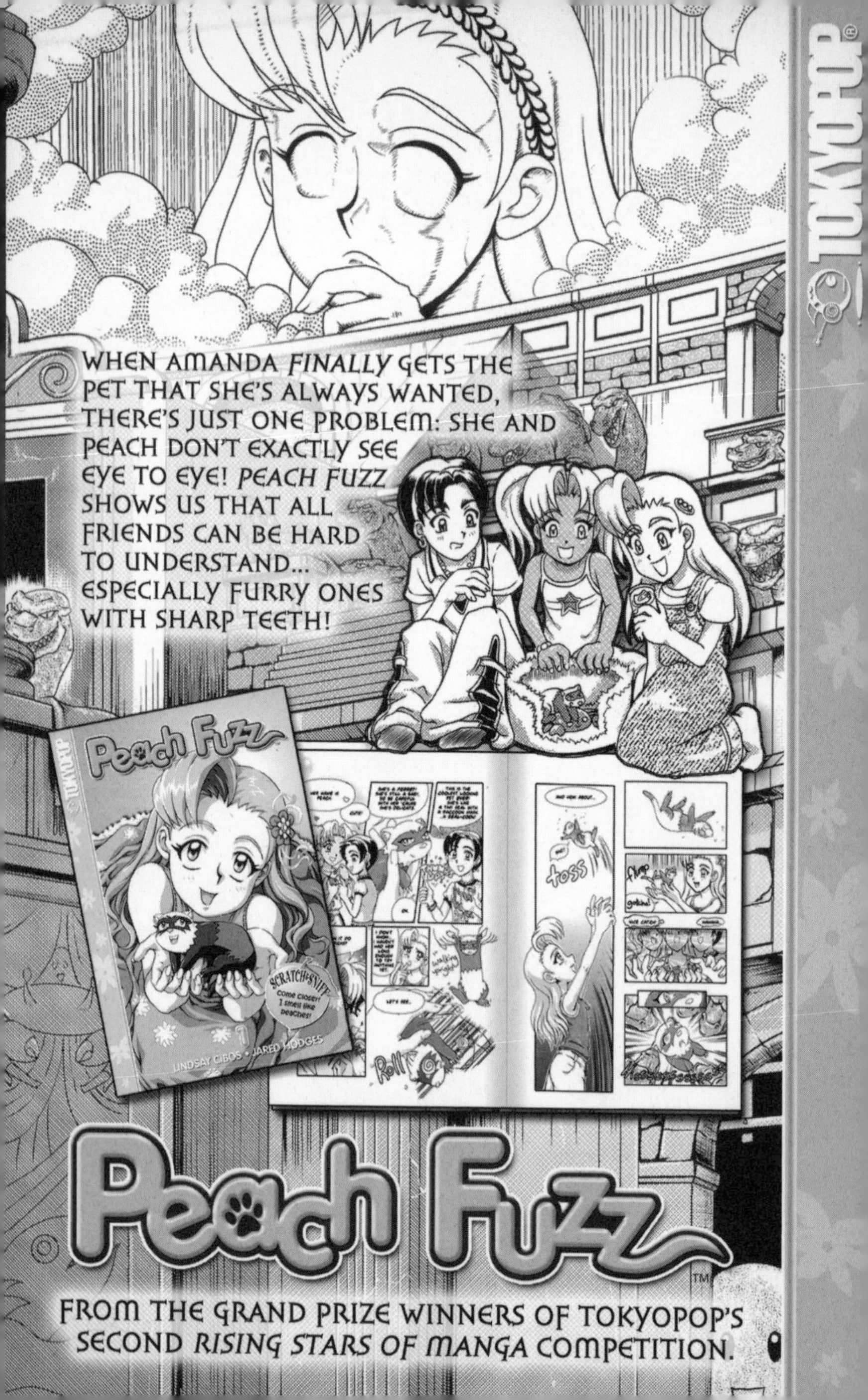
TOKYOPOP®
WHEN AMANDA FINALLY GETS THE PET THAT SHE'S ALWAYS WANTED, THERE'S JUST ONE PROBLEM: SHE AND PEACH DON'T EXACTLY SEE EYE TO EYE! PEACH FUZZ SHOWS US THAT ALL FRIENDS CAN BE HARD TO UNDERSTAND... ESPECIALLY FURRY ONES WITH SHARP TEETH!
Peach Fuzz
SCRATCH & SNIFF
Come closer! I smell like peaches!
LINDSAY CIBOS • JARED HODGES
Peach Fuzz™
FROM THE GRAND PRIZE WINNERS OF TOKYOPOP'S SECOND RISING STARS OF MANGA COMPETITION.

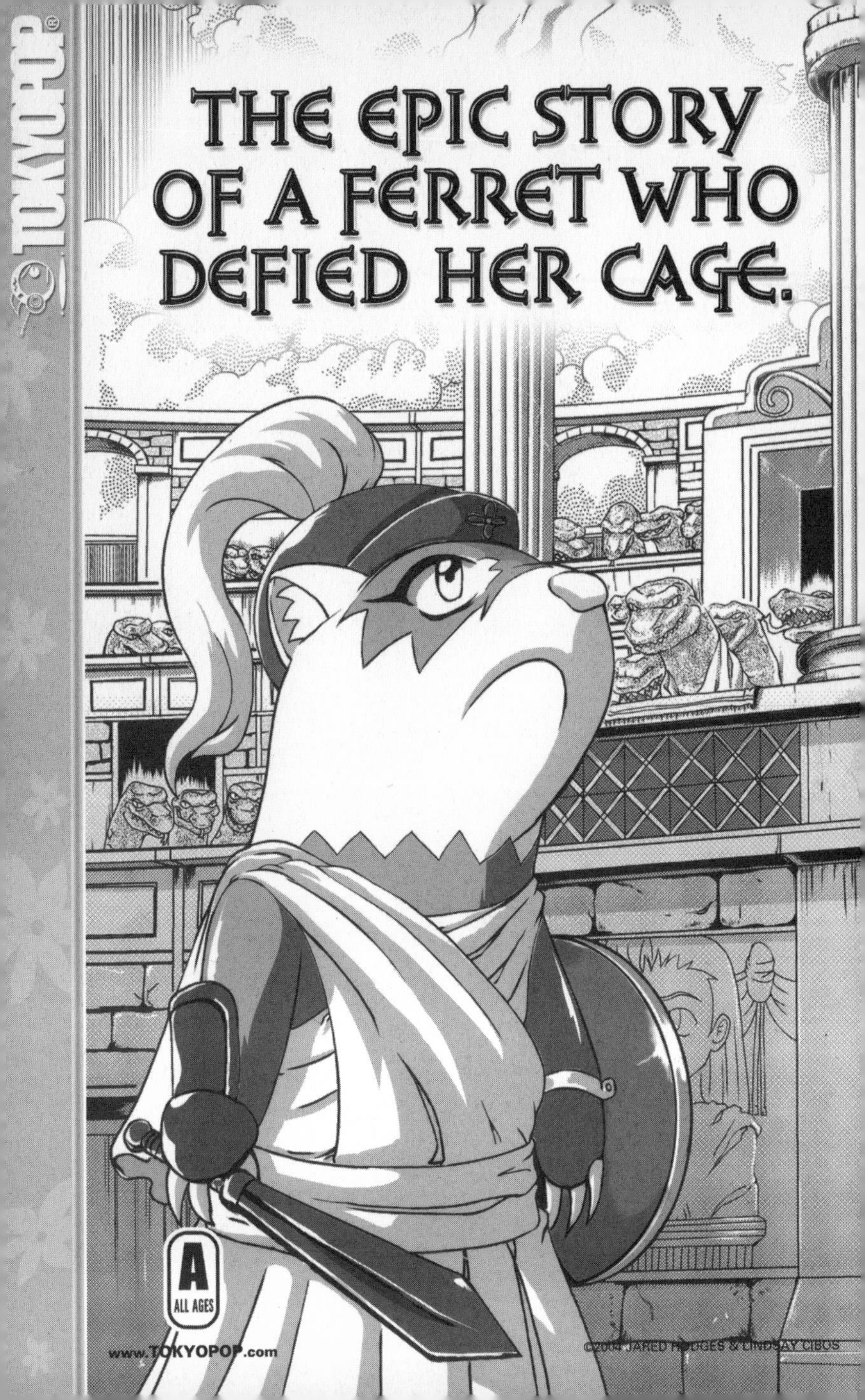
TOKYOPOP
THE EPIC STORY
OF A FERRET WHO
DEFIED HER CAGE.
A
ALL AGES
www.TOKYOPOP.com
©2004 JARED HODGES & LINDSAY CIBOS

When darkness is in your genes,
only love can steal it away.

TOKYOPOP

D·N·ANGEL